The Complete Poems

of

Louis Daniel

BRODSKY

Volume Two, 1967–1976

**Missouri Center
for the Book**

૪ૡ ૪ૡ ૪ૡ

Missouri Authors
Collection

Books by LOUIS DANIEL BRODSKY

Poetry

Five Facets of Myself   (1967)* (1995)

The Easy Philosopher   (1967)* (1995)

"A Hard Coming of It" and Other Poems   (1967)* (1995)

The Foul Rag-and-Bone Shop   (1967)* (1969, exp.)* (1995, exp.)

Points in Time   (1971)* (1995) (1996)

Taking the Back Road Home   (1972)* (1997) (2000)

Trip to Tipton and Other Compulsions   (1973)* (1997)

"The Talking Machine" and Other Poems   (1974)* (1997)

Tiffany Shade   (1974)* (1997)

Trilogy: A Birth Cycle   (1974) (1998)

Cold Companionable Streams   (1975)* (1999)

Monday's Child   (1975) (1998)

Preparing for Incarnations   (1975)* (1976, exp.) (1999) (1999 exp.)

The Kingdom of Gewgaw   (1976) (2000)

Point of Americas II   (1976) (1998)

La Preciosa   (1977) (2001)

Stranded in the Land of Transients   (1978) (2000)

The Uncelebrated Ceremony of Pants-Factory Fatso   (1978) (2001)

Birds in Passage   (1980) (2001)

Résumé of a Scrapegoat   (1980) (2001)

Mississippi Vistas: Volume One of *A Mississippi Trilogy*   (1983) (1990)

You Can't Go Back, Exactly   (1988) (1988) (1989)

The Thorough Earth   (1989)

Four and Twenty Blackbirds Soaring   (1989)

Falling from Heaven: Holocaust Poems of a Jew and a Gentile
  (with William Heyen)   (1991)

Forever, for Now: Poems for a Later Love   (1991)

Mistress Mississippi: Volume Three of *A Mississippi Trilogy*   (1992)

A Gleam in the Eye: Poems for a First Baby   (1992)

Gestapo Crows: Holocaust Poems   (1992)

The Capital Café: Poems of Redneck, U.S.A.   (1993)

Disappearing in Mississippi Latitudes: Volume Two of *A Mississippi Trilogy*   (1994)

A Mississippi Trilogy: A Poetic Saga of the South   (1995)*

Paper-Whites for Lady Jane: Poems of a Midlife Love Affair   (1995)

The Complete Poems of Louis Daniel Brodsky: Volume One, 1963–1967
  (edited by Sheri L. Vandermolen)   (1996)

Three Early Books of Poems by Louis Daniel Brodsky, 1967–1969: *The Easy
  Philosopher*, *"A Hard Coming of It" and Other Poems*, and *The Foul Rag-
  and-Bone Shop* *(edited by Sheri L. Vandermolen)*   (1997)

The Eleventh Lost Tribe: Poems of the Holocaust   (1998)
Toward the Torah, Soaring: Poems of the Renascence of Faith   (1998)
Voice Within the Void: Poems of *Homo supinus*   (2000)
Rabbi Auschwitz: Poems Touching the Shoah   (2000)*
The Swastika Clock: Endlösung Poems   (2001)*
Shadow War: A Poetic Chronicle of September 11 and Beyond, Volume One   (2001)
The Complete Poems of Louis Daniel Brodsky: Volume Two, 1967–1976 *(edited by Sheri L. Vandermolen)*   (2002)

Bibliography *(coedited with Robert Hamblin)*

Selections from the William Faulkner Collection of Louis Daniel Brodsky: A Descriptive Catalogue   (1979)
Faulkner: A Comprehensive Guide to the Brodsky Collection
   Volume I: The Bibliography   (1982)
   Volume II: The Letters   (1984)
   Volume III: *The De Gaulle Story*   (1984)
   Volume IV: *Battle Cry*   (1985)
   Volume V: Manuscripts and Documents   (1989)
Country Lawyer and Other Stories for the Screen by William Faulkner   (1987)
Stallion Road: A Screenplay by William Faulkner   (1989)

Biography

William Faulkner, Life Glimpses   (1990)

Fiction

The Adventures of the Night Riders, Better Known as the Terrible Trio *(a memoir, with Richard Milsten)*   (1961)*
Between Grief and Nothing *(novel)*   (1964)*
Between the Heron and the Wren *(novel)*   (1965)*
Dink Phlager's Alligator *(novella)*   (1966)*
The Drift of Things *(novel)*   (1966)*
Vineyard's Toys *(novel)*   (1967)*
The Bindle Stiffs *(novel)*   (1968)*
Yellow Bricks *(short fictions)*   (1999)
Catchin' the Drift o' the Draft *(short fictions)*   (1999)
This Here's a Merica *(short fictions)*   (1999)
Leaky Tubs *(short fictions)*   (2001)

* *Unpublished*

Louis Daniel Brodsky
(circa 1975)

Louis Daniel Brodsky
12/30/07
St. Louis, MO

THE COMPLETE POEMS

OF

LOUIS DANIEL

BRODSKY

VOLUME TWO, 1967–1976

EDITED BY

SHERI L. VANDERMOLEN

TIME BEING BOOKS
POETRY IN SIGHT AND SOUND

An imprint of Time Being Press
St. Louis, Missouri

Time Being Books®
10411 Clayton Road
St. Louis, Missouri 63131

Time Being Books® is an imprint of Time Being Press®
St. Louis, Missouri

Time Being Press® is a 501(c)(3) not-for-profit corporation.

Time Being Books® volumes are printed on acid-free paper, and binding materials are chosen for strength and durability.

ISBN 1-56809-073-0 (Hardcover)
ISBN 1-56809-074-9 (Paperback)

Library of Congress Cataloging-in-Publication Data:

Brodsky, Louis Daniel.
    [Poems]
    The complete poems of Louis Daniel Brodsky / edited by Sheri L.
Vandermolen.
        p.   cm.
    v. 1. 1963–1967
    ISBN 1-56809-019-6 (cloth). — ISBN 1-56809-020-X (pbk.), volume one
    Contents: v. 2. 1967–1976
    ISBN 1-56809-073-0 (cloth). — ISBN 1-56809-074-9 (pbk.), volume two
    I. Vandermolen, Sheri L.   II. Title.
PS3552.R623A17   1996, 2002
811'.54—dc20   96-17149
                                                                        CIP

Cover photo and frontispiece photo by Stuart Fabe
Book design and typesetting by Sheri L. Vandermolen
Manufactured in the United States of America

First Edition, first printing (2002)

ACKNOWLEDGMENTS

For nearly five years, Sheri L. Vandermolen, Editor in Chief of Time Being Books, has labored over all the manuscripts and books, published and unpublished, that I produced between 1967 and 1976, making certain that each of my poems was given its proper order within the individual works and the collection as a whole. She has also been responsible for determining the ultimate version of every piece presented here. Moreover, the excellence of her editorial overview has made this second volume of my complete-poems series authoritative and definitive. My gratitude to her is inestimable.

Jerry Call, Managing Editor of Time Being Books, has worked side by side with me to support and augment the editorial review process. Without his insight and steadfast commitment to enhancing the quality of each poem, this book would not fully reflect my life's dedication to poetry. To him, I am deeply grateful.

I would like to thank Dr. José Schraibman, of Washington University, for his careful correction of my Spanish verse in the poem "*Una noche oscura del alma*" and for his insightful suggestions in translating that work.

I also wish to give due mention to the publications in which certain of my poems from June of 1967 to July 1976, some in revised form, have appeared, including the following magazines and journals: *Amelia* ("Helen Among the Twelve Disciples" and "The Isle of Lesbos"); *American Scholar* ("A Sky Filled with Trees"); *Art Times* ("Father's Den"); *Bitterroot* ("Breaking Through"); *Cape Rock* ("The Casket Truck," "Catching Fireflies," "The Flower Store," "The Perfect Crime," "Redbuds," "Triangles," "The Voyage of A. Gordon Pym," "Waving Good-Bye," and "Word-Seeds"); *Chariton Review* ("The Books, the Woods, and Us," with the later title "Of Books and Woods and Us"); *Florida Quarterly* ("From Out of Nowhere" and "Rent-Controlled"); *Forum* ("Buffalo," "An Early Muse Awakens," with the later title "Cabin by a Lake," "The Fishing Dock," "Morning's Companion," "The Point," "Running in Packs," and "Tortoise and Hare" [00126]*); *Four Quarters* ("Ancestry," "My Flying Machine," and "Weeding in January"); *Harper's* ("Death Comes to the Salesman" and "Rearview Mirror"); *Hiram Poetry Review* ("Sitting in Bib Overalls, Work Shirt, Boots, on the Monument to Liberty in the Center of the Square, Jacksonville, Illinois); *Kansas Quarterly* ("Easter Flood," "Plant Manager" [00667], with the earlier title "Plant Manager no. 3," "Suggestions," and "An Evening in the Trevi Bar," with the later title "Trevi Cabaret, 1944"); *Karenjen Review* ("Beginning to See"); *Literary Review* ("The Expectants," "Jan's Song" [00105], "Lament," "Schoolteacher," and "Visitation" [00347]); *Literati Internazionale* ("Ancestry"); *Midwest Poetry Review* ("Paean to Jan and Trilogy"); *Mill Creek Valley Intelligencer* ("The Sisters of Fiesole"); *National Forum* ("The Books, the Woods, and Us," with the later title "Of Books and Woods and Us," and "Closing In"); *Newsart* ("Grandfather," with the later title "Grandfather Desires to Die in Bed at Home"); *Parnassus Literary Journal* ("Firefighter" and "Spider and Fly"); *Phase and Cycle* ("Crocheting Solomon's Seal"); *Pulpsmith* ("Panning for Gold"); *Roanoke Review* ("Lepidoptera"); *Route One* ("Accident-Prone," "Bill," and "Nocturne," with the later title "Conception: A Recollection"); *St. Andrews Review* ("Great-Grandmother"); *St. Louis Jewish Light* ("Epitaph," with the later title "Hebrew Louie, Shoe Salesman"); *South Carolina Review* ("Mutoscope Reel," with the later title "The Mutoscope," and "Their Song," with the later title "Our Song"); *Southern Review* ("Between Connections," "Joseph K.," "Manager of Outlet Stores," and "Résumé of a Scrapegoat"); *Sparrow* ("*Dopo il diluvio*: Firenze," "Eating Place," "Endless December," and "The Poet"); *Texas Quarterly* ("Late-October Sunday Service," "Reverie," and "Thanksgiving Misgivings"); *Whetstone* ("[First, the silent stirs under covers:]," with the later title "Eye in the Sky," and "Race Day"); *Windfall* ("Pieces and Tatters"); and *Wisconsin Review* ("Thirty Miles Southeast of Duluth," with the later title "Interchanges")

I wish to thank these anthologies as well: *Anthology of Magazine Verse and Yearbook of American Poetry, 1980* ("Buffalo," "My Flying Machine," and "Weeding in January"); *Anthology of Magazine Verse and Yearbook of American Poetry, 1981* ("Ancestry," "Death Comes to the Salesman," and "Sitting in Bib Overalls, Work Shirt, Boots, on the Monument to Liberty in the Center of the Square, Jacksonville, Illinois"); *Anthology of Magazine Verse and Yearbook of American Poetry, 1984* ("Great-Grandmother" and "Redbuds"); and *Voices from the Interior: Poets of Missouri, 1982* ("Death Comes to the Salesman" and "Rearview Mirror").

Several of the poems in this volume also originally appeared in my early poetry manuscripts, including the following: *The Foul Rag-and-Bone Shop* (1969, expanded), *Points in Time* (1971), *Taking the Back Road Home* (1972), *Trip to Tipton and Other Compulsions* (1973), *"The Talking Machine" and Other Poems* (1974), *Tiffany Shade* (1974), *Trilogy: A Birth Cycle* (1974), *Cold Companionable Streams* (1975), *Monday's Child* (1975), *Preparing for Incarnations* (1975) (1976, expanded), *The Kingdom of Gewgaw* (1976), *Point of Americas II* (1976), *La Preciosa* (1977), *Stranded in the Land of Transients* (1978), *The Uncelebrated Ceremony of Pants-Factory Fatso* (1978), *Birds in Passage* (1980), and *Résumé of a Scrapegoat* (1980), some of which were published by Farmington Press, from 1974 to 1980, and all of which are available, in revised form, from Time Being Books. The book and poem titles are listed in Appendix 2, with brief descriptions of each volume.

Certain poems have also appeared in my later works, including books and pamphlets.

"The Flower Store" and "Grandfather," with the title "Grandfather Desires to Die in Bed at Home," are in the unpublished pamphlet *The Ash Keeper's Everlasting Passion Week* (1986).

"Breaking Through," "The Flower Store," and "Redbuds" appear in the unpublished pamphlet *A Transcendental Almanac* (1987).

"An Early Muse Awakens" (with the later title "Cabin by a Lake"), "The Fishing Dock," "Marianne" [00011], "Morning's Companion," "Pieces and Tatters," "The Point," "Prayer," and "Thirty Miles Southeast of Duluth" (with the later title "Interchanges") are comprised in *You Can't Go Back, Exactly*, released as first and second editions by Timeless Press (now

Time Being Books) in 1988 and reprinted in 1989, and are also in a compilation translation of the text (Paris: Éditions Gallimard, 1994).

"Death Comes to the Salesman," "Grandfather," "Manager of Outlet Stores," "Panning for Gold," "Résumé of a Scrapegoat," and "Willy" appear in the Time Being Books volume *The Thorough Earth* (1989) and in a compilation translation of that text (Paris: Éditions Gallimard, 1992).

"Ancestry," "Between Connections," "Breaking Through," "Buffalo," "Casket Truck," "Country Cemetery," "The Flower Store," "Gulliver's Departure," "Helen Among the Twelve Disciples," "The Isle of Lesbos," "Joseph K.," "My Flying Machine," "Rearview Mirror," "Redbuds," "Running in Packs," "Sitting in Bib Overalls, Work Shirt, Boots, on the Monument to Liberty in the Center of the Square, Jacksonville, Illinois" (with the later title "In Bib Overalls, Work Shirt, Boots"), "A Sky Filled with Trees," "To His Coy Wife," "Tortoise and Hare," and "Word-Seeds" all appear in the Time Being Books publication *Four and Twenty Blackbirds Soaring* (1989) and in a compilation translation of that text (Paris: Éditions Gallimard, 1992).

"At Rest," "Bill," "The Books, the Woods, and Us" (with its later title), and "Eternal Triangle" are comprised in *Mississippi Vistas: Volume One of A Mississippi Trilogy*, which was originally published as a first edition, with no subtitle, by University Press of Mississippi in 1983 and was then issued as a second, revised edition by Timeless Press (now Time Being Books) in 1989. The poems also appear in the compilation translation of the Time Being Books text (Paris: Éditions Gallimard, 1994) and in the unpublished book *A Mississippi Trilogy: A Poetic Saga of the South* (1995).

"An Evening in the Trevi Bar" (with the later title "Trevi Cabaret, 1944") is included in the Time Being Books volume *Falling from Heaven: Holocaust Poems of a Jew and a Gentile* (1991) as well as in a compilation translation of that book (Paris: Éditions Gallimard, 1997).

All of the poems from *Trilogy: A Birth Cycle* and *Monday's Child*, listed in Appendix 2, with the exception of four ("And Our Child Asks, 'Where Did I Come From?'"; "Cruise Ships"; and "A Strange Kind of Birth," from *Trilogy*; and "Necromancers," from *Monday's Child*), appear in the Time Being Books volume *A Gleam in the Eye: Poems for a First Baby* (1992), which comprises their later versions. "Continuities" (with the later title "Continuities: A Dream") and "Nocturne" (with the later title "Conception: A Recollection") are also comprised in *A Gleam in the Eye*.

"Butterfield Inn" (with the later title "Butterfield Stage Pub"), "Closing the Old Café, Opening the Butterfield Inn" (with the later title "Workers of the Word, Unite!"), "Crystal Café Clock" (with the later title "Capital Café Clock"), "Disciples Gather at the Farmers' Lyceum," "Eating Place" (with the later title "Out of the Cradle, Endlessly Grousing"), "Helen Among the Twelve Disciples," "Hirsute," "The Isle of Lesbos," "KKK" (with the later title "KKK: Ozymandias Klavern, Laputa, Mo."), "Merchant Sailor," "The Origin of Species," "Private Judgments Made Public at the Butterfield Inn" (with the later title "A Cradle of Civilization"), "Round Table Café," "Running in Packs," and "Truckers" are all in the Time Being Books volume *The Capital Café: Poems of Redneck, USA* (1993).

The *Foul Rag-and-Bone Shop* pieces listed in Appendix 2 are comprised in the Time Being Books volume *Three Early Books of Poems by Louis Daniel Brodsky, 1967–1969: **The Easy Philosopher**, "A Hard Coming of It" and Other Poems, and **The Foul Rag-and-Bone Shop*** (1997).

"The Crows" (with the later title "Dreamscape with Three Crows") and "Teleology" (as part IV of a later poem, "Schreiber, Bard of Belzec") appear in the Time Being Books edition *The Eleventh Lost Tribe: Poems of the Holocaust* (1998).

"In the Synagogue" is included in the Time Being Books volume *Toward the Torah, Soaring: Poems of the Renascence of Faith* (1998).

Because two or more poems bear this title within volume two, the Time Being Books database tracking number is listed, to indicate the appropriate text.

*For my mother, Charlotte,
from whom I inherited an artistic sensibility
and a love of language,*

*and for my father, Saul,
who instilled in me the boundless energy and discipline
to shape endless hours into poems*

Poets don't have biographies. Their work is their biography.
— Octavio Paz, in an essay on Fernando Pessoa

"Fool," said my Muse to me, "look to thy heart, and write!"
— Sir Philip Sydney, *Astrophel and Stella*

Then read from the treasured volume
The poem of thy choice,
And lend to the rhyme of the poet
The beauty of thy voice.
— Henry Wadsworth Longfellow, *"The Day Is Done"*

CONTENTS

Editor's Guide to Volume Two of the Complete Poems Series

By the summer of 1967, Louis Daniel Brodsky had started his transition from apprenticeship to professional writing, and in the years that followed, he composed hundreds of poems, from short lyrical verse to long narratives, in an effort to capture both the singular and the commonplace events in his life.

His original intention, after graduating from Washington University in the spring of 1967 with a Master of Arts in English, was to be a poet. However, when he applied to San Francisco State University's creative-writing department, he was accepted into the prose program. Fearing that his poetry might come to an end once there, he spent the summer writing new verse and collecting previous poems into manuscripts, at his parents' home in St. Louis, and then drove to San Francisco, for the fall term, with expectations of becoming a fictionist.

Once there, busy penning two novels (*Vineyard's Toys* and *The Bindle Stiffs*) as part of his coursework, he had little time during the next year for the poetry so dear to him. Nonetheless, he was mentally formulating books of verse, carefully saving what he'd written that summer (fifteen complete poems, one prose poem, and two poetry fragments) and what he composed in his spare time during his year at San Francisco State (nine complete poems, six incomplete, and a half dozen fragments).

After receiving his Master of Arts in Creative Writing in the spring of 1968, Brodsky, still unsettled romantically, professionally, and emotionally, opted to seek solace by spending his summer as a counselor at Camp Nebagamon, in Wisconsin, where he composed several poems and used the quiet time to settle his thoughts, ultimately resolving to head to Coconut Grove, Florida, on the outskirts of Miami, in late August, to begin a teaching career at Miami-Dade South Community College and be with his future wife, Jan. However, shortly after arriving in Florida, Brodsky found he was still plagued by inner turmoil. Disturbed by the political climate of the country, the escalation of the Vietnam War, and the personal misgivings he experienced during his teacher orientation, Brodsky began to reconsider his decision to dedicate himself to the pedantic, bureaucratic world of academe. Within days, he resigned from his position and returned to Missouri, to pursue a job anchored in practical knowledge.

In an attempt to bring stability to his personal and professional life, he started working at a men's-clothing factory, owned by his father, in Farmington, Missouri, a town with a population then of approximately ten thousand. He lived in Rosener's Motel, in Flat River, just outside of Farmington, during the week and traveled to St. Louis on weekends. Because of this hectic schedule, he was not able to keep a regular writing routine, producing only nineteen poems and half a dozen sets of poetry fragments from October 1968 to March 1969, which he hoarded away with his other verse.

He purchased a home in Farmington in the spring of 1969 but still traveled to St. Louis periodically to combat the sense of isolation he felt and to help lessen the pressure he was under to prove himself in his job and his romantic relationship. When he eventually married, in July 1970, the forces of a fledgling career and home-life pulled him even further away from his writing. Although no longer forced to devote time to his prose work (which had come to an utter halt after leaving San Francisco), his first love, poetry, continued to suffer, with Brodsky authoring fewer than thirty poems, along with thirteen poem fragments and one prose poem, in a nearly two-year period.

During these transitional years, he finished only one book of poetry, *The Foul Rag-and-Bone Shop* (1969). He had developed its first manuscript in 1967 but came back to the work two years later, adding twelve poems he had written from June 1967 to September 1969, which he then meticulously blended into the 1967 manuscript. This expanded version remained unpublished until 1995, when it was printed by Time Being Books as a second edition.

The other writing Brodsky had been generating in his late twenties became the basis for *Points in Time*, a pivotal volume chronicling Brodsky's personal and vocational growth from the summer of 1967 to April 1971. Originally a manuscript-in-progress that contained forty-three poems, the book took on new life in 1994, when he added twenty-three other poems from that period and, using the typescript designations found with the book's inchoate drafts, fulfilled his authorial intention of dividing the text into parts defined by the geographic locations in which he was living or visiting when he composed the work (St. Louis; San Francisco; Lake Nebagamon, Wisconsin; Redington Beach and Coconut Grove, Florida; and Farmington). The reworked first edition was printed by Time Being Books in 1995.

The last piece in *Points in Time*, "A Divinity from Within," from April 1971, was the only full poem he produced in a seven-month period. He did not recommence composing verse regularly until August of that year, after adapting his writing schedule to suit the demands of his work and family life.

By late 1971, as Brodsky settled into a more stable work routine, he again gathered a full head of steam for his poetry, typing away furiously at home, composing on company letterhead at the office, and even scribbling on various scraps of paper while on vacation. Having come back to the rigorous writing schedule he had adhered to at Washington University, during his apprentice years, Brodsky encountered a new challenge: in earlier days, despite his prolific output, he had had time to organize his book manuscripts with great care, working through several drafts of each table of contents to ensure that his chapter divisions grouped images and tones precisely; now, faced with the ever-increasing duties of his daily life, he had to apportion his time wisely — shaping books took valuable time away from writing new poems.

Consequently, it was during this period that Brodsky began arranging manuscripts solely chronologically, with no overriding thematic structure. He finished *Taking the Back Road Home*, his first book created in this manner, in early 1972, gathering over fifty poems he had written between August 1971 and February 1972 and excluding only one full poem, two incomplete poems, and nine poetry fragments from the same time frame. He then set it aside, looking forward to new writing pursuits, leaving the work unpublished until 1997, when it was printed by Time Being Books.

Moving away from the more imagistic, mystical pieces he had written in the past, Brodsky's style took on a grittier tone in the months to come, capturing the mixed emotions he felt with the continual increase of his professional responsibilities. As assistant factory manager, he was a driving force behind the company's expansion into the outlet-store arena, overseeing the opening of an outlet in Farmington in 1970 and another, in Tipton, Missouri, in 1972. While this success gave Brodsky a true sense of accomplishment, it also brought him increased stress, requiring him to spend several days on the road each week.

The sixty-eight poems Brodsky wrote from April to December 1972, comprised in his next book, *Trip to Tipton and Other Compulsions*, which was completed in 1973 but left unpublished until Time Being Books' 1997 printing, reflect his struggle to incorporate the idealistic, romantic world of the artist into his "real life" as a young, recently wed man fighting to retain his identity and poetic sensibility while immersed in the corporate world.

Although this task was daunting, Brodsky was up to the challenge, never missing a chance to write, even during daily meals. Spending time in local cafés and diners allowed him to immerse himself in small-town culture, and the characters and dialects to which he was exposed quickly became a focus of his poetry. He began to relish those moments as respites from the work world, when he could disengage from business and revel in the realm of imagination.

Charged with energy, he pursued writing with increasing fervor, both at home and on business trips, letting the verse accumulate for months at a time, then collecting it into unpublished manuscripts. These books juxtaposed nearly every event in Brodsky's life, putting quiet weekends at home with his wife, friends, and family in stark contrast to his itinerant weekday existence as a traveling businessman. *"The Talking Machine" and Other Poems*, compiled in January 1974 and published by Time Being Books in 1997, contains fifty-three such poems, tracking eight months of his day-to-day rituals, from January to August 1973.

His next book, *Tiffany Shade*, created in April 1974, represented two important changes in Brodsky's life: it would be the last of his manuscripts to go unpublished for years (sitting untouched until offered by Time Being Books in 1997) and the last he would finish before he and his wife became parents. In several of the volume's fifty-one poems, composed from September 1973 through March 1974, he still touched on his travels through the Midwestern heartland, but in others, he turned to gentle images harvested from his relationship with Jan, celebrating love and contemplating their wonder as they faced the imminent arrival of their first child.

Detailing their hopes, fears, and joys as expectant parents, Brodsky composed a number of poems focused specifically on his wife's pregnancy. He also wrote several pieces about the birth of his daughter, Trilogy, who arrived on May 13, 1974. As an awestruck new father, Brodsky gathered this collection of eighteen poems shortly after Trilogy was born, dividing it into short chapters, to form a volume titled *Trilogy: A Birth Cycle*.

Focused on creating poems, not books, Brodsky had never pursued finding a publisher for his poetry before, and living in the small town of Farmington, he had few publishing resources available to him and little time to explore outside options. When these "baby poems" came along, however, he felt compelled to have the manuscript printed, for himself and for his wife, in honor of their daughter. Thus, he sought out the services of Farmington Press, which produced his first book, *Trilogy: A Birth Cycle*, in August 1974, offering it as a signed, limited edition of three hundred copies, with cover art by Jan Brodsky. It was also released by Time Being Books, as a second edition, in 1998.

Although it was a small book, Brodsky was thrilled with its publication, since it satisfied his poet's desire to see such beloved verse in print and his fictionist's impulse to have it arranged thematically. More important, it was a beautiful present of adoration for his wife, given in appreciation for the incredible gift she had given him just months before. In fact, he was so proud of the book, it inspired him to publish another collection of "baby poems," *Monday's Child*, which was finished just one year later.

A five-part book containing twenty-six poems written from May 1974 to April 1975, *Monday's Child* was published by Farmington Press in July 1975, as a signed, limited edition of three hundred copies, again with cover art by Jan Brodsky, and Time Being Books introduced the second edition in 1998. Reveling in the discoveries both he and his child were making as she progressed from newborn to toddler, the verse came straight from Brodsky's heart — a tender tribute to his daughter's first year of life — and he again found it extremely gratifying to have those poems in print.

He was also exploring other forms of poetry at this time, tapping new sources of imagery and language wherever he happened to be — from small towns in Missouri (Farmington, Tipton, Columbia) and Illinois (New Athens, Jacksonville, La Salle–Peru, Naperville) to big cities (New York, St. Louis, Fort Lauderdale). He was especially drawn to Florida, having visited the state throughout his college years, and he and Jan sought refuge there as well, often vacationing at a family home in Fort Lauderdale.

He wrote eleven "Florida poems" while staying there in April 1974 and eleven more during their next visit, in July 1974, causing him to ponder a new thematic project — a book in three parts, whose front and back sections would consist solely of these Florida pieces and whose middle portion, as a contrast, would contain poems written in the Midwest. A drastic departure from his other manuscripts, this book, titled *Point of Americas II*, was the first large manuscript he had attempted to prepare comprehensively for publication, and he wanted the poems, and the overriding concept behind their organization, to be as polished as possible. As a result, he continued to revise these pieces extensively and, before finishing them, even published another book of poetry, *The Kingdom of Gewgaw*.

Although two years would pass before *Point of Americas II* appeared in print, Brodsky was still hard at work penning other pieces through 1974 and 1975. His time was now divided between obligations at home, in his manufacturing career, and in his chosen profession — writing poetry. Thus, finding the hours necessary to arrange and revise *Point of Americas II*, or any book, became a lower priority, if not an impossibility. Although determined to finish *Point of Americas II*, Brodsky was overwhelmed and, against his own wishes, decided that, next time, he would return to the simpler manner he had resorted to just years before when arranging texts — grouping the poems by chronology instead of by theme.

Despite making this concession, he was resolute about forging ahead rather than becoming mired in work from years past. While he could have simplified his life by slowing his writing pace and concentrating only on the finished manuscripts he had prepared in the late 1960s and early 1970s, which were all still unpublished, Brodsky decided to keep an eye to the future, not wanting to retreat to images and styles that had grown cold for him.

Still making frequent business trips and writing at an increasingly feverish pace, he recognized the need for a more portable writing system. Although he had always relied on his typewriter when in Farmington, traveling made it difficult to keep handwritten scraps organized. He consequently opted to start setting down his verse in 8½-x-14-inch blue-ruled notebooks, which he uses to this day. Having written in bound notebooks only sporadically before mid-1974, he began carrying one in his attaché and composing in it regularly.

Now better equipped to handle his creative output, Brodsky could assess the chronology of his work more precisely, not having to depend as heavily on memory or side notes for pieces written while on the road. And the verse continued to flow at an exceptional rate, with Brodsky often creating multiple poems in a single day. But still he found time to collect his drafts into book form, placing forty-four of his recent poems, from July to September 1974, into a manuscript called *Cold Companionable Streams*, excluding just nine poetry fragments, one pair of fragments, and those poems he had already culled for *Point of Americas II*. He finished revising the text in January 1975 and then set it aside, ready to concentrate on the new material he had been writing that fall. The book remained unpublished until 1999, when Time Being Books printed the first edition.

Next, he compiled thirty-eight of the pieces he had composed from September 1974 to January 1975, leaving out five unpublished poems and four poetry fragments, to form another new manuscript, *Preparing for Incarnations*, which was completed in December 1975 and issued as a first edition in 1999, by Time Being Books. Providing intense studies of small-town life from the perspective of Brodsky's watchful poetic eye, his writing seethed with images of an outsider floundering in the depths of the often-restrictive community around him. The chaos of his younger years was now trailing him again, casting him further and further from his home.

As 1975 progressed, the poems accumulated steadily. Having to leave his wife and child behind for days at a time, Brodsky let his anguish reveal itself in his one release — his verse — ultimately lamenting, prophetically, that only his poems might survive his transformation. By June he had written forty-seven more pieces, forty-three of which he gleaned for the manuscript *The Kingdom of Gewgaw*, which he assembled in July and dedicated to his wife, in honor of their fifth wedding anniversary. He ordered the pieces chronologically, so he might spend the months ahead revising the poems, not the book's arrangement, and the finished form was issued by Farmington Press in February 1976, as a signed, limited edition of four hundred copies, with cover art by Jan Brodsky (its second edition was released in 2000, by Time Being Books). It was his third published book, appearing in print months before *Point of Americas II*.

Trailed by daunting realities, he sought another outlet for his passion, in Oxford, Mississippi, home to William Faulkner. Brodsky had started a Faulkner collection in the early 1960s, while at Yale, but had suspended his pursuits in 1968. However, in 1974, he was offered the chance to purchase twelve presentation-copy Faulkner first editions, renewing his interest. He traveled to Oxford in May 1975 to meet James Webb, a retired University of Mississippi professor and the curator of Faulkner's home, Rowan Oak, who shared with him information about the Faulkner conferences held at the Ole Miss campus. It was the first of many pilgrimages Brodsky would make there, as an adventurous collector out to soak in the culture, and subculture, that enhanced the Faulkner mystique. Rowan Oak, Bailey's Woods, the kudzu and loblolly pines, the characters that had so endeared Brodsky to Yoknapatawpha, and the South itself, still steeped in dark secrets — they all offered a surreal tableau into which this Midwestern outlander would eventually escape.

His fascination with the South bloomed, funneling away yet more of his time, but still he managed to keep sight of his other priorities, at home and on the job. In fact, his writing reached its most heated levels in the months to come, as Brodsky's trips to the Tipton outlet store increased. On his many nights away from home, he assuaged his loneliness with wine and music, letting motel bars absorb him in their anonymity. There, his creative juices flowed, allowing him to compose as many as five or six poems in an evening, often after having written one or two earlier in the day.

At this frantic rate, he composed fifty-two poems, two incomplete poems, seven poetry fragments, and two sets of fragments from June to October 1975. Brodsky later selected forty-seven of those poems for a new book, *Stranded in the Land of Transients*, again arranging them chronologically due to time constraints. Because the poems were still piling up around him daily, the book was not published until May 1978, when it was produced by Farmington Press as a signed, limited edition of five hundred copies, with a photo of an original ceramic by Jan Brodsky on its cover. The book was released as a second edition in 2000, by Time Being Books.

Feeling scattered and disoriented from his demanding schedule, Brodsky continued to seek relief in his verse, composing forty-six poems from December 1975 to March 1976. In these pieces, mixing reveries about seizing the day and pleas for guidance, he recorded not only his physical journeys throughout the Midwest but also his mental navigation through the bouts of happiness and melancholy associated with these travels. Together, the poems formed the whole of his next book, *The Uncelebrated Ceremony of Pants-Factory Fatso*, a chronological volume that was first published in December 1978, by Farmington Press, as a signed, limited edition of five hundred copies, with another of his wife's ceramics pictured on the cover. Its second edition, by Time Being Books, was printed in 2001.

The backlog of poems seemed never-ending, but Brodsky had a new understanding of his timetable — he simply had to have patience with the production of his books (which often went through multiple proofs and were now being printed two or three years after the poems' composition), in order to keep creating new verse. In fact, it was not until 1976 that Brodsky sent the majority of *Point of America II*'s forty-one poems to the printer's office. The typesetter worked on the book intermittently, while waiting for Brodsky to finish revising certain poems. After incorporating changes Brodsky made to three sets of proofs, the press finally received the go-ahead for the book in July 1976, offering it as a signed, limited edition of four hundred copies. It too had Jan Brodsky's artwork on the cover. The book's second edition, by Time Being Books, appeared in 1998.

Also, in 1976, Brodsky came back to two other sets of poems he had written years before — the texts of *Cold Companionable Streams* and *Preparing for Incarnations*. Dissatisfied with the writing but hoping all his work from 1974 and later would reach print, he began to drastically revise the pieces from both books and combined all but two of them ("New Year's Celebration" and "The Orange Bowl") into a single manuscript, an expanded edition reusing the title *Preparing for Incarnations*, which became his fifth published book. Arranged chronologically, this volume was originally printed in December 1976, by Farmington Press, as a signed, limited edition of five hundred copies, with cover art by Jan Brodsky, and released in 1999, by Time Being Books, as a second edition.

Busy finalizing *Point of Americas II* when time allowed and revising the new *Preparing* even while on vacation in Fort Lauderdale, Brodsky continued writing as much as possible. He had truly become a "road-poet" at this point, composing almost exclusively while away on business trips, often while driving, with his notebook beside him in the car. While this process was tricky at first (as confirmed by the wild, jagged handwriting in the manuscripts from his initial attempts), by 1976 he was a master at authoring pieces anywhere and anytime, even while flying down the highway. Indeed, almost all of the forty-nine poems in his next book, *Résumé of a Scrapegoat*, were written away from Farmington, many while he was in transit from one city to the next.

He authored those pieces from March to July 1976 and then set them aside, not coming back to them until 1979 and 1980, when he began drastically revising them for publication. The book, printed in the winter of 1980, was offered by Farmington Press as a signed, limited edition of five hundred copies, with a photo of another of Jan's ceramics on the cover, and the second edition was issued by Time Being Books in 2001. (Because most of the poems were dramatically changed during 1979 and 1980, generally only their original 1976 versions are shown in this volume. Their later versions, printed in *Résumé*, will appear in the final volume of this series, which will be devoted to poems that have undergone drastic later revision.)

Those poems became the last group to be arranged solely by chronology and placed into book form. Brodsky's output of verse had become too staggering — he could no longer continue compiling manuscripts, especially as his devotion to expanding his Faulkner collection and establishing its bibliography became a primary focus. He would publish only two other poetry books in the next six years: *La Preciosa* (1977) and *Birds in Passage* (1980).

He had still been writing verse about his daughter Trilogy, off and on, since 1975, so in 1977, to celebrate Trilogy's third birthday, he gathered thirty-three of those poems (ranging from June 1975 to April 1977) into one book on childhood, titled *La Preciosa*. It was printed by Farmington Press in the winter of 1977, as a signed, limited edition of five hundred copies, with cover art reproduced from one of his wife's etchings of Trilogy, and released by Time Being Books, as a second edition, in 2001.

Brodsky's only other Farmington Press release was *Birds in Passage*, containing twenty-seven of his poems that had been published in journals, magazines, and anthologies through the years. The volume was issued in October 1980, as a signed, limited edition of five hundred copies, with cover art by Jan Brodsky, and Time Being Books completed the second edition in 2001. The text contained some of his favorite pieces, ranging from 1968 to 1976, and all of them had been included in earlier Brodsky manuscripts. But unlike his other books to that point, which had been grouped by aesthetics or by the poems' composition dates, this group was arranged only by the dates the pieces had appeared in the various publications. Not a "true" book by Brodsky's standards, in terms of getting previously untapped poetry into print, he created *Birds in Passage* only to serve as a gathering of his best work — a collection comprising the majority of his verse published to that point, which would serve as a calling card, of sorts, at poetry readings and other functions.

Because *Birds in Passage* contained no new pieces and the later poems in *La Preciosa* (from July 1976 through 1977) were only a smattering of the writing Brodsky did during that period, the natural break for volume two of the *Complete Poems* series comes at the end of his last wholly encompassing chronological book, *Résumé of a Scrapegoat*. Thus, volume two comprises all the poetry Brodsky wrote from mid-June 1967 through the composition date of the final poem in *Résumé* — July 2, 1976 — including all fragments and incomplete pieces he wrote in those nine years. The only writings not shown are the few prose selections he authored in the late 1960s, since Brodsky's desire, after his graduation from Washington University, in 1967, was to be a professional poet.

The pieces in this volume are ordered by their dates of creation, which represent their original composition, not their revision. If a poem has more than one creation date (i.e., if it was started on one day and not finished until another, with extra stanzas or closure coming at that later time), it is arranged in the overall text by its first date, because Brodsky's poems typically have their intent, as well as the majority of their content, in place at that point. All creation dates are listed at the end of each piece (with bracketed numerals indicating sequence of composition, if two or more poems were written in one day), and the tracking number assigned to the poem in the Time Being Books database is included there as well.

If a creation date could not be verified, a question mark follows the unconfirmed portion, which may be the month, the day, the year, or all three. On rare occasions, the entire date is in doubt (in which case it is bracketed and followed by a question mark), indicating either that it may represent revision instead of composition or that the drafts were undated but were found near other material written at that time. Likewise, the date may appear twice for the same poem, once with a question mark and once without, signifying that it is accurate for at least a portion of the text but may or may not apply to the whole piece.

The dates and tracking numbers will eventually serve as cross references between the standard *Complete Poems* volumes and the two concluding books of this series: the index of Time Being Books' database records and the volume of ultimate, later revised versions. The index, to be arranged chronologically, will detail where each poem was composed and provide its publication data. This information, in turn, will link the standard set with the final volume, which will show the corrected, most recent version of every poem drastically revised years after its original composition date, often for a new publication. Any poem in this second volume that will have its later form printed in the terminal book (either because it has already undergone such revision or because it has been assigned to a future publication and will, presumably, undergo such revision) bears a delta symbol (Δ) after its title.

Thus, in the *Complete Poems* set, the standard volumes will present the text of each poem, the penultimate volume will chronicle its creation and its publishing history, and the final volume will show its subsequent, revised version, if applicable.

To retain the poems' original authorial voice from the period of composition, the editorial staff of Time Being Books has not fully revised any of the pieces in this volume except those culled for new publications (which have their early versions printed here, carrying a delta sign, and will have their later, revised versions in the last volume of this series). Even pieces in undeveloped form have not been edited stylistically, because they illustrate the evolution of Brodsky's writing, in juxtaposition with his more advanced works. To alert the reader, fragmental pieces have a dagger symbol (†) after the title, and incomplete poems bear a double-dagger symbol (‡).

Brodsky did revise the vast majority of his poems after writing them, however, with the intention of refining their grammatical form. To help him achieve that goal, the editorial staff has worked with Brodsky to make all pieces in this series meet Time Being Books' current standardizations for language usage and mechanics, correcting spelling, punctuation, grammar, and syntax as needed, in accordance with the *Chicago Manual of Style* and Edward D. Johnson's *Handbook of Good English*. Bold and italic typefaces have also been used as appropriate, and preferred spellings (as listed in *Random House Unabridged*) have been added as well. While his use of neologized words and compounds has been preserved throughout, hyphens have frequently been inserted in them in this volume (unlike volume one), to prevent ambiguity and make the usage more uniform.

These editorial changes are meant to standardize the work and enhance its readability, without any relineation or substantive revision, and they have been made only under Brodsky's direct supervision, bringing clarity and order to the pieces presented here, in volume two of *The Complete Poems of Louis Daniel Brodsky*.

Sheri Vandermolen
4/9–11/01
Phoenix, Arizona

INTRODUCTION

As May of 1967 drew near, I cast back over my protracted, four-year seclusion in graduate school at Washington University. I would soon receive my master's degree in English literature. Jan, my girlfriend since 1965, would get her BFA in fashion design. We both would attend the same graduation ceremony.

Having been accepted into the fall 1967 graduate creative-writing program at San Francisco State University, to pursue my second master's, in fiction, not poetry, I knew it was time to give permanent order to the poetic phase of my apprentice years. Indeed, the possibility existed that I might never write poetry again. By June, I had fashioned two books, *The Easy Philosopher* and *"A Hard Coming of It" and Other Poems* from the extensive *oeuvre* of my poems, incorporating many of the pieces from my first poetry manuscript, *Five Facets of Myself,* which I'd completed in January. I spent the rest of that summer sequestered in the upstairs back-hall study at my parents' home, in St. Louis, writing poems that would fit in my next two books — *Points in Time* (which remained incomplete for decades) and *The Foul Rag-and-Bone Shop* (a book I would not complete until 1969, containing favorite pieces from my apprentice years, with a handful written within the first few years after my graduation from Washington University).

In truth, that graduation was traumatic. For one thing, it didn't really mark my matriculation into the "real world"; rather, it nurtured additional procrastination by allowing me one more escape from reality, yet another reprieve from fastening onto a career that would support me, let me become fully independent of schooling, parents — essentially fostering the same sheltered, affluent existence I had known. It also marked the beginning of my separation from Jan, which was painful beyond reckoning. Soon after graduation, she left for New York City to begin her career as a fashion designer.

Conveniently for me, the five members of the English Department who sat in judgment over my master's orals (apparently, I was too complacent, probably because I felt that I had already overextended myself in writing an optional hundred-page thesis on animal imagery in Faulkner's fiction) decided that I was not "qualified" to pursue a Ph.D., at least not at their institution. Evidently, I had shown contempt for critical protocol in writing and defending my thesis. According to all my jurors except Stanley Elkin (himself a Faulkner devotee and, like me, a nonconformist with an artistic disdain for the conventional), I had footnoted far too few references in support of my conclusions and, therefore, must have borrowed from phantom scholars. Their insinuation made me grow sullen and resentful. Since there wasn't a large, sophisticated body of Faulkner criticism in the early 1960s, it had been easy for me to do the obligatory reading before proceeding to break new ground. If these panelists had determined my fate, I was grateful, because they had really shown me that I was meant to be an artist, not a scholar or professor. Creative writing, not teaching, would be my calling.

In August of 1967, I drove out to California, primed with an excitement bordering on messianic zeal. The preceding spring, I had submitted, with my application, samples of my fiction and poetry and was selected for the fiction component of San Francisco State's creative-writing program. I eagerly accepted the opportunity to attend, even though I would rather have been concentrating on my poetry.

In San Francisco, I settled into a rented apartment by the Pacific Ocean, two blocks from Playland at the Beach. Mornings, I would inhabit the kitchen, on whose table I had set up my typewriter, where I would work for five to six hours, pounding out what I hoped would be innovative works, not be just imitations of *The Sound and the Fury* and *Absalom, Absalom!* In the afternoon and evening, I attended classes on campus.

During that era, San Francisco was an education itself. The climate was hysterical. The Haight-Ashbury scene fueled a rampant abnegation of morals. San Francisco State and nearby University of California at Berkeley were cauldrons of radical politics and melting pots of the most anarchical of the Bay area's war protesters, political insurrectionists, and artists. Bill Graham's Fillmore West served as a lodestone that attracted a miscellany of music lovers, substance abusers, disaffiliated youth, lost souls, and me on weekend nights away from my typewriter, always in the company of two ex-cons, neighbors in my apartment building whom I'd befriended and who filled in the gaps of my education with street wisdom. I was overwhelmed by such iconoclastic performers as Janis Joplin, Grace Slick, Pigpen, and Jimi Hendrix. And certainly San Francisco was a writer's mecca, with its own distinctive literary style, born out of the individual styles of Allen Ginsberg, Lawrence Ferlinghetti, Gregory Corso, Robert Duncan, Jack Spicer, Richard Brautigan, Ken Kesey, and Brother Antoninus.

For nine months, I gestated my two novels, wrote almost no poetry (to me, the two modes of expression were inimical), remained unswervingly faithful to Jan, and grew increasingly lonely as a result of leading an almost monastic life for the promise of literary celebrity and the eventual resumption of my close, secure relationship with Jan. Mine was a worthy sacrifice; my goals seemed reachable.

When I was not composing what would become the novels *Vineyard's Toys* and *The Bindle Stiffs*, I indulged myself in the more relaxing art of epistolary writing. In myriad letters to Jan (who, literally, was working her way up from the selvage-strewn cutting-room floor as a fashion designer in Manhattan's Garment District), I could explore my fantasies and wax embarrassingly sentimental and romantic, a style I dared not use in my fiction. But all the time, I feared that I would lose her to New York.

In truth, knowing that Jan was a gregarious person who was not likely to spend her nights home when she could be out socializing, I suspected that she was into the bar scene, meeting men. On my one visit to her there, at Thanksgiving, she did take me to a number of her favorite hangouts, like Yellowfingers and Maxwell's Plum — hot spots of the youth culture's emerging sexual freedom.

Too soon, the school year was over, my second graduate-school graduation a *fait accompli*. *Vineyard's Toys* made a fine splash in the English department, but less than a year later, it would garner nothing more than a disingenuously positive rejection from the editor in chief of Random House. In my naive and arrogant insularity, I had dreamed grandiosely.

By that time, I had already subjected myself to an additional humiliation that made the stillbirth of *Vineyard's Toys* seem like child's play. What had begun as a strategy to bring Jan and me together resulted in a personal debacle. Perhaps out of desperation, certainly against my principles and good judgment, I persuaded myself to apply for a teaching position at Miami-Dade South Community College, in Coral Gables, Florida, within minutes of Jan's apartment in Coconut Grove (she had accepted a fashion designer's job for Suntogs, a Miami children's-wear firm, and was beginning to gain a degree of name recognition). To my surprise, I was accepted for the position of English instructor for the coming fall.

I spent that glorious summer in northern Wisconsin, thirty miles east of Duluth, counseling teenagers at Camp Nebagamon for Boys, where I myself had been a camper for seven years and a counselor for five. Realizing that this would be my last summer shielded from the real world, I wrote a number of nostalgic, sentimental poems by which to record the end of my youth. Twenty years later, when I would accompany my son, Troika, to Camp Nebagamon for his second summer there, I remembered these poems and gathered them, along with other "camp poems" written over the years, into a paean to Camp Nebagamon, titled *You Can't Go Back, Exactly*.

In late August of 1968, I flew to Miami, set up house with Jan in her tiny apartment, and prepared to brave Miami-Dade South Community College's hotbed of academic apathy. The faculty was too laid back, invisible. I began denigrating students I hadn't even met, for their lack of interest, their fractured attention spans, their listlessness. And as the days of the training period passed, I grew more and more terrified that I had made a cosmic mistake. I was now on the brink of indenturing myself to a career which, in principle, I not only hated but which would prevent me from ever freeing myself from its clutches once I fully succumbed.

I confided in Jan that although I cherished our intimacy, I feared I was close to committing spiritual suicide. Furthermore, I was not being honest to those who were counting on me to set a responsible example. I didn't want to be in school one more day, even on the other side of the desk.

I lacked commitment to the job, and I shamefacedly resigned after four days of training. I terribly regretted leaving the administrator with such an unexpected dilemma; moreover, I knew this move would anger and disappoint my mentor, Muggs Lorber, director of Camp Nebagamon, who had used his influence to secure me the job despite my lack of a Florida teaching certificate. I'd come to realize that teaching would not provide me with the experience of working with working people. I felt that if I was to be a well-rounded writer, I would have to develop a new sensibility, with its own distinct language, different from the one I'd employed to complete four books of poetry, six novels, and a novella during the previous seven years, one more muscular, broader and deeper in scope, and more authentic, which could speak to readers not trained in responding to esoteric literary devices only those connected with academia could appreciate.

Moreover, I was experiencing a very bad feeling about Jan. The same suspicions I'd had while she was in New York and I in San Francisco now came back to haunt me. I had met some of her new coterie of "artsy" friends in Coconut Grove, and I could tell that they were fast and loose. She was always gravitating toward such types.

With a single phone call to my father, who owned the Biltwell Company and had just purchased a factory in Farmington, Missouri, a small country town of ten thousand people, seventy-five miles southwest of St. Louis, I arranged to enroll in my next, and ultimate, postgraduate school, the proverbial "school of hard knocks" — Farmington Manufacturing Company. Although I agonized in saying good-bye to Jan and flying back home, I wanted to believe that I was on the verge of undertaking an education that would provide me with material to further my creative energies in unimaginable ways.

Although I had no certainty as to what might be the outcome of my quixotic flight from south Florida to rural Missouri, I trusted that the move was the right one for me and for the future of my work, my writing. If what I envisioned transpired, I would spend a few years in Farmington, working as an assistant manager, and learn enough to say that I then had a firsthand understanding of blue-collar America. With this newly acquired knowledge, I would be able to write with a more authoritative voice, one that wouldn't smack of bathos or pedantry.

What I didn't count on was that the job would be so consuming, not just physically but emotionally exhausting, that it would rob me of my free time, drain me of the desire to write new fiction. At best, I might be lucky enough to jot down an occasional poem. Factory work was demanding in a way I'd never known. This came as a rude shock to me.

In my first days with Biltwell, in 1968, I toured its Salisbury, Missouri, manufacturing and warehouse facilities and immediately isolated an Achilles heel: the company's inability to dispose of irregular garments. I was challenged to find a profitable solution for getting rid of the thousands and thousands of slacks relegated to the junk pile due to manufacturing defects. But my solution, an outlet store — retail garments at wholesale prices, sold right from the factory — would have to wait almost a year, until I'd assisted John Gulla, the plant manager, in starting Farmington Manufacturing Company from scratch.

For the first six months of my work in the factory, I lived in a motel five miles from Farmington and commuted to St. Louis on weekends to visit my parents and do some dating. I harbored a sinking feeling that in fleeing Coconut Grove, I had proclaimed my relationship with Jan finished. I was on my own, and to the extent I could gain time away from my new job, I began seeking female companionship. But after those first six months, I found myself sorely missing Jan. Dreaming that she and I might live together, I purchased a fourteen-room white-clapboard Victorian house, built in 1896, in Farmington, on the town's silk-stocking street, West Columbia, and invited Jan to join me in Smalltown, U.S.A. In November 1969, she accepted.

My life was in flux. I was experiencing the turmoil of dislocation. Working in a sewing factory required different disciplines, skills, and energies than any I'd previously known, and living in a rural community that found little value in formal education or culture was a challenge, especially for an outsider with three college degrees, a handlebar mustache, and an exaggerated afro.

Jan was also in the throes of dislocation. Having been used to a very active social life, she now found herself in Farmington with no job and no friends, certainly no excitement. We had no one but each other for companionship. The novelty of living together, "in sin," buoyed us at first but soon began to vanish. And while the quiet country life satisfied me, it became unbearable for Jan.

Around this same time, my idea for an outlet store was coming to fruition. I convinced management to allocate nine hundred square feet in the piece-goods-storage area of the factory to house my infant operation. I cut a hole in the outside wall, installed a door, set up bins to hold the stacks of flawed pants, which I'd had sent over from the Salisbury warehouse, and with a cigar box for a cash register, I was in business. Through local word of mouth, the store grossed $50,000 in its first year. (Unbeknownst to me then, word would soon reach St. Louis and beyond, helping the store gross $250,000 in its second year and eventually grow into an operation of 2500 square feet, with half a million dollars in annual sales, in the years ahead.)

Despite the additional demands on my time, I was experiencing a kind of spiritual euphoria. I no longer felt obligated to maintain a good intellectual front. No one in my new environment cared whether I had academic credentials or could quote Shakespeare, Shelley, and Roethke. Hallmark cards were adequate, superior. All that mattered was my being thorough in administering my duties at the factory, treating all the workers fairly, and rolling up my sleeves, sharing in whatever needed to be done, whether it meant working overtime, coming in for half a day on Saturdays, or being in the factory by 6:00 each a.m. Because I was a provider of jobs, many lives depended on my sound judgments. I had become one of the town's stewards. I began to take pride in the community and even joined the Farmington Chamber of Commerce.

In July 1970, Jan and I drove west. I'd dreamed of one day getting to share with her the haunts of San Francisco I had discovered during 1967, the Summer of Love, and 1968. The entire drive out, neither of us discussed marriage, let alone considered it. We were far too "liberated" to be beguiled by such traditional dependency. But in the back of my mind, I kept feeling that something radical, a significant change, would have to happen or our relationship would wither. And once we were in San Francisco, I was able to transform this fear into an abrupt marriage proposal. Spontaneously, we held our wedding ceremony outdoors, in Sutro Park, overlooking the Pacific. Our vows were officiated by a diminutive, red-headed leprechaun of a Presbyterian minister, symbolically named Glenda Hope. Our marriage, on the eighth day of July 1970, became our mutual high-water mark.

The late summer of 1971 ushered in the rebirth of my poetry. From August of 1971 through February of 1972, I composed fifty-four poems, which formed the basis of a new book, entitled *Taking the Back Road Home*. My excitement for the medium had been renewed. The act of creating a poem seemed to be perfect for me, considering the limitations my job imposed on my time.

After almost four years of hit-and-miss composition, I had taken fire again. In truth, before these new poems appeared, I had come to believe that my writing career was a graduate student's ephemeral run at immortality. But once they had achieved momentum, I was determined not to discourage them. Poetry, not fiction, turned out to be my saving grace.

I also realized that, with some maneuvering, I could have a continual taste of two worlds: I could play a role in the operation of the factory — be a businessman after all — and I could utilize the skills I had developed during nine years of undergraduate and graduate school, dreaming of one day becoming a professional writer. More so, I could be a responsible family man.

Marriage changed everything in our relationship for a while. Now, Farmington, with its small-town mores, embraced us, and we began to make friends. We felt welcome. Yet this new sense of belonging, which seemed so appealing, eventually began to wear thin. There wasn't any culture in Farmington. The closest movie theater was in Flat River, five miles away. St. Louis was an inconvenient hour and a half to the northeast.

My wife was the first to feel disenchantment. During the initial years of our married life, Jan busied herself with shaping our old house into a home. She painted pictures, played with her dogs, planted a garden. She cooked for me when I walked home from the factory for lunch and dinner. She became a recluse, progressively feeling confined, trapped, longing for escape.

In the fall of 1971, Jan's desperation took a bizarre turn. An old fellow camper and schoolmate of mine, who was living in Florida, came to Farmington to visit us for a few days. One afternoon, he confronted me. He was leaving immediately and claimed he was taking Jan with him. At first, I was completely stunned. Jan was nowhere to be seen. I became enraged, slugged him, and actually shoved him out the front door, without his suitcase. In my naiveté, I believed that he was irrational, crazy. It never occurred to me that for him to have screwed up the courage to disclose such shocking intentions, Jan would have had to encourage him. I think my violence surprised her. She never said another word about the incident.

I was so absorbed with factory work, the outlet store, and my poetry that I failed to notice her disaffection, or if I did, I would dismiss it. One attempt I did make to help lift Jan out of her malaise was to plan a trip with her to Europe. We hadn't really had a honeymoon, and this would be it. In April of 1972, we visited Lisbon, Madrid, Rome, Florence, Venice, Zurich, and Lucerne. In Venice, I wrote a poem called "Marriage in the Basilica di San Marco Evangelista" to belatedly celebrate our wedding. However, at the end of our trip, I also composed a poem about returning home from New York by myself. Without warning, Jan insisted on remaining behind for five or six days. I later found out that she stayed with a homosexual male classmate from her fashion-design class and five of his acquaintances.

In June of 1972, I opened up a second outlet store, in one of Biltwell's factories out in the middle of Missouri, in Tipton, not far from the college town of Columbia. This, though I could hardly realize it at the time, was the beginning of my life as a peripatetic, my career as a traveling salesman and a wandering bard.

In 1973, my parents bought a condominium by the ocean, in Fort Lauderdale, Florida, in a building auspiciously named Point of Americas II. Jan and I spent Christmas of that year there and returned again in March of 1974, when she was seven months pregnant with our first child. We would come back again in June, after our baby's birth, and in December, to celebrate Christmas and New Year's. Fort Lauderdale would become a great refuge for us. For me especially, it provided the serenity that I couldn't find in Farmington and allowed me to relax from the pace I was keeping. I would write many poems about those magical shores.

Jan and I rejoiced in the birth of daughter, Trilogy Maya. Jan, the fashion designer and painter, and I, the poet, placed on our baby the mark of our own creative souls. We named her Trilogy because we considered her to be one of three equal parts of the trilogy we constituted, and she received the middle name Maya because she was born in May and because we deeply respected Maya Angelou, whose book *I Know Why the Caged Bird Sings* and whose good deeds and compassion for others inspired us.

This miraculous event sparked many poems, which eventually found their way into three books about our first child: *Trilogy: A Birth Cycle*, *Monday's Child*, and *La Preciosa*, the first two of which were ultimately incorporated into *A Gleam in the Eye: Poems for a First Baby* (St. Louis: Timeless Press, 1992), a volume that carries an endorsement from Maya Angelou herself.

By the end of 1974, I had four outlet stores up and running, three in mid-Missouri and one in southern Illinois. They were grossing in excess of a million dollars a year — a tidy accomplishment, especially since the men's dress slacks I was purveying were factory seconds. The stores success required me to take to the road more and more.

But this traveling was anything but a hardship; in fact, it provided a very necessary escape for me from domestic tensions. I would come home tired from work, and Jan would be irritable from the lack of sleep that accompanies caring for a new baby. Then our constant arguing would begin all over again.

Now that I was driving so extensively, I learned to distract myself from the rigors and the boredom of rural road travel by devising a desk in the front seat of my Ford station wagon, one consisting of my attaché case securely pressed against my right thigh — it was the perfect size to hold my Boorum & Pease account book. (To this day, I do all my composition in similar record books, with the same kind of Bic ballpoint.) I had initiated a habit that would soon grow into an addiction to feed what I discovered was a ferocious compulsion to turn my road meditations into road-poetry.

With increasing eagerness, I looked forward to taking off in my station wagon to write "in flight." But what I failed to realize was that my time away from home, from Jan, was widening the fissure in our romance, our marriage. I misconstrued her plaints of loneliness, her pleas for me to stay home, as expressions of love, not cries for attention. I, too, was lonely on those trips, but I would keep so busy that I hardly had time to brood, and if I did, I would shape that brooding into poems that I deluded myself into thinking were love poems, albeit ones about love unrequited due to separation. When I was off to the stores, I doubt I ever imagined Jan's sense of emptiness in that big house or her growing aloneness.

Aside from providing me needed freedom, my time on the road made me feel like a stranger in strange lands, a Moses wandering through rural wilderness to purvey raiment. One night, while eating dinner at the Ramada Inn in Columbia, Missouri, having worked all day at my stores in Tipton and Salisbury, I wrote a poem titled "Breaking Stallions," and all at once, my entire world was transformed. I realized that I was seeing myself as the scion of Eastern European ragmen and bearded Russian tailors.

In a flash, I knew my great-grandfather, my grandfather, and my father. I had inherited the mantle of my Jewish ancestors. From that point on, a part of my writer's identity became a character named Willy Sypher, an ordinary but nobly spirited road peddler for "Acme-Zenith Trouser Co. of St. Louie, Mo." who, from Monday to Friday, day in, year out, plied the heartland, calling on small-town merchants, deriving a paltry commission from meager sales. Willy Sypher, schlepper, was me, a part of me, anyway, with which I had yet to acquaint myself. He was my undiscovered Jewishness.

I would continue in my capacity as manager of outlet stores for fifteen years. Whenever I'd drive to one of the stores (at one point, my modest chain grew to seven), Willy and I would merge. More than a few hundred "traveling salesman" poems document the intimate meeting of minds Willy and I experienced before we said our last good-byes in 1987, when I would leave Biltwell to pursue my writing full-time, leave the highway to Willy's memory.

During this same period, I revived a hobby from my university days: my William Faulkner collection. In 1968, upon moving to Farmington and immersing myself into my new business career, I had put the wraps on my collecting. But given a serendipitous opportunity, in 1974, to acquire a dozen first-edition presentation copies Faulkner had given to an old friend, Hubert Starr, a lawyer living in Los Angeles in the 1930s, I rekindled my passion. In May of 1975, motivated by my recent acquisitions, I paid a visit to James Webb, who, in his retirement from Ole Miss, was serving as curator of Rowan Oak, Faulkner's house in Oxford. After spending an afternoon with him in late May, roaming Faulkner's property, Bailey's Woods, being given a personal tour through the house, and visiting with the professor and his wife, I was moved to write one of my first "Faulkner/Oxford/Yoknapatawpha/Mississippi" poems, "Of Books and Woods and Us," dedicated to Dr. Webb. Little did I know that this would spark a love affair with Faulkner's mythical Yoknapatawpha and real Oxford, Mississippi, and an outpouring of almost 160 poems over the next fifteen years, which would eventually be comprised in three individual volumes — *Mississippi Vistas* (1983, 1990), *Disappearing in Mississippi Latitudes* (1994), and *Mistress Mississippi* (1992) — and the unpublished 1995 compilation *A Mississippi Trilogy: A Poetic Saga of the South.*

On June 23, 1976, Jan, two-year-old Trilogy, and I flew to Memphis, then drove to Oxford for the day to visit the Webbs, as if to formally stake claim to my next territory, have my wife and child give their tacit approval. In early August, I attended my first Faulkner and Yoknapatawpha Conference at Ole Miss. The experience would redefine the course of my life.

Louis Daniel Brodsky
4/29/95 . . . 5/7/01
St. Louis, Missouri

THE COMPLETE POEMS

OF

LOUIS DANIEL

BRODSKY

VOLUME TWO, 1967–1976

[The patient-weighted elevator] †

The patient-weighted elevator

6/16/67 — [1] (03335)

The Fate of a Poet No Longer in Vogue

Nouns that were proper cease to be of consequence,
For the density that enshrouds published sensibilities.
In an age crowded with greenhouse poets and preachers,
The laity pays lip service to his untended cenotaph.

He is the vehicle brought out on a dusty tray
To be displayed and bought by arcane curators
Who value the perfect stasis of his antique forms.
Yet, alliterations are underbid in this auction room,

Rhymes die on his end-stopped face, and steeples plummet
To pedestals that once held the graceful weight of God.
Syllables erode; worms undermine his oblique conceits;
Decay gains headway on the body's critical verbs.

With a loud squeak, the naked savage is laid to sleep
At the base of an extinct metaphor portending upheaval.

6/16–17/67 — [2] on 6/16 (01075)

The Golden Age

Spider monkeys and chimpanzees
Hang from ropes tied to his eyes,
Dangle over the flattened nose,
Their toes touching his fatted lips.

His fists are Pleistocene clubs;
The legs are petrified tree trunks
Sunken in swamps of stomach and thigh;
The forehead is a hot anvil;
His musty pea pod of a skull
Contains a cluster of rotting seeds.

He is progenitor and widower alike,
The last of a breed that has survived,
Each generation, in whiskey bottles,
Garbage cans, and tenement eyes.

A rummager among discarded keepsakes,
He lives beneath the drum's taut skin,
Within the sax's blown-out bowl,
And under a chauffeur's sweaty cap.

He is living proof to evolutionists
That progress is measured with calipers,
A scientific oddity whose facial hue
Has resisted change, whose pain
Is registered by daily failures
At agencies that restrain his labors.

Yet, he is a persistent creature.
Consistency engenders in him a calm
Not even the smallest pond
Can imitate for unexpected squalls.

Time, or God, has passed him over,
Arrested the leopard's curves in his mate,
Sculpted unique girdles in his palms,
Made poets of them, whose souls
Breathe perfect verses in the clay,
Songs from the nostrils' passageways.

Someday, interpreters living in caves,
Ranging out to find ancient cities
Crumbled or washed away, will say,
"The greatest civilization known to man
Was that of the neo-African in a displaced land."

6/18/67 — [1] (01076)

In the Dying Hospital

Fragile membranes strain at their stitchings.
The eyes twitch disconsolately without response
From memories that dance across their screen.
Although they have seen afternoons at the zoo,
Nights unwinding from a spool of thirsty lights,
*

And cool April mornings dawning with dew,
Nothing, not even slender sheets strewn
Or an "I love you" softly spoken in June,
Can undo the hazy hue a million tears make.
The little body beneath sheets is subdued;
Arms and legs are weak. The peaked face
Partakes of a gloom that fills this room
With waste, waste that shades the eyeballs,
Devastating the lids' quiet sanctuaries.
This girl who lies in wait in this bed,
Head propped against a pillow's breast,
Cries silently, listening for footsteps,
For a telephone's importunate ring-ring,
Or another sun to run its hot fingers
Down the closed eyelids of venetian blinds.

Life has cornered her; it winds her up
Into one small bundle about itself.
She is all crying; all coughing owns her.
The febrile moan that fills her throat
Belongs to all who shout songs of love
Out there; it shares their pain unborn.
Though she will never know their hatefulness,
She is doing the dying for all who dance.
Her life and death, so finely infused,
Are Dioscuri that, with each light breath,
Illuminate this night with a newer life:
A moon too bright for daylight to hide.

6/18/67 — [2] (01077)

Pacemaker

All along the glacial hallways,
Machines bleep, keeping pace
With distressed hearts, as death
Congests their waning springs.

The fluorescent screen is a face
That imitates each tortured gesture,
Traces every unsteady decline
Of a regulator clock about to unwind.

The body's economy becomes corrupted.
Irregularity dismantles the beat.
Only the electric plug's connection
Can arrest its inevitable defeat.

When writhing dies behind the door,
Silence subsides to an overtone.
Only heat from the machine remains,
And the screen's faintly fading mirage.

6/19/67 (01078)

In the Dying Hospital II

Dahlias, roses, two cymbidium orchids
Pose in cut-glass vases and bowls.
Odors ply her frozen nose; colors talk.
The chalky taste of barium escapes
As she stares at a store-bought bouquet,
Those sown in backyard gardens and cut,
And the pair that grew to unequaled hue
In moss-strewn pots suspended in air.

Already they have begun the wilting.
Their thirsty stilts, half submerged,
Once taut, soften like waterlogged ferns.
Imperceptible rust touches petal edges.
The bouquet withdraws its rosary.
Sweethearts that were virgins' bodies
Open wide, beginning their certain decline.
Only the orchids prolong their perfection.

Nurses and interns make hourly rounds,
Feeding her and attending her personal needs.
Patients she meets on occasional strolls
Down corridors swollen with heart machines
Pause to reflect on the gifts she receives.
Except for the flowers, she has no friends.
Their sympathy depends on suffering emblems,
Recommends life to her through dying things.

6/20/67 (01079)

[Silence swings its pendulum]

Silence swings its pendulum
Across this house — an omen
Owned by no ears but hers.
She lies bedded. Terse breath
Disturbs no birds between glass
And further space. Downstairs,
A nervous coffee pot totters,
Drowns out the wall clock
Clicking a hundred tinny tocks
A minute. The basin's spout
Leaks syncopated drops: water
Without end, running down pipes
To its outside source once more.

6/28/67 (00783)

The Turning In

For Ladd,
who has taught me to see,
on his sixty-sixth birthday

The sky is an architect's cardboard display,
Layer piled up and splayed upon layer
As though someone would have it redesigned.
A small plane walks across the horizon,
Its drone prevailing over the locusts' moan,
Which follows me like a lonesome ghost.

                              I am noises.
I am voices that crowd this thick night air,
Sounds that crack the malforged ears.

                              I am, in July,
The quail's unsung "bob-*white*" or peach trees
That squeak deeper, each season, into the earth,
Grass matted under feet, roaches in dank repose.

                              What I see is me,
For I am every rotting object I perceive
Through the mind's dried-out melon leaf,
*

Or each fleshly thing that grows and dies
In this tangled patch, where the coon lies fat.

What I am is tumid root
Without its fruit, vine void of writhing food,
Severed stalk leaking milk-white juices,
Pink-diminishing odors of the mimosa's bloom,
Shadows swept out by the pine's full broom,
The ribald scent of steaming horse and hog.

In this antique store behind my heart,
Nature's dusty faces clog shelves with dross.
They peer out at me through untouched cracks,
Through unfilled fissures in need of repair.
They stare as though I might come back
To rejuvenate these legacies of summers past.

7/16/67   (00415)

[The pewter heirloom hangs off to the right]

The pewter heirloom hangs off to the right
In a sky so filled with rank perfume, July
Lies down in its fenced-in pen. Crickets whine,
Spinning telegraphy across the vacant mind,
Whose missing code, once found, unlocks
The vast, illimitable road that goes to light.

7/19/67 — [1]   (00970)

[I cannot write. The mind gives in. . . .]

I cannot write. The mind gives in. A painful isolation
overtakes its prey. I kneel down in muddy gutters, a
cripple maimed in the war against the self. Help is
a whore; one barters for her with his self-respect; he
turns slovenly, a pimp to his own intellect. The worst
in a man spawns in the vast recesses of the swamps
*

forming in his vagrant hemisphere, the heart. I am brought low out of the throne I alone inhabited. I was king in a land where rhinos and lizards and scaly cobras and boa constrictors squeezed dry the individual spirit, spat the poison through the imagination. I kneel, bow, fall down on ragged knees to whisper to ants and gnats, "I am me. What I came for is me. There is no other way out of the self save through night's myriad, resplendent sphere. I am the voice no one hears. I am I, but which I is I?"

7/19/67 — [2] (00971)

[Yesterday,] †

Yesterday,
    The shoeshine ape on 43rd
Was black.
    Now, I cower behind his rag's
Crack-crack across my shoes' face

8/8–11?/67 (00943)

Phantasms of Sleep

From The Garden of Cyrus,
Sir Thomas Browne

Leaves of the silver-maple tree
Turn down, anticipating rain
That crouches in the sated west.

Beyond the lop-eared crests
That whine on certain nights
With echo-broken sounds
Of vagrant, outbound trains,
An unwound sun runs down.

A lady masked in topaz lace
Paces across a waning sky,
Reclines in a naked chasm.

Rain rumbles from tumid wombs,
Tumbles through fetid eventide
To line the spider's cable-stitch,
And now the leaves fall down
Upon the rabbit's matted back.

A girl undresses behind my eyes,
Touches me from a sifting leaf,
Sprays me with a seething rain.

8/25/67 (00412)

FDR Drive and 78th Street

Landlocked atop the cement abutment,
He is free to breathe the river's salt,
To see the gulls mediate both bridges.
His feet hang listlessly above the water.
Beneath his stolid vigil, he watches bottles,
Half-submerged, bobbing toward the Battery,
Rancid cans tottering like drunks they fed,
And matches he hurls catch the breeze
Before consummating their downstream course.
A Tracy tug looms faintly north of time,
Then takes the bend, nudging its barges
Beyond him in coupled recession.
Again, the river slows behind its banks.
Its tireless flow subdues trucks and cabs,
Fast-spanning cars, cycles, and vans
That chase each other along the Drive.

Beyond his perimeter, a jet sails low,
Falling through slack air of a landing path.
Overhead, a copter chops the wind apart,
Rattles his rib cage, then disappears,
While the sky and water wait for silence.
In this thick congestion that is night,
He sees activity at the white hotel:
The swinging doors, cars that loiter in line,
The working girls and prostitutes
And misguided Carries, who emerge
To be swallowed alive by this saw-toothed city.

His sedentary omniscience overwhelms him.
He is Homer's fisherman at eight bells,
Racing toward the lee of a Gloucester shore,
Or Thoreau waiting for the Fitchburg train
To break his amber quietude.
Nothing eludes him except the pious bum
Who comes out of nowhere to beg a dime.
When he turns into those porcelain eyes,
His own reflection detects him.
Once, he would have waited here
For a dark, decent girl to appear.

8/26/67 — [1] (00419)

Introit

Autumn leaves fall like deer hooves —
The breeze's speedy feet.
Summer closes its eyes and sleeps
Under a lumbering muscatel sky.
The dry creek that bracelets this land
Is a precious antique. No griefs
Lie beneath its serene patina.

A dry-wood fire is quietly consumed
Inside an outdoor pit. Pious flames,
A cardinal's embroidered surplices,
Twist high into the atmosphere,
While its smoke, the unkempt beard
Of a parishioner come to Eucharist,
Veers low as if to kiss his feet.

In this valley no city has fortified
Nor man been forced to compromise,
Nature has set aside her prize.
This is a garden of graceful repose,
Where creatures pace and people go
To expose the ghost they closely hide:
That love which He alone can know.

8/26–27/67 — [2] on 8/26 (00418)

Poet-in-Residence

In this time of tatterdemalions,
An extravagant bum
Lumbers down alleyways, rifles cans
Rancid with yesterday's news,
Runs after his shadow
As it climbs walls evasively
To elude intruders
Who would beg his autograph.
He hides in basement haunts
When his taunted thoughts
Crawl out to seek an audience.

He once worked at the university,
Gigging stray scraps of arcana
From the turf with a wit-pick.
Now he holds an honorary post,
Stoking bituminous coal
Into the school's boilers
When winter blasts empty classrooms.
By his careful choosing, he carries
In his shoulder-slung knapsack
Spare pairs of socks and shoes
That molder like useless beatitudes.

In spirit, he is an undone Lucifer
From the numberless crew
Whose few new gestures
Arrested time, briefly etched beauty
From lines the Lunatic's pencil drew.
By nature, he is a scavenger,
Removing refuse from heathen minds.
He knows his tasks go unnoticed.
In this time of lotus eaters,
The poet-in-residence gets drunk,
Throws all of his verse in the furnace.

8/28?–29/67 (01080)

[I am all loving.]

I am all loving.

You and I lie together
Under a cricket-night,
Lighting the fireflies
Plying the moon-slate sky
With brightness from our eyes.

We exist in each other,
Covered like rain-drenched grass
With a moisture so pure
That even the bee refrains
From taking our hidden fruit.

And I am all loving
For that gentle girl named Jan.
In dreams, her hand in mine,
We walk down paths lined high
With berry-fruit of the infinite moon . . .
We walk in that other region:
The Land of the Sacred Tree.

8/31/67   (04662)

[He stands in his driveway, coffee in hand,]

He stands in his driveway, coffee in hand,
A rusty Balboa surveying land
Humanity has not yet happened upon.

The trees he sees on the front-yard lawn,
With the sun behind, might be measuring tapes
Someone unwinds from their rooted bases.
Their shadowy trunks are caterpillars
Shimmering out above the grass, enlarging,
Portending the length of future days,
As he passes within the cooler grot
From an ivied walnut, which covers the garage.
The green Valentine leaves are tufts,
Clusters of lustrous acanthus or yew
*

That cover a tomb of arthritic roots
And chunks of bricks once used to ring the grave.
Now, a spider attaches itself in life
To the ivy that encircles the marriage
Of life and death and dissolution.

8?/67   (00797)

The Old Beauchamp Place

The pendulum of a regulator clock
Chops air behind glass, captured
Within its black-backed case.
Its stained walls reverberate
To the chime that keeps pace
With the pacing daylight hours.
At night, time stands still,
For no ears pierce its thoughts.
Montgomery Ward's rural phone
Stands alone in a quiet niche;
Its business has died.
The dry cells hidden inside
No longer record the dizzy motion
Of fingers winding its crank;
The tarnished, frog-eyed bells
Knell no hayloft fires
Nor inspire three-way conversations.
A Grover & Baker sewing machine,
Mounted on an encased maple table,
Rests atop cast-iron stilts.
Embroidered quilts and lace
Drape this implement. No legs
Peddle its static treadle.
Decay reeks of outgrown muslin
In trunks. All gears are numb.

The mattress of a Simmons brass bed
Still wears a man's restless form.
Its worn head-posts bear scratches
Where nails sculpted epitaphs
*

For a heritage buried in clay.
He alone survived the plague
To hear the frequent, irregular tocks
Of the regulator clock, at night,
Grow farther and slower apart,
To listen to the croaking bells
That never tolled for him,
To undo the rawhide belt
That once circumferenced
The life of his loving wife.
Children driving out on Sundays
Still speculate about the crazy man
Who died three decades ago.
They park by the road, peer inside
Through rimpled windows to see
Relics sealed in an unlit museum.

9/4/67 (00796)

[A saxophone grapples with the wind,] †

A saxophone grapples with the wind,
Lending an unblended resonance
That coalesces, hinders comprehension,
Beyond the green-screaming eyes.
That sound hugs the ground, climbs,
Falters like

9/4?/67 (00969)

A Touch of Turning †

A menthol night brushes past my nose.
Feline breezes assault unleaving trees,
Rushing pervertedly to fill their bustles,
To see beneath their neat embroidery
Arthritic limbs

9?/67 – [9/22/67]? (00968)

1513–1906

And when the fire finally subsided,
Quietude sifted the Roaring Camp
Like a miner siphoning nuggets
From the blood of a rugged stream.
A city without a history had been branded.
The hilly land lay leveled.
Masts of packets and side-wheelers,
Cape Horn clippers, slipped away,
Casting indelible daytime shadows
On the ragged, outraged bay.
Somewhere high on a rocky cleft,
A scrofulous Balboa knelt and wept,
Then drowned in his deep discovery.

9/23/67 (04651)

Song for Jan

Under whose roof do you sleep
                                        tonight?
Beneath the roots of what tree
                                        do you hide,
While I see the fog from the ocean
                                        divide
Through the city and over its
                                        countryside?

Beside what well do you go
                                        to confide
All the love you are forced to hold
                                        inside
Or the fantasies that your dreams
                                        belie,
While I lie awake to the foghorns'
                                        cries?

Where will you be when this water
                                        rides
Into Ozark springs that have all
                                        gone dry?
                                *

You will be where this fog and ocean
                        reside —
With me, long after this song
                  has died.

9/24/67 (04652)

[I taste this day!] ‡

I taste this day!
Salt sprayed in unseen gusts
Encrusts my lips, seeps through
Like rain leaking between
A window's unsealed sill.

I share the air
On which these gulls suspend themselves
Directionlessly, hovering above me
Against the bristling breeze
Swooping beneath my feet along the colonnade,
Covering the beach with tilting reflections.

My ears burn with unscourged rebuttals.
I whistle a poem.
My song is carried from me,
Huddles in the tide's wide backwash,
Then flutters, not quite kitelike,
To mix with landlocked clutter
Accumulating before me
On this stretch of peopled land,
Which reaches beyond the eyes' perimeters.
Ah, but is this not where the sun
Funnels down the furthest corridor
This country has ever seen?
Will this song not return?
Will it not concern the night
With its very silence?

Down there, an auburn child
Dips to pick up a Popsicle stick
From the littered world she owns,
While the heady waves crochet speeches,
*

Whisper uproarious lullabies
To her benevolent ears,
As they slide in along the serpentine tide
Surfers ride with precarious pride.
She leans into the wind, falls,
Gently lies on her mulatto side,
While, bikinied against the hussied sand,
Her mother, nursemaid, enigmatic friend,
Sends admonitions that bend the wind,
Divide her simple, unintended antics.
She comes running, her hands busy
With gifts she's sifted from the beach.
Beyond her, closer to the inching foam,
A lone terrier eludes its shadow,
Abandons its feet as it turns,
Landing on its chin. Unlike the gulls,
Who cautiously peck to the shore,
Then soar above the ocean's wash,
It is caught, its retreat clouded.
Beside the auburn child, whose friend
Dries her naked features, it

Now I come down off my perch to see
With my own eyes this beach.
My feet avoid a predatory tide,
Whose unending tongue leaks foam.
Where it has retreated now,
In among the musky, outgoing ocean,
Leaving only a darker print,
I see opal beads of spume.
The blue collar that wraps my neck
Flaps, slapping my ears.
The eyes turn in on themselves,
Blinded by the salt-misted gale
That twists the spectacles' frames,
Engrains the glass with pumice.
People are dull masqueraders.
The gulls collide. Orange peels
And cigarette butts, driftwood,
Unsealed soda cans fail to materialize
Behind the diminishing windshield
Through which I awkwardly peer.

Yet what I see I undeniably am,
For these eyes, divided slightly,
Preclude the rest, resist the child,
The enigmatic, bikinied friend
Who may have beckoned to me
As I passed her for the colonnade.
Yet now I am home again,
Alone,
Sheltered by this weathered wall,
Hiding behind an unending poem.

9/30/67 – 10/1–2? (04657)

[A slick deer] ‡

A slick deer
With a year's horny growth
Peers quickly from the brush,
Then rushes clear of us.
In this dank, lush hollow
No fire has yet destroyed
Nor flood swallowed alive
Nor earthquake shaken from its roots,
The feet tread lightly;
The eye defines time by space.
This is a graceful temple,
Whose columns, with burling,
Are caryatids of Leda and Demeter.
Laurel trees,
Like helpless millipedes
Turned over on their backs,
Send their bay-leaved limbs
Writhing toward what sky
The giant redwoods don't absorb.
Bracken ferns crowd the turf,
Where miniature Douglas firs
Squirm for recognition.

Only in this forest
Can the eye not see the tree,
*

Not the entirety of the thing,
For the sheer, sleek simplicity
That steers straight upward,
Defies longevity. Only when it's dead,
When man has razed it
To display the dismembered trunk,
Its brain, does he discover
That its life, a single year,
Like the dove shot in flight,
Is composed of two layers,
One black, the other white,
And that each ring, combined,
Registers more life

9?/67   (04656)

[Then-descending day scrapes across nylon horizons,] ‡

Then-descending day scrapes across nylon horizons,
Dragging lumbering clouds like dray-drawn carts.
An opaque sun, swaddled in hues of granite and clay,
Gives way too soon to a filibustering moon.
Pressed between all this breathless immensity,
A certain slow snow, pied like glycerin
Or an unfixed mixture under an optic's glass,
Plies the eyes,

9?/67   (04653)

[We stood within the green silence] ‡

We stood within the green silence
Of Muir Woods,
With the Pacific tissue sluicing
Toward dusk, children trying to speak,
Teetering on bumptious feet,
Seeking to taste the brook, twisting
*

Atop rocks locked in timeless grace.
Rain sifted from echoing space, through limbs
Hoisting a thousand turned-up earths
Upon their backs. We lay down, looking up
Through the drops washing dreams with sky

9?/67 (04658)

The Hyde Street Pier †

Along with anonymous windlasses, capstans,
Rust-encrusted anchors, and launches,
A fossilized paddle wheel from a packet
Stands upright on the piling;

9–10?/67 — [1] (04654)

The Everlasting Nay

I
Can't handle this shit
One bit!

9–10?/67 — [2] (04655)

[A sick, thick aroma of quick-frying hotdogs]

A sick, thick aroma of quick-frying hotdogs
Cloys the free, climbing spirit
As it lifts high above the eyes
To hide inside that one long instant
The roller coaster fails to annihilate,

Then plummets again, the eye, spirit,
Held there only momentarily
As the body seeks out the peopled beach.
*

Startled from reality, the eyes incline,
The neck strains, while the astonished mind,
Subdued by those reckless necromantics,
Divines the bodies, pierces their guises,
Descends to the bronzed flesh that squats,
Rests erect atop the mottled rack.

The fat lady, taking a brief hiatus
From the carnival in season next door,
Unfastens her tresses, drops her canvas dress
Down bubble-buckling legs, then flops headlong,
Her burden pegged to the eroding land.

Girls and old men lie back, unrelaxed,
Distracting themselves with fleshly groans.
Their distended thoraxes, sunken stomach cavities,
Signal skeletal pulchritude
Admired by vicarious multitudes above the wall —
That perverted crew Lucifer led from Heaven.

Behind the restless eyes, a naked Spanish child
Totters slipshod, jiggling its Lilliputian life,
While a Negress fidgets with her crimson wig.
Everywhere, bosoms, budding, heaving bulbously
In secret abbreviation, compete for freedom,
Repeat Manichean epistemology.
Each heart beats out the sum of all its evil parts.

Negroes and Chinese squeeze concupiscent sand
Through their toes, expose their adolescent fat
To those who defile them even as they lie,
Legs apart, breasts distended, minds drawn out
Line by girdled line, in the beach's open palm.

The hooknosed men in sandals and dark glasses,
Their short-sleeved shirts hiding unclean sinews,
The mustached boys with taut, bare feet, muscles
Bulging, trellised hair cut square at the nape,
Gape,
All of them scavengers on the make. Each waits for
The rotting bodies to broil, then boil down
To carrion for their insatiable maws, before
Their lawless claws scrape away the prey.

Once more, the flustered spirit tries to soar,
Seeking surcease in an unshrined retreat.

There are no lovers here, though those two kiss
Like angelfish.
What is missing here is . . .
The waves bark at distrait dogs
That bite lice and weeds from their tufted coats.
What is lacking here is . . .
Gulls screech; pelicans cull the troughs,
Plunge. Their bloated sacs explode like flak.

There are no lovers here, though unclothed maidens
Touch each other, disgrace themselves,
While little boys dig castles where they play.
What is missing here is . . .
The sun growls as it runs away from this place.
The sand stands up in the softest face.
What is lacking is . . .
Seal Rocks blocks nobody's view, while people
Eat at Cliff House, conscious of their gout.

There are no lovers here, though a beautiful girl
Straddles the beach, screams, writhes, climaxes
Into a mound of towel-covered sand.
What is missing here is . . .
Her juices spew down glistered legs.
What is lacking is . . .
Her blistered feet have six toes each.

The eyes go blind. They fail to see the fat
Float out to sea on Stygian rafts,
And the bones leak marrow, then petrify.
The mind recedes as the ocean rises
With the rotting weight of rounded breasts
And soft-fleshed bellies and aging thighs.
The spirit dies as heads fall off
And faces bob in disembodiment.
Only the ears hear those troubled tongues
Clucking litanies beneath the outgoing tide.

10/8/67 — [1?] (04659)

The Funny House

He holds up his fingers before him:
Bitten nails on these trembling pales
Are tattered robes of sailors
Strapped to a ship's listing mast.
And his hands can no longer grasp
The glass that sweats his blood.

He whistles, but no sounds issue.
Only the void behind his mind balloons
And ghosts' white shrouds inflate.
At his back door, harpies scratch,
And whores thrash barefoot
Through corridors his eyes can't penetrate.

He chews ice to cool the ague
That clogs thought, but the teeth
Go numb, and his gums bleed semen.
His dry throat explodes. Phlegm
Congests the vocal passageways,
As words wrestle to free themselves.

The nose that once knew love's odors
Burns with febrile exhalations.
Nocturnes breathed in other sleeps
Leak out in tissues.
They alone keep his nervous vigil
While vapors unweave his dreams.

One drum rumbles as a faceless child
Tumbles down his Eustachian tube,
Toward that thin-skinned membrane.
It breaks. A hundred unchaste songs,
Like gorgons' gongs, awaken him,
Scrape the brain's flaked paint.

His legs are pegs that gyve him
To a cave's coruscated floor.
The water that slowly flows over them
Macerates his flaccid limbs.
Composed from head to severed waist,
His body drains into the disposing day.

10/8/67 — [2?] (04660)

[A naked Pharaoh kneels down to kiss the ground,]

A naked Pharaoh kneels down to kiss the ground,
While buzzards swim with graceless disinclination
Above the blighted landscape.
Decaying skeletons of ancient dynasties
Bathe in mud, huddle in putrid graves,
Awaiting some ultimate laziness,
While the buzzards flay fleshless prey.

Communal death has set high its sights,
Taking the clarion from Hebraic warnings.
Swarms of beasts, insects, infect populations
That sway from their Maker's incantations.
This is a pestilential battleground,
Scourged, decimated, so that only now,
I alone swat the maggots that gnaw the bones.

10/24/67 (04661)

[As sure as I'm standing here now,]

As sure as I'm standing here now,
Urinals and one-armed bandits
Serve the same purpose:
Human amusement.

I watch this city, these buildings
I see soaring erect against the sky
Like elongated rain whose spray is
Caught in the camera's slowed eye.

These buildings are hospitals
Whose occupants are surgeons
Operating on patients, extracting
Their life, replacing defunct parts
With goods, items on order sheets.

And I have returned to this city where
Everyone sleeps on the surface of a coffee bean
And the taxis' doors are manhole covers
And their meters measure the EKG of the
City.

And God, how the inside of my dress collar
Is rough, dirty as an elephant's hide,
And the women are barely beneath their hair,
So new are they up from puberty,
These women, girls, children in loin skirts,
Who work behind a front desk or rest on cutting tables
While young men wrapped in scarves spread their fabrics,
And the textiles of their body, exposed, show wear
Like seconds unreturnable, cloths from Tyre, confined,

And I feel, not see, know less, these people
Returning to their rent-controlled apartments
In the 60s, 80s, climbing inside a beer,
Brandy, or random assortment of pills.

Yet, here is where each Jill, every Sister Carrie
Finds her Jack, her kicks,
And all the vested men in ads, boys in toyland
Find their Faerie Queens.

I have been here before. Was it in the college
Poetry class or seated in tall grass somewhere
Beyond the Meramec? Good God, get me out of here!
Let me return to that sane time before time *was*.

11/20–28?/67 (04650)

[Coffee vapors caper through New Jersey,] ‡

Coffee vapors caper through New Jersey,
Sloping from New Hope to Princeton,
Rattling into Grand Central Station.
    I see a girl, in an office
Just up from 6th, on West 39th,
    Drafting patterns, sewing flies,
And the dust rustles finished garments,
    A rag girl whose twirling hopes
Imagine high fashions,
    A rag girl who swirls through me
Like granules of hard-cubed sugar —

11/30? – 12/15?/67 (04682)

[Through the glass I muse.]

Through the glass I muse.
A noose goes loose about my eyes,
And I can see. Frost alabasters
Straight gray slate that's splayed upon
The roof. It is another time.
One more death descends, aloof.
It is another time of radical decay,
And I am witness, pedigreed heir
To immigrant trees and shrubs
Come deceived to this country
On promises of a glossy futurity.
This is a time when I am seen
By every invisible creature spored
Between storm window and brittle screen,
For there is nothing meta-terranean
That stalks the chalky turf. Each one
Has settled to earth behind the breeze
That tears, with witches' nails,
The very air. Only the sun, an eye
Impaled on opaque metaphors,
Sails along this shadowed floor.

Before I left, bereft things danced,
Thoughts in chiaroscuro spoke to me,
People were steepled with soft loftiness.
Now, in the dead of winter, I cower.
The noose goes taut. I am brought back
To myself, as though what were inside me
Might abide in inviolable repose.

12/19/67 (05189)

[Already, since last night,]

Already, since last night,
Through the day's faltering light,
Two inches of rain have been pinched
From the grayness overhead.
Though we were given warning,
*

The rainbow sign, there is no end
To this slave-making water.
The naked-limbed trees,
Tumbled by elliptical breezes,
Sway like elephants
Afraid of an unseen enemy.
Tumescent springs and creeks
Explode, overreaching bounds,
Resounding with contrapuntal debris.
Even the wheat-colored grass is matted,
Mated to the grating sky
That smothers it sensuously.
And I walk out, garbed in rubber,
Booted, unsuited for this freedom
That minimizes perspectives.
Yet someone needs to feed the pony
That falters, out of halter,
On its mud-clogged underpinnings.
Somebody has to tend to the dog
That waits behind its fence,
Defenseless as an entrenched soldier
Under fire. Outside the house,
I joust with an armored wind.
My toes go cold. I am at odds
With my senses. When I return indoors
From these morning chores,
I wonder, will I have the energy
To assume the responsibility
Of taking care of myself?

12/21/67 (05362)

[A million unseen collisions occur] ‡

A million unseen collisions occur
As the snow, like souls leaving a corpse,
Whirs earthward to seek purchase,
Take shape, displace more common forms.

Each green leaf of the three magnolia trees
That flank this wintering patio
*

Is a ski slope. Below their coronas,
Fibrous streams

The mimosa's pods are faceless lips
That kiss the day. They are vertical slits
That split space, twitch in graceful disarray

12/21–25?/67 (05363)

[Chartres is the result of a great fetish — H.D.] †

Chartres is the result of a great fetish — H.D.
                    Time in history in time
          composite — superimposition —
                    Living is the thing we are doing!

                    permanence and change
                              the hidden unborn experience
                              a new cadence of living
presentiments
                    the spirit of forms —

                              the adventure of our race
                    animated by analogous passions

— the critical spirit has become a poet —
call to the pre-Socratic spirit when poetry was all

          Time is at the disposal of the spirit.
          Time is a child playing with breezes.
plasticity of time
                    Time is a hag, sagging under endless
                                        wrinkles,
                    Supporting itself on
                              plastic legs —

3/26/68 (04685)

[Having flown in from San Francisco . . .]

Having flown in from San Francisco to White Cross,
going from temperate breezes to this weird April in
the Midwest, I am full well knowing, now, that a phase
has come around to its denouement.

This day, so opaque, whispers intercession into my
mind, the memory, for in space, suspended, it is green,
hueing, congealing, burgeoning everywhere in time-
less redolence of renewal, of cyclical growth: the orna-
mental plums in purple fuzziness, dogwoods, forsythias
low to the ground, full, yellowing.

And on this day going cold and fluffed in gray, opaque
shades of sky and light, I know snow will drop through
holds, hatches,

for rabbits huddle into themselves against the wind,
rabbits I once hunted through December, January.

The place where I have grown, built into my mind
ideas of permanence and familial bonds of slow affec-
tion, this place, graced by slowness, deliberate quies-
cence . . . and now I know that I am being impelled
toward newer destinies, newer formulations that will
redound upon this place yet exist in different inter-
stices of time.

So strange how the eye can smell snow in the weather,
how the horizon vies with the day.

I see that ancient memory here in White Cross,
memories of the time when I schooled, wrote here,
hunted, drove out, made love, ate dinners at Hesperide
Road,

because where a person is born, grows, is that space
where he will return to die, to add his chemicals to the
loam, where home was the shell for his rich constitu-
ents, for here, from here, no matter how far the mind
goes out, away, something, the compass's twin needles,
sway together, are drawn back, for to deny that growing
time in youth is to deny the immediacy of the matur-
ing mind and the outreaching spirit, which enlarge
with each new encounter, every new acquaintance, in
all new milieus, ambiances,

going out and ahead, for to sink back is to place

the mind, the being's spirit, in mounds no archaeologist
will ever bother to excavate,
    so that I must not submit to the easy return. Reluc-
tance must enter in, else the inquisitive, searching mind
falls down in puddles of the child's mild dross and be-
lieves that maturity is something to be attained,
    because I know that the mind, the body, must for-
ever be about maturing, that there is simply no temporal
demarcation at which, arriving, the man can convince,
should accept, himself as *mature* —
    Maturity is reached only in
        death.

    So much has transpired. It always does, so long as
one continues to perceive changes, so long as one en-
genders alterations by allowing the mind free run over
keyboards ever expanding and contracting with the psy-
chic weathers of the imagination.

4/4/68 (04681)

[She waits at the station,] †

She waits at the station,
Preyed upon by her own despondency
Creeping, like dreams down spines,   Where is economy
To that breach he left bequeathingly   of reason
                                                    and meter?

                        The harbor barge charges its lock,
                        Blocks the canal, reeking of garbage,
                        Before creeping through to the river.
                        At Hoskin's Landing, the pilot
                        Will order delivery, steam away light.

    Due to mechanical difficulties,
    The plane
    *

Has been delayed
Unavoidably.
Oh, say, can you see

By this dawn's early light?   Due to insomniacal sleep,
The man   The man
    Scans the runway   Yawns a runway
                                     Metaphorically
                                     By this dawn's early light.

                                     Due to curiosity,
                                     The crowd
                                         Repeats its vigiled
                                     Anxieties.
                                     How proudly we stand

4?/68   (04686)

[How delicate the tracery of her fine lines] †

How delicate the tracery of her fine lines

A tight fog strips clear the eyes,
Stipples the horizon with emery wheels,
Predatory creatures, beasts ready to seize sheep
Leaping from summits, creeping away from their blood

4–5?/68   (02309)

[Living in a metaphor by the ocean,] †

Living in a metaphor by the ocean,
He smelled the foghorn.
He seized every opportunity
To study in depth the foghorn's formation

4–5?/68   (02308)

[Somewhere, locked in somnolence, in a police station,] †

Somewhere, locked in somnolence, in a police station,
Somewhere, a night clerk, his pants unbuckled

4–5?/68 (02301)

[Silence spills from lakes, trees.] ‡ Δ

Silence spills from lakes, trees.
Leaves, giving away their secrets
To the breeze that gnaws our flesh,
Fall, filter, feather to the beach,
While beyond, across the water,
A shadow fills the void, screeches
Behind a voice the wind wimples.
For this hour, all thought is spent,
All notions of freedom bent,
Cauterized in green by a

6/25/68 (00007)

The Point Δ

The long day lengthens out,
Sprays pink inks
Across the lake's soft blotter.
Sailboats, buoyed in the sky,
Feint and tack while navigators
Chart their ancient courses.

From the Lumberjack Point,
A boy with hands in his pockets
Stands new in the sandy earth.
Though close up into the breeze,
His dreams run wing and wing.

6/27–28/68 — [1] on 6/27 (00008)

The Fishing Dock ^Δ

Above the dock's rotted planks,
I cease to hear the echo
Of reckless seconds that pass me by.

Mayflies swarm in the warming air.
Fish at feeding
Needle the lake's taut fabric;
Like seedlings,
They break through to life.

Swallows follow the lowering sun,
And now, the red thread of cloud
Is shed of night: day is done.

Cabin lights
Across this clear breathing
Stretch moons halfway to me.
They reach out,
Touch me, teach me to sleep.

6/27/68 — [2] (00010)

Invocation ^Δ

For Jan,
in her absence

This place, tracing the mind's furrows,
Trails me nine months a day,
Like the making of a child,

And now, God, and now,
I have arrived again to where
The air is decent for dreaming
And the moon has no lascivious thoughts.

And I have come here to loose myself,
To release a thousand dreaming balloons
Into this air, where the raven and bat
Scatter themselves like confetti
Above this land where you boys parade.

I am a child again, one of you boys,
Reteaching myself to speak with the eyes,
To sell my soul for that undefined dream
That seizes, in moments of reverie,
The peace of an eventide like this one tonight.

6/27/68 — [3] (00009)

This Pendent World

Trumpets blend; wars end inside the ears.

The searing heat dissolves.
Eyes, empty as rifled safes, swing on rusted hinges;
Limbs, like worms, squirm deeper into upturned earth;
And widows walk home to dress.
Those who once loved on private heaths
Weep, reach out to retreating crowds.

In defeat, Satan's crew hisses
                                exultantly.

8/8/68 — [1] (00402)

Marianne △

          I am thinking of you tonight. I am living
the dreams
              of a
                      twenty-three-year-old Swedish woman,
          seeing
                  through the evening's heat,
                  looking deeply into my mirror.

      In the glass, where antique bottles glow,
              my fantasies blow like flags;
              my dreams run slowly into that day
when you will return to
                      Stockholm,
                  with me behind the glass.

Yet,
yet, when days pass between us
          where we stand across from each other
                                        on the street,
     when the years salute like soldiers on parade
     and others' wars are fought and lost,
yet,
yet, we will not die with the days passing days passing day.

8/8/68 — [2] (01058)

Marianne ^Δ

     We drive a winding thread
To Hayward, through birch and spruce,
Watching for eyes that line the retinas:
Red eyes and green, leaning toward our speed.
          And the moon is a spider,
          Caught in its own white web of clouds.

She flees Sweden, I San Francisco,
Quickly,
     Meeting on foreign, common soil,
     Beneath a circus tent,
               Beside antique railroad sleepers.

     Diana seduces Thanatos.
     Deer suckle the stars.
The bind holds firm,
     And the web gives in to weigh us
     Where we balance at the lips' edges.

A man and a long-haired, slow-green queen
     Spin
               Within
               The vortex
Before crawling up inside the moon,
                    Happily trapped.

8/8/68 — [3] (00011)

The Devil's Circus: Chicago, '68

For Jan,
in Miami

Spurious currency circulates,
Politicians worry,
And regular delegates lose their seats.
Outside, police widen the night,
Draw tight the vise about peaceful bodies.
Like foxes in traps,
Children bite each other,
Trying to free a limb to free themselves.

But the night belches.
   Locomotives churn out of roundhouses,
   Melting down the tracks,
   Burning away the sleepers.
People are fed in, all of them;
Then they are steam, air — they *were*,
And the machines run on, run out,
                    imperviously.

8/27/68 (00425)

[Up here,] †

Up here,
Where the air whispers thin, cold love,
Only the wings spare

Two razor blades

All I want to do is create what is floating about
in particles in the head, whose eyes see beyond this
time, beyond themselves, through the retinas, to
another time, another face, where the air is fat and
thickly warm. To write is to live for this being — me!

I love to breathe and to see moons all over. I love
that girl down there in Miami, because in her I feel
all that is slow and gentle and considerate and
passionate and moody. . . . God, let me live inside her,
for her, and let my work of creation continue unimpaired.

I must work away, stealthily, slowly, because I fear
that this is my place, my time, and my reason for being,
now. Can love and living and creating with these
words be valid? If so, then let me strive to endure
the selves outside the self that believes in itself.

9/1–10?/68 (05166)

The Onset

The castor bean's leaves lie fetid,
Shriveled as an old lady's hands.
Winter is coming back upon itself.

Out here on the patio,
This gap in torrid space,
The icehouse perspires,
And I place myself in its grip.
Whose grip? Whose cliché?

Although I might liken myself, my slow mind,
To blocks of crystal,
To cakes of freezing glacier,
I am not really cold.

Yet when metaphors are guillotined
And the closed words that synthesize run-
On lines are exposed, there still remains
The awful truth of the internalized rhyme:
Trust, justice, and dust to oft-quoted dust.

An old lady's body lies shriveled,
Dead under a covering of winter leaves.

10/14/68 (01100)

Indian Summer

These trees stand clumped in lumps of plum
And tawny beige. Through this land I knew
In youth, soothing hues renew themselves.
Music of maple and walnut, sweet gum, elm
Overwhelms the eyes in cool reprise.

Yet, with all this beauty, the leaves
Fluting earthward are sermons preached
On other altars in other seasons.
The funereal pomp of Donne's "Autumnall"
Rumbles the casket of an old man's mind.

10/18/68 (01082)

Pathétique

Kings have not changed.
The state still owns them,
And muses still choose
The least obtrusive exhortations.

Once, a carriage's rough pulsation
Awakened Beethoven from a lusty sleep.

Bless the whore who bore him seeds.

11/2–3/68 (01101)

Visitation

A blessing for Jan

This day runs out
Like water from a slow drain,
And I awaken to view a new moon
Spray the Greater Ladle with a hazy glow.

Snow, like locks of baby hair,
Hides in pockets up there in that clear, black eye.
Below night's timberline, I bend,
Ascending through naked ionospheres.

A hand or the shadow of a heated breeze
Sways me from sleep, unfreezes the seeds
That tree alleyways of forgotten dreams.
I climb inside a perfect whiteness.

Yet who ever hears the sacred flakes break
Without feeling earthly choirs sear the ears?
Too, who has ever churched brittle fingers
And not feared the nearness of another's death?

The prolonged yawn bears subtle witness.

11/9/68 (00347)

The Nuptial Bower

For my sister Babs

Over this whole frozen lake down here,
Where no motorboats skim,
Propellers still snag a former breeze;
Cotter pins sift through oblique waters
Like leaves coming undone in winter air.

A man and wife come down to the snow line
At the edge of no lake
To share each other's implausible lips.
Inside the fish shack,
By a dry fire,
No one spies that sidelong embrace,
Which belongs to the man with implausible wife.

The lake spawns no fish, no ice.
No water fills these banks; they overflow.
The fish shack burns; it never was.
Somewhere, the man and his naked wife
Gather up leaves that have decomposed
And lie down beneath no trees to sleep.

11/16/68 (01083)

Vindication

For Charlie and Gerald,
my factory friends

The handholes leak on the Lookout boiler.
Compound the color of rusty blood
Runs out along the basement floor
To clogged drains, over crusty bugs in corners.
Inside, fire and water conspire with destruction,
While the night watchman sleeps with a broom at his feet.

Upstairs, elbows, unions, and sleeves give way.
Straps that shackle the black intestines
                              collapse.
Vacuum lines back up, run north like creeks in flood.
Return traps explode, and seeping steam,
Like unseen souls escaping the veins in fear,
Squeezes through packings of faulty valves.

The cold air of the factory is soiled by heat,
While the man with the broom tosses lightly in sleep.

11/22/68 (01102)

The Sisters of Fiesole

In the convent on the neck of a hill,
Where a saint lies, stolid, in stately repose,
Awaiting something, a resurrection perhaps,
And the grass stays matted from mourners passing
And varnish flakes off of an ageless sky,
Sisters take down their robes and pray.

The retreat on the slope was not always there,
Nor that patron's call more than a godly hope
When these lands were filled with lolling sheep
And his seeds would flow behind the plow.

These sisters, once children from the town below,
With dolls and dogs and soft, blond dreams,
These sisters with their flabby bellies,
*

Shriveled breasts, and misshapen toes,
Nude as dew that never leaves the air,
Kneel down on cold dirt floors and weep.

Across the land, a chorus scores the sun,
An organ snorts, and bells knell hysterically
As that body lifts and disappears. A new moon
Slices space with its invisible blade.

The sisters run out, gather about a solitary tree
To see the day on fire, to watch for some mistake.
They rake their hands over the coarsest bark,
Draw them up and down continuously,
Until their female voices undo his faith
And they cry for relief from virginity.

11/23/68 (01103)

[Behind this misty crystal,] †

Behind this misty crystal,
Christmas spirit, another music,
More white and clear than blues,
Curls through mitered frames of
Carpentered memories and genuflects

From silence registered on flop-eared street-corner
signs, I imagine the specters of other loves lost and
wept for from some craggy metaphor on the brow of
a hill

I see her lodged in a dust-mottled confinement,
behind which the light inside the skull goes by unsul-
lied by the battery of discouragement

I love the whole idea of living,

12/16/68 (00924)

Marriage of the Shadows

For Jan,
New Year's Eve, 1968

Christ, this basement is alone and cold!
No one is here to warm my outdoors.
That clock, going, going, running on,
Snares the last glass of champagne from a tray,
Shares its insipid conversation
With an idle clarinet, rumbles a drum.
Numbness masquerades for drunken fun.

Exhaustion gnaws the bones in bed
Because this new day has come too late.
The newer year is slow with dispassionate cheer.
Just a newscast ago,
We were younger for our resolutions.
Now these vows are raucous sounds
Cloistered within a noisemaker's throat.

The gay clothes she wore float before me,
And in a grass somewhere, matted with silence,
Her thoughts still compose wind-songs.
Her light stride across a mythical campus
Still goes there inside those shelved books.
The marriage of the shadows is all in white,
As though death were purer than life.

We used to hide from the future so well.
Now, it can't find us in my lying awake.

12/31/68 (01104)

Schoolteacher

For David Olsen;
bless him,
wherever.

The cheap scent of rented rooms
Seeps beneath closed doors,
Reeks of the whore's bouquet.
*

Vague odors from coal stoves
Creep along unheated hallways
Like snakes let loose to decay.
His nose goes cold as frozen meat.
Outside, a sign preaches neon vowels,
Calls him to its tawdry altar,
But the abandoned eyes inside his face
Are afraid to leave their fortress walls.

In this nether darkness, between sheets,
Strangers inhabit his glands,
And beasts dismantle his dead, sweet dreams.
Fruitlessly, he grabs at frantic sounds
That round off the corners of his world.
Time climbs down the spider's pegs,
Bites his thighs, arouses the drowsy blood
That floods the cradle between his legs.
Solitude unlatches its black vagina.
He climaxes
As a thousand seething wombs entomb his sleep.

1/25/69 (00344)

Norrie

The thunderbird suspended from her small neck
Flowed out of clouded valleys without rain,
Above burial mounds, beyond painful echoes,
To that room brocaded sweetly with conversation.

A voice saw through cool nights in Wales,
Broke open closed hands of queers on Soho patios,
Spoke of dark lights in Hyde Park pubs.
The words were the eyes' silence,
And inside the varnish,
Particles of time became unplucked lashes.

Out there, beyond the dream's last haunt,
You laughed into my selfish fear,
                    And for a timeless while,
                    The unformed self beguiled me.

2/3/69 (01084)

[And he woke up with a goat in his bed] †

And he woke up with a goat in his bed

At best, he was a blue man,
Whose love had always been self-addressed.
There were days when he still felt well assured
That when night filled up his champagne glass,
High-class women would whisper their price.
He even thrived, for a time, on lies told him,
As though reprisals

2/10/69 (02307)

The Indisposed

For Norrie;
God bless her.

The mellow flutes are inessential.
Clarions wail penitentially
For the bride, whose face hides white remorse.
Her conversion has come too late.

Life, being love, will not wait on compromise.

The violin begins its strident lilt.
She dies down the aisle, like her wilting bouquet,
Tilting beside a boy with naked smiles.
His diversion has never been more assured.

Death, being love, will not wait for her to renege.

Yet she flies from the public charnels
To a private carnival behind her eyes,
Where dreams ride bareback on high wooden horses,
And she cries for the lady who is sawed in two.

Love being life, she will die living love.

2/11/69 (01091)

A Valentine for Sir Kells

Beyond this window where I lie buried,
Married to the day dissolving,
The town comes unwound with a dizzy sound
Like a lopsided top revolving.

While my throat swallows, in hollow silence,
A loud sensation of crying,
Snow stutters from night's gray mouth,
Saying something outside me is dying.

Her wedding gown is the air about me,
Flounced with sequins and beading.
Now, it surrounds my skin and hair,
As she once did in our breathing.

Ice on the streets forms a hazy pastiche,
Like mirrors of tears congealing.
Beneath each surface, I see myself
Reaching out for her without feeling.

Only this whiteness, like her last whisper,
Echoes that passional voice, repeating,
"Oh, oh, how I loved you so,"
Even as our dreams were retreating.

2/17/69 (01090)

Retired

Behind his gate,
A seldom man rakes bedlam,
Prunes the small yard's fragrance,
Disrupts the fated commonplace
Of two snakes mating,
And birds take cover
Inside the absurd hiding of their silence.

Children floating home from school
Pass his fence, importuning
A litany of fleeting years.
Those oldest oaks on his property
*

Choke the opaque eyes of his throat,
Explode with a growth of bloated seeds
As he trims the simplest eloquence from the breeze.

It is his eventide.
Through this still, slow time
Before night breathes knotted rhymes,
The habitual evanescence of grace
Patterns his saturnine face
With a peculiar jubilation:
He has seen to the end of another day.

2/28/69 — [1–2?] (01098)

[Perhaps the dog-eared moon] †

Perhaps the dog-eared moon
Will soon collapse
And stars borrow another species of light

Let there be light fixtures,
And there were,
             tubes and starters and fuses
To ferry current from the core,
The circuit breakers' paneled source,
To illumine the sewing-room floor
    And storage area —

The furious young man on the trampoline
Tears the air, caroms off straps,
Collapsing the lungs, grappling
                        strapping
                        snapping
                        flapping
                        trapeze
                        perhaps

2/28/69 — [1–2?] (00933)

[Vague thoughts form a peristyle about the mind.] †

Vague thoughts form a peristyle about the mind.
The straight line the mind has sewn with chain stitches
Comes unwound, untwined

2?/69 — [1] (05279)

[How I loved her!]

How I loved her!
Oh, how I loved her then,
When grasses rasped her thighs
And breezes creased her seething eyes.

We would sit by the lake
And fill the sails with song
When the breaking of the day
Would carry us along
Into night. We would hail the fading light
Like pilgrims. Children . . . we were children then,
Walking on waters where we wouldn't belong.

2?/69 — [2] (02311)

[Naked as an unnested sparrow,]

Naked as an unnested sparrow,
She reclines,
Wrestling with demons with harrows.

Her tits are drowsy as puppy runts,
Softly invisible and small.
Like Dioscuri seen through the optic glass,
They seem in sumptuous decline,
While the heaving chest
Receives their weightless fluff
With silent affront.

And in that humid room,
Alone, atop the covers,
*

She breathes the tumid hues of her leaking perfume.
Her fingers rake the unused flesh
Beneath her belly, thrash the matted hair,
Enter the well where the demons dwell.

She shares the terse reality of her barrenness.
The undiscovered paradise between her legs
Begs for harsher impersonality.

2–3?/69   (02312)

[While somewhere upon the savannahs,] †

While somewhere upon the savannahs,
A chill-worried wind

She is a New York Jew
Who

The *Mayflower*'s prow runs aground, each night,
On a

She is seized each night by sounds;
The humming of lumbering South Sea whales
Capsizes her dreams. She twists, turns,
Lunges in wounds, and the blood burns;
Then she plunges down the harpoon's line
To the dank womb where Ahab struts

3/11/69 — [1]   (03336)

The Beautiful Flowers

For Jackie's Gail

Spirits detained at crowded gates
Cloud the souls of those asleep,
Awaken contagions in the blissful garden.

A man and girl stand nakedly reposed
In a rented room, where no votives burn
And a leprous mirror on the cement wall
Remembers their faces from another age,
Indentures them to the princely Slave.
The departed are close at hand tonight.

Buried within time's tired groin,
The man grows out of his selfish hiding
To see his own boy become a rogue.
Arisen for an hour to breathe again,
The girl conceives integrity
For a daughter who broadcasts vagrant seeds.

In the fields behind the cluttered gates,
The beautiful flowers are too hot to pluck,
And the dead return from life to die.

3/11/69 — [2] (01089)

Widow

The russet groan of day descending
Follows the swallows' bending away
Into silence. A sickly glow
Elbows its way into her eye,
Shimmers the static crucifix she holds.
Once again, she has begun the dying.

Her prayers done, time has come
To turn back the sheets for sleep,
But the awful sounds of darkness burn.
Her ears return to cooler nights,
When his gentle lips whispered lullabies
And a child was cradled at their side.

So new was the air then, so fair
The sky's complexion, when, at dusk,
The moon wore her metaphors,
Stars borrowed his lyric odes,
And the eloquent explosion of every dawn
Prolonged their delicate reverie.

Now, the taste of wasted wine
Tinctures her dreams with faint reminders
Of war, remorse for a mortally wounded child,
A husband long lamenting a cause,
Drawn in a doddering sequence of steps
Toward death, a wife deprived of life.

3/19–20/69 (01087)

The Garden

A listing breeze, warm, slow,
Blows, breathes, heaves the palm fronds
That weave somnolently the quilted air
Above her apartment. These whiskeyed evenings
Destroy her poise. Equanimity ceases
To acquaint her with completed noises
That descend from pristine towers
Like monks fatigued from extended prayer,
And she tears away the flaming screen.

Shadowed within the mirror's ear,
She leans into her naked curves
To hear the heart behind her skin
Coming undone as heated ice.

Palm fronds straddle the stallioned air,
Dulling their scythes on her frigid body.
The meat leaks bloody, rotten juices,
And the feet go cold above the sheets
That swaddle her. Somewhere in dreams,
Nuns confuse her, while a child,
Wide-eyed, sits beside a mystic pool,
Sifting the coolness at his fingertips,
Whispering poems to the floating fish.

Day creeps through the dusty shades.
She emerges from grayness, stirs,
Before slipping away from the stranger
Who lay in silence beside her all night.

3/25/69 (01088)

On Leaving a Flat River Motel

After a five-month period of incubation

Surrounded by the automatic sounds of television,
Sensual flutes, shotgun blasts back to back,
They are responsive to the untuned voids
That pock the eyes' membranes. Each reclines
Behind the awful, gutless ambivalence of hero-
Worship, clipped of manliness, of womanhood,
That flourishes in toupees and elevator shoes.

But what do I write, sitting here alone,
Confined to this motel room, splitting apart
For lack of fascination? And all these words —
What are they, if not legacies Alcibiades left
To hapless few who choose to rape themselves?
Jesus, this warm night churns the brain's butter,
Leaves the clabbered milk to rot in hanging sacks.

The door to this clammy grot is locked. Open,
You stout bastard! Let night's warm skin
Wrinkle these tired hands, wet them with sweat
Until moisture cleans away the foul vapors,
So soft that the diesels merely heighten silence.

I sneak out, gasping for the full warmth.
Those returning from eating unlatch my shadow,
Pass through, running toward public sheets
To sleep in forms unknown to them, to me,
For their mutuality: children with sweet hands,
Graceful faces, and bodies leaking urgent juice,
Seeking that moment's rest, the quick release,

While I pass through their hasty subterfuge.
A mighty wind the color of truck gears
Shears the inconsistent soul from my body.
I am pinned against the pavement's edge,
Wedged between grit and the perilous air
That rides away for the void to crystallize.
Down here, a sheer voice disturbs the ears.

War intercedes. Demons unleash cacophonies
That echo across the guilty mind. Reminders
Unwind from the spool of naked reprisal.
Only a lonely spirit quiets this shabby midnight
*

As silence broods over raucous belfries
That have steepled dreams of myself. I lie
Awaiting the judgment that enlightens faith.

A vital civilization has arisen from the egg,
Unnoticed. Only the broken shell remains.
And in this nether sphere, stars reach up
To touch a clear, bearable nowhere, collapse
Into the vaulted apse, where the Child resides
Beside resplendent antecedents. I am invited
To a coronation of the forgotten soul.

4/1/69 (01092)

[Inside the wide, high night,] †

Inside the wide, high night,
Wind white as the lion's roar
Screams gruff signs of destruction.
Brittle green twigs let loose.
Tall grass weaves itself to death.
Patio furniture turns to dust

4–5?/69 (02306)

[Squeezed into that last sneeze] †

Squeezed into that last sneeze
Was the day's impeded energy.
Diseases squeezed in pustules
Dissolve in limitless granules . . .

4–5?/69 (02310)

[The collector of fine, gilt mirrors] ‡

The collector of fine, gilt mirrors
Sits before a silvered glass,
*

Staring at his chest, the hair
Exposed by an open-collar shirt.
The nails are badly chewed
On hands filled with bloody rivulets,
While the straining neck is a flooded delta
At breaking point. The eyes shrink,
Anointing themselves in blurriness.
Penetration is redundant, uneventful,
And the mind reclines in a broken rocker.
Somewhere behind the fine, gilt mask,
Demons conceive engines of war,
Angels scurry to battle stations,
While alarms shriek in quarter time.
Silence undoes the quiet belfries
That have steepled his dreams of himself

4–5?/69 (02304)

[The molded plaster of gilt frames] ‡

The molded plaster of gilt frames
Containing an ancient patriarch and his lusty wife
Cracks at the edges. Hedges grow up the chimney,
And the clapboards on this dim-lit day decay
Somewhere far deep in my basement life.

Wheat, harvested and bartered at crossroads stores
Or shipped by freight car to Chicago,
Is siloed on my lips' back porch.
The broadcast seeder and single-tree buggy
Are derelict vehicles of my junk heap inside.

The things of my life bought and sold
Go cold as a joke too often disclosed.
Phonographs, typewriters, and recorder clocks
Consort with the amiable auctioneer

4–5?/69 (02305)

The High Side of Night

For Gail Heffere

I

Stems came loose from their loam,
Yellow jackets ferried life home
Devotedly,
And that black-headed eclipse
Shed an houring coat,
Exploded red-orange and large,
Harvest-bound,
Above fields we found together
Beyond an under-the-weather town,

While we rode softly over
Staccato notes of the hillside
Inside a forested night,
And that masculine wetness
Of steaming horse, streaming,
Stretched a lazy breeze to tautness.
God bless the elderberry bushes,
Freezing like untented gypsies,
That pointed a proper path back out.

Later last night, the attic's glass
Netted the familiar street below
With a fine, crystal kissing.
God, what blissful thoughts
Skittered into timeless sleep
Up there where we breathed silence
A century deep,
Keeping those carpentered secrets
Inviolate.

II

Now, a long, young sun
Funnels through day's naked spout.
Elements of an outside world
Swirl across the master brass bed,
Echoing simple, new brutalities,
And we awaken to the pendulum's rattle.
Again, the lonely mind's room
Shudders under the clutter of antiques.
I leave you with hammer, nails, and glue.

Yet, as I go,
Something beautiful lingers inside me,
Like your delicate fingers
Reaching an overtone's unseen keyboard.
Fleet souls pass in crass procession,
And still the will to survive
Drives my eyes back to you
Through the unstained varnish,
To the natural tarnish of your purest love.

On this fresh, crazy lawn,
The wet grass makes my clean feet green.
And I see a valiant little kite
Pouch the heating air, tear it
In midflight, weave the tall sky
Tattersall,
As you fall to the high side
Of night.
What a fine, nice climb, huh, girl?

5/3/69   (01086)

[The curtains are drawn about his eyes.] ‡

The curtains are drawn about his eyes.
Time devours ritualistic darkness
In a momentless, measureless blessedness,
While unsaturated rays of light
Converge upon some future season of love.

A tender battering of the languid air
Shatters an image the public has
As he drives from the country fair

5–6?/69   (04684)

[Seven fat mangoes] †

Seven fat mangoes
Squat on the mowed lawn
Of a house in The Moorings.
Coconut Grove goes slow
*

To wash away its sins.
Rain spins earthbound
Behind the

The poem hides out there, away from the special reality of transients, dabblers in life's traffic. The highways are crowded with abused metaphors, while giraffes and torpid river horses race in graceless pantomimes toward some scrubby savannah of Tierra del Fuego.

Scott Fitzgerald hides in the cuffs Prufrock rolls up. He bruises his tender hands on the fellow's hairless, red-blotched legs —

That apartment contains her body as her mind her thoughts, dreams, and fantasies, but a house is not a home and a mind is not a grave until there is nothing left but the four bare walls and a caller for a severed telephone wire —

I am a home movie. My reel catches frequently where the eyes are spliced in time. The gradual dislocation of space travels a cormorant's course across a checkerboard of random gambits, and beyond the glued terminal we used so long ago to bond the cracking design and dedicated as a way station outside those recorded limits, she poses, caught as a painter's squiggly slash,

the plane is caught in the forceful arms of
its lover, the high, cold Zephyrus, who squeezes
the elongated body through its sinuous intestines

Too soon now, the I inside me shall take leave of itself, excuse me from the table, where the old ones sit, to play outside with a neighboring laborer's son and a dog with hair missing in places.

The lush grove fades, gives way to those stony hills of the Lead Belt country, and L.D. has traveled into, through, the veins. Now, the arteries course swift with rippling centigrades of passion and longing.

She has found home inside the warm air. Her furniture is the whining neon street globes and people scattered in sweet, gaming disarray —

Down on her knees to see the train coming

New York
Florida   Because I can see that when people
          begin to slow the process of growth, they
     settle back into the sweet, easy quietude of lassitude
and laziness —
     the day gets by the mind like an assembly line of
          parts passing a blind supervisor

Two restless trespassers,
The hot dry lips,
Slip through enameled space,
And as they go slowly
Away from the ocean

And as I go
Slowly away from the ocean,
Over the hazy waste of Everglades,
Something, the sweet, green jade
Of Coconut Grove, the park, the breeze,
Or the tinkling boom lines,
Informs the dehydrated spirit,
Calls the eyes back to touch
Their mother. Smothering
In love is all too beautiful —

6/23/69 (05227)

[Day's light leaves, collapsing] †

Day's light leaves, collapsing
Like a helium bag deflating

Rain on me, green sprinkler system,
And bend stegosaurus-stems around my knees.
Please excuse my madness. The word in print
Squeaks, speaks, leaks idiocy kept private till now.
And no one will understand the fouled, cryptic nature
Of these anagrams, secret codes cabled to Tojo

6–7?/69 (02303)

[Softly, the tendriled night] †

Softly, the tendriled night
and the sounds around my neck choke the blighted spirit.
The mind bites its own limbs, and cringing widows die

The eyes dive through amber hues of sherry,
Floating, sinking, hiding in shrinking tides
Of thoughts unlinking, dreams coming undone.
A child's laughter falls out of upstairs windows
Somewhere, and a priest's Tinkertoy blessing
Dies on the firing line, where we stood being wed,
And the white echoes of Decembering shadow-glisses
Miss proper ears, land in the sandbox at my side.
The sure, keen, gliding smile slides on fast ice,
Skitters through paid vacations, into next year,
And off there, against a fading blue velvet gown,
Appears a shaded fabric of that expensive bloom.
God, the mind lapses in boilers on gaseous fire,
Escaping its own final resolves, bursting valves
That diagraph the cramped imagination, for love,
That catty bastard that goes around in disguise,
Has dispensed its last change. The treasury is dead,
And now, the head sees itself through blur-green ports

I have just recently walked through acres of Coco-
nut Grove, lulled away fetid hours on lawns where the
dogs roam and by the harbor, where the gloaming boats
rap their tinkly shackles through night's long-distance,
dark, hollow rhymes, and spent millions of poems on
the wasting eyes of searching young girls in unzipped
breasts and open hearts bleeding for the long, bony
edifice of time.

And now the music screws its lips on the flattered air.
So much exasperation, so much dullness, and, son-of-
a-bitch, I feel like yelling out for all those young minds
that are making that sordid break into notoriety, while
I sit back, laughing away the febrile hours in the an-
tique mausoleum. What is the distance of infinite space
and the pace of the fat caterpillar that rushes to alien
doorsteps to be squashed?

And now the paragraphs lengthen out, and the cre-
ative mind that once encompassed all the sounds, hues,
and oscillations of nuanced day and night no longer
recognizes its own shadow, on a heated, bright after-
noon, walking there slowly beside itself, and I wonder
why the aging metaphor, that whore in night-robes,
has decided to parade down someone else's Via Veneto.

Something about not finding humor and rest. It's
that breakneck pace to rush toward financial success,
for all those hopeless bastards, and somehow I can't
take seriously all the stained-glass thoughts that falsify
the true purpose of breathing. Good God, there is a
beautiful girl lodged in my smile, and the truest smile
is that which is always just unborn, just hiding at the
corner of the next minute, never quite out, not quite
further than the brink of the thinking mind. She sees
colors and hears sounds as another might eat, taking
all the basic elements for granted.

The illusive speech patters my tongue with stray
syllables, and the light behind the eyes goes dim, and I
see a young, fleshy girl walking by with a child at the
end of a leash and a dog in her arms, clinging tightly
to her neck for protection from the human offspring,
and now the leaves of autumn fold and fall apart, leav-
ing only the leaveless stems and the green nubs, while
Willie Stark tells Sugar-Boy to park his chromium, black
musical instrument behind the courthouse, to be pre-
pared for a quick heist. Ten thousand white lives are at
stake here on the barbecue.

And now all the staid ladies from some turn-of-the-
century family album stand up for their rights, while
Ida Tarbell seduces Theodore Dreiser's chemisms.

The sherry fills my pockets like bugs corners of a
dense menagerie, and

From where I dream, cable cars scratch the belly of
A hundred different hills, and a beautiful Italian girl
Swirls naked from the brass chandelier that flashes her
Personalities like a whore on the rise.
And Sue, you were there behind the proscenium, beaming
Like a

Por todas partes, children wearing adult habits
Die in pairs, sharing their own special disgraces,
Tearing away the superficial layers of raveled lace
To find that the unwinding secret is without weight.

The one with the fat breasts presses the sheets

Those palm trees build natural curvatures up the sky's
spine, carrying the eyes' white corpuscles into battle
with the sun . . .

There are som

Why do the limbs go dull, get sherried, for the park
looms up through a thousand grassy tomorrows, and
the poetry reading dissolves in a leitmotif affair with
airy substances called metaphors, and I hear music
brewing from some newer American Gershwin Jew, a
Roth in loincloth, masquerading as a Jewish guru in
semitrailer truck . . . and the cocaine is really sweet
inside this sherry

Because that girl Gail is sitting inside a few lewd photo-
graphs, and there she is, just loving the presence of
my mind, dull, lapsed, now responding to all that
youthful beauty, which is hers without the need for
making even so much as an effort. God, how does
she make my slim mind conform to her standards of
happiness?

There is a household filled with some strange form
of extraplanetary lovinglivinglaughing, and she once
asked how come it took so long to become kissed, and I
knew that there was the umbilicus to hang from, dan-
gling like some crude Tarzan clamoring for a Janeingful
love, and the showers of April drift through clouded
stages of light, landing softly on her, breaking her
open into fragile bloom . . . fragile . . . fragile . . . what
a fine, fine word for anything that breathes, and Jesus,

I might cry at any time now, because, through the screen that keeps me landlocked and safe and secured, moored to the cobbled landing by ropes . . . I am hesitating . . .

I can see all those securing loves lying there on the deck of a night-bound swimming pool, and my mind cries because there are so many stories lodged within my head, so much that might make others happy, because you see, God, I have never been too damn good at anything other than making people temporarily happy. Permanence has always been a concept that has bugged me into the wormy earth. I have known for years, now, that nothing good, or bad for that matter, lasts, and worse, the moment of living that one most savors is that which he dreams either as having occurred already or as going to happen soon — it is the dream of the event that has the most graceful meaning . . .

and a mother walks down the beach, holding her own hand, and she feels the residual warmth from that child that left her womb twenty-eight years ago. Who dies was once born, and the dying is only an adjunct to some former happiness that happened between people, because one alone is not worth a good goddamn . . .

and girl, girls, Suzie, Gail, Penny, Jan, Norrie, Gail, I hear you all climbing through the trellis work of my front lawn, and the mind crawls through the knee-high grass . . .
the beauty that is out there inside the player piano's roll . . .
and so the bottle beside me tipples, titters, totters like a baby cow . . . and I hear the words, "Oh, I loved you. Oh, oh, I loved you. If I'd been born a different man, I might have tried to understand; I might have spent it safely in your hands." Lord, why can't I sleep?

and those words rupture my thoughts, waking, arrested in midstride, because I know that the lethargy that consumes me, harpsichords my music in busted strings, is that which surrounds the majority of the breathing world daily,

because now I have seen all those poor bastards to whom circumstance has dealt that horrendous blow of nonculture, and the ambition is that which alone is derived from necessity, and now I sit back, fat, full, drunk, and I complain to the essential brilliance of the collective universe, wondering why the poetry and natty prose have left my garage, my house, which god passed over me, spared me the creative pain of verbalization. Bring me a basket of soothing candy, and let my eyes fall back away from the late late poetry show for tonight. I wish that whatever germ has lodged itself within me would die from palsy and a broken heart. There is something strangling my sense of proportion and right reason and that impractical posturing I once knew beyond a shadow of a certainty. The Fairmont Hotel looms before my ears and eyes and feet running away from police warnings and the friends in long hair making it with each other, and me outside the scent of burning love consumed in fast, mad, passionate fits of rapid, rampant love, making the hair stand on end. In the end, the story turns out right, and Stephen Crane dies in some vermined tenement, with all those colors wallowing about his red badge of courage . . . poor, lung-corrupted, stinking, coughing bastard who could put his pen to such good stuff . . .

6–7?/69 (04683)

[The lawn mower slows to a groaning] †

The lawn mower slows to a groaning

Fifty rain-slick, brick-lined streets,
Hedge-grown, windblown,
*

Converge at the ears' edges.
Such heard traffic never believes itself,
Except when words blend with flesh

6–7?/69 (02302)

This Familiar House

This familiar house,
With jackpot machine for a living room,
Outdoor plumbing strewn about the attic,
A stereo blaring delphic skepticisms,
And a tight-assed mannequin
Dancing out an incomplete crossword mind;

This familiar house,
With three Fatimas, or a Wing and two Omars,
Sears buggy section covering the john walls,
Galli-Curci stirring the crystal lips of Zeno Jones,
And a compatible love machine
Wearing ankle-length bloomers and diaphragm;

This familiar house,
With three bell-fruits of concentric light,
Drains clogged with unthawed filet mignon,
Gears that unwind the inward circularity,
And a hundred identically packed Cleopatras
Neatly stacked between the brass bed's sheets;

This familiar house

Rises on its original cruciform,
Outlined in snow about his solitude.
And now, this perfectly beautiful structure,
Love, collapses in a quick flash of confusion.
The dweller's eyes are buried in twin sepulchers,
While the soul he fastened together with things dissolves.

7/7/69 (01093)

The Landlocked

The abalone fisher from Half Moon Bay
Was reported washed up on shore, one morning,
As if to punctuate some unheard exclamation.

That same afternoon, the three-masted schooner
Moored at the foot of Hyde Street Pier
Shifted ballast, as though a cold, old ghost
In the hold below took a chaos-spell,
Dislodged those massive boulders in the boat's well.

Two paid tourists, a fay and his Negro mistress,
Who happened to be idly passing the day on board,
Were reported badly scratched about the elbows
And given free passes, as adequate compensation,
To Queequeg's Seafood Shack, on Fisherman's Wharf.

All the way back to the hotel, both remarked the odor
From the small trawlers and fish-fouled waters,
Yet nothing could suppress their restless concupiscence.

7/8/69 (01094)

[Yesterday,] †

Yesterday,
A sane man jumped into the Seine,
While the hieratic bells

And where is that overriding talent, the intervening
creativity that soars at the touch of the mind's fingers?
I would just like to know where and when the next
Boo the Pack Rat will be, when I am spending so much
of my time doing unstudied surface investigation in
a factory, what kind of story could possibly make for
a good youthful, sex-filled movie . . .
      and the words fell down a well six feet by six feet
by forty-two and a half

cubits . . . cubits . . . cubits, and the schoolteacher spoke to
Jethro: "Spit out that gum, you little geek, before I call the
principal in here, and that goes for you too, Sneed," she
said as she turned to her left, raising a tired brow . . .

Hosey Hardesty walked home from school, each day, pray-
ing to himself that it wouldn't rain, that neither snake nor
chigger would molest him as he pioneered the fields be-
yond the cemetery. Two crones sat together on the brass
bed, holding their hands over their breasts

The beautiful newness
Of this last interlude,
So recently passed,
Intrudes upon the blue, wheat-gazing daze
That impregnates my eyes with wasting seeds,
And a sigh convenes where the lips' heat
Seethes with throbbing pusillanimity,
And nothing of consequence grows,
Nothing slows this ragged presage, time,
From numbing the few final paraphrases

To speak with indiscreet

7/14/69 — [1] (00691)

[The purest moonlight ever breathed by searching eyes] †

The purest moonlight ever breathed by searching eyes
Rode the bare soles of Isadora's feet, that night, for us.
The beautiful newness of absolute speech, not as interlude
But flowering with passional heat of a hundred lumbering suns,
Danced from one screen, through space, to the dream's
    deep place

7/14/69 — [2] (04663)

[The crass fortitude of fat-assed sows] ‡

The crass fortitude of fat-assed sows
Plows up the soggy earth about the trough.
Rooster sings clarions to his proud progeny.

Butterflies, white, bright yellow,
Are the day's version of night's fireflies.
They absorb the full, thick space and hang
Like clothes on a wavering line.

Before me, beyond the barbed fence,
Where the tender wings flutter and
Pigs wallow in their own raucous clutter,
Where the beginning bubbles of Saline Creek
Seep from a craggy terrain, the eyes strain,
Then penetrate the graceful escape.
        Even the tumescent grass breathes speech.

The consistent trickle of the spring — a rooster and pig
        Kick at imaginary victims —

7?/69 (00925)

Morning's Companion △

Once more,
for Jan

From this sandy bunk, on an August morning,
Where hunks of color funnel down through dawn
To buff the corners of a day in the rough,
I feel the body's unrepeated shiftings
And its dry dreams drifting to lighter degrees,

Until something like the child's slow smile
Settles to a tabernacle inside the eyes.
Sweetest surprise outrides the minute hand,
Returns to the upright birth of breath,
And in a sculpted gesture of gentleness,
The future wife of a newer man
Bends down to caress the artist her kiss creates.

8/4/69 (00012)

Cycles

Somewhere back of the sky, within a floating seed,
A child stands at the edge of warmest birth,
Emerges to plant the winds with crying words.
A whitely woman, waiting at the end of night,
Untangles vines that climb ripening runners,
Until man, blessed instrument of love, arrives.

A crisp, clear stillness chills the wet leaves,
Fills the ears with insistent whispering of years
Distant from this path, lawn, house of careers
Called life. And this poignancy is air, idea,
Philosophy born of purest carvings in a tree
Screened against the shimmerings of unseen wind.

8/7/69 (02176)

[The bad wreck of the lumber train] †

The bad wreck of the lumber train
Strains the jaundiced memory of the ol

8?/69 (00922)

Song

For Jan,
in White Cross

Mid-September drips into another winter
Faster than a ship listing slowly
Between fathoms of opaque aloneness.
Jan has returned to outlive this rain.

Elms come unattached from space,
While leaves scrape yellow off the soggy air,
Then sift the colors of her floating eyes
And thread her lashes with silver-fine.

A sudden sun unlatches the castle gates,
Scatters her garden with art-glass roses.
Even the snow's chemistry, unconceived,
Is cameoed in the scald of her perpetual heat.

Indian cold grows narrow on the horizon.
Souls clothed with autumnal penumbra
Press close in blessed confessionals,
Awaken to a consecration of Jan's whispered kisses.

9/17/69 (00408)

The Lynching

An unsmooth, metaphysical cool
Entwines the trees with drunken breezes.
Even a family of Model T's, dust-covered,
Shudders from some distant, inhuman sound
Rumbling up there where a rabid moon
Huddles inside a dark heritage of nowheres.

Beneath weaving shadows, shades and demons
Dance as though the breath of witch hunts
Were escaping black Savonarola's acrid censer.
Townspeople arrive like rumors to meet legacy,
Ancestral curses scar the pockmarked air,
And oaths droop like icicles from the eaves
Of wood-frames with fired lightning rods.

Swooping bats splatter the night sky
With sinister kisses. The heavens abort
The holy beast, clothed in inquisitor's ermines,
A hanging rope dangling from his claws.
Violence is the fast, final crack of backbone,
And the creature hosts the blood of another Negro,
Retreats from those crowding the recent gift.
Revivified and clean, people walk back out of night.

9/19/69 (01095)

[A shabby darkness scars the ruffled shadows]

A shabby darkness scars the ruffled shadows
That flute her bedroom walls. All is still
Within this blissful continuum, where life
Contrives a scimitar in eclipse, skulls
Dull the scythe, a hundred blades disintegrate,
And the end rolls up like an unfolding spool of thread.
Outside the air, behind the beetle's scales,
A solitary pair of angels, disinherited and cold,
Scold themselves silently for their temerity,
And in such utter abandonment, they kiss their eyes.

11/17/69 — [1] (04664)

[A jaded eclipse fades into the eastern creases of dawn.] †

A jaded eclipse fades into the eastern creases of dawn.
Old deaths, remembered through whiskeyed, hollyhock evenings,
Increase in depth with each breath. The children of Hezekiah
    lie down,
And the ground accepts them ungrudgingly. New deaths
Release the stigma

11/17/69 — [2] (04665)

The Return †

Live oaks and palms
    give way to red clay
        and the vegetation of palm leaves.
The factory weeps from pipes
    fixed in the heat of Florida's sun,
        while the patterns, hanging, come undone

    She lies awake, small in brass

11/21–24?/69 (00921)

[We come up out of Coconut Grove, drivin' . . .] †

We come up out of Coconut Grove, drivin' one of them U-Haul Super Vans her mother give her the money to rent {description — fill up the eyes and nose with color and smell and the ears with sound}

The wide eye of night
        Rides the fetid, fluid car of Cicero

Time clocks tuned in crooked tandem
        Slam the circles of closed space chambers

Model T's drift in tilted random
        Through movies viewed in
                        Afterthought

While all his personality was a
        Slogan on the Innkeeper's marquee

The mark of excellence, the time slows down,
        dignity rounds out the humble heart —

11/22–29?/69 (00923)

For Eldridge

The spirit of black decency smolders,
Aborts white nightmares like slugs.
The eyes' thin skin achieves transparency
In the blinding light of silent defiance,
And love, like an animal in a trap,
Consumes its best parts, limps away to die.
Only the molted soul will outlast eternity.

Atop Areopagus, oracles repeat themselves
Inside the brittle ears of disfigured senators,
While to unearthly music
A blue horizon fills up with polluted ashes,
Shimmers with an uprising of harpy feathers,
And the detonation of a million hymns
Sears the lips of the Minister of Death.

Somewhere beyond the soft, wet seacoast,
Inland from exile,
The youngest bodies are being dismantled,
Whose castles are pissed on by helmeted Gullivers,
Whose protests are quietly rethreaded in prisons,
Whose indentured hopes are taxed as chattel.
The old people are relieved to see justice done.

And the slaves of the last inhabitants of Babylon
Are returned to the outraged earth as seeds.

2/7/70 (01107)

Jan's Song △

A loquacious cool caresses our insides,
And daylight scribbles spacious elegies
Across the ears. It appears that the birds,
Caught in slowing metaphors above the ocean,
Will collide with our eyes swooping aloft
From this grot, where our warmth dissolves the dark.

Last night, your whole love infused these cold walls
Like gold mosaics inlaid with Byzantine intricacy,
Suffused the dove-perched web of my temple with odes.
Now, I invent litanies with which to church you,
Take up the search again for words to hymn your love.

Somewhere, wind chimes rhyme you into poems hung
　　from the sky.

2/10/70 — [1?] (00105)

Covenant

God gave Noah the rainbow sign,
No more water, the fire next time!
— James Baldwin, *The Fire Next Time*

Bloated toilet bowls float out to sea
With survivors of the recent plumbers' strike.
Through a soiled sky,
The Lunatic dangles his golden pocket watch
From a passing planet.
Everyone left behind to guard the flooded citadel
Stares up through an endless sweep of eternity
To see the Referee rewind his timepiece, then retreat.

Now, basements fill up with water; streets disappear.
Chimpanzees tumble from trees, cling to steeples,
While green, brass albatrosses ride up from the depths,
Freeze on galactic tides the roiling winds inspire.
Three fishermen on vacation from ancient Tyre,
Flying above the retiring civilization in da Vinci's balloon,
Drop their lines. Soon, the inevitable tug comes,
And ten million souls climb the sloping ropes to freedom.

Beyond Canaan and Bethlehem, to the Promised Land,
In Model T's and Cadillacs, sandaled, with backpacks,
They arrive by twos and threes, hand in hand.
Being the "chosen" few is not an easy task to do
Without electricity or running water. Suburbs of figs
And pecan groves, tented, rent for exorbitant sums
During the northern-wintering months. Sea resorts
Dot like sunspots the clotted beaches. Life prospers;

Deserts become cities. Great centers form dynasties
Whose medicine, law, and cultural filigree
Inform history, while the people prefabricate monuments,
Invent alphabets to house their greedy poetries.
Unrest circulates within proliferating tribes;
Bribery runs rife among those engaged in the slave trade.
From a crowded tenement, unattended, a flame blazes,
Horrid noises rage, and, in an instant, an entire idea expires.

2/10/70 — [2?] (01109)

Buffy

One afternoon, the crying hibiscus wilted.

So far from the darkness-star of day
You strayed without him,
Through depthless rag-ends of gray smiles.

Limbs of the laurel swayed,
Bay leaves sifted from the center
To peripheries at Land's End,
Where a foreign voice from the shore
Colored prayer in feathery circles of gull,

And you followed, piercing the ears' hollowness
To the source of the breeze.
A priest, dressed in breathless air,
Tilted to his knees, addressed the night lights
That lined your eyes like familiar way stations.
Destinations receded, while your own shadow
Preceded a body doomed to return to the morning.

Now, home looms like a sacred mountain
Snowcapped with Queen Anne's lace and madrigals.
A woman walks out of a frozen cave,
Awakens, fingers her large, warm breasts, alone
In a garden that everywhere blossoms her image.

She is the delicate unevenness of her breathing,
The perfect insecurity of her real being,
An absolute definition of infinity.

Somewhere, a laughing hibiscus grows toward love.

2/11/70 — [1] (01105)

Mistress Jan ᐃ

Her wet lips, like rained earth,
Infect my mind with the sensual beginnings of seed,
And now I need to heed night's contrite birth
To bear this hounding loudness.
The pain of the body locked outside love
Stains the perfect, gentlemanly aloofness
I wear like medals from meaningless wars.

Her wine-ripe lips harvest my confession.
Guilt congests the eyes, and Mother Earth arises
From the matted grass where lovers lay,
Her odor forever perfumed on the breasted air
That skies our cloudy atmospheres. We survive
Our lovers' quarrel with the raging sun,
Run for cover under the heat of each other's kiss.

2/11/70 — [2] (01108)

Jack's Bight, Coconut Grove

For Jan,
for Valentine's Day, for Ever

A fat, fat man
Sat in the park against the bay,
Making rings
And other complete thoughts
With the music of his singing fingers
While the winds refined his mind.

All the beautiful, naked bodies,
Female and boy,
Deserted their dreams
To come unto his streaming irrelevance
With toys
And spoils from the sweetest entrances of love.

The fat, fat man
Fashioned silver rings from the air
To bind his voice to their minds' unwinding,
Golden crowns
To ornament their renaissance
With the authority of unaging sounds,

And the beautiful, naked bodies
Made children,
Dedicated their days to his sacred ways,
Until the bay and shaded park
Faded into unrelated dithyrambs.
Now, only Plato knows of the fat man's grave.

2/13/70 (01106)

[Your private eyes] †

Your private eyes
Cathedral
Dogwood thoughts of adoration
That say
The sky is wide as spring is soft
And long as days that never fade are light.
Your sleeping smile
    among the trees that intertwine
Invites the
        love

5/1/70 (00934)

[A deep, green lake,] ‡

A deep, green lake,
Like a dream of dreams
Repeating themselves sweetly each night,
Seeps to an excavation
Within the eyes,
    With which she speaks to me in sleep,

And I listen to see the garden she breathes
    Growing freely as children weave fantasies
With baby's-breath

6/10/70 — [1] (00947)

Four Fragments for Jan

Party by the Gulf

A rabid, dark sky moans at us beyond the window.
   How safe that storm is
     From our viciousness tonight!

Nocturne

A skinny road walked away
Into the forest; only its footprints
Allowed us to follow it home.

At Forty

Every afternoon,
    At about the same boredom,
    We would walk outside among growing things
    To listen for a nosegay of echoings.

Cul-de-Sac

Man's actions resemble spasms.
Even the most well thought-out
And neatly executed intrigues
Reek of bad breath and foul deeds
Secretly buried beneath the cloth.

The disguised lover
Is always discovered
In the hog's trough.

6/10/70 — [2] (01111)

Prayer

What is there more sacred or beautiful
Than a family eating supper together,
Reverencing a silence that, for a time,
Weaves their separate souls slowly
Into an individual speech of peace in time?

6/10/70 (04671), originally part of 01111 — [2]

[Some newer form, conceived more freely, . . .] †

Some newer form, conceived more freely, needs
to be reached in the space of a dream. Look up below
your feet, Jones, and you'll begin to understand that
man is a small bird perched on the summit of some
irrefutable spasm

The critical exposure of the human garden to the
    elements comes from the many suns which pass
        it on the path to the maskers' ball in town,
            false suns, pretenders to the vast
            heated mass of warmth

The greatest books speak of the undying effort of
man and woman to express, not with words but through
soft actions, compassion and sweetest affection for
each other.
    Why don't people feel weak with happiness at
the opportunity to help those nearby who are weak in
misery and bent low by the stubborn, ruthless hand
of tragedy?

6/10/70 — [3] (00948)

For Jan

I love you so very much.
    You are my one true and good friend.
        No ending shall ever part us,
Because we are the green dream
        of each renewed spring
That slips softly as a saintly priest
        through cobwebbed portals
            of endless sleep.
        There in that eternal womb,
    *

where you and I
                    recreate ourselves
        as child,
        as baby,
        as love-seed living in God's eye,
We will survive even the inspiration
        that gives our love its final breath.

6/11/70 — [1] (00950)

Jan

Let us always be
    the world's
strongest friends
        and
    softest lovers.
Let us always be
    the world's.

6/11/70 — [2] (00949)

[A small, white boat] †

A small, white boat
    Crosses a dozen squally troughs,
        And the mind opens wide
            To engulf its intrepidness.
Two children pretend to undo the sun
    With slingshots made of night.
        They hold in their hands
            A secret legend

Two children,
        with gazes fastened on passing afterthoughts,
        pretend to undo the sun
        with slingshots made of night,
        *

While we hide behind the glass
　　behind the sky,
Hoping to read in the moon a sign

6/11–12?/70　(01357)

[For every foggy August morning,] †

For every foggy August morning,
A snowy November day comes ripe
To fill the landscapes of your eyes
With sidewalks, highways, neon lights
That direct the stanzas of the mind
To

10/8/70 — [1?]　(04666)

[Splinters, disintegration . . .]

Splinters, disintegration . . .
The recesses forget themselves,
And darkness seeps out into the wind.
Thoughts carry the trees' leaves to earth,
And the festering begins again as creeping things
Infest his cage of ribs and wrinkled skin.
Raw, rough particles of earth bite the eyes.
Patterns of shadow plaid the crypt from which he peers,
　　book-bound
Between two buckram covers, his dusty remains
Having decomposed, transformed themselves into print
The size of Gutenburg blocks, and the body, supine
Upon the brittle vellum pages, inclines toward the light
Like plants thirsty for strength, and I read that voice,
So long spent and unchorded, disconnected from the mind's
Underworld of duomos and university spires and garbage cans.
And between the lines, the light reads life yet lingering,
Tenaciously persistent, insistent upon coming back again
To love the objects, the prospects of beginning forms
*

Lifting, sifting through the filters of curiosity, of hope,
To lift on fourteen lines into sonnet, farce, woodcarving.
And the marriage is complete: God, light, fear, mind-freedom.

10/8/70 — [2?] (04667)

[Against a sky grown riotous with light] †

Against a sky grown riotous with light

The words issue from my heart
Like prophecies of Paradise grown cold,
And the words, like stones, become dust
In the mouth, from the hands, to the ears of them
Who, at the feet of the great believing Jesus,
Beseech mercy in the highest from a sun
Whose light once brightened the lives of their kin,

Words whose ways are those of the spider's web,
Devious in mystery, filled with guise and subterfuge;

Now the factory was dark, though no silence covered its pipes,
And no peace issued from its corners, for playing among

The boats came down the river, into the bend, with voices
so faint at first, trailing behind the near-invisible crews like
up-puffing billows of smoke rising from a stilled campfire,
so unlike anything resembling human articulation, that the
shells, going in simultaneous slithers, might have been liz-
ards of some prelapsarian vintage, climbing up onto some
distant land, murmuring the ridiculous and meaningless
Gorgon-sounds of their kind, until suddenly someone in the
stilled crowd burst out laughing, lifting all of them from
their trance, the laugh rippling in huge, embarrassing over-
tones from the roof of the boathouse, the laughter at once
multiplied from the stillness, although no one knew just who
or what had been the *"causa prima"*; for that matter, none

would guess that the pert blond standing beside Scism
had let the slow fart that caused him to break the
strained intensity of the climaxing contest. .

10?/70 (04673)

[An overturned incense burner] †

An overturned incense burner
Bears witness to the brass ashes
Of another dry day on fire.
Paper dragons, like effigies,
Arise out of a clear, green sea,
Inhabit the mask of a centipede

Inside the palm frond, breezing,
Teasing the sensual

10?/70 (04669)

[The wild sky, divided like a dreary parliament] †

The wild sky, divided like a dreary parliament
Over tedious contretemps, drives itself to rage.
The jumbled punctuation of walnut limbs and gum
Argues the rain's stressed and unstressed vowels,
While a hollow sound behind the wind continues
Touching a pair of frightened ears with insight.

A child crawls inside his wife to hide; night

It was not at all uncommon
To see

10?/70 (04668)

Nocturne

*For Jan,
in her leaving*

A bright, white moon, just beyond the twigs,
Floats high into its own cold hues,
Hangs there against a dark-blue zone of night.

A few stars pierce the bracing chill,
Fill my eyes with painless glints, then disappear,
Like the hundred inessential profundities
That, from year to year, have patterned my skies
With scattered aspirations, then died.

Out here, inside this wide, silent room,
The shadow of my soul, so long entombed by day,
Escapes along the ground, finds peace in solitude.

12/14/70 (01099)

Unwed Seraph

For Jan's other self

A little girl comes slowly home each night
With a littler child
Outgrowing her own unenlightenment,
And the smell of stolen love hangs thick
As a sticky negative
Over her wrinkled breasts and belly flesh.

In a stinking room she undoes her heart,
While the beat of the other,
Her unseen being,
Repeats the breathing she kneads like dough.
Only the rain, closing in on her garden,
Drowns out the sounds that unbury her sleep.

Red and blazing brass and evertree greens
Crash through the glass behind the bed.
Daybreak rearranges ecstasy inside her head,
And the toad she touched with her dreaming tongue
*

Becomes the minister of her unborn son.
The gift she bears declares her innocence,

Delivers her from the impotence of a perfect soul.

12/15/70 (01081)

[A conveyor takes faces] †

A conveyor takes faces
Past the plate glass of our flower shop.
Cars on a lighted merry-go-round
Bound endlessly around the Square,
And I sit here with poinsettias,
Resting in some quiet quarter time,
     Sublimely
           extemporizing
               the lines that, without climax,
Render fantastic developments
              undefined

Only the noisy neon light
  Reminds me that we're open late for business
    This Christmas Eve.
      Poinsettias sell two dollars a bloom,
      And there are only a few two- and three-
        blooms left.

Now, the hours bore out my eyes
  With

Moon burns eyes,
  Turns lies to bitter truth
    As Christmas Eve approaches.

A bleeding rose
  Fills sweet eyes
    With reminders of a dying age.

Blooming flowers
  Scent her dreaming hours
    With belief in unseen seens.

Night turns light
  To bitter truth of day

12/22/70 (04670)

The Progress of Dreams

*A premonition of death
that came true
the following day
for Robyn,
Jill,
and Uncle Morty*

I

Satin roses,
Set in the softness of Favrile glass,
Glow in space like floating junks
On a waterless ocean.

The *Gone with the Wind* lamp,
Dressed in mauve and brass on fire,
Is a belle caught between youth and love,
A forever-thought, the delicately balanced dance.

Even dust-spirals,
Waterfalling a billion unwashed volumes,
Smooth the unpatterned air,
Invite me to wear its see-through eyes.

II

Sleep, like the sweetest ivy,
Continues its sinuous choking.
Widening voids become unquiet and alive
With the slithering hiss of vipers.

Wintering trees with pendant seeds
Waste in a screeching climax of winds.
A mole creeps underneath my feet,
Disturbing ancient mausoleums,

And in this noisy death,
Hiding from angels in humming gauze,
Who whisper promises come due, I pause
To pray for the fatal redemption of waking breath.

12/24/70   (01097)

After the Untimely Death by Conflagration That Occurred at 2:31 on Christmas Morning at the Home of J. Martin Brodsky, Involving the Widower Father and His Two Daughters

Feathers sift softly to prayers
That church the bodies,
Share the heat of sleeping,
Line love in the nests of the eyes
Of three dreaming schemers at rest.

While night disguises its whisperings
In sequined dust-beams from Chaos
And liquidless stars spray fragrance
Through screens that bedroom the breathing
Of three people safely enchildrened,

An odor the color of deepest shadow
Closes the door on their unspoken words.
Fright chokes on its own self-portrait,
As a chorus of lightning unveils the sky
And charges the dying with silent repose.

12/31/70 & 1/2/71   (01117)

Honeymoon

The old people out walking our beach, this morning,
Pass with the slack abruptness of mechanical ducks
In a shooting gallery. My eyes take aim and fire
At lives on the other end of their prints in the sand.

That man, whose skin is tan and body thin as glass,
Stands ankle-deep in brine as the land gives way
To receding waves. For the last fifty-five years,
He has withstood the slow obituary of bachelorhood.

The aging fat lady in loose-fitting bathing suit
Bends down to inspect the shore's scattered jewelry,
Hands pieces of debris to her husband for keeping,
As though these children could fill their vacuity.

A widowed businessman and his three teenage kids
Enter the water, give themselves up to the surge
That purges their separate identities; he cries,
Seeing their mother through the eyes of the surf.

In bed, where my wife and I lie quietly asleep,
Sculpting driftwood in a cemetery of fleeting dreams,
We're awakened by the noise of a million ghosts
Toasting our recent love as it begins to grow old.

1/4/71 — [1] (01112)

Night

For my beloved wife, Jan,
1/4/71

Across the sky that wafts before my eyes,
A copse of clouds,
Dotted like the soft hide of a snow leopard,
Rides the air, stares toward the sun,
Preparing to repeat its placable retreat,

While the red haze of dying day slips away,
Fades into late afternoon, then drops off
Like merchandise into a shopping bag
Opened at one edge of the horizon,
And sandpipers return to their midnight play.

The black vacuum that remains grows loud
With the sanely erratic convergence of waves,
Which, like a billion sun-bleached hourglasses
Undulating, traps me in that numbing lapse
Between sleep and sound, at one with the sea.

1/4–5/71 — [2] on 1/4 (01115)

Relics of a Crucifixion

The beach has survived another night,
A siege not entirely without its defeats.
Horseshoe crabs and clams, vehicles of war,
Lie strewn along the shore; stray invertebrates
Relate the legend of existence and decay,

While prisoners echoed in sponges and shells,
Trapped within the scattered collapse of being,
Are reluctant to give up what they have endured.
The living sanctuary for the fragile soul
Goes cold in the silence of the ocean's roar.

The spokes of the sun funnel tons of space
Through clouds the loud air dissipates
From dropping pockets to tunneled straits,
And I stare upward in that direction,
Awaiting my reflection in a covenant of grace.

1/6/71   (01113)

The Baptism

An opaque, gray haze has straddled this beach today,
As though an elephant rolled over on its side
Atop an invisible sheet just a few feet above morning
And decided to stay. The weight of time strains my mind,

And I resign myself to the weather. A fearful creature
During this season of the year, it stalks discriminately
The lusty young in bikinis, desiring to come quietly undone,
And the aging, afraid to walk too far out into the sunshine,

As if it might be water under whose surge they would die.
Purgation is a lonely harbinger on empty days like these;
Rejuvenation becomes outdated merchandise on mannequins
When no humans convene to share extravagant savageries.

Now, a crowd of screeching gulls follows my derelict feet
To catch the glances I cast aside like cracker feed
As I scan this treeless Galilee for relics of a crucifixion.
My knees give way, and I bend to the wet sand in prayer:

"May my veins be always attached to the outgoing swells
And these arteries connected with the inflowing tides,
That my blood be ever dependent upon the axles of life.
I beseech Thee this and amnesty from the unsubsiding rain."

1/7/71 (01114)

The Tree of Temperance

A baby crawled, on pudgy knees, toward open space,
From under a family cluster of banyan trees,
Whose sinuous roots, throughout her nesting,
Suckled her restlessness with a purity of mind.

In a grove behind the house built for the town,
A child, beguiled by the leafy mystique of green,
Escaped her nakedness by undressing into her robes,
Running clothed through a smooth, blue, cooling breeze.

Soon, a wealthy elder from the house of the priest,
Confused by the gamboling companionship he knew,
Returned through the woods, stopped, and stood still
Where a girl lay sleeping beside a swollen stream.

A young lady awakened upon the steaming grass,
As new to herself as the man standing by her,
Who, from fright, placed his hands over her eyes.
Disguised as gods, they passed straight through night,

Toward the oncoming sun, which melted their flight.
A woman with her guide came to rest at the well
Near the house where the priest and his people dwelt.
Crying out to the keeper to permit their admittance,

An old maid watched the gate come open, then entered alone,
Where the famous deeds of nameless townspeople
Were inscribed neatly in rows she quietly passed by,
Until she crawled beneath a family cluster of banyan trees
    and died.

1/8/71 (01116)

[A tinge of paralysis] †

A tinge of paralysis
sprays across the keyboard of
the spine, and the eyes roll
up inside their skull like a window
shade snapped up wildly

A man so relapsed with the mind's

3/29/71 (00935)

A Divinity from Within

For Jan,
my faith

Changeling heather feathers to fairgrounds.
Gleaning eyes glisten like neon seas at night,
While a dozen waning moons, in softest unison,
Offer the naked body their sweetest delights,

And the horses go smoothly up and down
As spinning music fuses steam and wheels into being.
The circle draws quietly into night's private fields,
Where fingers funnel each other's earth. . . .
We lay us down in dreams of diminishing strife.

A divinity from within masks our vast afterlife.

4/15/71 (00692)

First Anniversary

Somewhere above this heat, unseen breezes
Dissolve like ice cubes in the mouth
Before they ever reach the brown extremities
Of our town, south of the city

From which we retreated three years ago.
A slow, easterly storm is a swarming bees' nest
In motion, flowing beneath the jet stream,
Which promises rain for the celebration

We are inviting ourselves to this evening,
After moonburst. Yet, the crowded clouds
Are dry udders, whose painful complaints
Have already been sated on another occasion.

We will be left with only the lightning,
Dripping like stalactites from night's roof,
And a moon to shadow with deft precision
The undefined vision of our purblind minds

As they linger within a chronicle of hours
Colored by comets and meteorites
No longer existing, then explode in space
As seconds reveal the nature we seek to find

In forests that liquefy inside our eyes
When they touch each other with heated breathing.
We are land creatures who will come to sacrifice
Ourselves with high esteem and appreciation

For an uncommon freedom bequeathed us by man
Or his creator. We will borrow the sky tonight
For an altar, consign the stars to bear torches
For our bedchamber. Before lying down together,

We will undo the translucent hue of the moon
And use it as a sheet to cloak our revelry,
Until we have completely dissolved each privacy
That ivies the fallen walls of all other times.

Then we will return from the festival of life,
Rejoicing in the passional strength man and wife
Enshrine with a kiss. And when daylight bursts,
Our first anniversary will have circled the earth.

7?/8/71, possibly 9/8/71   (00357)

A Divinity from Within

For Jan,
my faith

A dying sun divides the widening breach of night
From afterlife. We fly upward through dreams
Like freed seaweed creeping slowly to the surface.

The moon, locked in a blue profusion of Fahrenheit,
Veers from some remote reciprocal of fate
To arrive at the blissful abyss where touching begins,

And we reach out through sleep's sequined breathing,
A sun and his newest moon, in human illumination,
To feel the real heat of each other's consuming eyes.

8/16/71   (00351)

Morning Climax

The spider's noose wrings night's last dew from the wind,
And morning is warm.
The mind reclines in a sleepy cocoon,
Streaming with dreams beaded sweetly in song.

Two bodies emerge. Their insides unwind in the wind's eye,
And for a sigh,
They lie caught between deepest death
And the relentless breathing awake of time,

Creatures within deities, images without images of love.
Unsure at first,
They burst through their burning furnaces,
Into a being completely released from themselves.

8/17/71 — [1?]   (00353)

Premonition

Distant lightning,
White as leaping dolphins,
Arouses the placid face of my lonely night,

While, beyond dawn,
A girl in white lies dying,
Whispering, with the sweet tides, my name aloud.

8/17/71 — [2?]   (00352)

Sunday Morning Has the Smell of Love

Sunday morning has the smell of love,
As though a hundred heated dusks,
Refined by the musky lace of lavender,
Have come undone
                            in a sublime confusion of time.

Reposed in a silent quintessence of space,
We share the slow odors of pinking mimosas
Growing yet in the garden we seeded last night,
When a cold, white sun
                            exploded the red-
                                        crazed moon.

Now, our eyes, multiplied in the cloudy mirror
Of a filigreed hall tree, discover our nakedness,
Where we saw only snow leopards and cheetahs
Clothed
        in a floating half-
                    time
                            of colossal speed,

And we climb out of the last grassy hours of Sabbath,
Devoured by the flowering awareness of self,
As two new beautiful fools set out to lose themselves
In the black,
            fluid
                vacuum
                            of the pendulum's
                                        backswing.

8/23/71   (00354)

[The old locomotives that rumbled my youth] †

The old locomotives that rumbled my youth

08/24/71 — [1]   (03353)

The Prisoners

At the northernmost fringe of town,
In a field of jimson weed and lespedeza,
Where stray cows and sheep come out to graze,
A rotted "bob" fence stops no trespassers,
And a small creek sags into dry vanishment
Behind a knoll where we live in a wooden shack.
An everlasting crop of grass and poke reseeds us.

On hot nights, with a bright moon huffing softly
Like a hungry bear snuffing out garbage
And no wind other than the sloughing swishes
Off a car's speed, passersby can almost hear us
Discussing ourselves in behind the roadside trees,
Where, on the face of the black earth, on our backs,
We look for our unborn child among shooting stars,

Coming back, perhaps, through a natural-born womanhood
Of night and sky and hot, soft air, being held aloft
As if some force from the grass, lifting smoke-sweet,
Might be juggling its delicate little wrinkle-feet
On unseen hands. Janny, my wife, frequently cries
Quietly as nearly done rain, and in summer's endless street,
We run over hot cobbles, looking for one lucky penny.

Our daughter was never among the dancing hours' names,
And the seeds dispersed as we joined cicadas in sleep
Against the earth each evening, waiting on morning's heat,
Until the night we came out from eating supper to rest
Inside a slow, pink sun flowing low into the highway,
When a voice, sinking in against land's ear like moisture,
Filled the finishing day with a noise of blazing sparks.

We began running fast across the thick jimson weed,
Past the creek, through a space in the unlaced bob fence,
Janny following behind me, until we reached a wreckage:
We saw each bad dream that had chased us all these years
Come crawling back on broken knees. A woman was sleeping
In the flaming backseat, while her baby screamed blindly
At the man who would never again feed her bleeding lips.

Janny grabbed the child tightly in her arms; we retreated.
Then a thousand scattered beams were bright at our backs
As people emerged from their tedious spaces beyond night
*

To complete the final indictment of a meaningless fate.
When we finally headed for home, all stars had quit falling,
And we were together again, less alone than before, free.
A gift was given Janny to give that evening, and she conceived.

8/24/71 — [2] (00356)

[I planted a]

I planted a
whole field of lilies of
the valley
right beside you,
where I was sleeping last
night.
Pluck just two of them,
and tie them
together
to remind you of our
oneness.

With all my love,
L.D.

9/1?/71 (00743)

Elegy

For Jan,
these words I made.

We used to drive out to the last twisting end
Of afternoon, past clumps of sky and sun
Tumbling softly as bumbling bears at play.
Beyond fields growing with rows of planted space,
We searched for something we had buried somewhere

Or someone we might have stranded along the way.
That was in the beginning, when the love we knew
Was no mere freedom with commonplace indecencies
But a warm foliage weighted with crazy blue hues
And notes floating up from morning-glory moons,

And the people we loved wore their insides out,
Like reverse paintings on lamps to be lighted
For arriving guests. Even then, when white moths
Circled our thoughts, widening insight in flight,
We could barely suspect what had already been lost

Or left back there under the unmarked ocean-tree
Where we surcharged our vows by removing all liens
Upon our unique and passionate state of freedom.
The burden of individuality had been wiped clean,
And in an instant, comfort's numbing encumbrances

Overcame us with a sameness no mind could escape.
Later, we moved to a house south of all known cities,
Where sunsets were still happening and clumps of sky
Might rumble like bumptious elephants. We took turns
Watching at the gate for neighbors and aliens

As our three children grew silently inside greens
Behind a blue lake forming a moat around their youth.
First alone, then with others, they began their trips
To the last twisting end of afternoon, past clumps
Of jumping sky and sun, and we followed behind them,

Until they drove beyond the fields growing with rows
Of planted space for the last time and left us.
Standing free and alone once more, we began to realize
That what had been buried out there so very long ago
Were the skeletons of two immortal souls in love.

9/7/71 (00355)

The *Wish Book*

Dear Sir,

> I regret to inform you that your order
> For two three-jaw universal chucks
> Cannot be filled by us at this time.

> We can send you our #46289
> Drill-bit kit, which we do stock, if you
> See fit to accept this substitution.

Dear Sears and Roebuck Co.,

    I was in hope of receiving the chucks
By Christmas for two personal gifts
At the factory. However, the drill kits

    Will be acceptable, providing the shafts
Fit the 3/8" arbor on the machines we own.
I would appreciate a very speedy reply.

Dear Sir,

    After having done some further checking,
I find that our resource for kit #3248
Has discontinued its 3/8" and 5/16" shafts.

    We are in a position to make drop shipment,
C.O.D., immediately, on 1/2" and 5/8" models
If you feel either will serve your needs.

Dear Sears and Roebuck Co.,

    Pursuant to your recent correspondence,
The two worthy foremen for whom the gifts
Are intended would have no use for either.

    Please see if there are any other suppliers
Whose specifications comply with my desires
For a genuine 3/8" forged-steel bit kit.

Dear Sir,

    I recently took the liberty of contacting
Quincy Forged Steel and Traction Company
Concerning availability of drill-bit kits.

    For some unknown reason, they have just quit
Their entire line of the parts in question.
However, they did bring to my attention

    Their extensive collection of three-jaw chucks,
Put up in nicely finished, fancy hardwood boxes,
Which I thought I should mention in this letter

    In case you might still decide to favor us
With an order. Delivery date on these items
To our Wayman Street warehouse is late January.

Dear Sears and Roebuck Co.,

> Since these goods will miss the Christmas date,
> I have decided to surprise my goodly wife instead.
> Please ship your $36.95 Easy Riding Side Spring Buggy.

9/9/71   (00358)

Consortium

Standing here, alone, on a tilted cliff,
With a breeze corrupting the water below
And tearing away uneasily at the shifting grit
That unfastens me from the flowing earth,

I look down to see a hundred jumbled penumbrae
Thrown back as shadowy profiles of a child
Impossible to recognize for the space between us.
A supple spirit rises up from the dazed eyes

Like a pilgrim's face before a future Christ,
And the ancient crucible, containing chaste angels
And dutiful slaves, overflows. A streaming fluidity,
In which the child is bathed, cleanses the skyline

Of rising sun blazing in an undiscovered Orient.
Somewhere out there, I feel myself being unborn
Out of a womb, out of a woman out of another time,
Into a realm of perpetual incline, climbing higher

Through steep underbrush to reach a tilted cliff.
Now I have returned after seventy years' sojourn,
Conjoined in a fellowship of sky-breeze and seawater,
To retreat with my soul as it finally leaves the body.

9/10/71   (00359)

[The highway ends in the white haze of midday] †

The highway ends in the white haze of midday
> with no more poems
>> or life.
>> *

She is a wife crying from a freedom of blown hair
          and too many sandy tides ebbing
               in a million unnamed moons
Over a hundred famous places she's sculpted with her body

The highway ends in the white haze of midday
               with no more poems
                    or lives
                    to be.
She moans like a wife freed of a tight child born

9/12/71 — [1] (03338)

The Young People

Farmington summer Sundays arrive in the backseat
Of our front-yard Sears, Roebuck buggy
Like an unhurried spinster out looking for old beaus
At the close of a lifetime. Her few remaining acolytes,
On their way to a stained-glass Mass, pass our house
With prim brimstone religiosity, then disappear.

We awaken with a kiss into our own shared ceremony.

9/12/71 — [2] (00360)

The Lecture

From the Gorgon's mouth came war proclamations.
Word of an altercation had reached the beaches,
Where an unashamed people ate figs and peaches all day,
While they pledged allegiance each evening
To a hedonistic philosophy of mediocrity and prayed
To the god of sodomy for relief from each other.

Enclosed within a religion of tetrahedrons,
Conceived upon the essence of earthly tumescence
(Temerity, greed, unchaste love, and pomposity),
They believed themselves to be completely invincible;
Their leaders paid no heed to the Gorgon's musketry
As she vomited and slobbered like a bothered volcano.

Even when kindred ministers from civilized nations
Quit their specious occupations to negotiate peace
With the suspected enemy, she made no acknowledgment,
And her people remained as scattered tribesmen at play,
Absorbed in rituals to Pegasus and the hippopotamus.
One night, a soundless shroud of lightning exploded

A thousand miles away from their estranged city,
And colossal heat began rising from the bubbling sea.
A million fish rode in against the shore each hour,
Until their slithering whiteness obscured the horizon
For the stupefied few involved in their useless removal.
A stench no human had ever known grew up about the land,

Until a state of emergency was at hand. A scourge
Of the first magnitude had come to neutral inhabitants,
Disturbing an equilibrium fifty years of diplomacy
Had managed to preserve against change and chaos.
Spreading contagion made it necessary to evacuate all
Who survived to a deserted island not many miles away,

Where obsolete systems failed to relay any messages
To other peoples in the hemisphere. After a few days,
No aid had arrived, and extinction was nearly complete.
Then, as though a devious foe had recalled his grievance
Without giving reasons, the plague retreated, and air
Became fit once more to support breathing creatures.

Now we have concluded the material for this semester
In History 22. Just by way of quick review
Before we dismiss for the holidays, let us all assume,
As do our influential political leaders and teachers,
That the first attack could have been entirely avoided —
A miscalculation in preparedness, nothing more or less.

9/13/71 (00361)

The Patsy

I

On a recent journey to the Gateway City
To enjoy the freedoms of a weekend bender,
A junkie accidentally bumped up against me.
*

Actually, he may have been pushed into my path
By three policemen taking a Negro into custody
For drunken loitering on the downtown streets.
Perhaps he had been waiting for us to leave the grill
And really meant to make the touch all along,
Or was drawn by the crowds toward the brawny police
To see what activity was underway, when he spied me
Standing with gaze intently set upon the raving bum
And mistakenly took me to be a cash-paying customer.
Possibly, it was my mustache and unfashionably long hair
Or the patched pair of blue jeans and boots I wore
That hijacked his best sense of criminal intuition.

II

Whatever the case was, this well-dressed con man,
Clothed in a tightfitting double-knit sport suit,
With tie and shoes that resembled pigskin suede,
Whispered in my ear could I use a few new kilos
Of fresh Mexican grass. *"No, señor,"* I quietly replied,
Turning my back on the black man fighting the cops.
The woman who had sat down at my table in the grill,
And planned to be my companion for the rest of the day
And night, began to fade as I made negative gestures
To the man who had stuffed into my hand a small bag
Of fragmented leaves and seed of the marijuana weed.
When he refused to pull away, I swung at his face
With my fist, and his chin twisted back like plastic.
The man I hit passed out on the street at my feet.
I heard the woman mention something to the police.

III

And before I knew what had occurred, she was cursing me
As a thief and pusher with such unmanageable profanity
That the crowd grew quiet inside her loud testimony.
"He tried to sell my husband dope! Look at that bag!
And when he refused, this guy grabbed for his wallet
And slugged him!" She screamed something about indecency,
Until a cop grabbed both of my arms in a hammerlock
And placed my wrists in handcuffs. I was then thrown
In the backseat of a squad car parked near the curb,
From where I saw the Negro being freed and the man
*

Giving information as to name, residence, and occupation.
Each explanation I made at the station seemed futile:
"No, I have never blown grass, popped pain pills, mainlined";
"Yes, she was just a passing whore at a dollar an hour
For twenty-four"; "No, I've never met either of them before."

IV

Finally, after I'd passed that night in a cell
And one more and outlasted a battery of interrogators,
They released me for insufficient evidence
And on my own recognizance, whatever that phrase meant.
Then I went down to the bus depot, purchased fare:
One way to Farmington. I was already a day late for work
At the trouser factory when I made it back there
The following morning, just in time for coffee break.
"Hey, old snake! We thought you'd quit." "Yeh, shit,
If it was all that good, you never should'a come on back."
"It was so great, I actually lost all track of time,"
I mumbled at the lunch table that noon. "A young girl
I met took me to her apartment, where we stayed together,
Making it the whole weekend, and she did all the cooking!
We even got high on marijuana one night, just for fun."

9/14/71 (00795)

The Actors

Like a seaman's compass being perpetually reset
At three degrees east, I retreat from each night
Toward days breaking peacefully through a moon
Of liquid marble shot across by a desolate sky,

And too soon, you loft a thousand white balloons
Into the hemispheres that clear behind my eyelids,
Filling their vitreous chemicals with searing insight
Into green and red-blue capsules of sheer yellow light.

Lying together beneath green, leafy philodendrons
And dracaenas, atop cool sheets, we recognize each other
In morning's heat-diluted suffusion of mirrored life
As two muses preparing to introduce a musical prelude

Before the awaited play takes place on our living stage.
Then the parade through plaza after shady piazza begins.
*

We partake of each occupation with people acting in concord
And sweetest harmony: there are monarchs and lords

And serfs, thirsting for strengthened rapport, and artisans
Displaying their assorted crafts to scores of laughing souls
Passing through moving scenes on their way to other plays.
Occasionally, we meet with scoundrels hounding the avenues

For the last few scraps of decency they might exploit
From those resting their heads at the church doorsteps.
And yet, whore and queen must be cast and seen together
In a womanhood of being, flesh enmeshed in seething flesh,

Fired out of the same questionable scruples Eve breathed,
Just as man stands alone when he fights the inner animal
His spirit trees in its attack against insensitivity —
Both the beast and the human come away bleeding and old.

Now, for some reason, we have reached a point of denouement
At which reality deals us confusing cues. We reel about
To see ourselves in unfamiliar costume and lose our balance
As we slowly fall to the stage below the stage above us,

Floating through a spacious black zone into our own bed
Inside night. Survival has returned to us again today,
Like a priest praying for a wayward congregation,
And we settle back into sleep, our faith and love revived.

9/15/71   (00362)

Dale's Poem

*Toward higher education, high ideals,
such as equality, humility, and tradition,
and the highest right of all, to breathe
without artificial hearts if one wishes
to die free in peace, at peace with oneself.*

Children return to the university at summer's end
Like lemmings dependent upon instinct to guide them
To their dying, and their families are left empty,
As if war has commenced.
                    Nothing is denied the rich,
Who have accustomed themselves to the human condition
That looms up from each six o'clock news.
                                    Their sons
                              *

Run a tautly rigged tightrope with fleet feet,
While their daughters sneak beneath cordoning ropes
Set up to withhold straining multitudes.
                              Few of them
Are ever arrested by progressivism as they press ahead
Toward inbred deceptions of liberalism and charity;
Fewer still achieve the sinecures marriage promises
Or receive fulfillment from their memberships
In coveted clubs.
                    They persist in building Cyclone fences
Around newly commissioned houses, so that their families
Will be left safely alone, with their lighted tennis courts
And heated swimming pools in private disuse.
                                          Grandparents
Pass away like balloons drifting painlessly into space,
Until the children of children forget the place they held
In the family.
                    Soon, even predecessors will cease to exist
For the aging parents, who find themselves moving indoors
More frequently as cooler weathers September the trees.

Then, one day, when all their offspring have matriculated
To the university, and time, like an unfilled grave,
Opens its palm to be read, they'll suddenly break down
With a profound realization of failure;
                                    a wavy lifeline
Will engrave them in naked surrender against the earth.

9/20–21 & 9/27/71 — [2?] (00364)

The Expectants

For Eric and Bev,
I found these words.

A slow sun backs away from night,
Into a cold September morning,
And day is suffused with souls
Rushing confusedly toward work
To complete circles begun in dreams,
With reality beating them down.

A wife remains in bed with coffee
And a recent magazine. A child,
*

Incubating in a creation-sac,
Convulses with her nervous pulse.
Soon, the aging weight she carries
Will relax in a fast collapse
Of seething life. Darkness will pass
Into heated, breathing brightness,
And a renaissance will discover them.

Enlightenment will configure her heart
With God's most precious inventions.
When she turns to her child,
A permanent suspension of disbelief
Will recall all lost, loving wishes
Broadcast over seven unseeded years,
To be replaced with hymns to life.
Then, hand in hand, man and wife
Will know their own beginning of time.

9/24/71   (00345)

October

For beloved Janny,
this Tuesday

Little girls leave school in the cool afternoon
And return the next day to graduate September.
Brown and green-yellow Octobering leaves,
Tribed in family clusters within treetops,
Waft with precarious resilience before falling
Into gravity's most brilliantly faceted avenues,

While I remain content listening to the breezes
Fling their wind-songs in pleasing acrobatics
From trapezes swinging freely between tree trunks.
Hunks of fading summer fall off like stone chunks
Chiseled away from a solid block by a sculptor,
And soon, all the harvested hay will be put away

For winter's rationings, as the last heat retreats
And the farmlands widen to accommodate shorter days,
Beginning to bury the foliage in earlier shadows.
Already, we've brought the cacti and other succulents
Inside, fertilized the lawn and strewn bluegrass,
Upturned the garden, which grew zucchini and beans,

Sweet corn, leaf lettuce, beets, and green peppers,
And covered it over in mulch, much as a loving mother
Might unfold a crazy quilt atop a sleeping child.
Although there might be one final mowing, a slowness
Has set in. We lapse between stasis and anticipation,
As a new beginning moves us to patient contemplation.

9/27 — [1?] & 10/5/71 (00367)

Autumnal

Thoughts of declining summer provoke the mind
Toward a winter of reclining slumber with ghosts.
An unsoothing numbness makes me succumb to hibernation
During that season, as hours retreat with a slowness
Exasperating even to a monk in voluntary repose,

And I shudder as though something about the cold
Withholds more than mere providential ambiguity
Between its fluid lapses, as though, perhaps, collapse
Of the psyche is imminent and aloneness antecedent
To the soul's embarkation from the body's fetus.

Although no scintillant dusk has yet begun to set
Low against a flint-sparked, wintering skyline,
I feel myself, even now, entering a mountain pass.
Glancing backward as a last mirage unfocuses my eyes,
I see memories seated about a pond like sweet females

Repeating to each other the poetry I wrote for them
So many hours ago. Not far away, the men I loved
As brothers lie on the grass, at play with ideals,
While the city we built as a sacred precinct for peace
Shimmers in an unreal, icy haze at the mind's periphery,

Where I fight to widen the narrowing passage at my feet.
Breezes filled with the scurrying debris death breathes
Will soon hurry me past lawns valleyed in leaves, nuts,
And cluttered seedlings, until the first shrill chill
Of autumn finally returns me, naked, to hiding outside time.

9/28/71 (00365)

At God's Extreme Behest ‡ Δ

*Extractions from studies
in "paradox" and "inversion" taken
from the notebooks of a late
Elizabethan courtier*

At God's extreme behest, sunne arises in the west
And sets east of this solitary sandy stretch of beach,

While His people awaken beneath moon's easterly seat
And sleep where victorious and retreating forces meet.

At God's extreme behest, sunne arises in the west
And sets east of this solitary sandy stretch of beach,

While His people sleep beneath moon's easterly seat
And awaken where victorious and retreating forces meet.

At God's extreme behest, sunne arises in the east
And sets west of this solitary sandy stretch of beach,

While His people awaken beneath moon's easterly seat
And sleep where victorious and retreating forces meet.

At God's extreme behest, sunne arises in the east
And sets west of this solitary sandy stretch of beach,

While His people sleep beneath moon's easterly seat
And awaken where victorious and retreating forces meet.

At God's extreme behest, sunne (arises) in the (west)
                                 (sets)   (east)
And (sets) (east) of this solitary sandy stretch of beach,
    (arises)(west)

While His people (awaken) beneath moon's easterly seat
                 (sleep)
And (sleep) where victorious and retreating forces meet.
    (awaken)

At God's extreme behest, sunne sets in the west
And arises east of this solitary sandy stretch of beach,

While His people awaken beneath moon's easterly seat
And sleep where victorious and retreating forces meet.

At God's extreme behest, sunne sets in the west
And arises east of this solitary sandy stretch of beach,

While His people sleep beneath moon's easterly seat
And awaken where victorious and retreating forces meet.

At God's extreme behest, sunne sets in the east
And arises west of this solitary sandy stretch of beach,

While His people awaken beneath moon's easterly seat
And sleep where victorious and retreating forces meet.

At God's extreme behest, sunne sets in the east
And arises west of this solitary sandy stretch of beach,

While His people sleep beneath moon's easterly seat
And awaken where victorious and retreating forces meet.

9/29/71   (02284)

The Visit

For Charlotte and Babs

Who will recall without flaw
Kisses passing from mother to son,
From sister to brother to sister-in-law,
Or the few other events of human consequence
We shared under the sun of September's last day,
When we gather at Christmas, inside winter's chrysalis,

Or who will remember, next fall,
The quiet walk the four of us made
About the shady estate in Farmington
And the talks we had about growing trees,
*

Caterpillars, babies, scents of dogs and grass,
When each of us is some place other than together

And the past races up to grab us
Out of a casual taste of apple pie
Or descends through a transitory skylight
Seen from beneath a mimosa's spacious lacework,
Expecting immediate recognition? Will we respond
With a positive nod or just brush the cobwebs aside?

9/30/71 (00366)

Elegy for Mrs. Lycidas

One year, he had no fewer than six mistresses
Strewn about as many cities like Christmas-tree tinsel,
Who would ornament the scented avenues of trade routes
Laid out in tireless latitudes he traveled weekly
Or at any given hour to peddle cheap trousers and blouses.

That was the period during which his dutiful wife,
Who tended toward suppleness in her plump resemblance
To a pewter teacup, grew used to mysterious phone calls,
With all the surprise subterfuge stirs. After a while,
She even learned to wait for each exchange to dissipate

Or perpetuate its busy tones into a deadening echo
Within the bedroom, where she lay awake each night, alone,
Reading through the newest cookbooks or watching TV.
Middle age had secretly remarried her to a switchboard,
From which key she became party to the private listings

Her peripatetic husband recorded in his devotional retreat
From home, as he made wayward escapades into other estates
Of the mind, through the body's easily opened tollgate.
She could only guess at deceits he wove from daily defeats
She was equally sure could never impress mechanical ladies

He was meeting on three-day trips he frequently made
By car. She was the only one who had ever accepted him
For what he believed he was, not for a cigar-smoking
Size forty-four with prematurely balding pate at twenty-three.
He had always been her wealthy executive in vested suit,

Who would devote every second summer in heady pursuit
Of her wanderlust. Entrusted to her dreams, they toured
European countries together and spent endless weekends
In San Francisco and New York City. Only the loneliness
Of having no children intruded, and then not very often,

When they were being young in love. What finally happened
Was that nothing at all happened to him. No new loans
Were floated in the form of rewarded promotions. The years
Began to cast his appearance against a lackluster backdrop,
Until, at last, even he had doubts about the credibility

Of his stature within the diminishing civilization his wife
And he jointly inhabited. Yet, to her, his sample cases
Remained treasure chests of the Forty Thieves, containing
Swatched tapestries and velvets of rarest foreign origins.
Even when his disloyalties began, she refused to share him

With other women he might be dining and sleeping with
In strange towns whose names she could never pronounce
Without stuttering. She actually came to accept the fact
That he was readjusting to a necessary change in life
And that her role as wife was more important than before.

For a time, his home became a way station, a temporary place
To exchange dirty clothing for clean ties and underwear
And neatly pressed starched shirts he had always insisted
She have dry-cleaned. His wife was the obliging nursemaid,
Indulging the irascible whims of a child in highchair,

Caring for her beloved husband as he cut back his schedule
To four, then three days, on their doctor's recommendation.
Good health began to slight him, much as a wealthy person
Denies others handouts, and his rotundity collapsed
Into an unmanageable quantity. For all her uxorial loving,

She could not stay death any longer, and he passed away
Beneath the passionate, gentle breathing of her face
Next to his, as being became obliterated, then unseen,
In the stilled movement of the body that had been hers,
Like a spirit in sacred keeping, for more than forty years.

10/4/71 (00368)

[A red-and-white Cherokee 140] †

A red-and-white Cherokee 140

10/6/71 — [1] (03337)

To Love First Discovered in a Cold
Country Cabin

One last warm afternoon passes a waving white flag
On its way to the final destination. Summer's end
Looms fast at the next bend, turns into an S-curve
As we swerve away from the main road, into winter lands
Snowed closed like Yosemite mountain passes in April.

Wide, white winds scourge the sky, brightening it
With an artificial saline chemistry, surging ahead
Into forests in a feeble attempt to dislodge creatures
Bedded down against the first blasts. We shiver out here,
As if a part of the tree beside us has taken root within;

Only, we are caught inside the tree, between the mortar
And the freezing chinks of log cabin, lost in a space
That continues to enlarge as though connected to a pump,
And we recede within a quilt-covered Queen Anne bedtime
As blizzard hours convert us from body heat into sleep.

Out of a cauldron, we see ourselves being carefully poured
Into twin molds, which, in their extended cooling state,
Will fuse two souls into an absolutely perfect love-piece
That no anger nor personal hatreds, ephemeral though they be,
Will ever annihilate or the greatest patience ever outlast,

Since, in this snowy dream we live together, it often seems
That the flakes embrace our hot tongues and face and lips
Without disappearing. We have been kissed with a deep sense,
Special to people being young for the first and last time,
In which each new dawn breathed leads into a million
    new moons.

10/6/71 — [2] (00369)

A Belated Anniversary Gift

On our fifteenth month

I love to hear you breathing near me in sleep.
It's as if you were creeping toward me
Stealthily on feeble knees to reach safety
From the giant who chases your virginity

Or, like a tiny, shaking rabbit huddled low
Against a snowy land, hoping in its quietude
To elude hunters and dogs passing slowly by,
Settling instinctively within my geography

And remaining there, neatly as a sealed fortune
Inside a Chinese cookie, beneath sweet sheets,
Waiting to be discovered and have small truths
Translated by my gentle, seeking hands. On waking

From night's brief hibernation in dream-caves,
We are born again into another cold morning,
Alive as pure-burning flames that never expire,
Naked as your breathing being borrowed from God.

10/9 & 10/12/71 (00371)

On Approaching Allhallows Eve

Demons in squirrels'
Disguise skitter across my lawn

                         sideways,

Like hypnotized
Filings drawn to a swollen

                         magnet,

Then freeze upon
Sensing me seeing them being

                         seen,

While creatures
Conceived as garbage wasps and

                         flies

During this brief
False heat preceding

                 winter

Spiral high upon
Miniature thermals about the
                                        eaves

Before stalling
In the icy turbulence surrounding
                                        night.

Their crisp husks,
Collecting like sifted seeds at my
                                        feet,

Are pulverized
With the swiftness of
                                electricity,

As bagworms
And tent caterpillars undo
                                nature

With colorless nudity.
Soon, they'll encroach upon my
                                        oaks,

So that the snow
Will have no place to rest in
                                space.

Suddenly, my eyes
Recognize a highly personal
                                enemy

Lying back
Between shadows that flatten
                                out

As afternoon
Returns with me to its cold
                                womb:

It is death,
Come calling in her costumed
                                voices,

Repeating obloquies
She remembers from other
                              seasons.

I reach out,
Impatient to repossess intangible
                              April.

10/11/71   (00370)

The Rise of Silas LeBaron, 1865–1929

Bareback in mid-October,
Running crosshatched down railroad tracks,
Just Jessie and I escaping carefully
From town
              on graduation day from senior high,

Steel kissing steel, and glass
Rushing past our vision in blurred precision,
Just the two of us, hiding away in smokers
Up and down
              that crack passenger express.

A bridge speaking in loud shadows
Passed us along into New Jerusalem
Like two molecules chasing down a millrace,
And we were lost
              in a faceless marketplace:

Babel in a tenement,
Italians renting from Irish, Jews choosing
To hide behind their own Hebraic newspapers.
Two hoosiers
              with our shingles out for hire —

Shoes, hardware, drayage —
Maintenance wages exchanged for our youth
Faster than that crack *Lightning* that bore us,
Pouring ourselves
              into molds high finance heated,

Only keyed so low
That five a week to drum clothes seemed sweet.
Jessie and I were a team, entrepreneurs peddling
Our smartly dressed souls
     to millionaires and urchins,

Whom we'd meet
Between Lake Shore Drive, Monroe and State streets
For the rest of the decade, molting storefront
After stenciled door,
     until a whole block owned us,

I tuxedoed for grand openings,
Picnics, fetes, plays,
And gala outpourings of sentimental yearnings,
Posturing with young ladies,
Finally just one,
     undone in a ripeness marriage delays

And infatuation
Hurries along to its last great harvests
In the initial years, when a mansion was picked
From architecture books and children planned,
Jessie and I
     each possessing reputations and a family,

Being exceedingly wealthy,
Because greed had probably never entered our minds,
Wearing luck like inlaid watch fobs, eating too well
For beginnings
     we could still see pushing us out,

Until the knell
Of perpetual workish years broke the spell
About Jessie's heart and exacted retirement
From me. Eventually, with infrequent, routine trips
To the firm,
     as prescribed for board directors,

I rediscovered myself,
Receding through a hazy maze the years construct,
Alone again for the first time since that night
I decided to invite
     Jessie to run away from home with me,

Bareback in mid-October,
Past any decent age for a man of my stature to feel free,
Running unencumbered of the baggaged years,
Down railroad tracks,
                    back to my land to be buried.

10/13/71 (00372)

[We could hear the fog creeping over everything] [†]

We could hear the fog creeping over everything
On the earth's surface that evening, very late,
Even before we saw it settling in ant colonies

10/18/71 (04674)

Sleeping Man

Quietly, poltergeists creep out on crippled knees
Each night and fly away from the cemetery
My breathing uneasily creates with its noisy silence.

There, a frequency of urn burial and cremation occurs
Inside an original space saturated with freezing light
Fused whiter than polar ice against a black sky,

While beneath the surface uncertainty has perpetrated
Against a dirty, purblind mind, kept women in cells,
Clothed only in a smooth-flowing nudity of breasts,

Slender legs, travertine fingers, toes, and feet,
Reach out toward each other to complete lesbian freedom
With dolphined sensuality. Togaed stoics masturbate

Within a clean-sheeted hygiene their indignities require.
Fires encircling this sacred desolation are leaping eyes
That see out, from watchtowers, over a vast civilization

Contained inside the tufted confines the pillow upholsters
About my hibernating imagination. Soon, the underbrush burns
Out of control. The eyes leak blindness through the mouth.

All deathly atrocities and delicious sexual inconsistencies,
Compacting as the gap between dream and daylight comes
   closed,
Disintegrate in a painless explosion of the six o'clock alarm.

10/20/71 (00373)

Late-October Sunday Service

For Danny and Cindy and their Amy

During this dying season,
Each tree is a preacher,
Unswaying at the base,
Casting off pieces of itself
To form a rounded congregation
Beneath it on the ground.

A very Sunday ceremony
Is being tabernacled
By each twisting carcass
As it passes through space,
Boasting, even as it goes
Toward a final enactment of gravity,

A graceful immortality
Scratched upon sensitive plates
That capture crosshatchings
Each leaf engraves, bending
End over end over end
Before achieving complete purgation.

Nature's stately ministers
Will receive one sun more
Before their speeches are done
And winter's pale gray skies
Veil their naked vacancies
In anticipation of May.

10/24/71 (00374)

Taking the Back Road Home

The boisterous lands we planted with eye-seeds
Gathered from people fleeing in exile
Flower sumptuous pollen that bees devour
Weaving freedom into a tapestry of hours.

Fields we discovered spread under the sun-line,
Yielding memories drilled in season,
Fill up after harvest with mellifluous dreams,
Like Van Winkle redeemed by a kiss.

The feline ocean, stalking an antelope beach,
Lying quietly beside us at night,
Makes its way yet through our jungled ears,
Though no pets have entered this house in years.

The empty sky we colonized with child's tunes
To illumine the spheres God neglected
Is a huge music box with smooth duplex combs
Musing us into taking the back road home.

10/26/71 (00375)

[A white cathedral dome] †

A white cathedral dome
Shimmers on the bright Tuscan horizon,
Yet I am with my wife,
Passing through a pagan desolation,
And what we see we saw

10/27/71 (04675)

Dr. Terraqueous

Just this morning, we heard the word
That another human being is on the loose.

It always did seem strange to me
How different the same species could be

When occupied by their game of freedom
Or when allowed to sift through histories

For justifications of their existence
And meaning of bleak, vacuous pastimes

They pursued within elaborate cages
Called "cities" for lack of translation

For "maze." Bad connotations
Accounted for many temporal changes

In their routine. Muted reputations
Frequently exploded a creature's habits,

While even his entire feeble reason for living
Was seriously questioned by us.

I can remember how their forced complexities
And nonconsequential measures to escape

What they concluded to be mortality
Used to amuse us in the very beginning,

As though they really believed in something.
For all our eavesdropping and peeping,

We never discovered their meaning of "religion,"
A code word they well concealed from us.

My own theory is that the human beings
Never knew either and that they used it

As a fantastic excuse to circumvent life.
Yet death forever devised awkward ruses

To upend their philosophical tendencies.
The twins, charity and war, threw a noose

About their good intentions. Peace died
Without us ever even lifting a directive.

That was what we found utterly astounding
About that thrombus of people down there:

They displayed such deft fascination
With self-annihilation that it developed

Into full-scale genocide. In defeat,
Each one finally took to his own retreat,

Afraid to be seen in public or private,
As though his own shadow would club him,

Set his house afire, or shoot his eyes out.
Silence became the commonplace equation

During the ultimate phase of disintegration,
As fewer humans ventured out each afternoon

Into the sunlight. Fear had imprisoned them
Within their own lonely cells, solitary

As smooth, useless rocks locked in a box,
Doomed to an unannounced end of time.

10/28/71 (00376)

Ultimate October

All the fall leaves have ceased their flights.

Only smoke seeping from their dying carcasses,
Like condensation trailing a high jet,
Remains ubiquitous against a blanching sky,

Then goes stale as weekend cigarette ashes.

The treetops are detailed maps whose byways
Are naked limbs; these miniature invisible roads
Run off into white sky like dry desert creeks,

While the unemployed eye registers a total void.

People deeply involved in outdoor chores
Fail to heed changing night and hoarfrost
As winter beckons with slightly sinister winds

And an irascible mean streak that bears watching.

How beautiful things are just before they die!
Even if we've not seen them growing, flowering,
Something about an ultimate liberation let loose

In the going out blows apart the prismatic minds

Of those who dare stand at the question's edge
And accept the unanswered paradox without fear
Of reprisal. Even a dumb understanding of nature

Is sometimes a bounteous kind of blindness.

10/29/71 (00377)

Velocipede

Her tricycle squeaks like a spooked monkey.
I wonder why her father, my unseen neighbor,
Can't at least find the time to grease it
Or have it aligned here in town. He never seems
To be around when that queer child needs guidance.

Just now, that screeching noise borne loose
By his eight-year-old girl is a preying banshee
Making naked the clothed poetry I've undertaken
Within my brain's fold-up cage. Her play
Is a crazy voyeur fixed on undoing my soul

When I'm most at extremes with aging emotions.
What's she doing driving that thing on my lawn?
First, forward engaged, then going madly in reverse,
She's succeeded in seducing my mind, distracting me
To such a degree I could run outside and slap her,

Perhaps drag her from that three-wheeled machine
And toss it into the street. It grows very late,
And this sheet of paper spits back vacancies
Like cheap-motel signs speaking neon affirmations
At midnight. Once again, I've completed nothing,

Created no great silhouettes, because this outrage
Upon my privacy has confused the diffused light
With which the muse used to illumine my quiet eyes.
In a flash of insight, I see history passing me by,
Riding a tricycle across the sky like a small child.

11/1/71 (00378)

A Valedictory Against Insensitivity

In which the poet mourns the loss
of poignancy among friends
and people he just knows
and might someday meet
or possibly seek out
for his last needs

Two consecutive days form an alliance in time,
A demarcation in the spatial variation of souls
Floating in limbo and those awaiting confirmation
To abandon their stately desolations on earth.

Forty-eight hours fuse two hemispheres with news-
Worthiness, as though man's fatalities and successes
Were sufficient catalysts to bind all life in peace.
Secondhand sympathy overwhelms the nervous psyche.

The revolution of twice sun and moon comes too soon
When a man and woman, planning to escape common-
Place strictures glazed upon them by their bodies,
Discover they are identical in every human limitation.

Only stones, washed oblivious by pellucid rains,
And seashells and trees, small things and mountains,
Go undisturbed through an unchronicled continuity
Of unconsciousness, being free to be absolutely free.

11/2/71   (00379)

[Summer has finally come] †

Summer has finally come
To

The trees wear a scant coat of leaves

Yesterday evening, I seen three dogs
Comin' up the street behind us fast-ass,
Like maybe they were aimin' to take a big bite
Or eat the air just behind us from hunger.

Whatever the reason, we never waited around
To see what would happen, 'cause

11/3/71   (04672)

House
Fly

All the warm-weather flies   Something about being deceived
That were alive two days prior,   By Indian summer's quick-change trick
Colliding in continual divisible frenzy   Was the only reason a surviving queen fly
Like crazy-patients passing in an insane asylum,   Could conceive. I'm sure she was being facetious
Lie brittle, silent, between two pellucid panes of glass.   In the face of a forty-foot winter breaking so close behind.

11/4/71 (00380)

The Slacks Factory of Farmington, Mo.

Dedicated to the employees of . . . ,
11/6/71

Another week has reached its denouement,
And all the factory people are leaving
The familiarity of their sewing machines
For a brief weekend at home with family
They haven't seen in more than forty hours.

This quick retreat from perpetual routine
Is motion caught between parentheses,
An isolated return to humanity, interlude
Without room for brooding about quality
Or lost production due to possibilities

Too numerous for them to completely control
On an individual basis. Although each depends
Upon the least capable, necessity dictates
Their ultimate well-being, and transcendence
From poverty becomes only gross achievement

When loaned out biweekly on a payroll check.
A certain decency has brought all these people
On streets and back roads fifteen miles deep
In each of three hundred unmapped directions,
Like a continuous emigration from idleness

To a new land with a million unhewed acreages.
Seated in daydream, some have come to fertilize
Unproductive fields left by harvested children;
Others to colonize a community of mutual friends
Backwoods isolationism has always neglected.

A few use it as an excuse for anything else to do,
Yet none is a charge upon our unweaning society,
Which encourages the beggar to continue his trade,
Retired athletes to atrophy, and the businessman
To sell his brain for a hundred-million-dollar ad.

Honesty, like oak trees, reseeds itself in soil
That never goes fallow when carefully nurtured.
These workers share their quiet kind of docility
*

With a heritage they help perpetuate, celebrating
The dedication of the self to useful occupations.

11/5–6/71   (00381)

The Rough Beast

On going to visit Dale in Palo Alto;
for her I heard this poem.

The slumbering giant rises slowly,
Like war grinding to a close.
His lumbering hulk, stark against dusk,
Like a crane along Thames's quays,
Is a mute moving through a noisy universe.

Although in face he remains the same,
No one will recognize him for changes
That have devastated the sated landscape
He is fated to return to this lonely day.
Even in fear, the people felt safe,

Knowing this was the place he domained.
Their security grew out of intimidation
They transformed into religion: they prayed
For peace; they came together to mate
In congregations and, without being aware,

To protect themselves from themselves
And not from the giant, whom, from pride,
They had grown to hate and misunderstand.
Later, they even learned the secret
To his weakness and defeated him in bed

One night, when they were sure his head
Was filled with repentance for his sins
Against them. When he disappeared
And all traces of his madness were erased
From collective memory, they celebrated

The beginning of nonworship, freedom
For the hedonists and believers of self,
And though cults and schisms grew into trees
*

Whose leaves filled every breathing space
With people, nowhere could there be seen

Beings meeting to share their privacies
With beings meeting to share their
Privacies with beings meeting to share
Their privacies, as they had done
When the giant funneled them together

Into a oneness of conscience from a terror
Of dying unnoticed. That was too many years
Before a prolapsed season for the old mute
To rehearse. Now, he lumbers home again,
In hope of finding a familiar place to die.

11/15/71 (00382)

"Enlistment Notice" et al.**

Enlistment Notice

Volunteers needed to join in the hunt
For the ring-tailed, saber-toothed elephant cunt
That escaped from our local zoo last month.
Apply at library. See Miss Amelia S.* Grunt.

*Stein

The Connoisseur

Being a worm and lover of the earth,
I'm compelled deliciously by my birth
To explore and adore the exotic lure
Of a faraway garden spread with manure.

Of Human Desires

A lonely hippo,
  The color of stone,
  *

Wallows and groans
 As he arches his bone
  To overtake the throne
   Of a mate who lies prone,
    Waiting to sate her erogenous zone.

Large-Breasted Stewardess

Nature, in her wondrous ways,
Endows each unequally with special displays.

Final Approach

Monopoly box-houses
At Phoenix's outskirts,
Set briefly in sand,
Somehow withstand the variations
Of a monotonous plan.

Farewell on Boarding

And
Be sure to tell Aunt Myrtle
That her girdle won the high hurdles.

Pericles on America

Our civilization
Reached its highest degree of sophistication
In the era of immediate prefabrication.
From the Nashville Parthenon,
It was a downhill slide all the way home.

Seat Belt

Please release me
From this brief stay
That holds sway over my insecurity,
But not until reaching the taxiway.

Dinner Flight

Trees that look like poppy seeds
Dot the hills of Yosemite.
I wish we could eat them all,
But the hungry eyes' appetite
Manages, through abstinence,
To satiate the stomach's walls.

TWA 727

Flying from east to west,
We're myriad players in a game of chess,
Testing the nature of our variegated fates,
Patiently waiting to learn the outcome
Each placement of the pawn will cause,
Flying from east to west.

** *[Written with Jan Brodsky]*

11/17/71   (00383)

Three for Sister Dale

Palo — 11/19–20/71 — Alto

No Contest

Despite the lack of proper magnifying glass,
My ill-defined mind finds it necessary
To search between the lines for meanings
          To the fine print
That legally binds me to my sister Dale.

It seems that every time court reconvenes
     And briefs are again presented,
Each of us enters a plea of *nolo contendere*.

Littermates

Two beautiful animals behind zoo bars,
Confused by their various-paced monotony,
*

Chase alien sounds with slow ears,
Knowing nothing lurking will disturb captivity.

After the Invasion

Half a dozen ants dance across the breakfast table,
Making advances on the rancid can of freestone peaches
That stands as a timeless reminder of last night's supper.

11/19–20/71 — [1] on 11/20   (00385)

Bonfire

For Dale and Jim,
who shared this whim

Even with the forty-degree night air,
The heat kept inching out
On caterpillar feet, eating away at space,
As though the black background
Were a green leaf and the people veins
Netting night with intimacies
It well intentioned to leave behind.

Its silence spoke high into the night sky
With flighty vowels
And consonants sparking the darkness
Like eloquent bombast
Yet said nothing to its rapt audience,
Who listened intently
For the release of secret mysteries

To the meaning of their being there
On such a pagan evening.
Soon, the crowd began to capitulate,
Retreating like sea waves
In measured undulations, as the fire
Crawled out of its body,
Become not butterfly but dinosaur.

11/20/71 — [2]   (00384)

Above Love in Sausalito

For beautiful Jan,
11/21/71

Fog interlaced with silvery haze
  Drips over distant Sausalito cliffs
    Like Chantilly spaced in assorted lengths
      For a Victorian store's bay-window display.

People come down from higher climes
  To exchange rain from other time zones
    And plain-bleached snow for water flowing
      Through afternoons stained with sweetgreengrains.

You and I, wife, in a soft floating
  Of streetlights, are sailboats and gulls
    Frozen in flight, whose slow-blown motion
      Holds up all sky above Earth, beneath God's eye.

11/21/71 (00386)

Pescadero Beach

For my sister Dale,
with all of my love

Moving
From Palo Alto shallows
Into cool-breathing La Honda Canyon,
Where California redwoods still pursue
A drowsy arrogance and crowded circumstance
Settles back into chill, black backwashes of nontime
To negotiate no new contracts with Captain or Mrs. Fate,

Crossing
The supple roughness
Of slumbering elephants' bellies
That define the hibernating high ground,
Thrown confusedly behind its ocean coastline
Like unglazed clay ready to be slaked out of shape
For weather-fingers to remake it into newer landscapes,

Emerging
To take up residency
Within the sea's choreography,
Which we three have come here to score,
We play at being free, entranced by the dance
Each creates at the dense green edge of immensity,
Until our sensuous bodies enter its strenuous endlessness.

11/22 & 11/29/71   (00387)

Endless December

                                        Defeats
Repeat themselves like timepieces machined to
Know the same twenty-four hours each new day.

People are piteous leaves that become unattached
In graceless eventides bestowed by evil seasons,
Rise on vagrant eddies to fly back up to trees,
Irretrievable for an unreasonable natural law.

Returning to my trap lines, set out last spring,
I find captured myriad feeble strays, nameless
Even in species,
                        identification tags rotted away,
Strays with disease, crippled, maimed in spirit,
Whose pursuit would discredit a lame vagabond.

Something within infinity paces inside of me,
Chasing reason like a cow running precariously
To free the butterfly fastened to its dry nose
And squeeze it underfoot.
                        I leap onto a rainbow
To see the earth below slowly gathering momentum
As it flows away,
                        then throw myself to that sea.

12/7/71   (00388)

The Other Woman

Like the Hydra, sprouting two new heads
For each defeat,
Her specter chooses unoccasioned nights
To frighten me.
Surely, I'm no strongman, no Hercules.

When I least
Expect to see her, she dissolves atolls
Nightmares accrete
Just beyond sleep. Coming naked up
From the sea,

She swims into my lagoon for safe keeps,
To be released
From the oblique prison amnesia creates.
Her breathing
Finds freedom to enter my secret prisms.

I reach out
To touch, taste, take her between the legs.
Dreaming ceases.
Only my screaming silence achieves climax
Before I retreat

Into the warm fortress my wife affords me
Each evening
Against a completely impotent concupiscence.
She still believes
My tossing is caused by implausible ogres.

12/13/71 (00389)

An Attack of the Heart

The rarest blood, type AB,
Tears through the aorta, misses the
Beat,
          Repeats a distant systole.

The body reacts with violent con-
Tractions
*

As the cruising fluid chases it-
Self through tissued contiguities,

Onto confusing spur tracks and sid-
Ings,
Trying hurriedly to unload nonmone-
Tarythings beings require to survive

The futilities of limited perfection.
Infections arrest the trans-
Fer of mer-
Chandise; vehicles switch directions

To avoid demons picketing the system,
While fatigue, like f l o a ting ash,
Settles overneath
        The crystal of a sprung timepiece

The brain used to look through to see
The   UNIVERSE,
As a last diastole calls all blood home
And the closing eyes fill fast with God.

12/15/71 (00390)

Deaf-Mutes

Two deaf-mute children,
Passing through a latticework afternoon,
In search of a single thought
To occupy their lifetimes,
Pretend to undo the sun
By filling their slingshots with night.

Soon, dusk hides them in its wide silence.
Their eyes cry out
In voiceless litany beneath the moon
To be advised
What destination they might pursue
As blue youth fuses into sepulcher black

And a sweeping second hand runs backward
To catch up with their activity.
*

They listen to *brujas* and poltergeists,
Whose green-red eyes illumine the mind
With misguided expectations
Of lush new lands lying low on a horizon

That eludes the psyche's importunate drive
Toward immortality, and then reject
The wisdom of demigods.
Bereft in old age, within a forest
They never really left,
Entrusting the remainder of their stay

To grave calculations contrived by death,
They touch each other's supple lips
With shivering fingertips
And cup hands to ears, as if to hear,
In a universe their naked kiss creates,
Whispers of future truths come due.

12/20 & 12/22/71 (00391)

[The way the Sunday section exposé] †

The way the Sunday section exposé
Froze her

The way the Sunday magazine exposé
Encapsulated history in

1/3/72 — [1] (02459)

The Kiss of Oblivion

> *For George Hampton,*
>   *teacher of Renaissance English literature,*
>   *on being involuntarily committed*
>   *unto state's keeping*

As master of his vast and isolated plains,
Where excavations for dragon remains
*

Were being undertaken,
He felt obliged to perfect disguises
That might frustrate the thrust
Toward a scientific explanation of himself.

In the end, receiving-ward orderlies
Forced him from his horse
By lacing each quarter-day with a pill.
Under the weight of stately chain mail,
He lay dazed beyond the portcullis,
Awaiting a flaming tongue to singe his brain.

1/3/72 — [2] (00392)

Each in Its Ordered Place

I

On cleaning day,
We were always so careful
Not to leave his furnishings and books in disarray
Or the room with a general sense of desertion,

As though no one should be led to believe or suspect
That the professor,
Returning after lengthy night classes,
Might be afraid to be met

By an unwholesome ghost he'd neglected to settle with
Or an unexpected change in the protective perspective
The tufted sofa
And cheap Monet prints gave to his leased principality

Or that, possibly, he might not have a wife
To tidy up for him, to let him use tired clichés
Upon a timid, outreaching Leda,
Allowing him to pursue man's paltry possibilities.

II

We were always so careful not to destroy
Or disturb the voiceless harmonies between things,
The medieval balance of worn Belgian rug, stained basin,
Torn lace curtains, enormous Victorian bedstead,

Which said he had mastered continuities in space
By arranging, to his own unexplained taste,
The most congenial placement of vacated afterthoughts
Within the husk that housed him these past ten years.

Perhaps all that time had been a study in dying,
His life an ordered sequence of flights and returns
From no one to nowhere, preparing for the day we found him
Tucked indistinguishably between sheets, alone no more.

1/4/72 (00393)

[A different kind of sickness,] †

A different kind of sickness,
Fickle as cunning,
Ivory-tan in airy shape
Like the coat of a snow leopard,
Visited us this Christmas with gifts

Who knows why hallucinations are the color of love

1/7/72 — [1] (03747)

Death by Water

My fishbowl existence,
Slightly murky from recent negligible activity
In defense of privacy,
Is filled with too many finned ideas
To search for feed that trickles gratuitously
From a distorted Above.

A shadowing curse disturbs the lighted surface,
Settling a net around my universe.
I rise without fighting silence,
Disperse slime,
Breathing out old, cold air from dry lungs,
Dying into a timeless, free-floating peacefulness.

1/7/72 — [2] (00394)

Sea Dogs in the New World

*A bad imitation of John Donne**

We speed through youth's trade routes
Like two pirates plundering loot
They don't know where to hide
Or how to use in the tired world,
Where people wear out their lives
Thriving vicariously on others' daring deeds.

We pirates succeed to such a degree
Of thievery that even envious nature,
Blazing with finite, transitory beauty,
Can't bequeath her greening offspring
Such delicious blooms as those we sneak
From storerooms filled with love's mystique.

And yet, the acquisition of our riches,
Gathered without suspicious authorities
Making accusations as to their veracity,
Goes untaxed as a beneficent donation
To a most charitable humanitarianism:
The organization of united, outgoing souls.

*Written while thinking of Janny lying awake in the hospital,
awaiting a morrow on which she will see the swirling circles of
sodium pentothal and feel the silent probings of friendly,
alien men at work with nature.

1/10/72 (00395)

Reflections upon Waiting for a Patient to Return from Surgery, 1/11/72

Strange laughs, lost
As cave echoes, carom
Between wide, gleaming corridors.

Steps connected to misdirected feet,
Lost as strange laughter
Belonging to healthy people,

Repeat an uncoded progression,
Whose busy sequences
Keep increasing as daylight recedes,

Until doctors and nurses
Leave only skeleton crews
To attend the disruptive silences

That permeate an erratic quietude
Of charnel-house lives
Suspended in endless uncertainty

Throughout this blockhouse maze.
Maladies, pregnancies, surgery cases,
Crowding im-patient file cabinets,

Are lifted hastily from another world
With galling arbitrariness.
Such a stunning unreasonableness

Goes unexplained by ward orderlies
With mimeographed progress sheets.
Each is left in speechless dread

Of a nonfeeling final pain
He believes will precede death,
Without warning, during sleep.

An elusive dash of sunshine,
Funneling across dirty window sash,
Affirms a successful operation

For those returned to their beds.
It burns a slightly hot incision
Upon the belly of continuing indecision

For the few doomed to remain
Within a gloomy prolongation
Of noisy hours and restive seconds.

Daylight, climbing up the curtains
Drawn still around an empty bed,
Etches an elegy in abstraction

To commemorate all lost souls
Who actually felt the last stroke
The burin made upon their soft plate.

Soon, even that brightness will disappear
Into the room's shapeless interior
As a new recruit fills the open rank

And his fearful ears are besieged
By laughter and erratic footfalls
Of people being healthy in the halls.

1/11/72 — [1?] (00396)

Side Effects of Technology

Overhead, a highflying jet
Tears a blue universe in two
Before the sky closes in again
Over invisible vortices
Its floating motion creates.

I try to speculate on the space
That separates my eye from it
And the distance its wing-tip waves
Will take, in minutes, to reach me,
Awaiting a possible annihilation.

1/11/72 — [2?] (00397)

Tomorrow's Leaders

He and she
Wear excellently textured redundancies,
Like crumb-catching cummerbunds,
About their festive heads.

Each selects for the other

An evening wardrobe of lavish cynicisms
And flaccid dishonesties,
Fashionably accumulated from nude scenes
Used by desperate producers
And from loosely woven speeches
Given by rabbinical and political priests,

Before entering the familiar situation
Of their closest friends,
At the opposite end of the development,

To spend the remaining hours of a waning fantasy
They have dreamed about all week,
Playing hide-and-seek with each other's mate.

1/26/72 (00398)

King of Kings

> *Look on my Works, ye Mighty, and despair!*
> — Percy Bysshe Shelley, "Ozymandias"

I

Death's delicate squeeze
Was scarcely felt
Because the season wasn't right for dying.

The great king's protégés,
Deprived of the proper etiquette,
Knelt to weep like rose petals

Seized from stems by November winds
Speeding through a freezing July.
The utter disbelief of the thing

Caused every priest in the kingdom
To scale dusty belfry heights
And free silence from rusty bells,

Announcing the arrival of another ghost
Into the *Doomsday Illuminations*.
He'd been caught, between acts, undressing,

Groping for another regal disguise
With which to make a daring escape
From the fabled demon, he a rakish king

Confined by the palpable limitations
Of a false freedom, forgetting the flesh
Has no allegiance unto the self.

II

He was a reckless king,
Infected with self-esteem
And swayed to raucous invective

By people he'd never even seen,
Who refused, through strength
He didn't possess, to perpetuate

His insatiable lustiness, a king
Gone sallow as a fading skyline,
Laid to waste in fallow stateliness

In a vacant nave, just as he'd lain
In stony aloneness all his life,
Waiting for sycophants to plague him

With illegitimate favors and praises
That might buoy his drooping divinity.
Now, a pointless king, without children

To carry forth his anointed deeds
Before an unconscious people, hears clods
Of a stillborn harvest tilled under

Above his slumbering shell. A king
Sinks deeper into memory than history
Recounts, until those chosen to succeed

Eventually remove his neglected tombstone
From the sacred lands to make room
For housing units and a supermarket.

1/27 & 1/31/72   (00399)

Self-Recognition

A drunk digs deeply
Into an overstuffed garbage can
On a freezing night.
Finding no relief from the freedom
He defines by his impoverished solitude,
He inclines toward the abyss,
Barely missing kisses the whistling wind
Sends just out of reach
As he slumps in a tattered lump to the gutter.

Beneath the haloed miter
Of a white-glowing streetlight,
A peaceful prince,
Heated by a natural insulation
His dreaming creates, lies sleeping
Within an ethereal tradition of honor,
Until he is awakened by a drunkard
*

Wearing his own princely robes,
Who offers to share stale bread with him.

2/7–8/72 (00400)

Rachel into a New Dawn Runs ‡

Clouded sands recede beneath seaweed,
In a murky disturbance.

Whirling urchins surface
Like hasty bubbles from a drowning person.

Rachel cries,
She barely cries.

Night sounds settle like an ancient house
In a fluted universe.

New-silenced music
Moves through muted communions to the soul.

Rachel cries,
She cries inside her coverlet.

Unseen breathing subdues this sacred place,
Makes a clean space

For birth to occur
With the graceful symmetry of wet cymbidiums.

Rachel stirs,
She barely stirs.

Explosions domino over the spine's fine line
To her mind's depot.

A baby crawls out
From sleep to meet its deepest incompletion.

Rachel stirs,
She stirs beneath her freedom.

Sun and moon undo the collapsed death mask
Nativity casts

Against the past.
Her shadow finds her in air, sand, and sea.

Rachel breathes,
She barely breathes.

Rachel breathes,
She breathes the tears of Jesus

Each day she wakes is a shaking leaf
                                child born of her eye
For safekeeping

To be raised by her

Each day awaits her return to motherhood;
The burning search

For silent return

2/23 & 2/28/72 (00785)

As We Are

*For Eric and Bev, Dick and Jean,
with all of our love*

I

We've waited for winter to nearly disintegrate
Before leaving our private occupations
Behind a clapboard youth, which we indulge.

All down the frozen trap lines we set out
Go protests from specters waiting to be freed,
Fearful we'll leave them to fend for themselves,

Just as we've chosen to do in our despondency.
Perhaps these maimed creatures are pains we fear
From people who hurt with words, who never sleep

For their own reluctant mistrust of being praised.
Our life has been a tedium of friendly occasions
Without success, unable to join voices, touch hands.

II

Now we step outside, set a course from boredom
Toward love, hoping, as we go northward from home,
That no more winter will cripple our importunacy

Nor any absurd storms will engage providence.
We bear a gift of nakedness for you, uncompromised,
Our gift, our naked voices, supple, loving voices,

To sing you praises, to touch your latent songs
With naked lyrics and make them reverberate
To the great unending sensuousness of all our lives.

We bring with us the preposterous possibilities
Of hoeing gardens atop cliffs and finding gold
In tadpole eggs. Won't you take us as we are?

2/29/72   (00401)

Peru Saturday Night

Through a cool, off-red sweetness of wine,
My mind sees night's unsounded time zones.
It hears the subtle calibrations love constructs
From its simple designs; it reads the sun's braille,
Which trails behind a million supple shadows,
Translating meridional changes into forehead wrinkles,

And you speak ten o'clocks to my nonliteral eye
All year long . . . special nights with eight of us,
Every night my wife and I are alone, speaking lullabies
To our sleeping, lonely beings . . . eight of us apart:
Carmen and Greg, Bev and Eric, Jean and Richard, Jan and
L.D., sleeping between the emptiness of sky and wine,

Which seas us seeing each other from floating boats
On our own private oceans, blown by memory home
To this time, when laughter converted lips to kisses
And eyes to wide and unconfined prairies we seeded
With our preposterous love for each other's lives.
Perhaps survival will depend on how frequently we sail
    from port.

3/4 & 3/21/72   (00799)

Blessed Four O'Clocks

Corridors empty into empty corridors.
Crowded doors, like whales inhaling plankton,
Devour crowded floors of fatigued people
Fleeing the bastardized insistency
Company beliefs and letterheadologies
Inflict upon feeble, working mercenaries.

Streets retreat into their own blighted shadows
From fright, while clouds swoop silently
Through rising steam from screaming wops
And Chinese cooks. A fat draftsman
Fingers the clitoris of his imagination
To expose the genius of frozen spermatozoa
As health food. Success undresses him in bed.

Drooping night is a load of limp wash.
Skeletons wearing clean clothes
Rattle inside a tumble-dried lifetime,
Spin past each other in a vacuous brotherhood
Of shattered atoms, finally converge
Within the urgent confines of expanding glands.

Day after fading day becomes the loud sound
A driving river makes cascading over a planet,
The loud sound lifting into a vagrant wind,
Moving away from its breasted tongue, going quiet.
All the tall buildings fill up, fall down.
Vultures and buzzards hover above the uncovered stench,
And still bulldozers tease the tired earth.

3/16/72 (00474)

Flight from New York to Lisbon

We rehearse each new stage of our beings
As though performing on perfect cue
The ocean's whisper in a chambered shell.

A terse wish, spoken in the Fisher's ear,
Halos the sky with infinity's scripture,
Skitters down eons, involves us in time.

Currents suspend us upon peaceful stretches.
There's no need to scream out. We are saved
This time. This time, we climb down
From the throne, where tabulations are made
In minutes, fates dictated in breaths,
And death, in somebody's borrowed costume,
Pontificates like a sacred transvestite
To a gay coalition of feeble prelates.
          Thy will be done,
                    Thy words become one
On earth as they are in heavenly days.

We are saved! We are indeed the saved!
A godly apparatus informs our naked eyes,
Graces each life of every day with sweetness
And quietude, as only a saint's uncommon belief
Could ever exact in a bargain with God.

Now, we leave the land, like consecrations
Going forth from a weeping preacher's lips,
Being benedictions of our own adoration,
Creatures keeping each other's secrets,
Custodians of a loneliness neither has lost,
Hands reaching out to an outreaching hand.

4/10/72 (03900)

Vino bianco †

We waded through half of yesterday's rain
Today, sneaking in and out of alleyways
Like children imitating war games, half-crazed
And loving the blue spaces that played with us
Having each other, hovering alone
As we climbed a greening Pincio Hill to see
History flowing into Piazza del Pòpolo, below us.

4/16/72 (02299)

The Spanish Steps, 1725–1972

A faint historical whisper of French donations
To build a solid house of worship for the fat nuns
To climb toward before vespers and descend from
After matins' mysterious end still kisses the air.

Long after the monastery of Trinità dei Monti arose,
They slid and stumbled in sunny rain showers,
Buckled in the mud on their way to Italianate prayer
For the long-dead soul of a rabbinical Son,

Until Specchi and de Sanctis devised a suitable design
For overstuffed icons to use. Then the church
On God's chin ceased functioning. Its twin horns
Tolled truths, while inaccurate bells knelled birth

For beauty's selfish sake, death for a lonely poet.
Wrapped in this stony, white, walked-on blanket,
He sits yet, pondering in celibate stupefaction
That argent locket with the blind man's paradisiacal hair,

Listening to the singing meters he imagines seething
Beneath that skull fired by genius' ignited filaments.
In an instant, Keats sings love ballads to the fat nuns
For God's sake and peace. He reaches forward, toward them,

On the mud-slick hill, slips into a vacuum of sickness,
Rolls slowly through winding tunnels, to warm fields
Flowering perfectly elegant stanzas, blooming pentameters
And bee-increasing couplets and odes. Now, these fields

Are stairs. My feet, like fingers touching harp strings,
Pluck each step, beneath which sleeps a Keatsian verse
I seek to awaken. People spill around me, liquescent
As lake waves. I am in search of a burning ocean-sea.

4/20/72 (03901)

A Sunday Morning in Florence

Big bells from monumentally small towns
Well up in unison,
*

Resound the Angelus to personal prayers
Each dweller shares with Dante.

All go out through crumbling fortress walls
To the old call
That runs from feeling to feet to kneeling
Against cold cement,

Repeating an invisibly flowing namelessness
In lame solemnity
As they climb the shameless base of altars
To reach a sacred place,

Then rise with the wasting wafer's taste.
Their ghosts walk close
Behind, unweaving humility from their silence,
Sleeping in their shadows,

Though day is still the ocean's rising tide
And the low horizon
The highest trough of life's triumphal night.
They are the wind,

These spirits passing passing spirits by,
The persistent wind
Nestling in the flowering hillsides of our ears.
The bells' sweet timbre

Resembles wedding bouquets laid in place
Upon a tabernacle
To consecrate the marriage of our eyes
With their dark faces.

The gates' creaking makes wrinkles shiver
Upon their foreheads,
As they go closed forever on their visions,
Frescoed by the wind,

The wind, and we're left with disappearance.
Only terra cotta,
Sightless, without odor, no fingers to touch us,
Speaks our tongue.

4/23/72 — [1]　(03903)

Dopo il dilùvio: Firenze

There are no signs of a flood here
Except trunk-to-tail tour buses,
Disturbing the convergence of turbulent *vìe*
That cringe in hiding between *palazzi*,
And guidebook mannequins, who stand for days
With their hands and eyes in their baggy pants.

Il Campanile, resembling a choking bouquet
Grown with tedious green-and-red concern,
Wilts under the weight of such recognition,
While Giotto becomes a kind of erudition
Costing an entire education to possess —
Death at those heights requires frightening devotion.

Santa Croce is violated. Michelangelo, Dante,
Galileo are wet to the bone, soaked in sludge.
The priest recites Ave Marias for Cimabue,
Who disappears under a hundred tons of Arno.
Renaissance worms finally surface to meet death.
What a long encore for such dispassionate mankind.

Autos squeeze through alleys meant for thin Franciscans,
And Europabuses, like legions of crossbowmen,
Unleash their motorized horde against the fortress,
Set fire to the stores, destroy the ordered serenity
Of Florence. Once more, barbarians complete the siege.
Deities can be seen laying cobbles throughout the streets.

4/23/72 — [2] (03902)

Marriage in the Basilica di San Marco Evangelista

A plump Franciscan monk,
Trapped in the fantastically simple
Yet complex ecstasy of his white ropes,

Hovers in a zone of holiness,
Whirls, and is gone, like an oracle.
We listen, with our backs to the cold wall.

Perhaps my wife and I would be warmer
Kneeling in the apse, beneath gold mosaics
That have seated Him in the highest throne.

Our marriage is in progress. Two flutes
Chant the sweetest bouquet of rose spires;
Their smooth voices shimmer dim church lights

As we walk toward the altar behind our eyes,
Lip to lip, then drink from the tongues' chalice.
The Minister of Infinite Space embraces us,

Takes us into the quavering censer's arc.
We become sun and moon, chasing each other
Through slowing pendulums, finding ourselves

Involved in a perfectly Renaissance worship.
We two, renegade Catholic, unknown Jew,
Are fused in hymn in God's musical house.

4/24/72 (03904)

End of April: Venice

Even the golden horses that ride the Basilica
Di San Marco, like windsocks for the pigeons,
Freeze their solid tails off, refuse to move
In the ripsaw cross winds that cut the piazza
                    in two.

    I must say that for the price,
    The elements might have provided us
    With less temperamental service.

I think it's this cold, wet weather. Whatever,
My head is just one more of those mosaics
Laid in the wrinkle-worn forehead of the floor
    St. Mark's wears when she's very sad.

4/25/72 (03905)

J and the Beanstalk

Excited by the height,
A willowy man disappears into a tree branch,
Emerges amidst perched birds,
Who form a crown of thorns about his improbable trance.

He becomes a steeple of every cathedral,
With pieced eyes of Tiffany glass and beaded leaves
Looking out over green land
Forever tied to the breezes his breathing achieves.

A three-day-long night,
With rain running under the sun like escaped saints,
Causes the tree-stalk to elongate,
Consigning him to the giant in a blissful constraint.

Now, the golden hen lays base-metal eggs,
And the plant grows top-heavy with clergy and sycophants.
Escaped, a willowy man stands tall at the base,
Poising his ax for a lasting act of salvation.

5/9/72 (03906)

Flight ^Δ

James Gatz, Minnesota

Monday morning in mid-Missouri
Is a stream meandering
                through my eyes,
Lined in sleeping, deeply seeded in breathing.

Its highways are filled with catfish
And bass — little tractor-trailers
Fluting through dim visions
            I use to detect you
                beneath the water,
                    where my dreams
                        lie in unmade rainbows.

            I fly from this life
Toward quiet Cheyennes
*

               and other crisp-air
                              fairy tales
          Americans still write
          To read to each other late at night,
          When the green light at dock's end has faded away.

5/30 & 5/30?/72 (03907)

Looking Through Mutoscopes

I

He screens his thoughts
Discreetly as a movie producer doing retakes
For an audience he'll never see.

Sequences that might be taken from real life
Fly by him onto reel after reel
Of documentary forgetfulness.

Through the Mutoscopes, which huddle
In a cluttered corner of his mind's arcade,
He views stiff-jointed burlesque,

Whose antic nonplot resembles his own
Soundless miscues, his dubious successes,
Digressions into sexual regressiveness.

II

Diaphanous nudes, fading into negligees
Like a full haughtiness of peacock plumes
Disappearing into mere earthbound bird,

Remind him of his seabeach youth — oceans
Green as whale spume rolling over him,
Naked bodies swimming to his head's surface

To breathe in the eucalyptus exuding
Down all the shores of his sweet anatomy —
Washed out to sea by a retreating hurricane.

III

The crank his hand spins is a throttle
*

That forces a steaming iron horse
To course erratically across a prairie fire.

He chokes on the smoke from the stack;
His knees go weak. The trestle between youth
And leaving home collapses. A huge looming,

Like a locomotive at high speed at night,
Spews through an opening, a hole in life,
Burying him beneath seventy tons of scrutiny

By insurance agents and railroad detectives
Who have come to prove his judgment
Defective by all existing standards, dead.

IV

Dead to his early years, he sees the cards revolve.
Like a sacred number, he comes to final rest
Below the pointer, a champion barefisted boxer.

Through cigar-stuffed crowds, he hears the bell,
Jumps up to beat a nameless opponent
In a three-second duel for fame and trophy

Recorded in an oak-chambered hall of deeds
His eyes shuffle past like heavy feet,
Until time runs out on his waferlike penny.

V

Outside, there is an afternoon happening,
With the awful stench of hot dog and popcorn
Sticking to the leaves of nostril trees

Like bug spray. Soon, the Pacific waters
Drain away through night's plumbing.
The Great Highway becomes adhesive tape

Over the feverish slice in which he lives.
A rosary of cars passes where he stumbles,
Balks; one may even stop to offer him passage

Aboard the next Cape of Good Hope clipper
Or a whaler shipping out of Hyde Street Pier.
He may even captain his own packet from Tiburon.

6/5 & 12/5/72 (03908)

Stillborn

Even the basest elements rush toward burial
In this desert by the sea.
All that's washed ashore
Could fit inside a paperweight with my thoughts.

The decayed bridgeworks of incomplete corpses
Connect me with death,
Accuse me of having neglected
No subterfuges in pursuit of our stillborn child.

My footsteps in the sand are ill-formed bird tracks,
Erased by retreating tongues,
I try to follow until
Invisibility envelops the search for her spirit

And waves reach up from their secret coverts
To unglue my handmade parts.
A black cascade of mourners
Passes beneath me on the ocean floor, laughing

As though nothing were dead yet were dying
A clown's water-pistol drowning.
My stare carries me downward,
Toward one little girl with a snow-cone frown

And popcorn cheeks, whose eyes are my wife's
Undeniable birthmarks.
We've seen each other somewhere
In patches beyond sleep, where dreams begin,

Running from orange beasts who would eat us,
Finding no safety in freedom,
Hiding in green longitudes
Stretching across night to abrupt awakenings

I alone survive each day to remind my wife
Of our dual pariahhood.
In this desert by the sea,
We can almost hear the sand being worn away.

6/6/72 (03909)

Impasse

Black, abstract
    scratches
    shadow
    patches on the white
               writing paper.

    They may be words
Gasping for a fresh
            vocabulary
      or just
Late-night
          lashes
Fallen from raw-rubbed eyes.

Blindness knows only the color
    of stuttering.

6/9/72 (03910)

Peace Talks

The wasting bones
Of unknown souls in flight
Float by me through early-morning light
Like chalky residue coming loose
From the hide night uses
To protect herself from complete nudity.

Incorrigible demons, dressed in dreaming,
Are clouds of costumed queens and bishops
Held in awkward hovering above nothing
Save the endless darkness. Lightning is
A crippled Hitler, hurling anathemas
At statues capable of committing suicide,

Or a kamikaze pilot on fire, diving at me
As I drive through three hours of a century
Besieged by the roar of war's gadgetry.
*

I am the storm's nonsensical target; it's
The secret enemy assigned to destroy me.
Maybe if I stop for coffee, we can discuss peace.

6/11 & 6/13/72 (03911)

Out with the New Line

Even within the city's netted web,
No people are spidering to work
At this hazy hour. A talisman,
The colored shape of sun, hangs
Through a cloud-breach
Dripping tasteless gravies over
Another roasting day's consumption.

Tractor-trailers that pass fast
In slender statistical margins
Cover my eyes with backwash,
Force blindness to guide this car
Toward cliffs where buffaloes leap.

Morning's run and evening's plunge
Repeat themselves in daily rituals
Of tribal survival. Soon,
An aging chief will ride away
To a peak's height, lie down,
Die beneath a Burma Shave grave.

6/19/72 (03912)

Ernie Resides with the Angel of Grace △

Somewhere beyond night's blue-black purlieu,
Out there
            beyond the depthless, flattest land,

Beyond spheres people haven't bothered to name
Or chart
            for limitless excesses of corn and soy

Covering spaces where they might choose to go,
Even beyond cosmic audition,
                                              a speeding car

Parts the darkness from the road, then closes it,
Rolling in fateful geometries, a fleet hound
Outracing an imaginary feed-rail rabbit,

Breaking, for a chill flash, all godly silence,
Shattering the black, benign incline of night
With lid-scratching brightness. The latitude
Collapses lunglike, with fabulously minuscule
Tremulations, as the vehicle crashes into truth,

The truth as impact, seismic contraction,
Truth as a too-real, tasteless diffusion
Of anesthetics passing through anatomies.

And all the past, like a wrecking ball swaying
From a crane's flexing boom, wells up
Behind the innocent head to undo its future.
Demolition becomes a brick-by-brick situation
On a structure refusing to make way for newness.

Somewhere out there, beyond gold-green moat-fields
Enclosing this hospital, an old tow truck
Hauls two defeated dragons toward the city dump.

6/20/72 (03914)

Jacksonville Reveries

Imperceptibly new backyard shadows
Sneak through the den window,
Surprise me to a kind of silent fright
Reminiscent of being in school
The first day my dark ages began.

I turn to view afternoon's fading,
Run from its punishing regimen
Into a truth of phasing qualities,
Moving toward my childhood sweetheart,
Who blooms in half-light palpabilities

Like trillions of greening pea-pod seeds.
We run supplely through Lisboan monasteries,
Locating music on remote trajectories
Where timepieces used to undo silence,
Singing songs not yet composed, making

Paintings on the eyes' excited color-cones.
We feel ancient breezes squeezed from tubes,
Hear dry colors, and touch brush strokes
Artists placed there in poignant release
To outreach the mind's sweeping extremity.

A sweetness slides across the shadowed lawn
Behind my seated body. Saints and angels
May be preparing to assault my solitude,
Or perhaps I've only finally recognized
The fleeting give and take of living poetry.

6/25/72   (03915)

Overview of the World Through a Dusty Window of the Tipton Drive-In

Morning's intrusion on sleep
Is an isolated violation of privacy

Followed by eight hours of working
Out the fears of five sow teats
Dreaming placed upon my forehead.

Day's end takes on the unmitigating
Odor of a mud-caked farmyard,

And I find my hollow, solitary
Self out hunting a trough mate
To share the body's tasteless buffet.

6/26/72 — [1?]   (03916)

The Porch

Two people,
Too old for weeping,
Cry through stifled silences
Shared by the meeting of their eyes,

While the spirited automobiles
With supple drivers
Pass in single-circle file
Through space and out of time,

Into a new century,
Without offering a clue
To the dying that only the two
Hear happening very near at hand.

6/26/72 — [2?] (03913)

[Driving through heat lightning,] †

Driving through heat lightning,
Like an auto being towed
Through an automatic car wash

I drove 175 miles,
Being towed automatically
Through a car-wash storm

A half-hour after stopping
To rest and think,
The body still reverberates.
Driving from one thought
To another when the old passion's gone
Ain't all that it's cracked up to be

Playing hide-and-seek at night
With sporadic beams
Becomes a matter of chance,
A ghastly game when the opponent
Shows his face across the line

Keyed-up people reading menus'
Bastardized Deuteronomys
Repeat a culture's secrets
Over a hundred screaming babies

Our people are the walking,
Waking, working standard-bearers
For a fat civilization.
We are fat reactionaries,
Protesting unrest in lean minds,
Who respond to discipline

Cows stand knee-deep
In a field of mown hay,
Eating through the afternoon

7/9/72 (02297)

Stopover

A postlude to our second anniversary

As I celebrate a hiatus in this long drive
Home, the blood of the lamb goes brown
As coffee, sweet as greening pea pods.

The eyes fall back into the dazed head
Like those of a Jumeau fashion doll
Lost last century in an attic and left
On its back. Even my jointed kid-leather feet
Incline toward sleep in this deep day.

Although home is a hundred miles away,
A mandate to return before night arrives
Is strong as compulsive yawning. I pray

That God may guide my sight with songs
The ears can follow and a spirited near-
Ness the mind might assign to His love.
Her waiting kiss is His fired covenant,
Kept ignited by my enlightened designs.

7/10 & 11/13/72 — [1?] (03917)

Yearly Run

On a salmon run, I'm almost caught,
Mistakenly thought to be spawning,
When all that's happening is my escape
From the cluttered city-riverbeds.

While all the worn-out weekend species
Return to funky Sunday evenings,
Completing elongated rehearsal dinners,
I swim wombward, toward strange beds

In an alien stream of nighttime life.
First, I go with the strangling current,
By outlying environs, then against tides,
As complaints well up behind the eyes.

Finally, only briefly scattered whales
Surface in my bright beams,
Spewing black exhaust through blowholes
Before diving into lengthening longitudes.

Still I go, slower now in new territory,
Finning fast, letting up off the gas pedal.
Fluting through slick vacuums, I feel
There are no assurances that an eel or shark

Won't dare interrupt my hypnotized course
Toward tepid Atlantis, where forever occurs,
Or that I'll ever reach Mediterranea
Or even return to mid-Monday-morning's reports.

7/16/72 — [1] (03918)

Overnight en Route

Flying quietly beneath a striated cloud-dome,
Driving in silence, alone as white smoke at night,
No less invisible, he's concretized by the highway,
Pressed neatly as fingerprints into each mile stretch.

The syncopated whisper of tires over tar-filled ruts
Stills a loud complaint the fatigued brain repeats
To quit this futile goose chase: the celebration
Of a new brand-line, dawn of a brand-new season.

A station wagon weighted with black sample cases
Bulging with swatch cards and mimeoed price summaries —
The Emperor of New Threads sits fatly at the wheel,
Heading out to subdue a zealot's thieves' market

With offerings brought from out the lion's jaws.
Or is he a prince, going in quest of old dominions
To control? In fact, he's the road-weary clothes salesman,
Who, for thirty-five years, has done well to survive.

A bleeping "Vacancy" neon identifies his eyeballs
Out of the clotted procession of vehicles on their way
To somewhere specific. He pays dearly for a cheap room,
Finds sleep, knowing his presence won't alter the sign

Nor the space his breathing occupies have made any changes
In the person he'll leave behind when he finally awakens
Any hour next morning and takes to the highway again,
The fabulously happy Jaffe, sturdy merchant of Persia.

7/16/72 — [2] (03919)

By Way of Explanation

A rising egg-hazy sun and I
Were the coffee shop's first customers.
Buttered toast, a side order of silence,
Juice were served as triple sacrifices
To the genius of day's lighting hours.

I wonder what consequence dawning sun
Suffers by undoing all that quietude,
*

Rushing away in cyclonic upheaval.
My world watches carefully to see
That loneliness doesn't find me hiding.

Now, as I pull out onto the highway,
Something overhead bellows my heated soul
Ahead with devastating speed.
I'm drawn westward, in its shadow, toward water,
Past all cities and cows, by all clocks

And old town halls housing fire engines,
Across history's vast grassland poetics,
Through galactic cut-glass passes, to flats
Of tasteless sand, to Brigham's saline water,
Without a semblance of anyone's religion

Urging me to heed an unwitnessed prophecy.
There are no reasons for my erratic actions,
Whose pattern no Hebrew David favors
Nor brass St. Christopher ever dictated.
I am original sin, committed to deification

In the liquid worship of archetypal motion
My mind converts from thought to sleeplessness.
Night passes like an unfamiliar stepparent;
Daylight is Shakespeare reading Greek to me
Beside my bed. I am attired in soft weeping,

Like the smooth, pastel soothing of wisteria.
Not in Utah or time, riding very westerly
To intersect the sun in midday flight . . .
Such a union of spirit, stretching to burn,
To reach an apogee, toward this my life turns.

7/17/72 (03920)

Morning After the Grand Opening, Crystal Café, 6:30 △

Round, rough, potato-like faces,
Glazed by the sun, glare hatefully at me
Through suspicious lenses. Greasy space
Involves me in vacant pasteboard staring;
*

I focus on a cardboard American flag
And a Day-Glo slogan for patriotism.

I can see them conspiring against me,
Not even bothering to show the decency
To remove their yellow advertising hats
Before piercing my hearing with calumnies.

I'm an epitome, something quite rare
In this community, quite undefined indeed.
Perhaps it's the heavily waxed mustache,
Bulbous nose holding gold-rimmed glasses,
The dressy clothing bought at wholesale,
My overly polite appearance and poise.

They believe me here for special dealings
With the IRS or other federal commission,
Come to finger one of their kindred souls.
They're certain to know the whole mystery

Before dusk. I'm the new Jew, come to town
With the Diaspora, bringing remnants, shoes,
And cut-rate slacks they can't refuse
Despite a crude persistence of prejudice.
Something about their too-shrewd ineptitude
For bargaining with truth will make them beg.

7/18 — [1] & 7/21/72 — [3] (03922)

The Poet

He chooses only incongruous occasions
To know himself on a first-name basis,
As though everyone within his radius
Should be certain he's in the flesh,
When actually he is out of his head.
Just now, he stands, naked to the socks
On his feet, in the middle of the street,
Stopping cars with cross-of-gold oratory
And frogs he throws into their open windows,

Shouting, "I am me! For this I have come!"
This evening, he'll meet with the girls
Retreating in bare feet from nunneries
*

And trapezoids to coffeehouses lining
Their bloodstreams. He'll recite a few
New lines commemorating freedom and sin,
Then finish in a synthesis all the world
Has awaited, achieving inexorable silence
As his audience rushes to tear him apart.

7/18 — [2] & 11/13/72 — [2?] (03921)

The Outlet Store

Now that all the stitching is com-
Plete and the items properly fitted
Into bins and labeled table locations,
We wait conspicuously around, anti-
Cipating a consumer stampede
To buckle the floor's creaking supports,

   And we wait
For heat accumulating at the ceiling
To abate. Yet the first waves
Of people never leave their cave dwell-
Ings, and our hands remain locked
In mildewed pockets. Something strange
Is besieging our brand-new enterprise,

   And we stand by, waiting
To apprehend a sign from the deity.
Maybe He'll create a palpable reason
To stimulate the need for cheap pants,
Such as tricot feed bags for elephants
Or double-knit cup cloths for priests.

7/19/72 (03923)

Intimations ᐃ

Running parallel to this false-
Fronted Main Street is track
For the nearly defunct Mo-Pac.
*

Only a ghostly whistle rushes past
Anymore for its erratic passing.

The nontimely myopics of change
Rearrange debris floating in Limbo,
Mo., a home away from nowhere,
Unfortunately. The old pants factory
Teaches the limited vocabulary
Seniority prescribes for penury.
It provides the invincible stimulus
For decay by subordinating time
To a motion analysis of menial tasks —
Ultimate paralysis for active minds.

Just once, I'd like to ride away
Inside that ghostly whistle as it shrills
Through town and leave the present behind.
The sheer idea of arriving — anywhere —
Survives the knell of the 4:30 bell.

7/20/72 — [1?] (03925)

The Olympics

The miler is tiring; the miler's dying
From heat exhaustion and body fatigue.
His brains leak vital juices; they spew
Where he lost them in the third turn
Of the fast first quarter he ran last night
In the obstacled miasma dreaming set up
To be cleared before the actual track meet.

The high hurdles are set way too high,
Not wide enough apart. Pull the pins;
Let the pack pass at an advantage
Before hitting the water jump. He's last,
Weaving space into deadening somnambulisms,
Pleasing a disbelieving crowd's clouded eyes,
With his bowels flying out behind from fright.

They've pilgrimaged to this sacred place
To bear witness to a psyche's wasting away
*

In public disgrace. A new religious order
Is being forged out of forced revelation.
Pain and weakness, as jealous teammates,
Leave the stadium gates with three gold medals,
While the miler picks cinders from bloody knees.

7/20/72 — [2?] (03924)

Prayer ^Δ

For the children of Camp Nebagamon

Three seasons have passed beneath my feet,
Like the separate choruses of an elegy
Composed for me. Something, a leitmotif
Recurring in each scheme, every daydream,
Has touched a chord with sweet sympathies,

And I lean forward with all my toned weight
Pressed against the escape hatch. The latch
Gives easily. I course freely through night,
Toward pine-whiny Wisconsin, with my soul,
Self, and whole head out of control totally

And ready to climb back out of time's boat,
Onto your floating island. Take me in again
To begin again a slow growth toward sunlight.
Make me an ornament in your gorgeous forest,
Suspended among unending memories and seeds

Recently planted. Cradle me in this retreat
Conceived by boys echoing friendly greetings
And men spending their adulthoods teaching
Beliefs from the Kingdom of God's Great Good.
Shake golden fruit from every wishing tree,

That nobody should ever discover me buried
Beneath my fantasies. Break fast, eat with me,
For we are all children the past has wrought
Upon this dawning day. We share its heritage.
Together, let us bless each other's blessedness.

7/20 — [3?] & 7/24/72 (00014)

Eating Place ^Δ

Conversation in this stifling café
Sounds more like the sickly moanings
Of war victims than informalities
Between easy townspeople and farmers.

Pronouncements about hogs and cows
Preempt the seven o'clock news, squeaking through
A cathedral radio. Profundities surrounding
The nature of rainfall, their state of grace
In raising a corn crop this season
Emanate from this radical School of Athens,
Frescoed on the cloister of my pariah eyes.

The cradle of Midwestern civilization
Resides here, between State Highway AA
And the Lake of the Ozarks, fifty miles away.
Nearby, Ozymandias, in bib overalls, awakens.

7/21/72 — [1] (00432)

4:10 Freight to K.C. ^Δ

At first, there's just the distance,
Space laced with black latticework,
Tracks laid before the Butterfield Stage,
Rail tacked to cracked wooden sleepers
Hooked to man-made gravel beds settling
Forever into hard-clay earth at Tipton,

Just distance, then faint tribal scrapings,
Steel wheels scratching out metallic tunes
As if the train were player-piano paper
Coursing over windblown reed-trackings,
Almost visible behind the quick whistle,
Coming fast now, like a crash,

Spastic in its trembling gigantism,
Passing alongside a plot my feet occupy,
Then stride for stride with my eye's eyes,
Inside the brief introspection fear breeds
*

When the final line of certainty disappears
And the whole body plunges into total sound.

The diesel freight is a spring I wound
Too tightly. With an urgent lurch, it balks,
Roars by me, away, out of town, sight, sound,
Spraying smell and grit, like dry nosegays,
Against the heated day. Nothing is left now
Except grasshoppers daring to fly boot-high
And a signal-crossing ringing in my ears.

7/21/72 — [2] (03927)

Taking Stock

Saturday morning is the highest peak
In this week's chain of daytime hills
And sinkholes. I've reached the summit.
Looking in one direction, behind me,
I can only remember tomorrow today.

7/22/72 — [1] (03928)

The Returning

Somewhere on this long trip home,
I should lose my week's companion,
The shade that has stayed so close
Through loneliness I've known. My wife
Waits four hours away in space, praying
For my safe passage. I hear her saying,
"Please . . . please . . ." The rest is glazed
In the unfading ripple effect her lips,
Touching my ears, set forever in motion.
I see small white birds flying toward me,
Turning, offering to guide me in peace.
As I arrive, these creatures float into her eyes.
I step out of myself, into her greeting.

7/22/72 — [2] (03929)

Epitaph ^Δ

I belong to the cult of pressurized thoughts
And sedentary deeds. In my seat, I dream
Seas into being, to be navigated and mapped
For posterity. People clustered beneath me
In minicities know my passing for sheet-metal
Glints shadowed against their sunshined eyes,

Daytime flights from heaven to ethereal regions of
    Conformity,
Made by a deity in bright tie and loud
Even in a crowded thieves' market —
Impresario of the bargain basement, that's me!
Hebrew Louie, purveyor of shoes new and used!
Now, what can I do for you, sir, Mr. Death?

7/28/72 — [1] (03931)

Rosehill Cemetery from the Air ^Δ

Downwind leg, low to the sooty earth.
Below this goblin, a funeral procession
Of rush-hour traffic, bound for midtown
Interment, goes in soundless slow motion,
Mesmerized by the deathly magician.

The eyes trip from gray haze to green
Momentarily. A brilliant maze of gardening
And bushy trees shimmers kaleidoscopically.
Strange how this incongruous preservation
Is the lifetime achievement of a city's dead.

7/28/72 — [2] (02177)

Thirty Miles Southeast of Duluth ^Δ

Cold, wet weather, heavy as a dull crayon,
Colors children's eyes, outlined in green
*

And chipmunk auburn, with spongy registers
Of punk and fungus. Decay, as her mate,
Undoes what nature replaces. Now, we set forth
To explore their friendless interchanges,
Through this pine-silenced rain, straining
To approach the hushed, hidden substance
With which life touches us in dreaming,
To taste the delicious, sweet divinity
Only privileged lips kiss in intimations
Eternity offers us every other eternity.

7/29–30/72 (00013)

Thirty Miles Southeast of Duluth II △

Now, we've passed through gray silences,
Into brightness. The lake swells proudly
As a sated priest leaving a godly feast;
It undulates to the shore like a hundred
Softly floating nuns coming whitely, as one,
Toward wormwood church doors. We stand
Ankle-deep, freezing to the kneecaps,
Preparing ourselves for immersion in time.
Awaiting the plunge beneath taut surfaces,
Where breathing ends and being outlasting
History begins, we shake for a lifetime,
Pained by the expectation ecstasy holds forth.

7/31/72 (03934)

Sold Out

Leaving becomes the least unpredictable act
In our routine performance. Forgotten lines
On faces in nameless memories, missed cues
Whispered by the few good friends who remain
Confuse this husband-and-wife team. We've played
All key towns and cities beyond our peripheries,
*

Hoping to introduce new drama to ancient stages,
Been greeted by empty theaters and circus halls
Filled with three-ring comedians and freaks.
No one even wanted to see me saw my love in two.
"Sold Out" stickers pasted over old show posters
Proclaim the shameful status we've finally achieved.

8/1/72 — [1] (03936)

Jan's Song

Like cities beneath these clouds,
Which can't be seen by people
From other galaxies, we're invisible
To those below this floating machine.

Caught tenuously between time zones,
Inside identities unknown to each other,
We're free to choose our dislocations.
I breathe you smiling in Sutro Park,

Churched within a perfect spire
Of wedding vows forever drawn
Above Pacific winds. We touch lips.
These curly clouds must be kissing us.

8/1/72 — [2] (03935)

Lament

Until right now, I've not had time
To introduce me to myself. Faces
Forget me frequently, escape memory's
Magazine of black-and-white slides;
Thus the reason for my social uneasiness.
This evening, I almost failed to recognize
Shades imitating my awkward walk, my gaze
Focusing on quarter-time syncopations,
My nervous hands holding coffee cups,
*

And talk falling from my twisted lips
Like bird feet scratching hieroglyphics
In sand. I stand before this mirror glass,
Trying on different gestures in private,
Dissatisfied by the profound silence
That roars up from my public image
Hiding out there beyond me, everywhere.
A numbing pain of knowing I'll never
Be invited to explain my idiosyncrasies
To ungracious late-night TV audiences
Or play lead frenzy in a rock operetta
Annihilates the presumptuous shades
That stayed with me throughout the night.

I awaken from a gauzy nonsleep in time
To see a trim, taut body stalking away,
Leaving behind it, for me to confront,
The stunted form that, in recent years,
Has adopted me as its roommate, sharing
A cell without number or bars. I see, now,
In the immediacy of its fat reflection,
A man, or statue, perhaps the sad shadow
Of an unachieved promise, made to me
By my self in childhood, to reach toward
A destiny of self-belief and faith in love.
It's almost too late for new introductions.

8/2/72   (00346)

[The dogs aren't barking.] †

The dogs aren't barking.
Silence surprises me, lying here
By myself. Bedsheets and used towels
Depict the ravages of nocturnal warfare
Conducted inside this air-conditioned box

8/3/72 — [1]   (00745)

Passing

Lionel train sets, like those I owned,
Race through this miniature layout
At unscheduled intervals. No faces pass
Anymore through the clanking crossing gates.
Freights the length of sideways skyscrapers
Scratch at rusty tracks with weighty scrap
And new automobiles, repeating a voyage
To and from the car plant, ad infinitum.

As children, we were taught to operate
The transformer and switches. I dreamed
A million electric miles of side trips
From a thousand feet of energized track.
Now, even those desires to ride the rails
Fail to materialize in our brief adulthood.
I don't believe my child should ever be told
To wait on anything until he's grown old.

8/3/72 — [2] (03938)

Hecht's Café $^\Delta$

Rain falls erratically as pinballs,
Jumping from one cushioned minute
To another, this summer afternoon.

Main Street shops are tropical fish
Hiding under seaweed, in silence.
The air smells of a live box

Filled with bait. Drains overflow;
Gutters purge dirt from tarred streets;
Small, crawling bugs line sidewalks,

Legs up, as though in slow protest
Of foul conditions. A freight train,
Like a bullet shuttle without design,

Slides through the opaque networks
Woven across the hours August spins,
Then disappears with diminished whines.

I peer out, through rippled windows,
To distinguish the slightest familiarity
In a dismal encampment. This small town

Abounds in one-way alleys, down which
The mind rushes, trying to find escape.
The roads are slick; futility skids

At every corner. Even street signs
Register "Dead End." Just when I think
This maze will spill me headfirst

Into a birth of peaceful landscapes,
My feet breach a sore orifice. Heat
Scorches the dying body inside of me.

8/3 — [3] & 11/3/72   (03937)

[A real, live cattle drive]

Watching The Virginian,
10:30 p.m.

A real, live cattle drive
Stampedes the recessed valleys
Memory has almost washed away.

Only a few late-night strays
Race across today's staged plains,
Chasing me back into the 1890s:

Cheyenne, false-fronted Main Street,
USA, sod huts, longhorn steers
Clearing a mile-wide swath across the west,

Civil War cannon standing apart
In the shaded square, lighting the day
Like a chandelier revealing a dusty past.

Just today, a range war took place
In Munich. All the world witnessed
The useless feud between two families.

8/5/72   (00748)

Calling Card ^Δ

The erratic hands on my wrist watch
Register time in miles and roadside signs.
Afternoon's late assailants chase me down
With arresting gestures I recognize.

There I am in the rearview mirror,
Overtaking my image with maddening speed
As my lengthening shadow, like fiction
Outdistancing history, eludes the truth

My being constitutes. I'm only a ragman,
With Cadillac and double-knit tongue,
Heading out alone to find Sutro's lode
In dead-end shafts of Midwest heads

And atop hills wet with small-town regret
For the slightest threat to set progressions.
Frontier shopkeepers still fear the Jew
Who deals swatch cards in handsewn suits.

8/20–21/72 — [1] on 8/20 (03939)

Ramada Sunday Night ^{† Δ}

Without wife, the mighty Beelzebub
Reels, collapses on clean sheets
Leased by the night. By the month, he dies
A private demise inside these cheap rooms,
Outside the mainstream of festive life
They lead in the city. So very wide,
This territory to which he nominally holds claim
In the name of the mind's untamed ambition.

8/20/72 — [2] (02296)

Sunday . . . Monday

Whatever creature be the soul's keeper,
It floats in liquid sleep toward me.
*

Like a white form behind a screen
Seen by a blind man in a half-dream,
It assaults the mind's demonologies,
Calls up assignations from active pasts
That relate us to people we've neither loved
Nor controlled, hated, in truth, if truth
Be followed through to its futurity.

Battling God's contraptions
Resembles a perfectly intact apparatus's
Pumping of collapsed lungs. Pursuing the task
Of subduing snakes that constrict consciousness
Is life's only rewarding source of endurance,
A minimal satisfaction at best, yet the best
Alternative to extinction by enemies in hiding.
A sharp pain awakens me. I reach for my wife
To heat the silence insulating us from night.

Daylight erases all the scribbled writing
I've deciphered. Naive to consequences our wake
Disturbs as we push ahead together, we arise
To the haphazard clatter survival requires.
Lonely as land, ocean, and sky supporting life
For human beings universally lost in eternity,
We go in search of the soul's keeper slowly,
Hoping to find its peaceful secret coverts
And be released into each other's sweet custody.

8/27–28/72 — [1] on 8/28 (03940)

Reverie $^\Delta$

Schools reopening call back all lost souls,
Vagrants, little waifs and vagabonds
Who ran ragged through summer heat,
To retreat down green, echoing corridors
Bordered everywhere by squeaking lockers
And imperious wall clocks parenthesizing hours,
Confining their bodies to hard maple seats.

June and August become mere old friends
Too soon forgotten as new ones are made
*

From classroom incarceration.
Face replaces face in changeless procession,
Until each day accumulates a legacy in space.
Waifs emerge as lawyers, grocery clerks;
The vagabond becomes town drunk, friendly cop.

Something is lost with each exchange
As the pace quickens. The graceful, wasted days
Pass away. Nothing remains beyond the paintings
To remind us of berry picking, kids at play
In games of snap-the-whip and kick-the-can.
My child has never even slept one night
In the musty Pullman of America's last dawn.

8/28/72 — [2] (00436)

Crystal Café Clock △

An all-seeing advertising clock,
Rimmed in blue neon tubing,
Flips a hundred painted cards
Every hour. I watch fifty pass
Like knighted souls going into battle,
Reading their Day-Glo slogans.

Nothing here breaks expectation.
The names reappear each fifteen minutes
With unfamiliar sameness: car parts,
Furniture, trucks, the one barbershop,
Sears, ready-mix, liquid gas — pre-
Packaged America at factory prices.

At a nearby table, nine apostles,
Whose titles ride the lighted hours
Above the cluttered front counter,
Preside over six o'clock in togas,
Contriving credos and promotions
To further their gospel of greed.

I'm a stranger to this conclave, Judas
The Jew, unseen in my corner booth,
Come with plans for a vast shopping mall.
*

Although the plug is in its socket,
The clock's hands have stopped. Probably
No one will notice it's broken, this month.

8/29 & 11/4/72 (03941)

Confessions of a Traveling Salesman ^Δ

Dogs and fleeting people press their identities
Against my eyelids and ears. Vague cacophonies,
Like caged slaves, pound at my iron bars,
Making raucous nightmares inside a pleasant day.

Frequent leave-taking is the fitful tedium
Both the ambitious and needy share. Over-
Night tent pitching on floating motel grounds
Lacks the profound insanity of Gullivered pursuits.

I am as tactically rational as any madman
Accused of producing too many perfect children.
The only abnormality in my uncracked slate
Is a slight misspelling of my Christian name.

I am my purpose for being here; the reason
For this business is me. Greediness thrives
Like termites in the woodwork my heated brain
Keeps moist with fears of being ignited.

Something in my makeup cries out for fame,
Yet were anonymity breached and celebrities
Recognized me as elite within their company,
Would I not revert to the family-tree roots

To assuage the treasonous misgivings wealth
Newly achieved portends? Small men, contrite,
Shuttle through generations threaded with meekness.
I am of quiet ragmen, decent shopkeeping people.

No one ever suggested, nor was the word written,
That I should either be destined or doomed
To emerge from the relevant purity of dirty socks
And rented rooms, into the temple of fat-ass Solomon.

9/26/72 (03942)

Stopover $^\triangle$

Before, when I'd come in for coffee
At 6 a.m., the whole movie crew,
Here to do *Tom Sawyer* in a river-
Town nearby, gave a gay illusion
That they'd found a new utopia
Within the boundaries of this motel.

That was when I had to be here
Every week to set my new business
In motion: nostrums relabeled, soaps,
Patent medicines brightly encapsulated,
Bitters, elixirs, and tonics for "Bronchitis
Of the Little Toe & Related Maladies."

Now, when I light out for the territory
To make a monthly installation check,
I stay overnight, take coffee in silence
Before going on to my final destination.
No 6 a.m. steamboat whistles awaken me
From the dreamless lethargy of daily routine.

9/27/72   (03943)

The Last Breakfast

Vague satellites and hazy constellations
I've passed by, unnamed in space,
Have all gathered in the Crystal Café.

Their unique fusion of plastic faces,
Drawn out like rubber bands to breaking,
Querulous, garrulous, gregarious

As a nation of Beelzebubs at peace,
Adjudges my silence, accuses my loneliness
With its aloofness and suspicious gazes.

My presence here threatens no one now
Except me. Perhaps it's time to return
To the core's source for transmigration,

Before I'm reborn within this courtyard,
Where Leonardo's fresco of me still dries.
Dying has always seemed such needless trial.

9/29/72 — [1] (03945)

[This wayward conveyance guides me]

*Lines briefly composed in transit,
remembering Shelley's "Ode to the
West Wind"*

This wayward conveyance guides me
Over country roads. Splattered life
Patterns the windshield, registers speed
In minute deaths. I praise life
That stays by my side, beside me
In the driver's seat, while I spectate.

Outside this dial-controlled inside,
Winter narrows daylight's wide screen
Into a closed circuitry of cold components.
Bleached trees, corn torn from stalks,
Sows, cows, rusted plowing shears,
Frescoed in damp abandon against the wind,

Divide my frightened eyes from future horizons
And a shimmering now. Trapped by time,
I scan the remaining hours of my being
To see if I'll yet breathe another spring
Or whether these autumnal prophecies
Have come to retrieve me from my daydreamings.

9/29 — [2] & 10/14/72 (03944)

Interior Monologues

Husband

After driving one half-hour,
We finally penetrate the cloak
*

Of smoke and decomposing lives
The city wears loosely as leaves
Upon its grimacing Tree of Evil.

Leaving behind bequeathments
Becomes easier each time
My wife and I decide to suspend
Normal breathing for freedom
Stretched between now and dying.

Wife *

Morning with my husband
is a rare beginning.
Creation climaxes at 10 a.m.
in deep-chocolate coffee.
Intense heat spills over
the sides of our porcelain bodies.
We hold hands,
smiling until evening closes its eyes.

["Wife" portion written by Jan Brodsky]

10/5/72   (03946)

Truckers △

Six-thirties in Tipton are dark
As the space inside a tight fist.

Two black phantoms climb down
From the cabs of their tractor-trailers,

Run toward the café, into light.
Inside, all the white men disappear

Behind a screen of opaque silence.
Two Negro drivers, seated at a booth,

Populate the filled room's emptiness,
Drink from fate's steaming thermos,

Then leave, like two Moseses retreating
Between impatient waters of the Red Sea.

10/12/72   (03947)

The Auction: Setup

The evacuees from a fated Ozark museum
Came in two tractor-trailers and a small truck.
The only thing broken en route from foothill,
Through city, to auction barn was a cast-iron stove.

Now that these exiles have suffered a transience
Even the new environment's silence can't reverse,
They prepare to sail on seas the diaspora created
With heathen debris, to become objects of piracy.

Fifteen years has been a century-deep eventide
For heirloom antiques, notions, and dusty oddities
To be on permanent display. Soon, motion will
Overcome them, dislocate affinities and continuity

Man so fastidiously assigned them in his passion
For order. Collections will go out fast as atoms
From a cyclotron, until the hour comes full tilt
To that singular, invincible image of house women,

In bustles and calicoes, heaving frayed quilts,
Broken wicker rockers, and boxes of outgrown toys
For the junkman to disseminate from his wagon —
History doing housecleaning each quarter century.

10/21/72 & 1/9/73 — [3?] (03948)

The Auction †

October ends its restlessness
  By fighting against indefensible armies
    Of deathly legions. Crisp, brittle leaves
      Remind me of sick flies in tailspins,
        Out of their persistent minds. Blindness
          Touches the moon's darkest recesses,
            Reaching my eyes

10/23/72 (00329)

The Auction: Leaving the Village of St. Francois

The village is still, inside a shrill, glistening freeze.
Early morning breathes shafts of blinding sun
Against empty log cabins. Abandonment preempts
Incomplete dreams that nursed fantasy's settlement.
I watch the slow rotting; it hears me retreating uneasily.

The circle from land untouched by man to crude museum
And back to knotted overgrowth closes like fog
Blowing in on an ocean resort. A startled garter snake
Escapes my boot. Two winters are beginning today;
Only one will ever change the toad back into a prince.

10/26/72   (00496)

The Auction: First Day

A coalescence of diverse personalities occurs.
Sensibilities overrun like haywire motors.
Human communication fills this auction room
Like accidental phenomena. They've come from
Ottumwa and Alton's heights to sift through
Another's gold, in search of sow's-ear shillings.
From upstate New York, Ohio, arriving late,
They take elaborate notes, quote bid figures
To an aloof group of attendant gods. The stuff
Is ready for anatomical dissection. Insurrection
Of all integral parts has begun, and the cry
Goes out over raucous loudspeakers. Their
Three-day war against the monarchy is spiritual.
It starts with two preachers quarreling aloud
Over a wooden icebox. Tybalt bites his thumb
At timid Mercutio. They fight for high bid.
The rest is legend in this reign of terror.

10/27/72   (00499)

The Auction: Second Day

Few people of supreme consequence
Attended our ceremonial dissolution.
Only the cap-and-ball arsenal
And a few percussion flintlock rifles
Piqued excitement. All the dusty rest
Was an uninspired group from a saloon,
Old hotel, and twice-removed general store.

Fifteen years of festering had overgrown
The pieces like bacteria and mold
Over mushrooms in cold cellars. No experts
Had ever been consulted to check ills
The museum had caught over the seasons.
No wonder those who had come from so far
Were disheartened. Six grievous hours
Progressed like a rife terminal disease.

Thank God, the god who commanded one man
To assemble from out the dark night
This cosmos, fitted between a sunny dawn
And the black backwaters of his life,
Was not presiding behind the rubber-hose
Gavel. He would surely have been grieved
By this man's scandalous debacle of creation.

10/28/72 (00506)

The Auction: Last Day

Two hundred mechanical gnats rattle my ears
With cheerless inspiration. Incessant whispers
Spill over inside my bland imagination,
Fill this afternoon with anguish the womb
Can't turn to music. For three days now,
I've fitted this room about my rigid brain,
Concerned about wearing my presence in public.
The garment shows strain; its skipped stitches
Rip back along critical seams, and I leave,
*

Rush outside, into the cold, in short sleeves.
I see souls carrying off pieces of the body,
Ants returning to their colonies with debris,
While inside, excited flies are still swarming
Warm carrion. Soon, I'll take the carcass home.

10/29/72 & 1/10?/73 (00532)

Rainy Drive

There was no escaping the sleep-demons,
Who guarded every tollbooth along the way.
The highway was wet with streaked rain, slick
As fish scales. Fatigue lay beneath the surface
Like a gigantic lamprey waiting for slow prey
Or the back of a black manta ray to straddle.

I came this way, through day's opaque veil,
Suffocating within decompression chambers
Set up for the mind's survival of the bends.
My rescue was a complete failure. The demons
Drew me down through their glittering whirlpool
Of swirling yawns, into death's prolonged dawn.

11/6/72 — [1] (03949)

The Uncelebrated Ceremony of
Pants-Factory Fatso

Nine communities within a twenty-five-mile radius
Shimmer against night's lighted horizon.
Mine is the only one without a drive-up diner
In which to pass a quiet suppertime by myself.

I never seem to find quite the right time
Or place to furnish my spacious thoughts
With trappings from the mind's Chambord.
The estate of my being is ready for auctioning.

Nothing is ever left in such unfinished condition
That leaving for good doesn't make it complete.
The final irrefutability death breathes
Dissolves our dreams, sweetens the grieving tongues

Of those we leave to repeat the metaphors' chorus.
In the stark, loud, dark cloud enshrouding this room,
No eyes but mine witness such intense silence,
Nor other ears hear the years passing like comets

In distant spacelessness. I alone have come to know
The meaning of phantasmagoria. A noiseless voice
Inside an echoing semaphore roars at me to be cautious.
Instead, I leap beneath a train returning from Treblinka.

11/6/72 — [2] (03950)

At Thirty-One

Snow's first whisper echoes the quick westerly wind
Blowing through my eyes. A drive by pioneers
Going north along Denver's Divide, toward Wyoming,
A hundred years ago, thunders inside swollen ears.

I listen for the wind to issue its new conditions,
As it must have done for those stitching crazy quilts
Of unrelated states from Maine to San Francisco.
Decisions depend on the senses' length of hesitation.

The perceiving mind and the heart that knows grieving
Never could outguess its direction, intention, or color.
Even the hawk hangs precariously against the altitudes
When late-October wetness turns November to flakes.

Now, it is my season to decide whether the slow creeks
And streams of my dreaming mind will be locked in ice
Or if there is yet time for exploring new Columbias
Flowing into newer Oregons beyond closed frontiers.

11/7/72 — [1] (03952)

Intimations of Breughel

Doves take flight, take frightened cover
Inside a gray landscape
Like figures skating through a Flemish painting.
I hide inside my fur coat's lining,
Running feverishly to keep chapped hands warm,
Looking at the cracked canvas from without,
Searching deeply for people reaching out
From winter's immobility to touch a frozen soul.
The frame containing my loneliness collapses.
I enter the ancient oils a centimeter at a time,
Defining a world at peace with its own creation.

11/7/72 — [2] (03951)

The First Snow

Lovely Jan and her animals

Predicted last evening by mercurial smiles
On TV broadcasts repeated each hour,
The drastic change in weather seemed less
Spectacular — in fact, a bit disappointing —
When we awoke and peered through cold glass
As witnesses to the first coming of the snow.

Dreaming had somehow created giant machines
In the sky to silently shred ivory tusks
And alabaster crystals shipped from distances
Beyond science. The mixture would be perfect
For spackling cracks in the earth's surface,
Making graceful stasis for all things living.

The actual stuff, before touching the ground,
Had sifted through trees, taking with it
The remaining decayed leaves for decoration.
What lay spread over the whole front lawn
Resembled dough rolled out on waxed paper,
Dotted with raisins ready to run when baked.

After spectating half an hour in bathrobes,
We set our three shelties out in their pen.
*

They seemed to play forever, feet prancing
Through dry powder, chests high like prows,
Alive, as if driving sheep. Then we recalled
Our coming upon something for the first time.

11/19/72 — [1] (03953)

Sunday Dressed in Deathly Bunting

Yellow mums we planted just before the freeze
Are bowed over with the snow's white weight.
Even the boxwoods seem leafy with new irony.

All the trees are ballerinas, naked females
Flailing their dainty arms in a fierce dance.

Sitting warm inside, I've assigned to myself
The singular goal of rescuing from cold seas
A Sunday paper floating in limbo on the lawn,

To decide if dying is still our only surprise
And life the sum of seasons leaving and arrived.

11/19/72 — [2] (03954)

Thanksgiving Misgivings

The checkout girl completes her ritual
Of depressed keys and crumpled receipts.
She administers sacraments to tired buyers
Come for last-minute rites and other items.

You would think from the crowd's enormity
That an apocalypse, not Thanksgiving eve,
Were crouching to leap upon sensibilities
Or that people were pressing toward Heaven

Instead of fighting express lines to leave.
The streets they travel are Venetian canals
Lighted by mercury vapors. In a slow rain,
No one remembers sailors who found this coast

Or the names of those who came here to escape
Shameless persecution for religious beliefs.
Only children are taught meaningful reasons
For our being here. Even the ghosts forget.

11/22–24/72 — [2?] on 11/23 (00435)

Thanksgiving Day Parade

A prayer read at the Hofmann table

Talking wastebaskets informing McDonald's ads,
Giant snails and dragons ten-feet green,
Reticulated muslin worms, clowns skating —
These are Macy's images the eyes twirl
In time with glittering baton girls.

Morning is a friendly place inside the home
For those in love. Brass bands bob like floats
On a turn-of-the-century pond; they weave
Through a cold New York November like herds
Of buffalo sprung loose for history's pageant.

Three families have emerged from their privacy
To arrive for this celebration. Rites are said
With smiles; kisses bless this congregation.
On seas beyond the lawn, three small caravels,
Taut against a ginger wind, head toward us,

Ready to chart our convergence. We lived then,
Pilgrims bending endlessly ahead toward now,
Engaging God, praying for man's survival
In a new land. Today, we've returned to beg
Surcease from the plenty threatening peace.

11/23/72 — [1?] (03955)

Checked Before Boarding

Creatures with such distinct physiognomies
Pass like stereo views
*

Spinning on an arcade Mutoscope reel.
They race to completion, move through archways
Connected to metal detectors, to be searched.
Luggage disemboweled, officials quickly unplug
Suspiciousness from "potential threats,"
Assured by one blue bulb. Free to step aboard,

All fliers are aware of their shared fear,
Apparently very dissatisfied
With routine procedures taken by authorities.
They're uneasy about spending the next few hours
So cohesively, certain the worst will occur
From such bodily coercion and proxying of trust.
Somewhere, there must be another enemy to subvert
Besides ourselves, another species to mastermind.

11/30/72 (03957)

[Having just come from two weeks of snow and rain,] †

Having just come from two weeks of snow and rain,
We find a polar cold too frightful an animal to confront
In Florida. We saved

12/1/72 (03619)

Privacy on a Crowded Beach

> *For lovely Jan,*
> *12/3/72,*
> *Pompano*
> *Beach,*
> *Fla.*

You
And me,
The ocean's shells,
A sea gull, weed and kelp,
The feet being driven easily
*

Into sand by receding waters,
A regatta of white canvas, far out,
Racing against a black backdrop of clouds . . .
We stand at the edge, hands locked,
Prepared to kiss in plain view
Of these familiarities. Only
Bathers see the momentary
Incongruity we make,
Me and
You.

12/3/72 (03958)

An Occasion for Flowers

Where daylight tips pink-flowering night
At petals' edge, my eyes paint in the sack
Of wasting red intestines some soul left
In haste beside the highway. It's a canine

This time, arrived on its ordained date,
Not just another crazed human corpse
Inclined to genocide or stymied magistrate
Climbing cold rifling toward a loaded shell.

Day's bouquet of baby's-breath and heather
Has no face, no special occasion, no grave
Freshly spaded to embrace its gracefulness.
Once dry, it might remind me I was alive

Or that I'm dying and may be rearranged.

12/27/72 — [1] (03956)

Home for the Holidays

The brightest sun . . .
                            Christmas done in haste,
Like soldiers making love
                            on overnight leave
In Haiphong.

Clean streets . . .
                    New Year's Eve approaching
Like the beginning of war's
                              roaring tin horns
In Southeast Asia.

Mobile cities . . .
                    Another year clears puberty,
Like crawling man standing,
                              shooting, falling
In on himself.

12/27/72 — [2] & 1/9/73 — [1–2?]   (03959)

Heading Home

For fifty miles, I drove through this decade undiscovered
By others doing something similar or disparate simul-
Taneously. Even the sun's mechanism hung open on START,
Overfilling the powdery red horizon until it spilled over,
Exploding every sleeping creature out of night-hiding.

My eyes clouded with protective blindness as I approached
The first great arena of routine city traffic patterns
Enacted by people driving feverishly to get to desks
And lathes and e-lec-tronic machines. I passed through,
Miraculously, genuflecting to the freedom sustaining me

Against seditions and petty larcenies the cynical mind,
Confined to a purely suburban overview of existence,
Maintains in times of questioning individual purposive-
Ness. Then I merged into a sparse flow of showy cars
Being drawn along an invisible aqueduct like race boats

Tracking at speeds unregulated, cracking sound waves open,
Going from one lunar junction to another, past towns
Without shopping centers, streets, TV antennas, police,
Or telephone poles harpooning the bleeding heartlands,
And headed home to take up residence in a very elite grave.

12/28/72 & 1/9/73 — [1–2?]   (03960)

[The leap from poetry to TV] †

The leap from poetry to TV
Is that of
The sublime to the mindless.
If that indictment
Seems unusually cruel,
Then consider the Uroboros,
Who consumed himself
For lack of anything better to do

1972? (00747)

January 2, 1973

None of us saw it happen; we never even
Heard the jets slipping through the sky,
Toward corridors filled with enemies
No one had satisfactorily deciphered.
And nobody learned when, or if, it ended.

All we knew was that what was withheld
Withheld the truth. Condoning was easy
Inside a realm of silent invisibility,
Created by the Holy Dome of All-Knowing.
We were a people gone greedy as Nero.

Feedback became confused with reasons
We'd agreed upon to maintain sanity.
No new troops went overseas, yet bodies
Draped in new flags kept returning home.
We had been to the ovens and survived.

None of us saw it happen; we never even
Smelled their stench or watched sampans
Flee over phosphorescent lakes. Maybe
The entire annihilation was just a bluff
We made in a decade of preposterous peace.

1/2/73 (03800)

Buonarroti

A protracted ache at the head's base
Relays pain to the mind's brain waves.

Once again, the ragged cave dweller,
Caged inside him from dim beginnings
Before barbarians scarified Florence,
Tries to escape, breaks stone chisels
That restrain dismal prehieroglyphic
Depictions he scratches on the faces
Dreams project against pantomimic eyes.

The corolla opens. Space gains mass.
The creature inside the creature stirs,
Chipping away at marble encasements
To liberate the nubile captive slaves
Huddling in his mind's dank basement.
How remarkably they resemble the artist
In their unfinished state, how naked!

Somewhere beneath the unpolished edges,
His pained breathing pumps their blood.

1/3/73 (03802)

[Please, Mr. Genovese, give me a chance] †

Please, Mr. Genovese, give me a chance
To explain, to regain my option on life.

1/4/73 — [1] (02770)

The Coy Mistresses: A Persuasion to Love

If you and I stay silent for just a little while
Longer, we might be able to watch each other come
Together within this bottle from Merlin's vineyard.

Behind the thick surface, withholding an ocean,
Our eyes, fleshy breasts, nipples, apple-moist mouths
Float on clouded fumes, spawn heated sea-spume

At depths beneath natural wet-zones of touch
And saline taste bud. We nestle, barely weakened
By personal encroachments night's blind eyes and

Gluttonous teeth make on our irrational loving.
Throbbing tongues, in dizzy, clitoral fibrillation,
Explode within our minds' endless fenestration,

Hurling us past each other's actual physicality,
Toward the region of astral souls. We will be
Each in each other's future skin, see ourselves

As intermingled beings, twin metaphors unifying
Sight and naked craving to be appreciated nakedly,
If you and I stay silent for just a little while

Longer. Be still now. Listen to the quick-kissing,
Concupiscent moon and her suitors. Watch her
Waste hot lunar juices across the entire cold sky.

Wait until she passes from sight, then enter night
Through the bottle's smooth neck. Stand waist-deep
With me in the tide's highest going out.

1/4/73 — [2]   (03805)

Eulogy for Baker

> *God take his soul.*
> *He tried so hard to endure.*

Poor Orris is dead. He lies on the cold floor
Before us, reporters, police, assorted people
Recording the horrid details of sordid release.

He is red, torn to shreds like old check stubs,
Distorted beyond recognition by icy pellets
Tightly funneled from a gun. His assailants

Have passed into January's coldest night
Like spirits leaving a dying body's hiding
For another corpse just being born. Undetected,

They prevail, waiting to be discovered, to be
Brought back out of the whale's bloated belly
To tell the truth, to show eager TV viewers

That previously undisclosed motives make sense,
Give order, if not justification, to insanities
We usually assign to inferior creatures, habits

That accurately categorize each species without
The capacity to reason. A solitary log cabin
On a city doctor's river property, Twelfth Night,

Freezing beyond all human intensity to survive,
A Christmas tree still glowing in the window,
Below which we stand a week after New Year's Eve,

Trying to piece together what actually happened
To the watchman, who went to bed high every night,
Dreaming he could single-handedly withstand armies.

1/7/73   (03801)

[My wife rides beside me this morning.]

My wife rides beside me this morning.
I am shorn of the freedom of being alone
For the brief eons my business trips take.
Reduced from victorious athlete to coach
Dictating game-plays to keep her amused,
I lose my desire to drive further.
Bland landmarks and oversize signs
That once clothed the highway in familiar garb
Become tattered habits of fat-assed preachers
Exhorting me to give my last pennies for a diocese
No human mind could have ever conceived.
Today, my domain has two potentates.

1/16/73   (03803)

Butterfield Inn ^Δ

Blue- and green-felt, long-billed hats
Hover three feet above each tabletop.
Somewhere beneath, gnarled field-faces
Wade cow-solemn through spacious depths
Of row-crop, feedlot speculation, debating
The high school's financial condition,
Pollution from a nearby pool-table maker,
Cost of hogs, per pound, on the hoof.
None has yet taken necessary measures
To differentiate this new eating place
From the previous converted filling station,
Recently evacuated. Neon-patinated linoleum
On floors, brick decor mixed with flocked
Wallpaper form a Chambord-like sore thumb
Amidst the stalled squalor in town.
A thousand coffees a day won't pay the lease
Each month. It's as though nothing's changed.

1/17/73 (03804)

Planting ^Δ

This small, white field, which I sow with seeds
My calligraphy broadcasts beneath no rain,
Yields no harvest. My parallel thoughts
Become blighted each season. Unborn wheat
And corn are verses my forlorn poetry re-
Peats, while I pay a scarecrow, frozen
To the paper field's white, wintry sky,
To frighten creatures intent upon bounty
That will never reach market, get eaten
By eyes hungering for mixed garden rhyme.
When I've finished tilling this ground
And these seeds are buried beneath earth
In silence, like words lost in dead books,
Then will we wait in hopes of new blooms.

2/13/73 (03807)

Monday in Babylon

The paragraphs of love are barren fields
That run through a blood-rust horizon.
Even single words form solitary pyramids
No flooding Nile or your slightest smile
Can budge from their turpitude. Serpents
Wear our cold syllables like tight skin
Ready to be molted.
                              No Mosaical staff
Ever changed the spitting cobra's venom
Into hyacinths. Face to face, we gaze
Inside a space our eyes transliterate
From the alphabet of marriage we spoke
When the tablets were enlightened by law.
Now, our hearts are those broken stones.

2/26/73 (03806)

[February freezes like an old lady squeezed by death.] †

February freezes like an old lady squeezed by death.
All streets take on a glaze beneath dusk-to-dawn lamps.
Human beings walk around like dazed mice in a maze
Inside a gray hovering, stumbling early to assignments
Designed to occupy dull imaginations.

2?/73 (00741)

The Children of Messiah

Quiet Sundays are spent outside of time,
While spirits convalesce. Human faces
Attached to fat bodies glower in dour mime,
Tantalize our silent hiding like hunters
Confronting lion prides asleep after eating.
Abstractions protract the mind's disease.

People scatter the littered debris memory
Keeps warm in tepid shallows of the stream
We wade. Beings disciplined in forgetting
Seek to find their places through prophecies
Created by agencies. They become the concrete
Laid for each new subdivision foundation

Excavated along the mind's fissured hillside.
People poke at us with jealousy. They grasp
Our sacramental loneliness from a distance,
Like mechanical hands clasping tubes of cancer
Behind safety glass. They hang on our fence,
Claw the air with insults. They would shear

Our beards and long hair, tear the clothing
We wear from the image of us they've painted,
Were death's barrier not forced between us.
We are the elegies, verses the sun drizzles
From cities of unearthly light. We are poetry
Escaped into rebirth, beneath a searching eye,

To decree eternal purposes to people gone dry
In seas ancient as Creation, wide as night
First parted from first light. Something dies
Whenever life passes itself in mortal flight.
The eyes no longer interpret implied meaning
Or find disturbing the propagation of lies

By readers hired to preach the musical word.
The edicts have all been buried in mausoleums
Buried beneath the concrete. Even the children
Are trapped between their own closed end-rhymes
Of modern birth and death, worshiped by parents
Succeeding at war. Children aren't even taught

To read the astral alphabet anymore or listen
To grass growing tall in the smalls of their palms.
We have returned to the cave, hiding by day
Behind a sealed entrance, afraid that children
At play will notice our final transmigration
From this planet before the appointed silence.

3/19 & 7/6/73 (03808)

Closing the Old Café, Opening the Butterfield Inn ^Δ

The Crystal Café/gas station became an oasis
During their scraggly-faced fathers' generation.
They came each a.m., again at noon, to seed rumors,
Returned evenings to reap the harvested gossip
Their base mortality required for survival.

The town's scanty population gave condolences
To its passing, last December, sending flowers
Four months later to the newer institution:
A Crystal Palace of aluminum, brick, and plastic,
Where scraggly-faced sons come to monitor the rain.

3/20/73 — [1] (03809)

Fugue

Jan,
in waiting

Like notes muffled
        By the private, humming mind
Of a musician sleeping,
        My thoughts compose you
In soft symphonies,
        Repeat you with recent themes
To form a soundless
        Counterpoint of you and me.
Somewhere, a quartet
        Performs us in angels' ears.

3/20/73 — [2] (03810)

The Permanent Journey

Ascent

We leave forlorn our sweet, sunny country morning,
Exchange overalls and boots for suit and bow tie, shoes.
*

Reminiscent of monks walking flatfooted from altar to cell,
We pass down airport corridors, whose resilient polished floors
Cast up to us visions of shades in Hell outlasting eternity
In suspect penance, wait for baggage to be ransacked
By trained Vandals and Visigoths paid by the state,
Then enter the center concourse to be devastated by speed
As the earth's peopled surface recedes from our perspective.

Up here, there are no disturbances the scanners fail to
Understand. Only man's perfection is called into question
As the sleek machinery moves through the universal neck,
With all its myriad sands commingling us outside of time.
In a single, prerecorded lapse of humanity, the black vastness
Surrounding our passage explodes. Night's code is deciphered.
Its closed opening commits us to a controlled landing pattern.
The lighted runway feels our wheels peeling away the layers,
Takes our weights in fractions, gives us a place to wait

Descent

Until the next scheduled takeoff. After all that motion,
The horrible roar of civilized silence violates expectations.
Our aquarium eyes fill up with colliding objects. Humans
In flight, malingering in lines like links of *carceri* chain
Dangling from roofless cages, are magnetized by the city
In brainless chaos. We are committed to set progressions
Material success has perpetuated. The custom of rushing
Subjugates us to hasty lovemaking, prepackaged eating,
Street scenes where socially acceptable grotesqueries

Compete with the most recent movie-screen surrealisms.
The air goes cold. Nothing here has the natural hues
Of fresh-cut grass or its juicy scent. We are wrapped,
Like survivors of an auto crash, in expensive blankets
Against the truth of exposed landfills, open smokestacks,
Springlike skies blowing coal waste and hopeless choking
Over this dismal accumulation of the Age of Greatness.
No one alive here even remembers when any single morning
Had an actual beginning or evening an identifiable end.

Final Destination

City of a million elevators! We step from one to another
Like riding vertical subways all day.
*

Then they flatten out into endless conveyors that take us
Along a flooding tide of sideshow distractions. We sneeze,
Touch each other's noses to confirm our physical uniqueness
Among all the gaudy quackery of glass showcases and faces
Staring out behind counters lined with estate jewels, meats,
Perfumes. There seems no return from this soothing miasma
That purrs around us, waiting to scratch out our eyes.

We were the chosen souls, waiting for a total change
To remove our old clothes, freezing in that polar zone,
Where heat turns to rain-leaves and dry ice burns snow-trees
To a bleak and hueless melancholy in the mind's preserves.
We sweated from a fear that conspiracies of evil forces
Would devastate Heaven before we could complete our arrival.
Now, in the sacred monastery above and beneath firmaments,
Below oceans, stripped of bones and motors of war, we breathe
The sweet, sunny, country morning air, as we did before leaving.

3/22–23/73   (03811)

[Odors of smoke, roasting pretzels and chestnuts, trash] †

Odors of smoke, roasting pretzels and chestnuts, trash
Congest the nostrils' normal fresh-air traffic. Taxicabs
Are chain links scattered

3/27/73 — [1]   (02782)

Burlington House Viewed from a Tall Hotel

Plastic plants, signed prints . . .
Scanty people in closed compartments,
Holding coffee breaks, executive meetings
To project the week's lofty perfections,
Reside from nine to five, penitentially,
Behind shades raised in neon silence.

File cabinets with lies and half-truths
Compiled between Manila folders
Hold secrets upon which the pilings
Of this colossal mausoleum are anchored.
A hierarchy of concentrated inactivity
Maintains the weight of its machinery.

Scaffolded window washers decontaminate
The devious Mondrian persistency,
Painted in glass, framed in stained steel,
Which thrusts insults at a feeble sun.
Such tedious cleaning for a Grecian urn,
Just to reveal identical lifeless scenes,

Seems a bit inconsistent in an age
Disinterested in arresting history. Images
Created precipitate all violations by time,
And people conceived out of breech birth
Disturb no galaxies. We shut the curtains
To deprive those faces of our lovemaking.

3/27/73 — [2] (03812)

[All winter's discontents dissolve] ^Δ

All winter's discontents dissolve
In the sunshine Saturday sprays,
Sweet, small-town elixirs, small
Antidotes against endless melancholies,
These signs we look for like clovers
With four leaves in quincuncial lawns,
Sunrays sifting nickelodeon beehives
With fingers lengthened by possibilities
Of reaching the honey-dome people seek
Whenever they step out of their skeletons,
Into a pristine, crisp physical fitness
The cold air alone knows fifty miles out
To sea.

4/28/73 (00250)

[You are the morning being borne]

With all of my love, wife

You are the morning being borne
Above the soft horizon. My eyes
Accept your wafer as warm blood
Flowing from the source of oneness.
My mind is on fire. Becoming you
Is not an easy thing for me to do
When silence of sleep shapes dreams
I need to penetrate. Breathe me today!

5/4/73   (00936)

The Vapors

The music sends sylphs lunatic
On this moonless night, alive with heat
Lightning. We dance behind a screen
Concealing naked bodies from thirsty eyes
Driving toward total consumption. Eternity
Inside a wineglass invites speculations.
Moses' God may be very near at hand!

Drink to all the floating ghostly creatures
Who have traced our short course before.
Become the thunder, rough as dynamos,
Gentle as flying geese, demure, serene.
Be my tongue tasting, my eyes touching,
Gracefully, the sky, transposing storminess
Into another key, retrieving its melody.

God bless beings everywhere who can see
Themselves as fragrant, sacred blooms
Whose profuseness gardens the universe.
We are only gingerbread silhouettes,
Registering the wine's half-light designs
As tiny seeds promising no new growth.
The wind alone knows to choose our signposts.

Imagistic watch fires shimmer the glass,
Disturb an imperturbable rainy surface,
Then pass like civilizations on the plains.
When silence once more vapors the eyelids,
Visions of greatness fade. Space temples us
With its vast humility, while sleeping poets
Rewrite nightmares into mothering lullaby.

6/2/73 (03813)

Jean

Spoon River Jean
Reaches up to us out of her prairie
Heritage like a seed seeking completion
In fields growing green
All winter wide.

6/3/73 — [1?] (03814)

Up from Egypt

Outside, headhunters pass in legion,
Looking for suitable food to sustain
Their orgy of flight and procreation.
The jungle draws me into its odors.

Monkeys pantomime my credentials.
A mad zebra runs through the fence
It makes merely by being itself.
I run from poison bird-points spent

By naked warlords, hide inside night,
Where satyrs graze without privacy.
The neck explodes, goes steaming cold
As molten steel dropped in an ocean.

Tribal fishers arrive in hordes,
With nets to drape my closed eyes.
*

The opaque gauze dying provides
Dissolves. Before me lie saxophones,

Making love overtures to the moon,
And fields where soft, white ladies
Dream Dante's dreams in terza rima,
Conceive the chemistry of my new being.

6/3/73 — [2?] (03815)

Sunday in the Flower Shop ^Δ

Dear Mr. and Mrs. H.

Church bells reach toward the ceiling.
Day's heat has begun screeching orisons.
I hear them preaching sermons in Berlin,
Lucerne, Turkey, here in Jacksonville,

Where I peer through planters profuse
With plastic displays and crowded foliage,
Balanced randomly as dandelions on a lawn,
Behind these plate-glass manifestations,

Staring from this chair, where,
For thirty years, brides-to-be have sat
To select wedding bouquets from lithographed pages,
Musing upon the June-languid Square,

Where pedestaled Liberty guards her martyrs,
Caught in bronze, and the state's patients
Graze in crazy noontide solitudes.
Church bells skip down stitched frequencies

Drawn thin as invisible rain. Fragrances
From chrysanthemums, carnations, calla lilies
Touch time, kiss memory, taste delicious
To the sweet, honeysuckling tongue climbing

Wild to the ceiling of being, sheltering us
From the heat. Strange how our deliveries,
The week's most delicately wrought,
Will remain outdoors this evening, sleeping

Where all these church bells come to rest,
In Diamond Grove Cemetery. I'll take them,
Place and consecrate them in God's eye.
The dry soil is waiting on our arrangements.

6/17/73   (03816)

The Fishing Club

> *Greg and Carmen . . .*
> *beautiful!*

I

Mosquitoes dip to the lake's surface.
Ripples, stippled with natural spray,
Slowly fade into circles our eyes
Circumscribe as they try to contain nature.

Occasional dragonflies scissor the thick air
We breathe, their netted, leaded-glass wings
Hovering their short-lived fuselages forever
Before dissolving into sleepless anonymity.

No one knows where they go to hide their lives
Between the hours of their brief fighting
For survival and the silent, dying light
Of their final morning. Even the cicadas,

Like strident motorboats and garrulous
As washerwomen, leave no defined clues
To their unremarkable demise. They sing
Invisible elegies with perfect disregard.

II

Minnows peer through a murky liquid skin
The lake wears, nibble insects, grab warm air
Precariously, before returning. Inclined to freedom,
We follow their gracefully sensual submergence,

Find the evening inside a bottle of sweet Chablis.
Each of us, whole beings being pieces of the whole,
Reaches deep into our soul-grown entanglements
To touch butterflies fluttering, then tongues rain

Plunging over the earth's edge, to our planet.
We are the children of our children's parents,
Created in minds loving out of sheer passion.
Such irrational incest burns lines in the sun,

Turns the lake's surface to dust, lightens night
To such energized diamond that the eight of us
Reflect a faceted coalescence against the moon.
Soon, God's angel may announce a new birth line.

6/24/73 — [1]   (03817)

Sunday from Hauser Hill ^Δ

> *Jean and Richard . . .*
> *how we love*

Trains, with loud freight and long, and barges,
Awkward before the tow, traverse Sunday morning,
Warm as soft feathers. Neither river nor track
Discloses itself through pin oaks and maples.
The eye floats them across the length of sky
In a succession of lazy blinks. Motion is life
Registered in strokes, measured in light-years
From the poet's sun-source. No people approach

The mythical landscape, crazed in gray-blue haze;
None tries to leave. Still, the bells scratch glass
Through which their ghosts peer in at themselves
From outside the steepled culs-de-sac, strangers
Caught in a comforting alienation from all time.
Somewhere down there, those dispossessed of love
Rest beneath dirty sheets, afraid to raise shades
Against another prolongation of daylight saving.

The swampland separating the river from us bulges
Like a pregnant snake, threatening to contain
Fifty miles of dry prairie behind this hill house,
Forming an island privacy free of contingencies
Conceived in the city so below, so far, far away.
A train collides with itself; a barge runs aground
In twenty feet of Illinois silt. The bells crack,
And people come out from sealed houses, fill streets

In time to see stars, in broad daylight, bombard
The sun with dark argosies, the moon come up full
From the westernmost sea, still dripping water
Like rain occurring completely out of sequence.
Soon, the dispossessed return to their dirty sheets.
The rest dance inside neon tubes, anesthetized
By the boring normalcy of phenomena. We fall down,
Touching. Gentle kisses define us tonight, forever.

6/24/73 — [2] (03818)

Radio Station Watergate

John Dean's testimony

Not since Nero posted "CONDEMNED" signs on Roman brothels
Have so many faceless Patrick Henrys and Matthew Arnolds
Chased fire-engine sirens across the entire grudging terrain
Of a state of the nation (out of pure curiosity, unrestrained
By forgiveness or executive clemency) to see monuments blaze,
Victims prepare to leap from the oval safety of high places,
Patriarchal foundations tumble through water gates, to basements
Where all great statesmen are framed by plate-glass wall safes.

The Persians are coming! Xerxes the Crazy is gleeful with prospects
Of victory. The Greeks hide their secrets in wooden mythologies,
While the wives of magistrates and peasants await the final rape
Of sacred beasts. Thermopylae gives way. History is a weary runner,
Covering distances between foul conditions absolved atop Areopagus
And their repetition by future rulers in other cradles of civil-
Ization. The Potomac is cruel in June. Blossoms topple in July
As in a baptism by fire. Only new poets notice the metamorphosis.

6/25/73 (03819)

Breakfast Reflections

The paper place mat, a mountainside beneath my face,
Disclosing a needlepoint map of the United States,
*

Proclaims, "Welcome home, wherever we are," in red.
Coffee refuses to yield recognitions from eye-blinks
That dot four hundred locations in imitation green thread.

Although I've stayed overnight, birth never occurred.
I am nowhere whenever my journey transports me here,
Where identities are misplaced by identical strangers
Exchanging business conversations with stray waitresses.
Home was never the tasteless sameness of frayed decoration,

Nor did our parents welcome solid-state misrepresentations
By friends defenseless against eccentric needs for honesty
In dealing with each other. Our bedsheets never bore
The stained mystique of a thousand whores in car coats
And satin peignoirs. Chauffeurs didn't park before our door

To unload their sordid cargoes. No traveling cavalcades
Of migrant seekers ever reached our furthest boundaries
Without first stating their purpose in being there.
Within limits, there were never any limits to our sharing.
But the homestead became myth. Peace is on its knees,

At the mercy of those who, by degrees, would freeze it,
Like water into ice cubes floating in a neat martini,
Then leak it away in a seizure of evening repartee
Regarding recent investments in commercial properties,
Like this one, which welcomes me home so personally.

6/26/73 (03820)

Genealogies ^Δ

The new morning started many years before,
Taking the same course as the crack train
Freighting back and forth between the K.C. station
And St. Louis, passing, in a flash, each purlieu
In the between zone without so much as a whistle.

Twenty miles, in each direction, from a siding,
Tipton lies like a dusty flag waving hastily
In June air heated to slow motion by steel
Spinning over glinting rails. Once each century,
A presidential Pullman runs, slowly enough to be touched,

Through crepe-paper Main Street, spews steam,
Then speeds away, with its hundred bearded faces
Peering in isolated amazement at their enclave.
Not until the last visage disappears from memory
Does the town settle back into even tractor paths

To hide again inside a cycle of dying and rebirth
The earth provides without coercion. Tipton survives
At horizon's edge like a tired body tied to a log
Floating endlessly on a sea of dry wheat, a tiny island
Peopled by giants speaking in silence to ancient queens.

6/27/73 (03821)

Private Judgments Made Public at the Butterfield Inn [Δ]

Twelve pharaohs, seated four at each of three tables,
Compete to be heard. Deeds are being decided by word,
Laws analyzed for the most severe application to fact.
In the beginning, rectitude was their sole guide,
Providing it never applied to royalty. In flood time,
When people below the Golden City were wont to steal
From need rather than sheer greed, their leniency
Would commute hundred-year sentences to ten tilling
Olive groves. In good times, felonies and misdemeanors
Were treated with the same degree of cold obstinacy
Projected in the sack and raping of enemy city-states.

Public monuments must first be quarried, then sculpted,
As in days when the masters fashioned great pylons;
Wherefore twelve pharaohs meet in seeming consultation,
Each morning, to determine a nation's division of labor.
With so much peace to accommodate, they find it difficult
To exact servitude from work crews, especially when summer
Heats coastal beaches. They agree the people lack spirit;
Lethargy and fatigue are plagues brought on by Moses.
Today, they'll fabricate convenient laws banishing him
From their regenerative land of the Fertile Crescent,
Dooming him to become the forgotten father of ten lost tribes.

6/28/73 — [1] (03823)

Ahab's Obsession

A four-blade circular fan bats at heavy air
Heated, near the ceiling, to a hundred degrees.
Its blasts don't even tease the riotous flies,
Lighting intermittently on cups and plates
From which we eat with little enterprise.

It's on days like these I begin to realize
How Jonah must have felt inside the leviathan,
And I want to swim far out into an ocean,
Commit myself to its cool-breathing cave,
Buoyed deeply within a case of sweet spermaceti.

6/28/73 — [2] (03822)

[The sky has gone mottled] †

The sky has gone mottled
As a moldy potato

6/28/73 — [3] (02771)

Prague War Trials

K. has never been in any of the uncharted chambers
Of the compartmented nautilus. Yet when
He strays beyond corresponding boundaries
Consciousness arrests at its threshold,
He finds himself unable to properly make
Self-justifications in the abstract. Being
Becomes the seeing-eye dog for a mind
Blind to the formation of requisite metaphors.

Becoming is achieving a state of being defeated
By hung juries stacked against defendants
Brought to trial for suspected nonviolations.
Refusal to stand is punishable as treason,
Fighting predecided verdicts a falsification
*

Of intended victimization the nerve ends
Are subjected to, ad absurdum, by the creature
Dwelling in the shell's fluted convolutions.

Each day, heavy seas wash clean its covering,
Buffing, filing away. The persistent sounds
Attrition makes in the wearing away disconcerts
The thriving worm. He fears immediate eviction
From this apartment housing his reasonableness.
His dreams portend a being floating free-fall
Through ocean halls endlessly deep and wide
In five directions. The sky above turns purple.

6/29/73 — [1] (03824)

A Stitch in Time ^Δ

The three-dieseled freight that just passed
Came faster than a bullet-shuttle screaming
Or a perfectly timed feed dog drawing the wind
Invisibly across a gravel-bed throat plate.
Its evenly spaced cars were safety stitches,
Setting a neat back-tacked seam at eyes' edge.

The pieced garment I wear, walking down tracks
Empty of cast clatter, might be Joseph's coat.
Being alone out here excites fear of bodily harm,
And I run to find the mind's scissors, then cut
One stitch to free the chain, let the fabric
Come easily undone. No freight train ever passed.

6/29/73 — [2] (03825)

Smoke-Filled Rooms

By 8 a.m., the ballroom swells
With cigar fumes. To separate the clouds
We left outside from the great hall's sky,
The mind gropes for blue metaphors. Eyes
*

Fly wild from stolid faces to faces dying
Slowly without knowing when ends arrive.

Afternoon fills with smoke thick as minutes
Crowding out each hour. At meeting's dusk,
Horizon's chameleon hides in blood-rust hues,
Ready to leap into deep-jet undergrowth.
We leave through a normal June-night fog,
Caught in blurred arcs of brass pendulums.

6/30/73 — [1] (03828)

Three-Day Sales Meeting

Rank deprivation drives him to pay a hundred dollars
For a Swedish barmaid, who, after hours,
Arrives at his hotel door, begins devouring
Dark forms that haunt his psyche, removes
Phantoms that isolate him, each night,
From comforts narcosis provides, then leaves,
A tight fog going out on low morning light.

6/30/72 — [2] (03829)

The Salesmen

Thirty voices express their independent choices
Of model, style, and color combination offered
To the nation's apparel exchanges. They anticipate
Repeated increases. All reasonable men will agree
That people need to disguise their bodies
Behind woven screens. As disciples going abroad
With a new religion to teach in a world materialized
To complacency, they'll sell their martyred souls
From swatch cards, competing, in a vast wilderness,
Against weaker creeds to reach deepest pinnacles
Of highest achievement. And when they've passed,
Scribes will record the history of Joseph's tribe.

6/30/73 — [3] (03827)

The Impressionists

Jan,
together we make love happen.

Afternoon peers through streaked windows
Night lights from behind with five million moons
Splintering in endless permutation. Smoke balloons,
Diffuses on a shimmering air. Somewhere in wheat fields,
Bales catch fire from a sun's feeble

Dissolve. On a dusty road, two people, new
To each other, believe they see Monet painting
Beside a haystack. They stop inside their kisses,
Resisting easy distances that keep them from the truth,
Then leave, inspired by love's creativity.

6/30/73 — [4] (03826)

[There was a crooked man,] †

There was a crooked man,
Who walked a crooked mile
Awhile. His name was Milhous,
And he never wore a smile

6–11?/73 (03971)

The Sales Meeting: Last Day

Men step out of the previous night,
Struggle onto morning's patio like rumors
Homing in on their appointed targets.
Behind their eyes, vague shadows graze
Like blunt cows plowing through plains
Opaque as ocean-smoke. The room floods
With stale space. Voices trail away
As our speaker begins preaching gospels
Derived from Dead Sea Scrolls. Designations
*

Contain the tenable awareness of life
Thriving on a daily basis, removed from
Snowflakes and graceful hummingbirds.

Industries compete for peace, through war
Conducted by forces defined by price.
The men complain the hour grows late.
Someone sneezes. The speaker digresses
To change three ranges in anticipation
Of poor availability of piece goods.
Weighted jets take off from Guam for Laos
As the meeting draws to a tired close.
Men complete their lists, gather swatches,
Prepare to unleash bombs on a trade
Awaiting their arrival, escalation being
Justified by every threat to prosperity.

7/1/73   (03830)

Three Anniversaries

Janny

The mimosa explodes its blooms as profusely
As ten thousand soft rockets blowing dust
Colored in endless dissolve against dark
Tuned to perceive a genius's silence. We
Embrace a thousand clocks' weightless hands,
Fly through pendular suspensions, descend,
By climbing from the Children's Kingdom,
Into chambers served by old people clothed
In gold roses grown in clouds before birth.

We stop long enough, in our steep, free passing,
To touch each other touching feelings float-
Ing through trees blown by poets' breathing.
Somewhere far beyond high, a loud sea rises,
As if our coming were air filling its lungs,
Then plunges against ears we once shared,
When music contained cloves and bay leaves
And oregano. The waters compose our children
In uterine capsules released by sweet kisses.

A mimosa grows naked in the space in a hole
In time. We climb to its base, rooted in July,
Crawl eight days out on its strongest limb.
Our shadows dangle in perfect superimposition
Against the earth, while a marriage of body
And being eclipses all singular achievements.
People will know us who have only known us
As blooms cohabiting in a halo of floating pink.
Our seeds will fill their gardens with dreams.

7/8 & 7/18/73 — [2] (03831)

The Turtle

Silence rides a turtle's curved back
Through paths profuse as tall rain
Falling to the brain's surface. Under-
Growth, entwined from dismal histories
Recorded by the eyes' secret scribes,
Makes clear egress almost impossible.

Only portions of lives, unclaimed names,
Give way to memory, as crawling claws
Disturb silent sanctums, calling up
Gods and ghosts to reconstruct beings
And poems from dust. Scattered ashes
Pollute the space we waste in passing.

If only the poems had tongues to speak
Thoughts their beings never apprehended
Or caught in time. A million million
Ideas, being massed for encapsulation
Like the last glistening drips of wisdom
Sipped from lemon rinds squeezed dry,

Almost reach the pencil's tip to trip
Into light, then die. I thirst for words
Unprinted, philosophies never conceived,
Which yet belong to everybody imprisoned
In sleep's best collective dream-cells
As she rides the turtle's curved back.

7/13–14/73 — [1] on 7/13 (03832)

Farmer [†]

His only tenant is himself, his land
A suitable companion

7/13/73 — [2] (02772)

Escape Artist

The collector of fleeting perceptions
Screams down the highway, climbs inside
A security he's made by passing this way
One hundred times before. Filling stations,
Boarded up and derelict as creatures
Left unexpectedly dead by Hell's vehicles,
Glare at him like missing teeth in a clown's mouth.
He stares at crashed-cars-become-crumpled-icons-
Of-disaster just to complete his familiarity.
They stay parked in static frieze all along
The curved wall of an urnlike countryside
He races through to escape his self-image:
A wasting soul who intimidates him when they
Meet face to face in their rearview mirror.

For thirty years, nothing at all has changed
Except the depth of pavement and dumb number
Of cows grazing in numbing constancy beyond the glass.
His eyes have tried to see special connections
Between analogies his mind conceives and meanings
The brain assigns to undefined objects
Floating softly as lily pads in a calm estuary
Leading from birth to the great lake, where life
Evaporates imperceptibly. Just now, a darting bird
Scratches jaggedly against the onrush of sky,
Vacillates, then turns into his eyes and dies.
The emblem pressed against his radiator grille
Makes him nature's surrogate. He awakens in pain,
No longer insulated from the land he inhabits.

7/18/73 — [1] (03833)

Evanescence

She was sleeping yet when I left early
Yesterday, a sweetheart rose unopened
By day's heat, fragrance subtle as silence.

The critical essence of absence touches me,
Reaching to touch her fleet breathing
As afternoon closes its tedious argument.

The distance is Ishmael's, Ulysses's odysseys.
Such urgency as theirs destroys reason.
I survive the highway merely by fortune's

Oversight, pressing ahead because instinct
Is a steady hand in gripless fogs, intellect
A blind vision. I see you sleeping yet.

7/19/73 (03834)

Trilogy

I

Even the sirens collapse. The tired eyes
Are turtle heads drawing up inside lidded shells.
Feeding time
                finds the victims lacking appetite.
A charley horse
                grips the brain ascertaining needs
For survival during the next three hours
Preceding sleep.

II

Alone in a murmurous dialogue
Exhaustion engenders from sheer spite,
The body fights its way out of a paper bag,
Perpetuates workaday manifestations
Of godly purpose by kneeling to pray
For the release of another sunlit evening
Held captive in the resurrection cave.

III

The hours dissolve. Night collides with itself
In accurately accidental equations. Shadows
Stab the absolute lapis lazuli that dreams fashion
From unrelated romances bards transpose for me.
I sit in an uncharted corner, reading the stars'
Braille, waiting for an intruder to touch lips
With me, to set sail upon a galaxy of our two
Bodies moving in sweetest unison. Soon enough,
You enter my eyes, running smooth as couplets
Through musical verse, bursting focal points,
Exploding all notions of a heavenly descent
By the absolutely pure and human nakedness
You expose as you take me into your fantasies.

7/25/73   (03835)

The Talking Machine

"Jan,"
my tiny voice cries out,
"Jan..."

I sit alone, listening for distant whispers,
Letting the phonograph stroke itself
Like a satisfied cat. Its slow, even drone
Is past years molting, memories cast off.

Cathections and sweet, mysterious connections
Issue through a morning-glory horn formed
By hand-painted sounds coming through the air
From nowhere. I am surrounded by urchins
And minstrels, in search of Turkish minarets

To topple with their enchantments, and friends
Forgotten as love letters kissed by passion
In fleeting sequences on late-night beaches
Scented by fired driftwood and mild white wine.

They arrive yet through an opaque liquescence
The music sprinkles like missives set drifting,
On placid lakes, in ancient glass bottles.
Their messages are shattered; images pulsate
On vaguely familiar overtones, then dissolve.

The needle finally reaches its inmost soul,
Coasting into a groove of endless circularity,
Which scratches dissonant emptiness against
My ears — the only sound I can hear anymore.

7/26/73   (03836)

Friday Night Farmington

Sevens fill the sad air like swarming gadflies,
Persistent as ice crystals forming high in the wide eye
Of undecided rain. I am flying a scattered pattern tonight,
Sliding along a sloping trajectory toward the Plain of Jezreel.

Seven spheres appear to be in decline behind me,
Where life expands like ink on history's dotted blotter
And time is a poor writer recording deeds of beastly people
On Doomsday pages. The musical universe seems so far away
    from me,

Harmony's heaven a mere proliferating oscillation
Seen by a few Hebrews in ancient days. My eyes are filled
With wet deserts; no one crosses the sands in caravans anymore,
On his way to trade routes and spices I used to give out of love.

The sevens register their pain in strange relation
To the plagues that name me the one chosen to be mercy's
Scapegoat. They have finally traced me to the end of Paradise.
I touch ice crystals high in the eye, freeze inside heated ecstasy,

Cry out to be touched by the even suspirations God,
In His breathing, achieves as the world draws up inside Him
Each time He reaches through the clouds to inspire dying lives
With peace. His kiss expels doves caged within my mind's preserves.

7/27/73   (03837)

Just Jan and Me

Praise all who have lived and those of us
Who live yet in their stead. Getting through
*

The nimbus is as contradictory as being tried
For witchery and surviving its five-minute
Drowning. Few have ever achieved the stability
To freely choose their own guillotine. You
And I, at least, retrieve our dreams without
Preconceived designs, believing in trans-
Substantiation of minds made divine by self-
Proclamation. We were born at identical times,
Like colliding comets in darkness, exploding,
Fusing two new equations in a regenerative mass
That glows to show us a hole in the future.

Fields we run through register only one passing.
Garden leaves we gently ransack for green life
Brush up against us as if touching silence.
People we've loved call out a name we recognize
As belonging solely to us in the whole world.
Who are we if not twins moving blind in a crib,
Children of parents married to their planet
By God, docile creatures rejoicing in simplicity
Bequeathed us by beings whose teachings
Reach our feelings through eyes kissing tongues
And kisses speaking, in perfect wordlessness,
The union of man's body and woman's hot blood?
Jan, I know you totally in our separate sleeps.

7/29/73   (03838)

Among the Chosen

Mine is a 6 a.m.–to–9 p.m. existence,
Without morning menu, or clean sheets
To sleep on each evening, spent frequently
Away from home. My briefcase and luggage
Bulge like the belly of a fat man eating;
They contain an entire inheritance — life
Transported like the Bedouins'. Someday,
Only my voice will travel these many miles:
Cards in slots, properly keyed electricity,
Solitary dots on maps, representing accounts
Active as lungs pumping blood money from
*

Public wells, alive as thriving cancers.
The plagues were made to pass over. Chosen
Were we among all people of every nation.
Soon, I'll be the pharaoh of this territory,
With men working under me. Predestination,
It's been called, will lead me from bondage,
Bring me, well-heeled, into the Promised Land.

7/30/73 (03839)

[An island floating in an ocean of seed corn] †

An island floating in an ocean of seed corn
And soybean. Furrows seething beneath tractors
Turning up dirt heated to the burning point.
The people run from the sun to take cover
Under a shield they fabricate from drudgery

7/31 — [1] & 12/25/73 — [2] (00740)

Clockwork

Even the stopping continues on in silence.
Despite my arrival at a midway station,
There is never any stopping. Continuation
Is merely the reiteration of all resumptions
And every cessation logged on the odyssey.

Sounds, foreign as cows close up, huddle
Into my ears, form awkwardly as clay
Dropped to a concrete floor, then lose
Their accidental shape. Alien shadows
Dart by me like minnows below a surface
Made opaque by fading daylight. I am trapped

Between start and stop of the widening arc
The observation wheel makes reeling about
The greased axle. Life is a drunk's view
*

Of the world perceived by a blind child,
As I fly high above the fairgrounds, seeking
Landmarks and people from the familiar blur
Disturbing equilibrium. The spring is tight.

7/31/73 — [2] (03840)

[The land is a loom] †

The land is a loom
through which the train zooms.

Tractor zooming across the land-loom
leaves seeds like an even thread,
forming the pattern of next season's crop.

The mind is dormant,
storing its excitement
like bears hoarding their sleep in storm time.

People racing at the snail's pace
to fill their pails with the sweet marriage
of idle hours and tart berries.

O harried berrypicker,
slow your ass down;
dig this moment beyond the city.
There are no appointments out here.

A field of dual striations,
moving up green stalks to sandy-beige tassels
in an endless stream of Illinois acreage.

Driving through a labyrinth on a tar-ribbed roadway
cuts a solid field in two.

Fertility screams an incessant shrill.
It fills my dreams with a million seeds bursting,
a reiteration of all creation
caught between the kaleidoscope's peephole
and its screen dissolving and reappearing
like cosmic phantasmagoria.

Reticulated tar-ribs of the cemented snake
that takes us on its back into the lair
where the mongoose waits
to eat or be eaten.

8/3/73 — [1] (00695)

A Time of Butterflies

Butterflies born in late July
Flood our eyes. Their disguise
Eludes all sense of propriety
With a pure, naked coloration
And bravura. Transparent wings
Mingle an entire environment
Into gentle whispers we hear
Through eyes that see eternity
In silent things and beauty
In a cocoon marooned in a web.

Suspicious, lately, of nature,
We listen for wing-tip vortices
To set avalanches advancing.

8/3/73 — [2] (03841)

Mardie and Lloyd

A wide field, tall with corn and beans,
Whose sole purpose is for growing things
To be eaten . . .

A green tree, in the middle of the field
For no reason other than to shade itself
Underneath . . .

The upturned earth in a shaded space
Beneath the tree, heated and humid enough
To take seed . . .

A breezy air, carrying adherent seeds
From neighboring fields like disciples
Preaching . . .

The anxious soil, preparing to receive
A mixture of future to renew its lineage
Next season . . .

Two new plants, who emerge as one
From seeds in the earth beneath the tree
In the field,

Turn to us as though we are the sun,
Taking strength, acknowledging our love
As they leave.

8/4/73   (03842)

In the Ocean-Sea

Once again, I head out volitionless, pressing ahead,
This time through a fog thick as a soft feather bed.
I sleep through two dreaming hours, alive yet not alert,
A body trailing its head ten years behind like a yacht
Towing a ship-to-shore dinghy. I ride a tiger's back,
Lost between the stripes, highway and tiger difficult
To separate. My lifestyle stinks like gross ammonia
Freshly sprayed in a field. Time has the dry heaves.

I leave Jan so often of late, escaping the safety
Anonymity creates out of its own self-perpetuating
Privacy. We hide there from all the privy judges,
Appointed for life by the stationmaster. We pass,
In a perfectly classless, color-blind society, for white
Humanitarians. Now, the caravan undulates; the desert
*

Regurgitates it in passing. The Caspian Sea leaks,
Flooding all trade routes to the east. Columbus dreams

Monsters into being from waves ten feet high, islands
From floating debris. A deep fog surrounds his eyes,
Seeps into melancholy, suppresses reason. He fidgets,
Turns his ear to the ocean's megaphone. A colloquy
Determines his defeat. There's no question that death
Must deliver him despite conquest, his discoveries.
Everything he's done, he begins to see, comes back
To birth and the circle. I take up where he leaves off.

8/15/73 — [1] (03844)

Variations in Gray

There come times in a person's life
When living is merely the reenactment
Of breathing. The eyes see only themselves
In an endless inward multiplication
Of spiraled tunnels, eyes within eyes
Within eyes, showing no blinks,
Disconnected from suspended thinking,
Which once occurred with some degree
Of succinct expertise. Even the limbs
Lose their taut, supple musculature
And those splendid, fluid movements elevated
To beauty in the painter's poetic mind.
Mere functions have no mind or guide,
And I am directed by mine to breathe
And nothing more — an iron lung, vertical
As living yet horizontal as being dead.

8/15/73 — [2] (03843)

His Vindication Speech

8/15/73,
8 p.m.

Nixon
Is fixin'
*

To piss on
The queen's castle.
An entire populace
Gathers up scrub pails and wet mops
To wash away the sins of the lord,
Sweep them under the country's front-hall rug.

Gulliver splits his sides with laughter.
The ropes that have held him tied to earth
Give way. He and the three-legged cow
Hitchhike across the ocean, to Redriff, to die
　　　　　　　　　　　　　　　in retirement.

8/16/73 — [1]　(03846)

In Quest of Leviathan

Neat lanes of corn eight feet high,
Spaced evenly, seen from above
As cars parked at a drive-in theater;
Square-baled hay, stolid as sows
Wallowing in sleep, seen from below
The field in which both lie,
One growing, the other beginning decay.

Fake cows graze inside the haze
That makes the day a magical cape
Turned inside out. It bulges
With clouds that might be doves
Ready to fly from hiding at the wave
Of a wand; it might only be rain.
Green is a state of breathing deeply.

Gray weaves a wire-mesh screen
Over my tired eyes. No voice-beams
Give my position to the enemy.
The silence in which I survive
Disappears like air in a balloon.
Even the cows, reaching to hear
Brain waves, go deaf as ivory.

I take the road connecting trees
And creatures to every peopled city,
*

Lost as floating seaweed and white
As diseased fish, frightened to death
By life. Soon, I'll arrive home
To my wife as Ishmael, lone survivor,
To tell the tale of my incarnations.

8/16/73 — [2] (03845)

[Always leaving by back doors]

Always leaving by back doors
Leading from boarding houses we furnish
With tangerines, always entering front doors
Like breath penetrating sacred caves
Where dreams start, the body undulates
Behind the sinking, swift elaborations
Our tongues modulate, like soft, supple fingers
Wet clay, shaping a coronation
From space. We are wealthy beggars,
Seeking solace inside a perfect solitude
Our eyes shape in the Communion feast.

We sit facing each other, you reading,
From memory, the Oriental encyclopedia
Of erotic art, I deciphering the Chablis,
Reflecting through it, in pleasing distortion,
Your absorbed eyes, gauzed softly in incense.

The minutes of our night as one go naked
As dancing minotaurs leaping to sheer earth
From balconies above nothing. The hours
Race ahead of monsters challenging time
With deliberate forgetting. Years transcend
This evening, with us riding on their wings.

8/18/73 — [1] (00805)

[Everyone attends to the slot machines,] †

Everyone attends to the slot machines,
With inebriated fingers and legs
Swollen as Greek pillars. The bandits release
A pauper's treasure, squeeze every emotion
From victims left to die a slow life

8/18/73 — [2] (02773)

Soap Opera

We never reread the nights we write
In serialized form or return to edit
The obscure passages describing flights
From reason and deviations from normal
Body formation. The series we act out
Has run continuously for eight seasons
Without relief, with only a brief hiatus,
During summer months, for this small cast
To recuperate on the sands of Juan-les-Pins
Or bask at the Venetian Lido.
                                        Last evening,
One of the principal protagonists collapsed
As he prepared to disclose the fact that
Boredom had finally set in. The finish
He'd carefully rehearsed with a loaded pistol
Had to be postponed.
                                Only the prop man
Stopped to question the pure spontaneity
Of his solitary gesture. No one else
(His eighteen-year-old mistress, a doting wife,
Their only child, created inside silence)
Realized he'd been trying to leap off
The stage of printed script,
                                        into life.

8/19/73 (03847)

[Just another just-so afternoon] †

Just another just-so afternoon
Thrusts us toward evenings beyond

8/25/73 — [1] (02783)

Reflections upon a Dubious Public Servant

Elaine: we love her!

Words conceived by a pompous fat man,
Bloated even beyond the shadow he casts
Against the moon, complain of genius
Too well-schooled in conceits, strain
To find a new voice in the same cage.

Politics, begun like tentative grains
At the head of an avalanche, disintegrate
Into a million chaoses. His caustic soul
Is cursed from within. First the mouth,
Then its lost chords, explode. He pleads
To be set free from lies he's fabricated,
Without replying to their veracity and
By repeatedly,
                repeatedly,
                        denying re-
Peatedly their validity on grounds of
Consanguinity. Nothing remains except
The parched echo of his three-tracked
Videotape personality,

Memorized by history, paraphrased by gen-
Erations as a liturgy of curses
To blaspheme God's clean countenance
Without risking irrevocable condemnation.

8/25/73 — [2] (03848)

Emergency

Red   White   Red
White   Red   Red   White

Light speaks to me
Its own stuttering language.
Light screams speed,
Springs to life at death's behest.
Light spits syllables
Like hot, rotten dragon teeth.
Light guides an ambulance;
Its soliloquy stills my tongue.

White   Red   Red   White
Red   White   Red

8/27/73 — [1–2?] (03850)

We Are the Parents Our Children Become

We used to complain of arrangements
Too formally engaged in by our parents:
Their weekend disguises in formal coat and tie,
Their nightly hide-and-seek bo-peep society,
Steeped in raising families extramaritally,
Behind inherited deeds of trust, legacies
Somewhere far beneath the sonorous titles.

We had seen their sportive entertainments,
Squinting through a kaleidoscopic peephole,
Been dazzled by clay pigeons, floating like fireflies
On summer evenings, before total explosion,
Caught between heroic polo-team captains
And lathered horses steaming like locomotives,
Haunted by retrievers pointing up trophies.

The disease set in at a very early age.
They were the carriers of malignant greed;
We were indulgent hosts without knowing it,
Until our seeds were consumed in blooming
By the heat of our waning afternoons.
*

Forty summers ago, the Compsons invited us
For drinks and conversation, and we stayed.

8/27/73 — [1–2?] (03849)

Dim-Lit Dinner

Strange how two voices speaking to each other
Within a vacuum shatter the viscous mold, blow
The candle imperceptibly as lambent light-years
Barely disturbing a clouded universe. You
Stare at me, frowning, and I relate truths
That share their basis in our cold speculations.
We believe in nothing other than warm eyes,
Whose penetrations embrace the lives of saints —
Watch fires lighting our caravan, abandoned
Beyond peopled centers, keeping us together
From death to death, binocular visionaries.
A shadow of my breath bends the candle's flame
Toward your gentle face, framing a stained-glass
Tapestry to hang where we come to worship love.

8/27/73 — [3] (03851)

Flight from St. Louis to L.A.

Incongruities accompany us, like depressions,
Between earth and sky. We drive ourselves
Into clenched talons, through a needle's eye,
Like eagles dragging a lifeline behind them
In flight. Our clearly worshiped purpose
Is pursuit. An age of prefabrications
Colors our self-portraits, so that at times
We sit for days, waiting naked as nightmares
For the artist's arrival. A Tinkertoy set
Of connections interrelates the designs
We need to define time's relevance to the space
*

In which we find ourselves softly awash.
Speed dislocates the painter from his canvas.
Soybean fields persist against the immediacy
Of eye-blinks straining to change the scenery.
Superimpositions make cornstalks into people,
Like metaphors actually happening to dreams —
Strange to be walking among faces duplicated
By video dreams projected in rerun sequences.
How could a whole race have run out of beliefs
In things unseen and creatures God sculpted
For heavenly reasons alone? Omens of emptiness
Intrude upon the capsule that protects us yet
From death. Feelings we should have harvested
Turn to weeds in gardens the sun's neglected.
No human hands conduct the bleached tiller
Across brain fissures gone fallow with disuse.
Still, in quiet despair, we drive breech-first
Toward a rebirth. The idea, or its corruption,
That mortality is merely a visible landmark
On an impossible plain leading to realities
We've simply not yet learned to decipher
Directs the wasted soul to search the earth
For some lost clue to its port of origin.
Escape transcends mania. We are besieged
By ropes, scaffolds, pulleys, every means
Available to the mind to make its break
With the living spirit. A vision of idiots
Leaping in passionate madness from a ship
Ablaze in a burning ocean of petroleum
Fogs my nerves. I try hard to identify
These effigies terrorized by a conflagration
Set by themselves inside a common heritage.
Floating briefly atop the flaming waves
Are all the charred remains of myriad souls
That scream our names through mute hues
Of firelight as though they've known us
From another place beyond the present age.
Recognitions are slow in materializing.
Finally, the eyes undress those disguised
As victims of a fiendish holocaust — they're us.

9/5/73 (04041)

The Friends

White gardenias float on crushed-ice oceans,
Like Japanese boats gliding against the moon.
We speak in tones of paintings made long ago
By dreamers reaching out to catch the earth
With bare hands as it hovered at eyes' horizon.
Your *Mona Lisa* gaze plays against my memories
Jigsaw-quick yet slow in the piecing together
Of its withheld disguise. I know you as a friend
For life from another lifetime, like the angel
Arrived to Isaac's father, whose annunciation
Proclaimed love growing long as widening day.
You saw me through space as a man husbanding you
Across endless lands, in quest of a new planet
Beyond Chaos, far beyond humanity's sirens. We
Were pioneers of our own choosing in a settle-
Ment bereft of geographic expansion, traversing
Limited accesses to search out the Golden City
Beneath high plains in the brain's Gethsemane.
You and I have grown content to seed gardenias
In each other's kiss, repeating birth rites
Bequeathed us in sweet seasons of deep youth.

9/9/73   (04042)

Evel Knievel

> *Jan . . .*
> *she shared with me*
> *his perfectly pure absurdities.*

Imagine a full moon against a wide, black sky,
Like a one-eyed sailor, or one-legged Ahab
Pacing the taffrail, cursing the night lights,
Spewing anathemas on his watery passing
Toward personal oblivion. All our lives,
We dream such outrageous chauvinisms.
The egoism of madmen even excites teachers
Screaming to be heard in cork-lined cells.

Imagine breathing with perfect solemnity
Beneath volumes of sea fifty feet deep,
Seeing, through endless opacity, the sun above,
A giant kept alive by belief in the self's
Capacity to survive weaknesses the mind
Devises from duels with its environment.
Such rare idiocy, embodied in our species,
Creates the genius visionaries emulate.

Bless the poor bastard who dreams of flying
His motorcycle over an entire Grand Canyon!

9/18/73 (04043)

Growing Older

Now, almost all the row corn has compromised
Its grossest base nature. It no longer grows,
Merely stands still, wallowing almost piteously,
Like a man suffering protracted depressions.
Some green stalks remain, forgotten or left
Purposely for overfilled silos; the rest bend,
Arthritically brittle, toward September's end.
Not even a persistent vision of summer green
Redeems the present debasement that nature
Endorses as seasons disintegrate. Decay changes
Memories. You and I are two different people,
Though we traverse this highway in a horizon
Clouded with snow-gray pillows floating ahead,
Atop all these harvested beds, for us to choose.
Tonight, we'll lay our heads on one and dream
Pumpkins and zoo bears and dry, fallen leaves
To rake into piles to hide inside and be young.

9/19/73 (04044)

Soaring Home

People fly past, rapid as water cascading,
Faceting in the horizon's pink light-fade.
*

Two voices, like one image facing itself
In a pool, clasp at the point where space
And memory meet in synapse. Their meeting
Complicates a new moon dropping into place,
Makes it necessary to bend down and touch
The ground for reassurance. Weak mortality
Fills all the miles of my nerves. Fibers
Deciphering what the eyes reach to see
Through a million pairs of monarch wings
Participate in their silent mating season.

Once again, visions sift into my soft skull,
And I think how unoften I've shared friends
With myself, how few flew toward my sun,
Then how briefly. History's sweep barely makes
Mention of my odyssey. Eons rush past, rapid
As water cascading. Souls flash as facets
On an immense beveled hall mirror fastened
To a clear, black atmosphere; they remind me
Of butterflies mating. I try to recognize
Myself in their passing, imagine being trans-
Ported back to conception as by an aqueduct
Carrying dreams across an entire dry lifetime,

As though to resume something never begun
By someone never really conceived to create
From improbable seeds thoughts with wings
To soar in silence. Even feared apparitions
From the past appear as blessed messengers
Of peacefulness. I believe that my arrival
Was actually anticipated all the while
I was alive defending myself against death.
Each new day here explodes in tree leaves
Floating gently as butterflies in mating,
Grows like caterpillars walking weightlessly
As love-couplets across autumn's time lines.
Lady, this chrysalis you've made is godly.

9/22/73 (04045)

[Five hours separate us, and still the uproar] †

Five hours separate us, and still the uproar
Of a hundred tight-assed 281-class
Sewing machines converges with road noise,
    Sideseams the highway

10/2/73 — [1] (02821)

Fisher of Men

Rain
    begs the day for release.
Relentlessly, we press ahead against a brain
Unwilling to proceed.
                Rain
                      colors wide rays
Slightly gray. It remains contained
For the present, taunting us with tentative flashes
In a strange distance turning away from daylight,
Toward a dying, bright-purple dusk.
            Rain
                touches earth, rushes full-burst
Against glass. There are no empty patches
For the imagination to punctuate with speculation;
There's only the awful, actual fact of mastery
The rain has gained against me, its circumambience
Like a great white tide breaking late
From a body of land called Fallen Man.
                    Rain
Purifies; it also floods. It drowns those
It surrounds in soundless, somnambulistic glazes,
Behind the wheel at dusk, alone inside the
                      rain.

10/2/73 — [2] (04047)

Alphabets

Free-falling through dreams, awakened
By my uneven breathing, I left the house
In time to see a mute moon float alone
In night's wake, making hand signs to me
As though I were the deaf universe
To which she meant to communicate.

As I wrote in my study all afternoon
In silence, waiting upon night
To justify terminating my sacred work,
She became, by chance, the tongued moon,
The only one who spoke to me while I,
As pilot, guided the earth in blind pursuit.

10/14/73 (04048)

The Catcher

Who really gives a shit anymore
About
            anything as quintessential
As the seventh game
                  of the WORLD
                              Series?

By chance and not method,
The radio makes my car a stadium.
I am twenty-two minds at one time
      and yet one out of time,
      inside a dying tradition.
My whole life, I've succeeded in leaving behind
      scenes that form sweet romanticisms
      we reach back for with friends
      when seeking common playgrounds.

My left palm still remembers the quick sting
From the last fastball caught behind the plate
Fifteen springs back. That pain lingers,
Residual as dying: the stinging ferocity
*

Of youth against Youth, pressing through dawn
   in search of Psyche's threshold.

Why is it now, of all times, that I
   am drawn back, within this silence,
To locker rooms in the mind's dim basement?
I can almost hear that mysterious
                        jubilation
After winning
           in extra innings after dark,
Which happened just once in growing up.

10/21/73 — [1] (04049)

[Hot-damn for handlebar mustaches]

Hot-damn for handlebar mustaches
And tandem bicycles! Seventy-five years
Peer though smoky coffee cups that disappear
One after another. I sit amidst dissonances,
Considering an age that spawned my parents.
Voices colored by arthritis and emphysema,
Couples afflicted with common silences
Stare at me as though amazed to discover
That even "longhaired freaks" have to eat
To maintain the body's precarious symbolism.
This quiet dining facility becomes a beer garden
With trellises and a Wurlitzer orchestrion.
People become something other than facsimiles
As my speculating eyes reach for the ceiling
To escape the reality of a T-bone steak
Heated with microwave celerity. It seems
Strange to imagine critics of Dreiser's age
Complaining about such genuine indiscretions
As coveting another's mistress or young wife,
When we haven't yet mastered the easy poetry
Of rhyming our lives with peaceful feelings,
Neither in deed nor, for certain, in mind.

10/21/73 — [2] (04050)

[Can it be that man is still at work]

Can it be that man is still at work
In these brown fields now that fall nears
Its apogee? Even beyond the eyes' scope,
Missouri yields to cold-night moistures.
The passing has already occurred, witnessed
By almost no one. Only the farmer,
Stifled prior to harvesting his soybeans
For flash floods, knows the virulence
Of diseased seasons and overexposures.
All I see are empty fields and brittle corn
Awaiting a white mantle a month from now.

10/22/73 (04051)

Cows ^Δ

Cows, black and brown, converge upon the ground,
Lapsed in stupid abstractions, surrounded by sounds
Filling a late-October afternoon with colors of leaves
        turning colors. They see everything
Without perceiving, as though they were humans sleeping
Out their lifetimes with the briefness of slow breathing.
The fields and barns that circumscribe them,
        by definition, as specific entities of farmyard,
Displace them for a moment in time. They might be
        naked thoughts escaped from Leonardo's brain
Or elements of space-time equations Einstein pondered.
For one second, they even become dreams Freud peeled,
With layers of meaning beneath fortress battlements.
        These creatures evoke an entire environment
        without speaking to me, as I slip silently
As a hawk through fall's quick briskness,
                            alive to possibilities
        that the cows
                have succeeded in dreaming me
Into abstractions that make us equal in intention,
        if not ultimate consequence.

10/23/73 — [1] (04052)

[The hippopotamus thinks heavy thoughts]

The hippopotamus thinks heavy thoughts
of
us.

10/23/73 — [2] (02822)

[Different shades and gradations]

Different shades and gradations
Place us in separate stalls
Before we're called for the start
Of the last race to Jerusalem.

10/29/73 (00920)

Sleeping Through

A clichéd break in routine has occurred
To me: how strange to be just waking at eight,
After all of night has dissipated. The unexpected
Frightens. To see faces in the honest light of day
Changes perspectives, persuades me to return home.

In the past, I've made this trip in an ego-capsule,
Sealed in anonymity, arriving late, leaving at dawn,
Passing between factories to make recommendations
As to status of methodology and quality standards:
A Pope going in hopeless expectation of finding peace.

Now, self-consciousness dogs me like mortality
Coming toward the fore at death. Businessmen
Force me to sit in their company, listen to whispers
That promise success, mandates of sheer genius.
I slump behind coffee — in knit shirt, no tie — thinking
How I should never have dozed back after the alarm.

10?/73 (04046)

Visiting ^Δ

Not far beyond the universe you've sparingly furnished
With fraternity paddles, marriage, and granddad's walnut bed,
The green-and-yellow commuter slips through my view
Like slightly connected friends we used to dream of keeping

Forever. Somewhere, that track has to reach its terminus.
Perhaps the ocean laps behind it. I've often wondered
How far back to our heartland that line of acquaintances
Would extend, how many trains it would take to reach us,

Were we able to reconnect scattered leaves to their trees.

Disparate noises draw my attention away from deep reveries;
Hesitation distorts recognition. I don't know the meaning
Of a newer train freighting motorcars far into the heartland
By the millions, nor can I begin to presuppose its destiny

In a land where autumn leaves lie jigsawed on every lawn.

11/9/73 — [1] (04054)

Nocturne ^Δ

We sit listening to each other's heartbeats,
The babies breathing inside babies seeking
Peaceful regions beneath amniotic strata.
In this apartment, the beginning of things
Surfaces ancient and primitive as ritual
To a savage attracted to the moon's shadow.

Now, we fly to day's edge like dying light
Leaving the sky for a less distant universe,
Then join our blood under a wine-scented canopy
Of sleep. Discovery of a common soul is night.

11/9 — [2] & 11/11/73 — [1?] (04053)

Reflections upon Finally Dreaming a Child into Being ^Δ

Time is a carpenter continuously adding to struct
ures
already earmarked for demolition,
A scruffy goat rushing blindly to the hilltop   d
To survey each new ascending leap on its trip   r
a
w
p
u
to
the
ultimate
p
l
u
n
g
e.
Somewhere inside an echo traveling above the canyon,
we discourse on the merits of procreation,
reach impasse beneath surging white peaks
That penetrate sight. With astonishing lightness,
We press blindly through improbable Rousseau roofs
Of clouds, into a land breathing animal passions.
Two goats, leaping free as time,
dive through the universe
in endless search
for the origin
of future
human
features.

11/10/73 (04055)

Dedication to the Arts

Poetry uplifts with slight, ineffable whispers,
Like kisses dreamed in sleeping lovers' ears,
*

Not the colossal wrenchings of heated hearts
Impassioned by the immediacy of naked legs.

My restive muse undresses Milton each evening
After taking his dictation; she sleeps by day.
The path I take to her stable late at night
Passes where Beelzebub lays sweet Aphrodite.

11/11/73 — [2?] (04056)

And Our Child Asks, "Where Did I Come From?" △

Until recently, I was led to believe that birth
Is a matter not of extraction of a body from
Within a hot body but the relaxing of taut ropes
On pulleys intricately conceived by a genius
To connect from the floor of Beelzebub's fortress,

That each of us is born out of sinful deeds,
Into sinfulness, and that every step we take
Leads to the icehouse, where we'll assume
Final earthly identity within crystalline blocks,
Be transformed into invisible see-through cubes,

That we pass down a rickety flume, its length
Arbitrary as long, to the universe's cold edge,
To join the deep and dark unending as particles
Frozen in voice, in space, inscribed in isolation
Like pterodactyls locked in fossilized rock.

Only, now, as I move toward thirty-three years
And begin to assess my tangible accomplishments,
Without success, a godly spirit informs my mind
That a child will be delivered from out the flower
Of my slightly astonished, beautifully blooming wife.

11/11/73 — [3?] (00438)

Thanksgiving Day 1973

Vagrant hunters pass through a crisp November day,
Shaping courage, endurance, and skill from the sun.

They follow their shadows along a main-line track
Of the Illinois and Rock Island, as though a space
Were made in the land to proclaim neutral grounds.

No one can shoot, nor can any creature be wounded,
During their graceful prelude to the killing time.

Soon, they will leave this noisy openness of being
For coverts, be swallowed in gloom — poor Jonahs all —
Peering through deep waters, feeling along shafts
For rabbits, squirrels, quails, raccoons, possums,

Lost to a world driving cars, typing poems, tying
Ribbons around gifts given as reminders of loving.

These dedicated humans, isolated from other humans,
Forget the painful perspective of their intrusion,
Neglect the rules governing sacred balances, push
Awkwardly toward an arbitrary convergence of shot
And hot flesh rushing to escape the quick pursuit
They encourage with grainy fluids.
                              Blood gushes out
From helpless bellies. The forest covers its life
With an invisible sheet: night seduced with light
Falsely struck from a waning sun. They are caught
In a marginless thornbush, torn across the hands
And face by eel-like branches. Miniature scratches
Mar their imagined perfection. They begin to feel
Death's dumb weight packed in their jacket linings,
As though it were the Mariner's bird-burden/curse
They're inheriting. In a frantic act of disavowal,
They throw their trophies to the earth, race away,
Leaving graveless the tortured souls of afternoon,
To return as hunted and hunters to a neutral land,

Where man, forest, and railroad track almost touch.

11/23/73 (04057)

Traveling to the Capital City ^Δ

On each side of the littered highway lie pioneers
Foraging inconveniently for a meaning to Scripture
And seasons, gratuitous reasons for rain and flood.

Shiny combines, going like towboats in water,
Move smooth as heated glue through torn fields.
They lower horizons as corn becomes tiny stubble
To be burned off or disked under earth by plows.
Inhuman spirits swirl in prairie-wide smoke-fires
Rising above the land. The harvest sleeps
In barns and silos. Cows, in solemn retreat, unite
In wide space. Sows, with young hung to their teats
Like wash beneath pins on a windy day,
Repeat an awkward quest toward freedom.
Sheep disturb nothing at all for their bleatings,

As we speed to Springfield over the Old State Road,
Sliding by, behind glass, in abstract disdain, to shop
The city for plastic-and-glitter Christmas gifts.

11/24/73   (04058)

Omens: On Dreaming a Child into Being ^Δ

Leaving home frequently becomes a train ride,
A Lionel track-gang car going back and forth
(I see it yet, racing its plastic, orange body
Against itself, always out of the mind's corner)
Over a system of intermingled tracks whose net-
Work touches all prairie towns, kisses flats
Rolling down Mississippi valleys. No friends
Are ever waiting at strange gates to greet me,
No children tugging at my bulky briefcase,
Only people performing very specific services
To make me feel secure in the enemy's kingdom.
My blood courses with turbulent, washing strokes
Against my eardrums. A heavy rumbling, deep
Like a ship's turbine in the secret recesses,
Throbs; my pulse surfaces beneath the wrists.
The idea of being — and, then, completely alone —
Has blown imaginations far greater than mine
In scope. I can't resolve the base chemistry
Involved in turning human sperm into a species
Capable of reasoning and squirming upstream
For justifications of making money or hunting
In fields for surviving relics of sacred lives.
*

Each time intimations of an explanation creep
Inside a timely invitation to banquet with Christ,
Sheer fright brings me to my knees; white silence
Stings my brain, leaves painful, burning lesions
To be cauterized in a dumb numbing caused by God
In His grieving futility. The Son-of-a-Bitch
Doesn't want me to break free or see Him
Seated on a throne in a field of pure manure
Or know that He ordered the forces of Ethiops
To isolate me, keep me from creating, not out of sodomy,
A child, to defile, with its perfection, an image
Generations of nuns and fat, flatfooted monks
Have managed to blemish with too many pious
Improprieties. Goddamnit! My child will be
An angel washed in the somber, mortal light
Of an immaculate conception, baptized inside
An eye seeing from out a mind coerced by death
To endure an environment in its last stages
Of infinity. Bless my unborn baby girl
Or boy. May it be ordinary to the extreme
Edge of eternity's ethereal, peaceful regions.
May there be just a tiny piece of clean land
Upon which its decency can reach to one person,
That, together, they might form an open circle
Both closing in and closing out friends of man.

11/28/73 (04059)

New Athens Spacey †

Some dumb son-of-a-bitch hung a crescent,
Clear as pure alcohol in a black bottle,
Against my tired eyes — stars

I'm at it again, like a crazed hatter
Stitching madly to produce his quota
Of items for some arbitrary stipend,
Finishing the beginnings of another store.
Everything I breathe on turns to

11/29/73 — [1] (02823)

At the Midnight Hour

Like desultory speech, I stutter through night,
Leaping between strange lands to create sleep
For the combustion-chambered lungs to breathe
At a less abnormal pace for a brief season.

Nothing comes of insistent dreaming. Fantasies,
Conceived in gingerbread beaded with raspberries,
Camphor, and jasmine, explode phantasmagorically,
Leaving me more awake than before dozing deep.

Spiders come creeping like hot water leaking
From a rusty faucet — creatures suspended
Above my head from invisible umbilici.
I give birth to fears of inordinate weight.

Pains from false labor insinuate my eyes.
The lids flicker as though touched by fire.
A hundred public debtors pass, on their way
To private stockades hiding behind my brain,

Straining to break fetters my imagination
Has placed upon them. Who are they, anyway,
If not specters the spider has had trained
To come unto him, waifs made comfortable

In the inestimable dislocation isolation
Has branded into their faces? And even I
Am among them as fighter and fantasizer,
A creator of dreams that reduce existence

To viewing a group of traveling vagaries
Confined to timeless mime, caged in sleep.
Sometimes, no day dawns without debtors
Dicing with a Christ trying to make money

To pay for my silence. He at times belies
The sticky-footed spider who weaves me
Into my own dreams by setting a silk net
Of snowflake intricacy to catch the fly.

I am the net, the night, a dicing Christ,
The dream tortured by fine complexities
Answerable to no reasoning mind, the fly
Disguised as Savior, Godhead, tiny man.

11/29/73 — [2] (04060)

Looking Backward

Already, at 6 a.m., the sky is all red
Over blue, with just a few white striations
Piercing the great expanding overlay.
A bridge spans all time placed behind
My mind and a future too new to view
In perspective. My body enters the day
Like an auto surviving assembly line,
Crossing the bridge for the first time.
My system of highly refined components
Seeks to find a small piece of past
Adaptable to its need for peacefulness.
On the other side (but there's no stopping)
I see Copley's strait-laced women
Posing at sidewalk cafés with Sloan's
Dreiserian nouveaux riches and Homer
Rowing the Schuylkill with Louie Sullivan.
Laser beams fracture brain waves, life.
I choose to be John Roebling or Eads
Overseeing construction on his bridge,
Being transported one hundred years back
And forth, neither start nor terminus
Clearly defined, no tolls to throw,
Only the slow horse-and-buggy manners
Of people concerned, at least visibly,
With basic commonweal and the right
To be alone despite a species identity.
When there's no more fuel to move cars,
The bridge will still stand to take man
On foot, hand in hand, to the other side.

11/30/73 — [1] (04061)

Paolo and Francesca

The gentle bearing of his sweet disposition
Is the ocelot's languid flow at full speed.
She feels it most when he needs it least
For the easy security she breathes into him.
Musician soothing an entire jungle with flute,
*

Teacher reading haikus to a full auditorium
Of two, a priestess ordaining a sensuality
Both inspire by their very nakedness: together
They make a harmony of Yeatsian bouquets
To be worn by both for reasons of safety
Against demons disguised as love poems
Begging interpretation. She sees beyond bones
That form merely the crudest articulation
Of his extravagant being, beyond the skin
That amplifies his pulse to an atmosphere
Rarefied by a promise of their near arrival.
Her eyes wear a mysterious incandescence,
Rhyme with each other in perfect meter.
He repeats vows made in an oceanside park
Above a beach-blown eucalyptus grove. Slowly,
Gone silent as ten miles high, they go out
Toward distant Eden, leaving behind in flight
Their life, that they might repeat marriage
Forever, that two new dreams might meet
Forever, that man might not negate himself.

11/30/73 — [2] (04062)

La vida es sueño

The shattered patterns of my passing life
Scatter confetti-like across a horizon
Whose false brightness is afterglow, the high
Below euphoria, a lost future's expectations
Promised to youth, taken in the prime,
Then forgotten like the mottled designs
Obsolescence makes by pressing its face
To the glass behind which we dress for death.
Confessions are sought too late for truth
To have any consequence upon the state
Of a naked soul on trial for its life.
Crimes of hasty love, latent castrations
Of the psyche, blatant heterosexual tendencies
Emerge from the fading chrysalis, collapse
Icarian. The handcrafted wax formations
Dissolve. Disembodied apparitions disappear
*

In fires burning in fields filled with shades
Whose shadows recognize my base silhouette,
Braced against night like a precarious bum
Holding up a lamppost. A curious shrill
Stills the cosmos, suspends the earth's turning
Momentarily. A million familiar voices sing
Celebrations to the Messiah. Jesus, am I dying
Or merely suffering the lonely exacerbations
Of future pain? Am I capable of dying alive,
Leaving nothing behind but material ideas?
They bury me beneath my feet, a shadow
Confined to an unchanging season of noon-
Times, alive as a mute moon in a galaxy
Gone cold, reaching to touch a sun-cluster
Just above the false brightness covering me.
Sacred illuminations, you flabby bastards,
Receive my ministrations! Bring me peace
Through the prospect of this long, loud night,
About to conceive me in its great womb-wedge!
Is this death, or might I just be the child
Bulrushed beyond hushed gardens of Genesis
Into a temporal persistence of mortal dreams?

12/4/73 (04063)

[Even the strongest spirits cringe under the cold,] †

Even the strongest spirits cringe under the cold,
Imagine bodies floating into space, frozen

12/7/73 — [1] (02824)

Continuities △

One child, born of two mild children of God,
Plods over stones made of years, neatly laid
At various spots in the stream to make crossing
Easier, keep the journeyer from getting wet.

For reasons never questioned, he has never
Settled into patterns answerable to reason,
Never stepped into the precarious water
In his dexterous escape from wild creatures
That threaten his blessed, ineffable contrariness.

Only the hope of finding a sacred lady to mate with
Sustains his painful flight through a forest
Deeper than life, wider than the highest banks
That rise along the new stream he contemplates.
Her reflection on the surface sees him seeking,
Reaching, brings him to his knees to give a kiss

She receives in silence. Two mild children
Of God retreat beyond two eternities, meet
Their ageless parents where both streams touch
Beneath earth. Circles fan out like roses
Opening, close upon their disappearing union.
The family assembles to consecrate a birth.
A child strains. The stones take his mild weight.

12/7/73 — [2] (04064)

Litterbug

Shredded, foil-lined cigarette packs,
                                        abandoned
                                        beer bottles
Partially afloat in every hallway recess,
Odors released from coffins two weeks buried —
These are merely the manifestations, residue,
Stinking, sleazy cellmates of a long last night,
Gone stale as strokes on an overworked still life
I've posed for away from home over the last three days.

I have to pass these familiar landmarks
Each time I leave this high-class establishment,
Traverse with judgments suspended, telling myself
I'm a sensible man, aged to accept untidiness.

Yet what I can't quite understand is why I spend
One third of my entire span sleeping,
*

Stretching to touch smooth-breasted dreams
That veer past when I awaken. What sanctity is there
In ordered morality and clean bedsheets shared by people
Who've never undressed before each other
Or known the brief perfection of illicit lovemaking?

12/8/73 (04065)

Staying Somewhere near New Athens

Jan . . .
  first snow

Incipient snowflakes, blown wet
As miniature washrags against my face,
Hang interminably, create voids
In space that break Friday-night silence
By the speechless design of their form
In private conversation with my mind.

The white membrane contains visions
Of you swimming through atmospheres
Pure as aqueous humor. You blink
Inside my eyes' pergolas. Tigers
Leap through fiery hoops to stoops
Anchored inside iron environments.

We are flakes aflame, blazing hoops
Moving to encircle all leaping beings
Given to secret urgings. The fire,
Alive beneath the heat, singes both
Of us equally. Our blisters are finches
Riding a graceful tiger's flinching back

Into freewheeling. Once more, slow snow
Washes vision. Empty signboards
Advertise a circus three months folded.
Head-beamed flakes are splayed upon my windshield
Like carbide spotlights touching sequins
Beaded to your high-spinning body,

And I settle into forgetting near a mirror
Filling riverbeds with melting dreams.
*

We are forever caught in the brief passage
A flake takes on its way to complete re-
Integration, as passage and flake become one
With our original breathing mass of being.

12/14/73 (04066)

Dale

Her gift,
12/25/73

So many times I've imagined seeing you
In a monstrous universe of Goya's Black Paintings,
Tangled in animal seaweed, riding the back
Of a scaly pterodactyl, a queen's daughter

Lost within an endlessly acred estate,

Whose plaintive screams are beggars dying
In the streets for lack of something to eat,

Whose speculations turn to specters doomed
To live in monasteries frightened minds seek,

Whose tiny body is a mere battalion
Guarding an entire island set apart
From an earth quarantined for paranoia
And diseases affecting base sensitivity,

Caught upon the axle time's motor turns

In a balancing act, juggling a genius
Torn between falling into steaming vats
And leaping, through a hole in the soul,
Into Tiepolo's ceilinged fantasies. Heat

Touches the queen's sweetest daughter,
Disturbs an equilibrium that keeps reason
On visible paths through the deep forest
She's entered. Invisibility keeps her

From being seen during daylight hours.
Nighttime blinds her to the seeing beasts
That would draw her away from destiny.
The future is a focus her eye corrects.

Yet nightmares dissolve. Imagination soars.
The forest opens onto familiar expanses
Green as soft apples ripening. She comes
Running, breathing a million real kisses,

Intact, bathed in afterglow by the trials
Only she knows are born out of solitude.

12/15/73 (04067)

Drinking from the Edge of the World

Jan's canvas

Someone must have sneaked up on the sleeping lion
To tie all those violets to his scraggly mane.
So docile, almost social, is he beside the edge,
Perched with uncertainty of that depthless space,
Guarding, almost, if you will, an albino giraffe
Come from the mind's savannahs to drink gardenias
From the last great lake contained within a bag
Tied to a firmament on one side and blue horizon
On the other three. A peaceable silence dominates
The entire environment, where three sunflowers,
Stark in their gargantuan size behind the lion
Daring the albino giraffe to drink from a lake,
Grow ever taller toward a sun cracking apart
Like dry mud on a quarry bank yet held together
By law. Not even the purple leopard or its mate,
Dappled all in flesh except for flowered spots,
Recognizes what's about to happen beyond the frame,
Where one woman has already ventured, with palette
And brush poised, to encapsulate their land forever.

12/23/73 (04068)

Excommunicants on Christmas Morn

Still snow still fills Christmas morning
With slow resurrections. Masses happen
*

Beyond our scope, within cold, dim chancels,
Where only chosen souls go to rejoice.
We, the children cut loose from salvation,
Muse over our meager earthly alternative
Of loving each other as though we were
The Lord's disciples in loving and
Living under a canopy each holds high
With hopes of giving birth to new lives
Worthy of Christmases outside religion.
Soon, even the chancels will melt away.

12/25/73 — [1] (04069)

Note to Jan

Calm your ass!
Anticipating this flight
Will pass like the flight itself
Before sun sets . . . if you calm your ass.
Otherwise . . .

12/26/73 — [1] (00744)

[I love you!] * †

I love you! *

I admire you! — ugh!
You're swell!

The stained perfection of a tainted petal

*[This portion written by Jan Brodsky]

12/26/73 — [2] (02825)

Bill △

Only a madman, crazed   stained
                              attenuated   glazed/dazed
                              concatenated   fantasia-splayed,
Could have ever made such splendid tempestuizations as those exploded
Upon that isolated and highly restricted plain inside his nervous brain:

Quentin riding a train in both directions,
Flushing the same crap along both halves of the track
                                                    stretching
Between his solitary years and back
                              to the stained burl roots
His ancestors dug, shoveled, dragged, axed, fired, even, at times,
          Carved into lattice and gingerbread architectures
                    Mansioned in magnificent silhouette
                         Against a trammeled fanlight,
                                                    the South . . .

Ike thriving on ancient codes
Revived each season, deep in an endless backwoods pathos
The mind seeds with animals
                              and occasional old people to love them,
To hunt and seek the illusive ghosts of all their ancestors with
                                                    out
          Seizing the palpability
                              of their steaming blood and guts
Upon some cold autumnal morn . . .

Addie traveling in a wagoned coffin wombing Cash
     Inside his absolute philosophical carpentry;
                    Vardaman within a live fish caught and boned
Between the miasma of ten-year-old genius — an idiot, dolt, and dreamer;
Dewey Dell swelling within an unwanted fecundity;
          Darl and Jewel saddled to a maddened horse
Clearing the entire sky in a single nighttime, and lost forever;
Lastly Anse, taking a duck-legged wife,
          As though to protect an outrageous sanctity of family
                              sol i darity . . .

These figments of a kindled spirit reaching to speak to spirits speaking
          To each other in a galaxy resurrected from
                    Nonexistence,

Those pronouncements found in urns buried in an earth no other poet
        Ever broke open with his meager tools

Help to explain the perfectly beautiful lunacy
        He never could quite contain within a solitary paragraph
He could never quite refrain from embroidering with universal gossamer
He never could quite sustain for the limited years bequeathed him.

12/26/73 — [3]   (00063)

The Third Coming

The ghosts of past days gasp in desperation.
Even eternity approximates certain finality.
So total a death is dislocation for creatures
Grown used to changeless anticipations
That life becomes a last bastion, burning
On a plain tainted by human beings in flames

Lifting from disappointed souls sifting smoothly
From corpses passing through the tight neck
To ash heaps beneath glassy penitentiaries
Surrounding experience. Miniature pyres
Light the way to dusty caves engraved
In the earth's surface. A lady's wrinkled face,

Inviting sin despite her age, begs to be touched
By every son going off to war, every drunk
Hung by the salaried spike to a corporate wall,
All poets and charming, naked ladies of Lesbos
Dreaming deceits into being as sweet occupation
For their concupiscent existence. The ghosts

Whisper among themselves. Someone notices
The regulator clock has begun to stutter. Both hands
Catch, lock in slender bending against gears
Hidden beneath a yellowed circumambience
Framed by a million explorations and patents.
It's not, they know, as though time stops

But merely lags to recalibrate inner windings
With magnetisms aligned to the mind of God.
*

And so they wait as if this new preoccupation
Might project a profound philosophy of afterlife
To generations of ghosts not yet disembodied
Or gain them insight into a dismal unending

Only now threatened by abrupt discontinuation
As protean energy and protozoan slime collide.
In an isolate pond beyond Earth's peopled cities,
A colossus rises, breathing. The ghosts shudder
Behind a guise of all recognizable knowledge.
The creature slowly opens its eyes and gasps.

1/22/74 (04071)

Animus

The dappled spirit rises inside its dwelling.
        A slender privacy, at best, protects
The shell from a persistent wearing away
        One day at a time. Dawn shows black
As the scratchy insides of a burlap sack.
        The heart, seeking new frontiers to kiss,
Ventures out blindly, each beat as critical
        As a prospector's steps along deep cliffs
On his way up out of a valley, loaded with gold.
        Even the eyes fly ahead to scout aliens
Trained in the fatal arts of complacence
        And ugliness. A gap glowing roseate
Opens just ahead — chrysalis or dream-hole,
        Difficult to know. Two butterflies collide
In a sensual, bending spiral, alive as light
        Framed by their transparent wings.
It's the unseen design that reminds me of you.

1/23/74 (04072)

Repossessed by the Devil

"Christ Died For You!
What Are You Doing For Him?"

Above most of the city, sitting
On tarpaper, seeing these words
In déjà vu immediacy from the roof
Like a whole philosophy come to me
                                        intact,
Recognizing monads scattered over ages,
Rearranging meanings intended or other
                                        wise,
Deciding Christ never even realized
He died without notice or concerned Him-
Self with consequences beyond the grave,

I conclude there is no terrestrial reason,
No ethereal appointment needing keeping,
For me to leap from this tenement roof

Just to prove that I am dying for Him.

1/24/74 — [1] (04073)

The Old Trouser Factory

Off to one side, like a rotted log
Caught sideways in a sluice,
The factory trembles, its red bricks
Barely sticking to its weighty frame.
The last vestiges of its paint flake
Each time the freight to K.C. scrapes
The edge of day in fleeting retrograde.
People ask nothing of the mastodon
That forms two corners of Main Street
And First. They barely recognize
It as a creature with vertebrae,
Breathing, occasionally belching steam,
Eliminating residue. It takes strength
From thread, trim, and fabric, feeding
While lying prone in a lion's slow
Melancholy beneath heated afternoons.
The beast spews short, shrill snorts
As though sewing machines were lodged
In its gut, racing erratically
*

Toward overwhelming peristalsis.
The behemoth barely renews itself
With the seasons. The species retreats,
As the need for base survival
No longer matters and leisure time
Minimizes its purpose and reason
For being in existence any longer.

1/24/74 — [2] (04074)

Four-Way Stop

To be read responsively
by minister and congregation

All in dark,
                    The twelve apostles speculate
Like the morning of original deluge,
                    On odds out of Las Vegas.
Morning conceals its thieves, disguised
                    Religion has even reached Tipton,
As half-ton-pickup truckers and hundred-head-herd cattle-
                    Despite the catastrophe
Men come in from under the elements.
                    Illiteracy breeds through bigotry
Only one among them has ever kissed
                    And deceit. Each man sits
The earth that gives them subsistence.
                    Suspicious of each other man,
The others converse without knowledge
                    Fearful of his specious smile,
That death will infect their wheat
                    While dreams of basest fame
This season, rushing up to meet them.
                    Swell within the chosen one,
The sensitive one, gentle supplicant,
                    Preparing to carry out his mission
Dissolves into the darkness, his hand
                    Against all odds, against God's Son,
Reading God's will on a knife blade.
                    Within the hour, without restraint.
                              *

Afraid to refuse the black purgation,
                    A blemished victory is at hand
He stirs, steps out of cold marble,
                    As he presses the knife blade
Chiseled from all human record,
                    Against the heaving chest bones
Long enough for stony sinew to move.
                    Of his unsuspecting neighbor.
A latent sun explodes. Twelve men
                    Soon, all of the townspeople know
Scatter to repair their implements,
                    The one is dead who came
Conclude leases on their existence.
                    From the city to adjust his life.
Only one remains to squander the hours:
                    His lands are untrespassed upon,
A ragged scarecrow hanging on a pole.
                    As his name is slowly forgotten.

1/25, 4/3?, & 4/4/74 — [2–3?] on 4/4   (04075)

After Reading with Buck

The first words after the first steps after the first breaths after birth
                    Converge
Like Siamese ideas, back to back,
                    Upon the nervous psyche of the child
                    Surfeited with love, cursed by overprotection,
Words that first well up out of needs to satisfy thirst and hungry stomachs,

                    That attach themselves
                    To the Siamese ideas
                    Of feeding and sleep,

Words that leap through colored illustrations, from houses to people's faces,

                    Stairs and chairs to see,
                    To read from memory and
                    Pronounce aloud, a mouse,
                    Some cheese, a needle to
                    Thread with rhyme, clouds

To fill an unreal air with familiar friends, whose various shapes share a sky
               That widens as the imaginative mind
               Comes slowly advancing out of hiding places,
Words attendant to a new tongue tasting soothing fruits and concupiscences

        Consuming the fired soul,
        Touching another's lips,
        Skin, unwilling or unable
        To control a body's whim,

Words that finally turn to silences toward the end of certain persons' lives,
               As they were in childhood, before merging
               With clean waters filling dry streams
From nearby mountains, silences the old know as echoes of the lookout's cries

        From a high crow's-nest
        On sighting land-birds
        Far out at sea, a beach,
        Then figures resembling
        Men indefensibly feeble

           At the edge at the end of the world,
           Where excursions to the being's core begin
And first words after the first steps after the first breaths after birth
        Emerge.

1/26/74   (04076)

Redemption ^Δ

The men convene again to speculate.
Designs align themselves at season's onset
Like snowflakes on December windowpanes.
Surfacing patterns are images swimming in hypo.
Weave, texture, and thumb-feel congeal,
Solidify in type on white summary sheets
That pass down tracks toward destinations
Stationed on maps each individual draws
With his pulsing arteries. Lot numbers
Dumbfound; models and descriptions fit
The general complexity of the marketplace.

The men grow impatient, anticipating
Their new swatch lines. Their compliance
With taste dictated by committee of one
Becomes sublimated creativity wasted
On a herd selling itself to a greater herd
Waiting to receive word of the coming.
Yet their leader guarantees success.
"Go! Go on fleet feet! Go to the people!
Propagate philosophies cloaked in plaid,
Reversible rayon-and-wool-blended vests
And fully constructed double-knit suits!"

"Go! Take religion to the outer regions
Dressed in simulated suede and leather trim!
Even God, in all His naked humility,
Has never felt a more definite imperative
To go about His invisible ways bedecked
In fantastical fabrics, mystical garments
Stitched inexorably with golden threads.
Go! The meeting is ended! Suspend disbelief!
Sell yourself and you'll sell your soul!
The product is God, and each one of you
Is His Son! Go out! Return to your homes!"

2/1/74   (04077)

Skaters

Another country Sunday afternoon drains away
Inexorably as recollections fading with age.
This particular day glides yet on a surface
Not turmoiled by night, like a child skating
On slender ice above a lake, flying gracefully
Through an hour's fabled Arabian daydreams.

Only a few telltale scratches are manifest
On the buckled glass, beyond which cars pass
And clouds gather imperceptible momentums,
Scratches that might really be roadways
Made by a child's glazed runners, or maybe
Elongated cracks in a surface slowly breaking.

2/3/74   (04078)

Fueling and Loading

Gnomelike vehicles with headlight memories
Serpentine toward openings in the worm's belly.
One hides beneath the giant; perhaps it's absorbed
Or leaves in unseen retreat. The worm sleeps
Without suggesting its latent energies or that
It fears forces that would drag it down in flight
From an enemy close behind. The worm stirs
To resonances from liquid entering its thin skin,
Lumps of leather and cardboard being dumped within,
Sober feet stepping repeatedly along its length.
Soon, it sets up minimal mechanical responses
To charges generated from the sum total of tactile
Sensations embracing its stalled being. It flexes,
Writhes, checks its tentative balance and headings,
Changes direction twice, then takes off to survive
Itself, its insensate purpose being safe arrival
At its next destination, completion of the cycle
Ad infinitum, until it's ready to return to earth.

2/7/74 (04079)

Dreaming the Artist into Being

Awakening early into a complete nakedness
Of wrinkled skin and twisted bone unfolding —
A corolla opening without witness, clouds
Dissolving above a rain forest, abalone shells
Trapping rainbows beneath patinas — my soul
Sleeps yet between the V the legs make
Seated beside this thirty-fourth-floor framed canvas,
Painted in reverse on glass. Down below,
No concrete people scurry like acres of hay
Caught in a prairie wind or fly like saints
Congregating in destiny; no creatures hurry
From entrance to street to entrance to buy
Identities they might never wear, just carry
Endlessly in a plastic bag filled with air.
An engaging quietude congests my disbelief.

2/10/74 — [1] (04081)

Tiffany Shade

Oh, that New York were forever Sunday,
With Comfort Tiffany combing the beaches
Washed by the brownstone Sound, seeking glass
And pebbles worn smooth by the sea, questing
Gradations of iridescence lying in the sand,
Awaiting the heat of his alienated genius.

Even the rising sun, captured in massive reflection
Against the face of a truncated skyscraper,
Assumes a newer shape. Superimposed mullions
Form a leaded network on a burning surface
That might become apple blossom, wisteria, dragon-
Fly as bronze day heightens to golden night

And the shade fills out with pieces that might be
Translucent lives of those who illumine the city.

2/10/74 — [2]   (04080)

Skyscrapers

Even daydreams, like coins left in pockets,
Gather fuzzy dust, lose their gleam
When handled too frequently. Departures
Creep quietly, quickly, into the weaving hand,
Leaving unfinished seams, raveling edges,
At the mind's most fragile extremities.

Only the slender pinnacles, seen from above
Through three thousand feet of scudding cloud cover,
Help maintain a whisper of waning dignity
Knitted into man's fantasies of achievement
Conceived and executed in heightened exile
By a few for everybody to pray into being.

The vast, graceful immediacy of wrought iron
And concrete, cast, by genius, in colossal molds,
Whose unfolding is the cold rose holding close
Into its bud, explodes whole into ornament.
For moments briefly beyond belief, we sleep
Between the beams, inside the riveted sweep

Time assigns to destiny through humanity's
Monuments, like skeletons within skeletons
Inside skeletons, breathing the haughtiness
Of calculably feeble beings driven by desire
For self-mastery, almost retrieving the day-
Dream, as the slender pinnacles forget the eye.

2/12/74 (04082)

Carousel

For Kroid,
course clerk of the crack meet

All those bodies flying about an oval,
Bearing tribal motifs, coats of many colors,
Competing with each other's breathing apparatus,
Striding thought for thought, idea and psyche
Knitted into the tight, gliding, pistonlike legs,
Breaking into final sprint when even the arms
Are spent, dreaming possibly of diving wet
Into pools of naked, sleeping jigsaw people
Or taking leave of Earth through deep tunnels
Beneath the bleachers to the immediate right,

Until someone with a whistle and an insight
Decides to rewind all those graceful bodies,
Send them flying forever through memory,
Upon the sweep-second time has devised
To account for generations coursing the oval.

2/16/74 (04083)

The Ages of Man

Whispers of pre–Korean War boys,
Who grew in crew-cut, ducktail love
With pixie, cheerleading grade-school sweethearts,
Sift forward and back like electric stings
Barely bringing twitches to the eyelids.

283 FI Corvettes, two-seat T-Birds
Roar toward me. Distant drumbeats
Record the end of senseless defeats
In an Asia none of us had ever seen
Except through Brubaker's fear at Toko-Ri.

Reverence for memorabilia and trivia
Is our legacy, the leather handles
Of weighty baggage carried by people
Ever on the move, forever on the increase.
The near-fanatical insistence upon things

Sought for their palpability, solidity,
In an unfurnished universe persists,
As though loneliness were a saucy lady
Needing bought pleasures to survive
In a quiescent state behind the shadows
Each projects against the others' screens.

We grow fat. Our hair goes gray
Or thin upon the pate. Stomach muscles give way
Like hillsides sliding behind heavy rains.
Features we once achieved forget us
In the immediate flash. Death advances

The calendar's pages with bony fingers,
Plays croquet with fate, takes chances
From us clumsily. We grasp straws,
Cling to the things we've always agreed
Are perfect companions on our journey.

Only, toward the end, there's no recognition,
No passion. Remaining zeal is the body's dirt
Draining away after the last bath. Nothing's
Left except the two of us, absolutely bereft,
Senile, feeble, wrinkled as babies being born.

2/20/74 (04084)

Heiress and Novelist

Two people, one held hostage for her father's money,
The other in exile for tenets held against the state,
*

Both retreating, each in search of a kind of peace,
Eternal release from confinement, to walk freely
Through fields and city streets, to return now
From out the animal's den to the family of man.

It's almost understandable that wealth might spark
Such violence, but the threat derived from ideas
Buried beneath metaphor is difficult to conceive,
Considering that so few beings can really appreciate
The virtuosities used to disguise everyday speech,
Raise it above its communicative bark and growl.

2/21/74 (04085)

The Magician's Demise

The magician's physician administers him drugs.
The master of tricks and alchemical postures
Has been sick for almost a year. Prescriptions
Taken from coven logs and old-fashioned cook-
Books have restricted his recuperation. Age
Has passed down no written rules for undoing
The straitjacket that human physical limitations
Bind about the lunatic trying to survive against
The blind, three-eyed Cyclops guiding his life.

The high-hatted prestidigitator
Slips into a deep sleep. He sees his days
Leap like rabbits, ducks, and gay scarves
From beneath the hidden brim
Of circular music he once held in smiles
Given him to bequeath shining eyes laughing,
Who wandered uncalled unto his calling
From everywhere just to see him perform
Miracles and myriad inexplicable ambiguities,

A life's passion for dealing in unanswerables
On the chance that one might answer his need
To be identified. Now, the leaping rabbits
Scurry beneath the briars; ducks fly upward
And out of sight. Only light-blue silk scarves
Linger, wispy as angels' breath or sky.
*

He reaches out, grabs a cloth as it passes by.
Something draws it and him through a hand,
Turns him inside out, into disappearance.

2/25/74 — [1?] (04087)

Eggshell and Tempera ^Δ

Trees, silos, windmills, a single steeple,
Engraved upon a desolate earthen plate
Crosshatched in melancholic hues, highlighted
With snow, dissolve in passional tridimension,
Linger Rembrandt-numb in lackluster penumbrae
Recessed in stations beyond the brain's memory.

This country is silence. Within its spaciousness,
Predestination formulates lives, engendering,
For months at a time, a seminal evanescence
Of beings in waiting for seasons of growing
And death. Even cows are without noise or motion.
Each sunset is a covenant of graceful repose.

Perhaps an abandonment or massive evacuation
Has occurred throughout this region. Possibly, no people
Ever arrived with dreams, in leaky wagons, to seed
Permanence and harvest rooted denominations secured
By marriage and family burial. Maybe this solitude
Is nothing more than February being the demon.

2/25/74 — [2?] (04086)

Adoration ^Δ

Being born, seeing before the beginning,
Then flying back with you through vast expanses

To uninformed inspirations, breathing love songs
Composed along the way, singing children into being,

Conceiving three from two, two from one unification,
One from many fused souls controlled by order,

Being born in ginger fields powdered with curry,
Sleeping in the same dream, simultaneously dreaming

Two sleeps lined with ginkgo and bonsai trees,
Filled with sleek, sprinting borzois, elephants

Gentle as babies' bellies . . . scented in sweet oleander,
We emerge, dance with certainty, return in peace —

From none, one minute, to triumvirate, whose emergence
Goes noticed by every poet reaching his love poem.

2/25/74 — [3?] (00439)

Motel Stopover

A sole pariah in isolation this morning.
Too early for the cynic to scorn people
Or political misdeeds. No bodies stir.
On leaving this restaurant, I might expect
To encounter splintered bodies in heaps
And shrapnel scraps embedded in wood
Along the dizzy corridors to my number.

Last night's memory of a mistress found
And had is today's lucky penny lost
In a muddy gutter. Only the martini's
Aftertaste reminds me of hasty escapes
I might have made from identity tags
Hanging around my neck, on my cold toe.
No one claimed to know who I might be

Or recognized my features from the others
Lying on icy slabs. A thousand noons
And names wear the same face, speak like
Memorized routines of production-line
Operators soldering two mornings together,
Fusing dreams from printed circuits, as if
My purpose were to be the perfect machine.

2/26/74 (04088)

KKK △

The mailman in gray beneath fur hat;
Farmers waiting on their land
To wake from suspension, in town
For the purpose of reasserting their being
On the sleeping earth; the manager
Of car parts at the Ford dealership;
Construction boys in membership caps
And mustaches, mud-dried work boots —
All profane to an acceptable degree,
Repeating responsively patter expected
Of a particular assumed identity,
An entire community of thought
Locked like metaphors in motives
Ulterior to ships on smooth surfaces,
Withholding judgments for meetings
Hidden away in evening's recesses,
Thinking, "Look upon our mighty deeds,
All ye who dare trespass, and pray."

2/27/74 — [1] (04089)

Waybill

The hours are tractor-trailers
With names replacing dates.
I'm the highway, absorbing vibrations
Time dissipates in desperation
As it tries to reach brain-stations
Routed within the mind's terrain.

Such freight as that which sleeps
Beneath surface discouragements
Days keep locked in vest pockets
Is the main reason for going ahead,
Making the delivery without delay.
The fragile shipment is always me.

2/27/74 — [2] (04090)

Crocheting Solomon's Seal ^Δ

We are caught up in the fingers' exercise
As needles weave melody and crochet nets
In a perpetual letting-go of tensions.
My eyes are mesmerized by flying light
Unwinding from skeins of man-made plant
And animal; hers concentrate on the design.

Twogether, naked on our bed, being free
From prying eyes for a while, breathing,
We rejoice in the dazzlement of creation,
As though silence itself were the child
Growing inside her uterus, the fetus
Become bunting, a godly seal of Solomon.

Solomon's seal: an emblem consisting of two triangles form-
ing a six-pointed star, formerly used as an amulet to guard
against fever

3/17/74 (00440)

A Strange Kind of Birth

Terminal infirmities,
                                    futile recuperations occur.
The circle widens with each stone thrown
                                    at the lake's aging face.
Off in a corner of all being,
An opaque spasm of fluid; a bag of waters
Containing a helpless adult spirit convulses;
                                    contractions begin.

Pale-gloved hands stand poised at the womb
To shake the newborn to death, slap its back,
Send it flying,
                                    as the wasted, misshapen form
Passes out of the panting body, beyond life,
*

A harbinger covered bloody, mucous,
    Quitting the earth without so much as a whimper
            or tiny excuse.

3/19/74 (00441)

[Such dumb creatures, crutched by their comforts,] †

Such dumb creatures, crutched by their comforts,
Afraid and unable anymore to

Someone just born, an adult full-blown

3/23/74 — [1] (02836)

Thirty Years Has Janny

March 23, 1974

In the midst of spring's beginning,
When euphoria and traditional memories
Achieve coalescence in peaked birth
And hopes survive inside gardenias
Growing live on the air, just then,
Snow turns your lovely eyes' landscape
To valleys seeded in white ash,
Strewn with ravenous small birds
Desperate for food. Just then, people
Retreat into pergolas vibrantly fluid
As music, where staghorn ferns and snapdragons
Thrive. The mind's inside is in bloom.
Its silence is nutriment. Just then,
Despite the darkness, you and I find
Our shadows lost in the last sun,
Their patterns come home today as flakes
*

Racing from God to Earth to celebrate
The few beautiful hours of your rebirth.

3/23/74 — [2] (04091)

Turnout ^Δ

Reveries deep as twisted history
Surface from oblique centuries,
Stream by my mystified eyes
As we rise from the green table
Spread in springtime ginghams and calicos.

Memories of other, earlier flights
Redeem forgotten dreams from nets,
Return the sepulchral brain from death
To a soul-searching worship
Of birth. The earth diminishes,

And as we turn out and away,
I see innumerable babies cradled
On smooth air, or cloudy resemblances
Of devastated spirits long gone
From the common onrush and increase.

I dream ghetto faces and physiques,
Tenement eyes, the saintly lives
Of inebriated priests and testy poets,
Contrite, condescending, mere skeletons,
Whispers of beings previously dismantled

Or in the process of fetal creation.
In this sphere, all possibilities
Are easily conceived. Each resolution,
Every verse, imaginable crime,
And martyrdom coexists in an ice floe

Moving through eternity's two bluffs —
Congealed metaphors. They reach perfection
As fulgent stars, sun and moon mated,
Controlling the tides, cycles of lives.
I fly from birth to birth forever.

3/27/74 — [1] (00701)

Being Beach and Ocean ^Δ

The beach, lying
Beyond plate glass,
Inviting the waves,
Excites tender sensualities
Merely by being.

The notion of flowing
Reaches the beach with song.
Being itself
Is the essence of ocean. Its tides
Are always on pitch.

The poet, being
Mindful of ocean and beach,
Is possessed by each.
His verse is their sole existence;
Their being justifies him.

3/27–28/74 — [2] on 3/27 and [1] on 3/28 & 3/7/76
  (00703)

Arriving at Point of Americas II ^Δ

Just the quiet excitement of being at one with a beach
Beside a somnolent afternoon sea, stepping tentatively
To avoid breeched driftwood, corals, Portuguese men-of-war
Is sufficient reward for tender feet and flabby belly.

The sheer delight in seeing an abandoned sandcastle
Become Machu Picchu, and half-naked people at worship,
Posing in self-adoration, praying to their sacred skin,
Affords the proper ambiguity that frees imagination,

Allows the priestly mind to practice vows of abstinence
Without heeding resonances set up by the aroused flesh.
These people don't see my shadow or celebrate my arrival
As I take leave of the beach, the beautifully strewn beach.

I've arrived. I've finally reached my promised state of grace.
All that remains before sleep is to clean the tar off my feet.

3/27–28/74 — [3] on 3/27 and [2] on 3/28   (00702)

The Act of Writing $^\Delta$

I stream down the beach, dotted with bathers,
And race against my perspiring self without reason,
Inspired, perhaps, by the sheer lust of running,
Of feeling the blood steaming up the throat.
Watching my feet make deepening indentations
In the water-soggy sand, I look back to see
The visible fact of passage in continuous tracks
Attached to each other by threads made of speed
Weaving off a human spool of forward movement.

I rush ahead of the body's capacity for sustaining
An arbitrary beat of psychic desire to outdo
Human limitations. Legs and arms unfold;
Eyes go blind; the machinery composed of bone
And muscle conspires against the coordinating self
To throw off my timing, collapse my fired lungs.

Finally, the beach recedes from infinity, arrives
At a sandy point where the cramped feet converge.
My heaving chest is a furnace being stoked with air.
The body's blood runs backward, from vein to artery,
Toward a confused heart. Hours pass in minutes;
Seconds become consecutive daytimes, until the body
Prepares for its return journey against the breeze.
Only, now, as I retreat, my footprints stay hidden;
There's no factual proof that I ever passed this way.

As far as flat, the beach is a sheet of manuscript
Neatly erased, speckled with shell-fibers.
A strange sensation translates the entire landscape
Into a page ripped from my notebook and scattered.
Perhaps I never took off racing at all. Maybe
It was just my imagination running ahead of the pen.

3/28/74 — [3] (00704)

Still Life: Caladium

Green marbling corals the softest pinks.
Each leaf is suspended in vascular dazzlement.
*

An entire rain forest contained in a pot
Of white baked clay, a complete society
Of aging youthful leaves and new blooms,
Unfurls from rigid stems like sea scrolls
Ancients once filled with the lives of people
And read from sunrise to dusk continuously.

Caladium, arranged to seduce the inner eye,
Your silence stupefies all sense of sight
And sound. Your bright profusion is a beatitude
Spoken through God's body. Caladium, alive
Inside the breathing nimbus you radiate,
Whether divine corona, rainbow, or cloud,
You alone have been spared the keen awareness
That we are dying despite our radiant selves.

3/29 & 4/4/74 — [2-3?] (00705)

Point of Americas II: The Rocks ^Δ

This man-made spit of colossal rocks,
Lifted into place as if by a godlike race
Of giants, or gnomes, discloses Port
Everglades, sits like a ship's prow
At the point where ocean and harbor converge.
Fishing boats drone inside the opening
Like bubbles moving through brewing tubes.
Occasional cruise ships are misty crystals
Of white ice going out with the tide,
Returning through perfectly pure turquoise.
Brown pelicans float freely in the eyes.

Alone, nailed to the sacred rocks
To endure the curative Promethean purge
Of burning forever beneath heavenly fires
Or being eaten alive, we turn toward Zeus,
Appeal to his mercies to release our dreams
From such lusty presumptuousness. The sun
Composes us as lyrical notes unhung
From a composition flowing above the wind,
Emoting sensuality. The dance of waters,
*

Lapping at the boulders, draws us together.
We delight in being elements of an endless day.

3/30/74 — [1] (00707)

Walking the Beach ^Δ

For beloved Saul, my father

We go out together after all the bathers
Have left for the afternoon; no one remains.
The beach is ours for the sheer mastery
Merely by setting the feet a direction
To follow. The achieve of seashore distance
Is negligible as night to the wind and sand.
The liquid moon and receding sun,

Hung in a streaming substance of sky,
Become amulets we wear, accept us both
As partners reflecting basic fraternity.
The sun lives yet, as our lives parallel
The erratic tide with our moving shadows,
While cold waves, gently washing
Achilles tendons, heel bones, and toes,

Awaken a spirit of kindred generations.
Our feet are baptized in the same waters,
Cleansed and blessed by fates that breathe
Life into ideas inherited from Abraham.
No words spoken between old and young
Interfere with the subtle interplay silence
Has manifested, this holy day. The tongue

Becomes a sacred instrument, igniting love
Without ever tuning its intricate strings.
Soon, we weary. The pale skin
Begins to overheat. The beach disappears
In a matter of undreamed years. We two,
A father and son, come home together,
Having mastered a span of deepening shore.

3/30/74 — [2] (00706)

Port Everglades Nocturne ^Δ

A sibilant wind translates the dusk
From blue to paling hues of cider,
While a Chaplinesque moon cakewalks through clouds,
Moves in quarter time toward self-effacement.

Dressed in ragged makeup as if to highlight
The antic phases of my upstaged life,
It parades before my face like a third eye
Attached to me by my steadfast gaze.

Through it, we both see flowers blooming
In a universe illumined by sweet antinomies.
Hidden behind the ocean's ancient sheet
Of prophecy, we watch moons proliferate

As wave upon wave collides in endless rhyme.
Together, we sleep as lovers transfixed
By the vaudevillian timelessness
Of our naked appearance on this elevated beach.

4/3–4/74 — [1?] on 4/4   (00708)

Waiting for the Sun ^Δ

A gray-white nimbus stretches across the sky
Like canvas pulled taut on a painter's framework,
Awaiting its first design. No one knows
Yet what sketch the artist will translate
From notebooks: a squally rain, the fishing fleet,
A seascape splashed with waves, touched by gulls
And sailboats, whose ruffled feathers and luffing cloth
Are brush strokes flying in a rough imagination.
Perhaps he might even fashion a self-portrait
To hang on the blank wall of this sunless day.

4/5/74 — [1?]   (00710)

Wading into Sleep ^Δ

The inexorable continuity of sea,
Weaving waves into the crocheted beach
We wear, makes sleep easy
To reach. We lie on mottled sands,
Awaiting the perfect moment to disrobe,
Then merge with the comatose ocean.

4/5/74 — [2?] (00709)

Cruise Ships ^Δ

Every time day slips away,
A cruise ship disembarks from Port
Everglades; the tides run out.
It churns deep into the dusk, is lost.
Earth tilts, spills its bag of waters,
Creating a series of contractions
Felt, occasionally, as far away
As Illinois. A baby is evacuated
Every breath we take. The earth tilts,
Spills a wrinkled species; the aged
Drift out. Space closes over them
Like ocean waves consuming the sun.

4/5/74 — [3?] (00442)

Vacation's End ^Δ

All that remains of a month's anticipation
And a week's fulfillment
On a beach in Fort Lauderdale
Is this transitory three-hour stretch,
With me sitting between semirigid wings
With my very pregnant wife
*

And a miscellany of unrelated people,
A broken series of rain clouds
Containing potential tornadoes
Or bizarre electrical threats,
And a queasiness about fantasies
Of making a crash landing in the Everglades,
Which not even coffee will ease,
Stimulating thoughts
That just by chance my wife's
Bag of waters might collapse,
In which case the matter of timing
Contractions and breathing properly,
Not to mention all the other normal fears
Of not arriving (both ways),
Would give way to conundrums at hand,
And . . .
All that remains of a week's fulfillment
Is the grim reality that tomorrow
Will quickly recall all the amnesias
We'd hoped to leave buried in the sand.

4/5/74 — [4] (00443)

Serene Flight

I hear jacarandas blooming in my ears
And see butterflies lifting my eyes
Above fields seeded with lusty clouds.
My spirit rides inside the slipstream
Unwinding behind a speeding trajectory
As we move, unchecked by street and sign,
Toward cities beyond the radar screen.
In such a state of grace as this is,
Even the alternative to a safe arrival
Is merely the lesser of the two real evils.

4/5/74 — [5] (00711)

[Creation speaking to genius]

Creation speaking to genius
Is a child begging its mother
For freedom to climb a tree
To catch the cat it chased away.

4/12/74 (02300)

Mass: Easter Sunday

Everywhere, the air is awash with images of death
And icons pressed into service, this holy weekend,
To remind the congregation of special obligations.
The white megaphones of three-bloom Easter lilies
Project a ubiquitous dialectic of visual beauty
And inner wisdom. Subtly, they sift into decay
Like manifestations of greatness or soft illusion
Going out of focus at twilight. All these people,
Seated with backs to each other, have come, today,
Like gathering rabble, to purge the ancient scourge;
They had hoped to witness another crucifixion.

4/13/74 — [1] (00712)

Sitting in Bib Overalls, Work Shirt, Boots, on the Monument to Liberty in the Center of the Square, Jacksonville, Illinois △

> *The mystic chords of memory, stretching from every*
> *Battlefield to every Patriot heart and Hearthstone*
> *over all this broad land will yet swell the chorus of*
> *the Union when touched as they surely will be by*
> *the better angels of our nature.*
> — Abraham Lincoln

The names of those who fought and died
In civil strife are inscribed around the pedestal
On which I slouch, watching anonymous townsfolk
*

On foot, in vehicles, hurriedly enter the Square,
Then leave, return, retreat like blood
Coursing toward death. I imagine them in uniforms,
Caps, with bayonets, marching for a common cause.
But the vision shatters into pieces of ordinary citizens
Pursuing personal liberties and individual freedoms,

While the bodiless names raised on bronze plaques
Turn black-green from municipal neglect and weather.
Vigorously as Aladdin, I rub the lackluster letters
With my shirttail. A kind of magic brings images back
From shadow. Voices beneath the granite base
Come unentombed from the ageless incarceration
Of having to outlast the memory of their deeds alone.
They form a chorus only I can hear, this Easter —
A resurrection, of a sort, for a nonbeliever.

4/13/74 — [2] (00141)

A Sunny Pre-Easter Saturday in Town ^Δ

Cripples walk like pigeons
Squawking on the littered, mica-flecked sidewalks.
Their journeys begin and end at park benches
The Square guards like a frontier fort.
Blind and mute students arrive
From the two schools to converse
In manual geometries and locked elbows.

Farmers leave muddy fields
To deal soft goods and hardware
In Big Smith, Tuf-Nut, Wild Duck brands
And exchange views on state-hospital patients
On the loose. Motorcycles and tractors
Confuse the music traffic composes
On the washboard encircling Liberty.

In this lush, unacknowledged Gethsemane,
Banker gazes through leggy waitress,
Whose moony eyes are on the barber
*

Describing a recent poker game
To the slightly wilting florist's wife,
Detaining the sheriff, pursuing his own escaped image
Around the urnlike shape of public concern.

On this Saturday, halfway into April,
When everyone should be giving calla lilies
And gardenias and receiving blessings
They remind each other to make for them,
No one recognizes their prairie heritage,
Inlaid with mosaics of gold maize
Outlined in green soybeans.

No one, it seems, has seen the sun,
Hiding all morning long,
Roll back the stony cloud-wedge
And ascend from its cave of daytime hours.
Even now, none has felt its heat
Linking their skeletons in a cautery of love,
As it hovers like a cosmic period.

4/13/74 — [3] (00714)

Church and State

Political faces gape from places
Where the public passes daily, afraid
To walk out of painted slogans, into life.
Facades of churches, splayed with glass
Meticulously cut, pieced, and leaded
In sacred gradations, begin to fade.
The eyes search through a funnel
Of singular gaze, seize their object,
Distort the exploding rainbow, then render
Both church and state out of keeping
In an age decidedly antitheocratic,
Undemocratic, not even premedieval.

4/14/74 (00296)

[A family of country people] †

A family of country people
Preoccupies itself with stereoscopic views
In a parlor, reading commentary
On the back of each card

5/5/74 — [1] (03004)

Putting in the Garden △

My pregnant Jan

The raucous red gasoline engine,
Mounted to a welded tubular frame,
Is the horse. It doesn't even sweat
As the blades it powers unknot earth
And churn it back in my face. I hold reins
Connecting machine and pounding blood
To purposes conceived through nature
By man's simple ingenuities. Planting
Comes from seeds packaged and labeled,
Dropped in soft dirt furrowed by hoe,
Covered by fingers delicate as ballerinas
Moving across a stage of painted balsa.

The knees of my coveralls are brown.
Arms and legs shake from weakness. Ideas
Of growth and harvest fade like cloth
Being bleached under the sun. Sweat
Drying on gold-rimmed lenses turns seeing
Into daydreams. As I leave the garden,
An image of Demeter in my wife's likeness
Or my wife in her ageless simplicity,
Ripening fast toward the last hours
Of her nine months' cycle, approaches
To bless the completion of my seeding
And call me to come eat from her table.

5/5/74 — [2] (00444)

Genesis of the Poet

Being surrounded,
        Perceiving circumambiences
That contain the outreaching eyes,
        Breathing in and out sounds
That define environments the tongue explores
        Before daring to explain its intercourse
With the astounded mind —

These are acts of salvation
        We perform on ourselves,
Regardless of station,
        Merely by joining the journey toward life
And otherworldly pursuits
        Imagination derives from the dream.
Can you conceive what might happen if we tried?

5/6/74 — [1] (00715)

Instructor and Pupil

For my dear mother, Charlotte

He was born in his mother's trunk
And grew to do a soft-shoe
Across her stage.
        He became a fledgling star,
                a prodigy,
        Whose meteoric act was fantastic
        Yet brief by all measurements,
        Except to her. She applauded
                his childhood recital
Long after he'd quit taking lessons from her.

5/6/74 — [2] (00716)

Crew Practice: A Reminiscence △

Moving from crew shell,
        Outside New Haven's ghettos,
    *

Along the Housatonic River,
        To the gynecologist's office
In midtown St. Louis —
        A leap through twelve years'
Residue floating on a surface
        Dirty and bruising in June:
The daily practices for Saturday
        Races, the discipline, courage,
And nervous, sleepless anticipations,
        All of it leading to this day . . .
The momentum of perfect blades
        Recovering across choppy waves;
Breaking the finish line fast;
        Holding the throbbing trophy
High over the shoulders — a baby
        With whom to do calisthenics
When the last regatta is forgotten.

5/6/74 — [3] (00445)

Plant Manager

No persistent moan of sewing machines
Disturbs this morning's abnormal routine.
Sweet noises of birds and squirrels
Assail the astonished ears as though a bomb
Exploding an entire civilized idea
Has blown the mind into otherworldly atoms.
I'm an indoors person turned inside out
By merely having decided to leave work
For the day. Such simple freedoms
As walking through wet grass in boots,
Lifting the dawning sun to my eyelids,
Gazing at a robin feeding beaks
Nested in ivy remind me of ecstasies
I've been sewing up and shipping out
As fine men's sportcoats and trousers
For the last five years without realizing it.

5/6/74 — [4] (00717)

Last Days Before the First Baby △

How outlandish the dream that precedes birth,
Heralding its arriving being among the quick.
In the beginning, an early spring continues
Indefinitely; a heart beats in sweet sympathy
With another blood it washes clean, until lust
Rushes from my lady-in-waiting and her husband,
Leaving both within a delicate sweep of gravity
As her belly inexorably achieves tumescence.

All these manifestations surge toward release
From the divine scripture stored like a Torah
In the fleshy arc of my wife's ripe stomach:
The dream becomes fetus, the child the law
Reality keeps naturally balanced with death.
Soon, the idea of life, moving further down,
Breaks through the totally effaced opening,
Into a day bathed by a mother's radiant tears.

5/9/74 (00446)

Just Before Birth △

Everything takes on the tumid saturation
Of overripe zucchini as seething daylight
Expands toward night on invisible vines.
Rain contained by or containing the air
Seems to fill the sky with flying seeds
Sweeping overhead like white snow geese
Entering a gigantic ovary in mid-flight.

Birds, seeds, ovaries — blessed elements —
Poise long enough to exploit the horizon
With the mysterious symmetry of their being.
Something has set them free upon the rain,
As though its perfect sperm
Had spontaneously conceived a birth in dream
Or the brain had guessed the certain hour.

5/11/74 (00447)

Exponential Theories

Beyond morning coffee's acidity,
Stimulation begins. Outbound mysticism
Turns in toward myth and alchemy
Worked on a people's belief in fear,
The unknown, and holocaust. Earthquakes
And goblins clash with lost souls,
Hydrogen flashes. The planet levitates
From words spoken by poets,
Who translate the earth's waves to paper,
Making a new language to stave off
Demons of boredom. The Tower of Babel
Becomes a silo, stark against a sky
Widening over this May Sunday morning,
With people lining up at its base
For handouts of feed corn and beans,
Ideas and dreams in a time of plenty,
A time of famine. Neither the coffee
Nor the alphabets validate the poet,
The mystic, or the ghost being absorbed
As exponents of an irrelevant theory
In an equation of obsolete factors.
Only, the multitudes continue to increase,
Irrespective of everything except the flesh.

5/12/74 (00718)

Choosing Inducement †

Through inducement, there's a chance
Our baby will breathe today; of our choosing

Through inducement of our choosing,
There's a good chance
(The vessel containing our baby)
Our baby will breathe today
(Will break)

5/13/74 — [1] (01364)

At the Obstetrician's †

In the waiting room,
All the expectant Madonnas gaze
At the rubber plant, the painted photograph
Framing a stylized mother clutching baby
To her draped breast, the magazines,
Light fixtures, lamps, and furniture,
Every conceivable distraction to work
An adverse effect upon the hobgoblins
Dancing across each tumid belly's stage

5/13/74 — [2] (01365)

Inducement △

When the fetus finally reached full term,
We were given the gift of choosing
Whether to induce labor. If followed through
To elemental conclusions, the natural stride
Of childbirth would be significantly altered.
We would assume complete responsibility
For ordering the heavenly execution of ties
With predestiny. Severing the life cord
Prematurely might shatter the weaker links
In the chain of being, possibly even confuse
The reunion of myth and fate in birth.

Besieged by this awesome, God-like option
To preempt law and consigned by free will
To arrive at a viable motive for our designs,
We reached our decision diffidently
To wind up the universe for our waiting child.

5/13/74 — [3] (00448)

The Gathering of Pearls △

The grit has grown so slowly
Within the creature's quiet enclosure
*

Beneath the ultimate silence its sea
Emits. No foreign bodies penetrated
Its shell as the grain began spinning
About its silvery self a slender web
Protecting its delicate heart and brain.
Now, the vessel is straining to break apart,
Give up its most precious possession,
That others might reflect upon its perfection.

5/13/74 — [4] (00449)

Father's Den ^Δ

*Waiting to join Jan
in the labor room*

Beyond the modern walnut doors
They've taken my wife, taken my wife
Beyond the modern walnut doors.
Two slabs of a tree and a shiny corridor
Divide the time that keeps us from seeing
Each other, acts as a barrier
Between expectation and clinical despair.
Paranoia, in the form of sweet amnesia,
Sets in. I am beginning to forget
Where I am, where we are together
Separately, each waiting for the doors
To swing open and readmit us
Into the private world we've shared.

5/13/74 — [5] (00450)

Jan's Song ^Δ

Obstetrical ladies and men in green
And blue gowns peer over their masks
At the blond girl, birch-white beneath sheets.
Cautiously, they read the line charts
Running like extemporaneous soliloquies
*

From the mouth of Fetal Monitor 101B,
Whose two nervous tongues trace beats
And contractions as though a recent quake
Were registering incidence and intensity
Instead of a tiny baby begging release.

A bag of clear Pit drips consistently
Through tubing fastened to her breathing wrist.
Too soon, the contractions assume a new degree
Of difficulty, require prepared breathing
As effacement moves through hurried dilation
Into hasty transition: three to eight centimeters
In two hours, before she's moved from labor room
Into delivery, translated from rolling bed
To stationary operating table
Beside stainless-steel tools, below groping eyes.

She is almost ready to participate
In a final act of marriage between mother
And God. The sacred vows involve her
In a surging push toward a parturition
Neither machine can record nor doctor
Discourage as the creative ceremony unfolds.
First, the head emerges, the body advances
One bloody limb at a time, then life cord,
A whimper, placenta, needle and thread —
Debut, the hour, the day, in memory forever.

5/13–14/74 — [6] on 5/13 and [1] on 5/14 (00451)

Vestiges Δ

The alchemy of bodily change
Arranges for total effacement to free
A passageway for escape from the sea
The floating creature has survived in
Without surfacing to take a breath
For fully three seasons. Leaving the heat,
Introducing air into the collapsed lungs,
Opening eyes to first light after a midnight
Lasting clockless eons . . . such rituals
*

As dreams consist of in distant worlds
Are the only vestiges we are privileged
To see before all the heavenly trappings
Fall away and the tedious feeding begins.

5/14/74 — [2] (00452)

First Feedings △

The new baby has moved from her old neighborhood
And, with our permission,
Taken up residence in our private environment.
She has such strong sucking needs
That her feeding becomes a routine seeking of the stores
Of warm colostrum.
Setting up an effective expression of sustenance
With her loving mother
Is the only goal for her pilgrimages from nursery
To waiting life source.
Existence is no longer just a matter of floating,
Though dependence persists.
Now, each requires the other as well as God.

5/15/74 — [1] (00453)

Trilogy △

Her birth poem

A seismic enterprise, like a low sun rising
Slowly over an eastern horizon,
Enlarges gradually in her belly, growing
In proportion to the life floating inside.

The skin stretches taut as raw light
Spanning dawn, goes loose like blue rain
Flowing smoothly through Steuben glass.
Slight movements motivated from within
Change the basic shape. Rearrangements
*

Become transitory as refracting atoms
As the being drives actively toward peace
With a world shrinking by subtle degrees.

Finally, all motion ceases, and silence
Divides like ocean waves breaking close.
A child rides in upon the high tide,
Exploding against our beach, crying,
As though from relief, at arriving
From a journey taking many millenniums.
We gaze in not-quite-total disbelief
At an abstract fleshed into reality:

Two separate identities fused by love,
Split once, then divided again
Before being guaranteed to the third
In a covenant of pure earthly worship.

5/15/74 — [2] (00454)

Going to the Land of Canaan ^Δ

The stitches, the milk, tinges of jaundice
Still lingering; the nurse's final words
On feeding, bathing, holding, turning the head;
Bouquets and extravagant arrangements
Wilting in varying stages of decay . . .
The phasing out begins at week's apogee,
And as Sabbath arrives, we start preparing
To transplant our new flower to a garden
Far away. The city might be a safe place
For being born, but, ah, the country,
The country, for breathing, is irreversibly
Sweet and clean. So we leave at first glow,
Alone as we arrived, only surely reconceived
In the fascinating imagery of a Trilogy
We've conceived, a mystically born source
Reaching deeply to touch us with meaning,
To redeem our silent souls from emptiness.

5/17/74 (00455)

Paean to Jan and Trilogy ^Δ

Eyes closed,
Nose pressed against the breast
Of her nursing mother,

A baby rests
In eternal caress, a nested bird
Expecting warm worms

To digest wet
As liquescence. Such godliness
Can hardly be expressed

By mere peeps.
The miracle leaps from the mirror,
Like a perfect image,

Onto the body
Sucking from the earth's core.
The poetry of her birth

Confirms God.
The actual fact of her tiny feet
And uneven breathing

Reminds me
How we three are correlated
In overlapping metaphors

Of seizing time,
Squeezing dry the sweetest rinds
To taste of primal milk:

From my rib,
My wife; from her lush garden,
Our daughter, Trilogy.

5/24 & 6/1/74   (00287)

Strangers ^Δ

The day is a stranger's face we see
Through lattice gates and lilac trees,
*

A neighborly smile from a family
We know only for an occasional
Social amenity, a wave-of-the-hand day
Floating through no-man's-land
Like someone escaping from someone,
From us. The day runs from itself
Like a fugue, anticipating a debut
In end-of-May Xanadu before we arrive
At the midnight hour to celebrate
Another day of life for baby Trilogy.
Her time is ours. We are changing days,
Constant hours her hands point toward,
A stranger's face taking familiar shape
Through lattice gates and lilac trees.

5/27 — [1] & 8/16/74 — [2?]   (01403)

Of Nomenclatures △

*For "Muggs" Lorber,
the "Bull of the Woods,"
who aimed me toward manhood*

Magnolias, hollies, lilacs, and rye,
Clover, trees, plants, animals
Lesser and great — the naming claims them
For our dominion. We've become monarchs
Over all things living, and about to be,
Within the conscious realm we circumscribe.

Nature is a princely infant born to us,
Needing delicacy to cultivate it
And selective care to neither neglect nor spoil it
With too much fuss or not nearly enough.

Trees, birds, and grass, shadowed by sun,
Converge in the corridor between dream
And beyond. As we pass close, we hear them
Speaking praises to each other about us.

The objects are comforting in silence.
They share with us a peaceful coexistence
*

Based on a need for being unmolested.
In a sympathy binding all bodies that die,
We've agreed to do away with monarchies
And call each other by the names God gave.

5/27/74 — [2] (00719)

The Poet Is Asked to Give a Reading

The strangest sounds, like striking typebars
Clattering against a pitted platen,
Impress suggestions on the unbalanced cylinder
His mind rotates on the heart's rough axis.

The sounds control the message. The words,
Profound in their pure, crystalline silence,
Are secrets repeated through endless generations
To ears hearing only the truths they fabricate.

Sounds, ungodly and inhumane for elaborations
Churched in the worldly sermons and earthly
Homilies they reiterate to sinning men,
Emerge, abortive as dead fetuses, from the canal.

They exhort him to seek release from his soul,
Fly from the seat of his emotions, toward oration,
To save them. Only, the sounds confound freedom.
His tongue goes numb, as a crumbling rock slide

Tumbles down an invisible cliff,
Below which he stands naked before a hundred eyes,
Swallowing his precious touchstones,
Screaming to be heard above the colossus of his solitude.

6/7/74 (00720)

Dear Dr. Long △

Trilogy, Jan, and I,
For the last four weeks,
*

During the craziest hours of the night,
Have thought and thought what we
Might present you with for making us three,
And we arrived at a decision.

We decided that what you really need
Is a new flight suit,
Replete with contrast stitching on navy,
So that you might fly into Farmington
Or Lambert without having to change
To fit a different situation.

If, by chance, you require a slight adjustment,
We hereby extend to you our invite
To fill out a flight plan, check moisture
In the gas tank, reset your Kolsman window
For Farmington, and crank the prop.
Our day will be your day — any day at all.

Trilogy, Jan, and I
Hope your spirit will soar like a hawk
In your new aviator's garb
And as high as ours have flown
Since the special arrival, May 13, 1974,
Of the blithe creature you helped us land.

6/9/74 (03609)

Tortoise and Hare

The road from Willow Springs to Van Buren
Is sinew twitching taut, then loose
As my nerves compete with swift muscles.
It's the corrugated back of a tortoise shell
I navigate while racing the fleet hare
That scurries through my bored imagination.

Soon, I see it leave the course,
Disappear over back-country shortcuts,
Then arrive three hours late
At a gas station where my brain has waited
To reabsorb it for the long leg home.
*

A blown radiator hose, a flat,
And a thrown rod have dismantled victory
For the unwary rival my mind set free.

6/11/74 — [1?] (00966)

Van Buren Stop-Off: Commensalism △

Odors of hickory stick to the air
Above this land where weekend canoeists
From St. Louis come during summer months
To salt the riverbanks with tin cans
That glitter like pyrite in the sun.
Even though townspeople anticipate the scourge,
Despite hatreds, they remain polite
To the flabby cult that patronizes with tips.
They encourage a symbiosis that has allowed
Two very distinct species
To die upon each other without knowing it.

6/11/74 — [2?] (00721)

Pine Trees

Pine trees, lining the highway,
I drive past at ninety miles per hour
Are hitchhikers whose stubby, thumblike trunks
And fingerlike limbs scorn me as I race by
Obliviously. I almost feel they're telling me
I'm selfish not to give them a lift home.
I reduce speed, make a complete stop
To pick one up; only, none is going my way.

6/11/74 — [3] (00722)

First Father's Day ^Δ

From the greeting card he mailed
Special delivery,
The boy discovered relevant
Something shared with one of his parents.
He wrote, "God bless you, Dad.
Now that we have a child,
Recently born, I know fully
What it means to reach manhood.

"On this day, each of us is framed
In a hall of telescoping mirrors.
We look forward, toward memories,
Forever seeing our own images
In history surrounding the tree
Assigned to our family plot.
Bless you, Father! Bless me, child!
We are begotten of the same source."

6/16/74   (01404)

The Blind Man, the Square, and Sunday Morning

With each tentative step the blind man takes,
He converges on emptiness. The entire Square
Is quiet except for the gregarious chatter
Of his white cane's tongue touching curb
And sidewalk. To us, his staccato monologue
Is a telegrapher tapping in silent code,
A typist organizing another person's ideas,
A runner listening to repetitious strides
Inside a mind going blind with exhaustion.

Although he makes the same passage each day,
No one sees him for commerce and enterprise
Being freely conducted by greedy people. None
Knows why the blind man dares venture out
In such an undulant sea. Only children
*

Are aware of his unique and awkward pantomime.
They conjure the strangest misshapen demons
From his serenely helpless physiognomy.
Occasionally, they even play at being sightless.

We watch this man, on a mid-June morning
Too cool, somehow, for the seething prairie,
Making his pilgrimage to the motor hotel
For breakfast. His path chisels out a tracery
From boardinghouse, via town green guarded
By bronze Liberty, past our florist shop,
To the familiar entrance filled with smells.
Each storefront forms stained glass
For the rose window his ritual cathedrals.

He and this Sunday have become one with us.
His unmindful convergence on our early labors,
This Lord's day, is a blissful visitation
Informing us of a spirit breathing equally
Upon the land. The wisdom of inner vision
On earth is a gift bequeathed each of us,
To a greater degree or less, before we go out
To make peace with those who only see
And those who see only through kaleidoscopes.

6/23/74 — [1] (00723)

An Early Muse Awakens △

For Don Finkel;
he makes such joyful noise.

The very notion of cliché as a figure of speech
Takes the form of a faint aroma
From a cabin, long abandoned by me, behind a beach
Beside a lake lined with pine trees and birches,
I knew intimately in my youthful days.

It infiltrates both my mind and nose
Palpably, as though I were ten years old again,
Sitting here dreaming of a real boys' camp
Instead of just seeing blurry reminiscences
Dissolving hurriedly in the rearview mirror
*

Of my advancing years. I hear only your voice,
Teaching me to avoid cliché-ridden poetry,
Metaphor based on memory, flatly conceived,
And nostalgia trapped like dead air
Between clapboard and lathing of a mansion.

Yet, a fleeting glimpse of something dressed
In the odor of brocaded cliché shimmers before me.
I reach up from the typewriter keys to hold open
A screen door closing on a summer cabin
Where I've been sleeping for the last twenty-three years.

6/23/74 — [2] (00015)

Their Song △

How can any music be so churchly serene
As to make me kneel on cold stone floors
And weep? The song is my wife and child
Lying in mutual sleep beneath sheets.
Each breath is a sweet note released,
Scored by me while I tiptoe reverentially
From the room to keep from awakening them.
All afternoon, my eyes reshape their sound.

6/25/74 — [1?] (00349)

Coming Apart

My silent voice leaks through these old walls,
Floats out on a sea of sweet amnesias,
And I forget faces connected to ideas,
And bodies in naked frieze, cut off from light
By the boundless stasis of the mind in retreat.

Jesus, how silent and easy the dissolution is!
Each day "under the hood," I'm a tiny carpenter,
Busy dismantling, a nail at a time, the roof beam
First, then the endless complexity of framework
We spent so many theories and poesies building.

Soon, all that will remain of the gorgeous dome
That rose in asymmetrical shape, praiseworthy
For its exaggerated design and fierce gingerbread
Individuality, will be a vacant basement
In the cold earth beneath my feet, an open grave.

6/25/74 — [2?] (00725)

God's Apostles ^Δ

Riding high hog into the new season,
The men, affluent Judases, convene
To review summary sheets and samples.
From Pittsburgh, L.A., Orlando, and Dallas,
They congregate to cost out religion,
Agree on viable wholesale-price guides
For retailing the sacred saints' lives,
To be commemorated in next spring's line.
From all available data, forecasts
Related to man's unstable raiment

Suggest a definite trend by the masses
Toward blended double-knit spirituality.
After Adam's fall, the Lord ordained,
The Human Body Shall Be Brightly Clad.
They chant, "Praise be the graceful physique
Nattily suited in leisure ensembles."
"We clothe the whole naked world,
Anchored to a cross of mediocrity."
"Redeem your ragged souls, sinners! Please!
Salvation is our only feasible business."

6/27/74 — [1] (00727)

[The bones pull loose from themselves;] [†]

The bones pull loose from themselves;
A skeletal fractionation takes place

6/27/74 — [2] (00730)

The Sisters of Fiesole

A riderless palomino races headlong
Through a forest scented with silence.
Something other than a horseman is missing
To guide the sweaty beast. The harmonies
Animals and birds give off are as lost
As the origin of species inside history.

Deep in a rocky, green density,
Shadowy as blunt fish
Swimming upstream in a shallow season,
Nuns, or their ghosts, dance randomly
To music they improvise, before undressing
Demons that cling to their deathly skin.

The horse leaps from shadow into sound,
Rises in frenzied orgasm.
The maidens fall naked to the ground.
Only one among their order
Will unleash a centaur on the universe,
While the others nurse unconsummated lust.

6/27/74 — [3] (00726)

Priestly Notions Suggested by a Recent Sales Meeting ᐞ

Dictating public taste
Becomes increasingly sacerdotal.
The responsibility for matching models
To piece goods changes daily.
Fashion is flat-chested,
A naked whore on stage at night,
Dealing by day in smooth chiffon
Beside the Zürichsee. We're her pimps,
Stimulating demands for merchandise
To meet the needs of people dreaming
Of being led to bed by a bashful princess.
We're her pushers, cutting prices
On assorted surplus lots we consider
*

Drugs on the market. We're fabric junkies,
Hooked on noses, sold on clothing
As a universal nostrum for the naked spirit.
Dictating public taste
Becomes increasingly sacerdotal.

6/28/74 — [1] (00729)

[The men weary. Their tedious arguments] † ᐃ

The men weary. Their tedious arguments
Wither like leaves on unwatered plants.
The fouled, cigar-stained air grows heavy,
Descends painfully upon the gray heads,
Slightly lumpy bodies. They complain
The hours grow too late to retreat
To the days when they were suffering
And each little achievement was a Golgotha.
So many duties sloughed off, so very few
Contingencies fulfilled, achievements
Reaching maturity, all leading
To a similar and basic conclusion
Shared by each

6/28/74 — [2] (01302)

Panning for Gold ᐃ

They haggle over the gold teeth
In the ash heaps. Each
Prospector keeps an assay
Of daily accumulations. The dust
Was once handsome caps and fillings
For sophisticated Jewesses and brokers
Named Jacobs, Weinstein, Leiber,
Rabinovitch. Now, bounty hunters
Shake their sieves at Auschwitz,
*

Treblinka, thirty years later.
Still, on shrill air,
The death-rattles clatter soundlessly
As white noise floating on an ocean
Of sperm whales surfaced in oblivion.
The teeth are brought to auction.
Bidders become zealous, vigorous,
Wide-eyed, their ear-to-ear smiles
Exposing their own gold fillings
And elaborate bridgework. Dealers
Beg forgiveness for viciousness
In arbitrarily jumping their own bids;
They have clients the world over
Whose superior collections are complete
Except for the rare and precious teeth.

6/28 — [3] & 7/1/74 — [1–2?] (00092)

Song of Flight

As we leave the ground, Earth, propelled by urgency,
The lines converge further than we'll reach today.
The planes we separate will surge closed
Someday. Now, our destinations are charted, we three
Against gravity, held aloft on featherless wings
By airstreams strewn with fleeting phantasmagoria.

Are we fresh metaphors vesseled in shells of flesh
Suspended in a secondary shell above a celestial orrery
Revolving forever in a vast, fantastic hourglass?
Are we creatures capable of seeing a lifetime in minutes,
Second-guessing dream through a collective intellect
Inherited from evolving beasts, conceiving death?

Metaphor or beast — possibly both. In evanescence,
Our lives stretch toward soaring like silhouetted birds
That linger in heated brilliance beneath cloud forests.
On clear days, standing on grass or snowy slopes,
We can see ourselves up there, indelibly shadowed,
And we rejoice. In reaching, we touch close to home.

6/30/74 — [1] (00731)

Ex Utero △

Our tiny baby lies fast asleep
In a womb of human activity.
No longer does maternal fluid
Cushion her from polluted chemistries
We reluctantly breathe. She has emerged
In a debut celebrated by few,
Without bouquets of fragile flowers
Or the sheer, unmistakable perfection
Of hand-crocheted lace. She is Trilogy,
A rain forest of orchids
Blossoming all at the same time
Within her face. Her delicate flesh
Is a nativity robe woven of velvet
Or plush too smooth to touch,
Worn like a coat of many colors.
And as I gaze upon her helplessness,
Tears well up behind my eyes.

6/30/74 — [2] (00363)

The Kingdom of Innocence △

The widest eyes in the kingdom
Reside in her face, reflect
A fief owing allegiance
To a ruler who feeds her:
The queen, my devoted wife,
Her mother. The realm is secure;
Its stores fortified with love,
It will endure another reign.

The eyes go closed on dreams
Only she creates behind lids
We can only bless from above.

In quietude, a fortress rises.
Together, forever in peace,
We enter under its raised portcullis.

6/30/74 — [3] (00404)

Ancestry $^\Delta$

I stand knee-deep in the ocean,
Examining the tepid, eddying sand
Collecting about my feet like hungry minnows.
These particles are the oldest creatures
That still exist, older than Moses,
Younger only than the planet itself.
My own bones are composed of granules
That once came awash on desert shores.
Is it possible that I can recognize
My ancestry beneath these sunny shallows,
Associate blunt shadows with families
Buried a thousand generations ago?
I stoop to pick up a fluted rock
Alive with fossils. I can almost feel
Worms wriggling in my wet palm,
Almost hear captured voices
Asking me for my body to inhabit again.

7/1/74 — [1–2?] (00138)

Seascape $^\Delta$

Royal palm trees lean easterly.
Winds rifle the beach with sandy rain.
The shrill void fills with noise, like steam
Blowing a bolted lid off an exploding kettle.

Despite the storm, three sailboats
Penetrate the low fog and are lost; a plane
Churns the wet air and, like the rusty tanker
That left harbor an hour ago, disappears

Beyond the scope time defines by its horizon.
Now, all that remains is the jagged ocean,
A slime-green leviathan showing its teeth,
Its mouth open to ingest the whole beach.

7/3/74 — [1] (00733)

Rent-Controlled

They've moved into a two-room point of view
Overlooking streets busy with pushcarts
Loaded with doom and a river whose banks
Are filled with imperceptibly moving crude oil.

This district was once a highly desirable
Neighborhood, where man and wife might raise
Questions of national import, get valid
Answers as ideas grew through adolescence
Into mature adult solutions, and brainchildren
Had space in which to play out fantasies,
Watch their own offspring take shape
In the form of changes derived from sacrifice.

Now, they share a common backyard.
Their senile janitor neglects cigar wrappers,
Cans. Grass no longer grows at all,
For shortcuts they use to avoid deputies
Collecting rent on apartments the mind sublets.
Bulbs go unreplaced; plaster cracks.
Yet, they have no alternative to staying here.
Evenings, they thumb through albums, without recall.

7/3/74 — [2] (00342)

Jan's Physical Law #101

What goes in must come out.

7/4/74 — [1] (03063)

Changes in the Will △

My backyard is an ocean
Rolling unendingly out.
This morning, the eyes walk briskly
Toward an invisible fence
*

Defining where my property stops
And God's begins. A storm,
Set in silvery strata,
Makes a fist as if someone decided
To challenge that ancient abstract
Underscored by wandering tribes
Arrived by Heaven's floor.

Until now, there's never been doubt
About my imagination's sole ownership.
I alone was bequeathed this property,
From son to grandson, in perpetuity.
All my life, neighbors
Have waited patiently while I created
Frozen snowflakes, flowers,
And subterranean lakes from this ocean.
Today, the sun has trespassed.
He leads clouds, disguised as hunters,
To devastate my backyard.

7/4/74 — [2] (00734)

Spectator ᐃ

I

Only great plates of glass
Keep me separated from the heated beach.
I remain insulated from natural phases
By a simple, single electrical connection,
Which, like a hidden umbilicus, attaches my brain
To a tin placenta in the dark closet
Where man-made transferences occur.
A thermostat fastened to a plasterboard wall
Reads my pulse like a lie detector.
I sweat when trying to conceive rhymes
That neatly fit into poetry on loan,
Which I fashion from distant listening ears.
My skin goes cold after I've sat too long
Digging in sand for buried treasure
Maps tell me exists beneath the X-
Cavations I make into the paper's shore.

II

They bring me coffee, juices. I require
Complete silence at all times
While I write. I'm paid exclusively
By the typed and polished line. Just now,
My eyes raise from the vacant keyboard,
Walk along the beach, and stop by a child
Filling pail after pail with dreams
From a hole he's been emptying, all day,
Into waves lapping the shore where he plays.
What lies beyond the other side
Is his mind's China, the Spice Islands
I've searched for my entire waking life.
Maybe if I stay, the child might find them
Before high tide washes away
Every trace of his golden Cíbola.
Perhaps we might both share in its discovery.

7/4/74 — [3] (00735)

Two Doctoral Candidates in English Meet on a Fort Lauderdale Beach over Spring Break ^Δ

Slipping casually out of her bikini,
She whispered to me,
"A secondary effect of catharsis
Is hedonism." Blinded by the sun,
I gazed noncommittally.
"Pleasure is the highest philosophy
Yet conceived by man and woman,"
She asserted with emphasis,
Fingering her tiny white breasts.
I couldn't easily demur.
"It's the epitome of equilibrium
Between beast and soul,
The whole and naked truth
Executed with total ruthlessness,
The only cosmological raison d'être."

"Your small points are neat
And well structured, the crux
Of your larger argument disarming,"
I replied, tugging at my suit.
"The main body of your ideas
Precisely coincides with mine,"
I said pruriently,
"And your Aristotelian terminology
Excites me to metaphysical harmony.
But couldn't we at least
Leave this beach to lay down
The outline for our dissertation
On venery, before the police arrive
And give us the third degree
For indecent exposure of our literacy?"

7/4/74 — [4] & 3/7?/76 (00736)

Doleful Day for a Sailboat Race ^Δ

For Dick and Jean Hauser

Despite general storm warnings,
Yachts begin to collect for the regatta.
Within minutes, a choppy ocean plain
Is ablaze with infinite rigged masts
Passing like fat monks in billowing habits.
Quivering booms are jousting lances
Being readied to tilt at creaking windmills
That emerge each time a contestant
Unfurls his sails.
                              Blue occasionally
Breaks through purple-gray-white hues
In nubile rearrangements.
                                        Yet, the Lady
Dulcinea, who lives above, teases
Her suitors with crude, concupiscent ways,
Takes off one layer at a time,
Ultimately nude in becoming rain squall,
Monsoon. Then, in dizzying movements
To recover tacks, reach the lee,
*

Disenchanted crews are forced to abandon
The contest, forget the quest that buoyed them
Through a restive week of detail meetings.
With cracked battens and tattered spinnakers,
Captains return to their book-lined broom closets
To read of former winners' deeds, and dream.

7/6/74 — [1] (00737)

From Out of Nowhere △

All at once, a black mass of heat
Is wrung cool-dry like squeezed grapefruit
In afternoon's quick-shifting fists.
Pleasure crafts, fishing boats with antennas
Sensing anything other than schools,
And masted yachts eye the turmoil
Gathering close, slightly to the east.
Rapidly, they head toward Port Everglades,
Leaving the ocean erratically as water rats
Abandoning a sinking ship before boilers blow.

Day fills up with a unicorn wind
The size of thirty locomotives dragging a storm
Behind them like freight cars loaded
With war. What, until recently, was a beach line
Teeming with little people at worship
Has now become a screaming wind tunnel
Sweeping debris in every direction,
Turning fronds into lashing alligator tails.

Finally, a faint container of blue breaks open.
Since it's early afternoon, the heat returns,
Boats leave for the sea, and people
In bikinis resume worship services
As though nothing at all ever intervened,
Except a death and rebirth in the universe.

7/6/74 — [2] (00343)

Leda Among Pelicans ^Δ

Brown pelicans and lesser birds of prey
Crash daily through the ocean's surface.
Her constantly violated body membranes
Have learned to stay perfectly virginal
In their ever-changing adaptation to rape.

She's a shapely figure, resigned to fecundity,
Seething at her most calm, penetrable
Even in her least orgasmic state
When once aroused by a strutting sunburst.

The pelicans swoop and spire, widening
Then tightening, eying her voluptuousness
From above. Not quite voyeur-prurient
In their desire, they preen, screech, fight.

She excites them with writhing white flesh
Churning green, emerald, sapphirine,
Awaits a beak, like threaded needle,
To stitch her hot, cohesive fabric.

Anxious for the birds to curve near
Her swelling breasts and undulant thighs,
She trembles, smoothes the ruffled hymen
Of her turbid surface for the diving creatures

To drive right through, carry her off
Dripping spray. She moans her approval
Of their playful, indifferent lovemaking,
Agrees to remain their green-eyed mistress
On the promise they'll never impregnate her.

7/6/74 — [3]   (00732)

Mother and Child ^Δ

The baby became a hand grenade
Her nerves were holding.
Her growing lack of patience
Let it blow up in her face.

The baby became a spiny mine
Her fears had laid in silence.
Then raucous screams exploded
The whole field in her ears.

The baby became an atom bomb
Holding dreams to be dropped
On lonely people. The plane
Carrying it crashed taking off,

Yet the baby became a soldier
In a gentle enemy's army,
Writing poems about his mother
To comfort her during the night.

7/7/74 — [1] (01405)

My Flying Machine △

Once again, I'm integrated with machinery,
Insulated. My nerves are cables
Stretching from pulley to pulley to aileron
And elevator. My mind is a panel
Crowded with instruments and toggle switches,
A cockpit of fidgeting needles and dials.
My tremulous eyes become gyros
Functioning in vacuums, like silent worlds
Turning in space. My ears are tuned
To Pitot-static tubes
That check the speed of dreams along this odyssey.

The same flesh that protects my bones
Stretches over wings and fuselage
Fluting through zones of winds aloft.
This unearthly machine burns my blood,
Exhausts unoxygenated thoughts
And exploded harmonies, accelerates rhyme
Toward selected climaxes in time.
Only my voice, of the elements absorbed,
Remains unchanged and controlled by me.
It flies inside the slipstream
Each song I write leaves in its wake.

7/7/74 — [2] (00100)

The Voyage of A. Gordon Pym

Motorboats below are water striders
Cavorting. Their white rooster tails,
Trailing like slender prints
In sand, might be mere reflections
Of the vapor trails our jet leaves
Indelibly on the beach of sky
We fly through like a fleeting sun.

We enter a Sargasso Sea billowy
With floating icebergs. The plane
Shudders as though taking punches
In the stomach from kid gloves.
Now, the preset altitude is reached.
Even the icebergs are submerged
Beneath us, and we no longer float

Or fly, rather dream ourselves
Down lonely corridors, home.
The house that breathing keeps alive
Rises like white sleep, begs us
Come inside and rest awhile
Before leaving on the terminal leg.
We acquiesce as if we made the choice.

7/7/74 — [3] (00713)

The Fourth Anniversary

Bless my Jan

Fruits of every imaginable design
Realign themselves in the bushy trees
That shade memories of you and me,
Me and you, cultivating, in blessed profusion,
An orchard of widening years. The apples
Of the sun are golden; silver are those
The moon grows. Both appear in your eyes,
Melancholy and silent at times, fiery
As flames feeding on themselves endlessly
Without dying, at times inclined to blindness.

Your smooth, soothing physique is wet and waxy.
Its shapes, scents, and saxophone sounds
Are peaches and grapes, blood-ripe plums
Waiting to be tasted by a beautiful human
In perfect sin before the Serpent intrudes.
All the rest — the prunes, apricots,
Juicy pears, grapefruits — share complexions
Of past and future, the changing faces you wear,
Or have worn and will wear, as youth enjoys
And age recalls perfections of this harvest.

7/8/74 (00645)

The Tree of Everlasting Life

Solitudes and moods of uselessness
Are trees in a woods
Through which I stumble
As though something disposed to death
Were chasing close behind.

In their sheer arbitrariness,
They feign to guide my shadow,
And I follow, fumbling down
Ten unfriendly paths
Simultaneously.

Each intuitive fragment of self
Is a leaf; each tree limb
Contains infinity's part of my being.
Frightened, I reach up
To touch a fleeting lifetime,

Grasp a thin bough,
And hang precariously,
Hoping our graft might take
And grow me a thousand rings high
Under the sun and the thunderous sky.

7/11/74 — [1?] (00643)

The Everlasting No

All the days of useless searching
Have dissipated
                    into immediacies
That compete from hour to deathly hour
For each breath I take.

                    The search,
Like footsteps stretching out
Behind me
                    on a beach I've never seen,
Fades, by gentle degrees, into dream.

I've passed the last obstacle and still
Not discovered plausible reasons
Why privileged human beings
Can't survive indefinitely.
                    Yet,
Now that it's time, I refuse to leave.

7/11 — [2?] & 8/29/74 (00644)

[The very act of sitting] †

The very act of sitting

7/11/74 — [3?] (03319)

["Goddamn"s and "The hell they would"s] †

"Goddamn"s and "The hell they would"s

7/13/74 — [1] (03320)

Round Table Café ^Δ

Red, blue, and green billed hats,
Baggy pants, sagging facial landscapes
Eroded by seasons alternating heated days
In cornfields with freezing afternoons
Indoors all winter inform speech
Peppered with bold and bruising epithets
Slowly drawn like hot steel pressed
Through rollers. The green, blue, and red hats,
Emblazoned with fused and handsewn labels,
Display orders, dominions, degrees:
John Deere, Funk's G Hybrid, Pioneer,
The heraldry of an ancient grange community.

Green, red with mesh, blue with ribs,
The hats are easily misconstrued as balloons
And pennants shimmering above striped tents
Where a seasonal tournament is being held
To determine chivalry and highest valor
In duel-to-the-death pugilistics.
Here, honors are awarded on the basis of loudness
In jousting, tedium in fencing with broadsword,
Vulgarity in the art of verbal repartee,
And meaninglessness with spiked ball and chain.
Victor and vanquished are granted immunity
From all known precepts of fancy and reason.

Whether Christians whispering rumors of Christ,
Knights riding in quest of ladies
To save from disgraceful, barbarian rapaciousness,
Or grangers meeting for six-o'clock breakfast
Before advancing on hundred-degree labor,
Hog troughs, commodities, or retirement,
They converge beneath the billed hats.
Like ghosts rising in multicolored smoke,
They float, purging sleep's incubi from their eyes,
While beneath their chairs, in open runs,
Starved lions pace, waiting to be freed
From an older time to complete their deeds.

7/13/74 — [2] (00642)

Plant Manager

Afternoon passes by
Like a Saturday matinée
That costs a dime for the whole day.
Its silver screen is a tinted windshield

Whose glare distorts the mind's haze
As my eyes watch meaningless footage
Unwind from a gray-white highway
Under wheels of a projector I drive.

The concrete that paves daydreams
Is bereft of heroes and lithe creatures
On horseback, on beds, on themselves
In frantic and fanatical fantasies.

My dreams are "mov-ies" cast with cows
And hogs, spliced with overexposed
Images of women stitching trousers,
And choreographed with farmers on tractors.

Afternoon passes by
Like a full-length feature film
Whose ending I've too frequently seen.
From my seat in this empty theater, I grieve.

7/13 — [3] & 9/1/74 — [2?] (00641)

Theft

A stirring . . . a low-moaning disturbance
Occurs not far from town's edge.
The rails whistle an electric fugue.
Soon, the darkness evacuates two shadows;
Like contrapuntal themes, each repeats
The other's footfalls across the highway.
Two figures, draped in arc-light lakes
Unevenly splayed on the ground, dissolve
Into an isolated crime. Their lives
Are indentured to felonious entry. Fear
Bursts the seams containing their stability,
*

For a mere handful of merchandise.
Two shadows reenter the darkness, stained
Indelibly, tainting the mystical dreams
Of souls sleeping, still, without stirring.

7/16/74 (00640)

Islets in the Whirlpool

The earth's hurling whirlpool
Swirls us slowly toward total disposal
Through a drain kept freely flowing
By the brain's diluted dreams and fears.

Its elusive, susurrant vortex engulfs us.
We're drawn through a U-shaped neck
Of tubing that connects life with Life.
The passageway is abrasive to nerves

Turned completely inside out, uterine
To the dissolving soul descending whole
Toward rebirth. We race our defeated selves,
Trying futilely to explain our reason for being,

While temporary redemption is rewarded newborns
Moving on the whirlpool's outer edge,
Who cry without requiring prior knowledge
And are fed the breast without knowing why.

7/19/74 (00639)

Photo Studio †

The ancient three-blade GE fan,
Fastened to an oak roll-top desk,
Might be a raucous motor
Lifted from a Tin Goose mount.
The stale airstream set up
By its noisy motion cuts my face

7/24/74 (01300)

A Twilight Wedding

For Sharon and David Bayless

Despite the grip, one twist of fate
Can break the fist, shake the faith
That makes two clasping hands ache
With ecstasy. The blessed messenger,
In robes, takes two new angels,
Clothed in white light, unto his voice.
He reminds them of the precariousness
Of choice, their double, loving choice
To share a faith based on friendship
And gentleness until death intervenes.
Slowly, they kneel, then slowly rise,
Like sun and moon, newfound man
And wife, to illumine the cold earth
They populate and pursue each other
Through a universe that they create.

7/27/74 (00647)

Passing of Orders

Thank you, Camp Nebagamon!

Through the prism of sunlit kitchen windows,
Whose green ledges are strewn with cactus plants,
And beyond the backyard my eyes outline
With imaginary stakes, the years fly home.

Time is a line of musty Pullman sleepers
Drawn by steam and massive cast-iron sound.
A black locomotive passes between my legs,
Diminutive, possibly nonexistent, human,
As it drives on cold steel bolted to old ties.
My mind trembles as it goes by and retreats
Into a dense, endless profusion of birch forest
Deepened by Norway pine and blooming sumac.

Dearborn Station looms like a marble echo
Within echoes. Milwaukee is one dark night
On the quiet countryside, busy in heavy sleep.
*

Red- and white-painted dairy barns, silos,
Farmhouses are each pieces of stained glass
In a frame illumined by perpetual twilight
As the train threads destinations with smoke:
Chicago, Highland Park, Spooner, Hawthorne.

Each name is a punctuated, peripheral vision
Of a place no longer inhabited by my being.
Only my languishing soul still rides rails
Pulled up to make way for the highway
Connecting youthful deeds with aging solitude,
As though it knows that the chubby little boy
With curly blond hair, a mole beside his nose,
Is waiting at tracks' end to take me home again.

Through the prism of rain-stained kitchen windows,
Whose gray ledges are strewn with cactus plants,
And beyond the backyard my eyes outline
With imaginary stakes, the years go in flight.

7/28/74 (00648)

Stars for Juliet

> . . . *and, when I shall die,*
> *Take him and cut him out in little stars,*
> *And he will make the face of heaven so fine*
> *That all the world will be in love with night,*
> *And pay no worship to the garish sun.*
> — William Shakespeare, *Romeo and Juliet*

Old poetries I decipher from the crisp air
Above loves once in progress come home to me
This evening. A cool night in late July
Unlooses indelible faces I've almost forgotten
For the haste made in getting through my life
With as little inconvenience as possible.
Lusts, dulling as scopolamine, and vacuous dreams
Fall away, as faces, like Juliet-stars
Cut from love notes and glued in silhouette
Against an expanse I used to race through
In search of nerve endings to spark dreams,
Come alive against this clear night.

The stars are past faces floating in a fluid pool
That only occasionally deposits a speck or two
At mind's edge for my eyes' tiny fingers to touch.
These stars are my dreams screaming to burn again,
Dreams of being known on a first-name basis
By all who hoped to see a king rule himself,
Passional dreams of transcending the elegance of flesh,
Dreams of dreams dreamt by ancient dreamers
Lying in pastures, straddling mountain peaks,
Reaching the ends of continents to ponder
Why the garish sun comes funneling down,
Through moon-wash, to fertilize each new millennium.

I dream, tonight, the faces my poetry once painted
With smooth brush strokes. I recall the pain,
Now gone, vaguely remember all the vexations
Of names attached to faces, difficult victories,
Delights and pleasures of wet fruits eaten.
The dreams and stars become years, become facets
Forming a glistening marquise time holds poised
For me to kiss. Only, they are sharp and irregular.
They refract no light-ray ladders to the sky,
Provide no fantasies to conjure and justify.
Nonetheless, I kiss the dream with my eyes,
This most beautiful mistress, the dream of life.

7/30/74 (00646)

Flat River ^Δ

Its ghostly, false-fronted Main Street
Has reached a vacant, plate-glass impasse.
Lead miners who worked beneath the earth
Stay busy, now, in clapboard caves,
Drinking their waking hours from beer cans
And watching new flab accumulate
Like pumped-out slime piling higher
Atop a rising, widening chat dump.

The town is a derelict car being towed away.
It has no title, no license plates;
No owner claims it anymore. Impatient
*

State legislators will soon consign it
To scrap. Huge hydraulic bureaucracies
Will compress and bale it until nothing's left
Except a tiny chunk of lead heritage
To be placed on a museum shelf, behind glass,

As the mounds, ubiquitous as pyramids,
Become cenotaphs near an empty riverbed.

8/1/74 — [1?] (00652)

[Late in the day, and already the cars] †

Late in the day, and already the cars
Lock horns, fight for senseless supremacies
Lasting little more than half an hour

8/1/74 — [2?] (03259)

Waiting for the Final Release △

Dr. Frank B. Long,
godfather of the soaring spirit

We sit, husband and wife with a baby
Lying quietly upon her swaying knees.
She waits to be checked internally
For the final time — then blessed release.
Both of us remembers, through vague reverie,

The last occasion we waited here,
Anxious as actors approaching a stage,
Just us, united against the unexpected,
Come to behold the nature of a delivery
Impending, just two then. Now, ten weeks

Have elapsed. A profoundly delicate sense
Of helplessness overwhelms our tense minds,
Unbends all our selfish misconceptions,
Paints images of a fragile spirit
Arrived like a visitation into our keeping.

Who but the cruelest human being
Could refuse this gift, knowing well
*

That He who made death could conceive
In the shape of a sleeping baby a design
For all of us, busy with living, to emulate?

8/1/74 — [3?] (00406)

Beginning to See △

Converging before the eyes,
Opaque blurs burn through haze,
Turn into scintillating focus
As she grows a blink at a time.
Objects become noisy persons
Shaping words interpreting toys
Into voices. Unbending joints
Become mesmeric pivot points
On which the mind draws inward
All the colossal weight of shapes
Rarefied on the cathedraled air.
To those perceiving the baby
As a maker of grave decisions,
Choice is the flat, red side
Of a round, white toy
Turned slightly, like speech,
To reveal a naked metaphor.
Now, blue eyes that at birth
Looked through obscure pupils
Without distinguishing us
Describe the arc of friendship
We project as a silhouette of years
For her to fill up with our love.

8/1/74 — [4?] (00411)

Rainmaker

I: The First Coming

Caught by a spreading depression, his mind
Goes dizzy in nosediving spirals.
*

Stall-warning lights don't even cry,
Or if they do, his ears cannot perceive
Their incessant shrill, for terrible speeds
The machine achieves as Earth enlarges.

Only in a desert of brown-stemmed corn,
Stunted by drought, is the crash made manifest:
The surviving pilot is lost in waving acres
Seeded in memories burning in heaps
Within the maize; a flame maneuvers
Through brittle fields of unbending stalks,

Until the entire prairie is a wide fire,
Feeding its mouth with everyman's harvest,
An ocean whose molten-lava surface
Flows toward the polarlike icebergs
Bobbing in his bloodstream. Each day,
The level rises. Flood stage is reached.

The system cannot hold. Levees break.
Flames and cold blood alternate
Between, beneath, and above firmaments,
In a personal scourge of this emigrant victim
Alienated from himself in a strange Canaan,
Where he's been sent to awaken old pagans.

Seasons containing embittered spirits elapse.
His footprints dissolve in snow and mud,
Reappear in erratic and frenzied ant paths,
Until, one day, by accident, he emerges
At desert's edge. Whether from slow atonement,
Grace, or both, the pilot's escape is marked.

II: The Second Coming

Naked, infinitesimal against the stars,
He gains altitude in a smooth, bending dimension
Of depthless forgetting, achieves new heights
As his machine penetrates a trajectory set by God.
For the second time, he prepares to eject, explodes
In a perfect free fall all can see

Who have anticipated his Messiah-like return.
They know he's their lost soul flown by fate
Away from the tribe, a migrating Moses
*

Arrived from out of a clear night sky
Above the prairie, come to relate mandates
Of the flaming bush and the rainbow sign

To their group of penitential men and women
Ready to do anything to restore their faith.
Awe-inspired, they kneel. The earth trembles
As he speaks dialogues between lightning
And white thunder. Dissolving, he bequeaths
A drizzle they neither hear, see, nor feel

Yet stand beneath, wet to their bones,
As though the endless rain were clover cast
By angels gathering and throwing it over
Heaven's edge. Their lands turn green
As Bahamian sea shallows. From fallow soil
Comes vegetal abundance. The people thrive

Inside a cycle of rich years. Their pastures
Fill with calves and wheat. Colossal cities
Are glued to hillsides like gold-leaf mosaics.
Peace proceeds from every mouth and ear.
In time, citizens cease remembering the pilot
Who crashed in a desert of brown-stemmed corn.

8/3/74 (00651)

The Navigator

An everlasting madness always chases me,
Makes each passage over imagined oceans
Connecting the mind's Spice Islands a race
Participated in by the nerves. With neither
Winner nor loser, they finish in equal collapse.

All the way, this trip, the threat of rain
Becomes a major factor relating me to time.
It's as if my safe arrival were dependent
On somehow avoiding a downbursting storm
Or discovering San Salvador before other sea dogs
Can lay claim to new territory
In the queen's name. Only, everyone knows
*

There are no unsurmised continents
Beyond Atlantis, no natives to proselytize
In the ideology of Western democracy
And quasi-religious doctrines of material prosperity,
No intriguing crops to barter for fiefdoms.

I'm alone, tonight, in my lonely sea voyage.
Sighting a harbor before the skies gather
Drives me on from sheer conditioning. I realize
How the black hours, closing and reopening
In systematic perforation, form a music
That seduces the senses. Night becomes Circe
Inviting stray sailors into deep narcosis.
If not for a dread of going to sleep at the wheel,
I might follow the naked muse who calls,
Swim into her keeping, drown while breathing
Her too-sweet perfume. Instead, my destination
Rushes up from a neon marquee and invites me in.

Safe at last, I announce myself with a signature,
Take a key to a vacant cosmos, buy sleep
With a quarter's space of mechanical vibration,
Then board Prince Henry's caravel
And navigate the Tagus from Belém toward open seas.

8/4/74 (00650)

Leaving Sleep

My clothing has the crumpled feel of moist leaves.
One finger whisks away
The intricate net of cobwebs left
As nighttime residue, the axle grease
For dream-gears, deposited by sleep
To ease friction. The naked body has lost
Precious weight merely by breathing

As well as by vicariously helping to construct
The greatly ribbed, vaulted dome
The resting soul has directed its servant, the mind,
To hoist by pulleys, one block at a time,
Into place, then, with soaring inspiration,
*

Dive over the edge of without fear,
Clear of St. Peter's facade, into dawn.

The entire physical being awakens,
Reacts to hunger deep in the stomach,
Thirst. The eyes burst through blindness
To grasp fleeing visions, like a drowning swimmer
Trying to break a distant surface
As life dies one beat at a time.
Leaving home is not easily accomplished

By a renaissance man lost in a land
Caught between sleep and dream,
Bent on following the Arno's twisted flow
To its end, the Tagus into open oceans
Floated with sea monsters. This morning,
I cross the Tiber twice for good fortune
Before resuming work on my Vatican ceiling.

8/5/74 — [1?] (00656)

Buffalo △

Its flat, insect-blackened radiator grille
Is a buffalo's nose; twin exhaust stacks
Become the rugged creature's glistening horns.
Eighteen spinning tires are four hoofs
Churning concrete plains. Its screaming trailer
Assumes the shape of a humped spine,
Midsection and writhing belly connected
By ribbed muscle and corrugated steel.

Whoever said history slaughtered, wholesale,
All those sons-of-bitches had his ears
Fastened to the wrong rail spur.
Once again, America's prairies are overrun,
With snorting hordes breathing diesel fuel.
Perhaps another greed-inspired massacre
Might be an ecological blessing to protect us
From being trampled to death by stampeding beasts.

8/5 — [2?], 8/8 — [2?], 8/10/74 — [1] (00127)

Grandfather △

For Uncle Sam and Aunt Ann Brodsky

Damn it. Goddamnit,
        that dear man is dying of cancer.
He refuses to eat or be fed intravenously,
Desires to die in bed, at home, desires
To die,
        and here I am, lamenting his loss
As though I know him for the close friend
I wish he had become
                rather than
The mere shadow of a vague acquaintanceship
We made on all those High Holidays
And Friday nights. We're the keepers of their ashes,
Those gone souls devastated by wars
Of attrition conducted among their leaders,
People marked by scrolls on their doorposts
And frontlets between their frightened eyes
To be spared Pharaoh's famines and blights
For the cyanide.
                We're their keepers
In spirit, self-appointed, properly anointed
With seminal heritage we share through
                ancient marriages.
Our births, though fifty-five years apart,
Are sealed in a common ceremony, marked
By a family name. That dying man,
With whom I tried to reason only once
Concerning the meaning of a living religion,
Is reason enough for my lamentations.
His loss is me; his departing will deprive me
Of the shadow of that constant reminder
That all those gone people rely on me
To substantiate the decency of their existence.

8/5/74 — [3] (00096)

Haystacks △

The stainless-steel, streamlined diesel Amtrak
Has already faded into gleaming reverie,
*

Whose passage earlier today from K.C.
Awakened townspeople from their sweet sleep
Among the haystacks. Now, night
Is the same train, returning from its antipode,
Whining through red-eyed crossing gates,
Shining the rails to tracer-bullet brightness,
Gliding past oscillating semaphores
Green as holly leaves. This evening
Has arrived like *Aida*'s awaited overture.

The silent audience comes alive.
Everywhere, in plastic lawn chairs,
Old people by pairs, preparing
For death's onset or the mastery over boredom
And geriatric lassitude,
Hear and recognize, perceive, or see
The renegade train pass rapidly by
Like a rider of the Apocalypse with scythe.
They sigh at another day's punctuation
Before dozing again into mute communion
With the estranged souls they once married.

Beyond town's parched edge, women
Expiring inside private incarcerations
At the reformatory maintained by the state
Wave at the passing train they can't see
Yet imagine as freedom personified.
They transmute its distant whispering
Into sibilances of lovers, buried or lost,
Calling them to leave off loneliness,
Escape to cities beyond the tall corn,
Before resuming their garrulous blasphemies
And endless cadence of cigarettes and gum.

For a moment, Main Street is all gears,
Then totally neutral for a lifetime,
Like a truce delicately struck, peace achieved
Briefly before collapsing in deceits, lies,
As all eyes stop to read the signs
Clanging, lighting erratically as pigeons
Squawking for feed. Drivers wait impatiently
In silence, their old motors loud with cams
And clacking tappets: farmers' families
In pickup cabs, ripe high-school girls
And slick-haired boys drawn close

In their fathers' Chargers. Fourteen-year-old nymphs,
Whose supple breasts are mimosa blooms
Seen through tight shells, pause to watch
The others watching the train come fast,
Then disappear, absorbing their silence
As if it were tied with twine to the tiny caboose.
The little girls resume their smoking
At the curb across from Fred's Pool Hall,
Blowing their heated fantasies slowly,
In white O's, onto the thick air,
Hoping, perhaps, to grow up overnight,

Even as they're accomplishing that feat
Without knowing it. The town is drowsy.
Its timetable is printed with wide spaces
Where trains once passed with frequency
Irritating to all but the stationmaster.
The inhabitants, who once had an active past,
A promise of progress to keep them awake
And moving ahead, regard the Amtrak
With an oddly ominous regret as they lie
Beneath haystacks, fast asleep, dreaming
Of cows and sheep and steam locomotives.

8/5/74 — [4] (00649)

Gulliver's Discovery in the Land of Farmers △

Gulliver's yellow highway-department tractor
Is out, this cool August morning,
Mowing the inclined perimeter of a road
That slopes like a scaly alligator tail
Flailing to throw off parasites.

The highway divides miles of row-corn
And square-baled hay lying as stolid
As hogs slogging through golden troughs.
It connects farming communities at random,
Like ribbon tying up a massive package.

Pickups, combines, rusty feed signs
Tacked to poles, barbed wire, silos,
Billed MFA hats,
And suspiciously quiet eyes
Define the dialectics of a philosophy

That forms a kaleidoscope of fusing illusions.
Caught in the end of its elongated tube,
Strangers wait for Gulliver's hand to twist it,
Make it reveal simplistic intricacies
That formulate their secret existence.

Gazing wistfully through its narrow aperture,
His eyes focus on tiny men and women
Surviving on floating islands,
Then on giants thriving in a cyclic maze
Of constantly changing, changeless design.

Finally, his vision ricochets off prisms
Of sunlight infiltrating his irises.
He sees himself as ten beings
Sliding in and out of each other
And realizes he controls every twist of fate.

8/6/74 & 8/20–21/76 — [2] on 8/20   (00655)

Lucifer's Crew △

THE ARGUMENT

The fallen angels confer on the impending arrival of a fated Chief Executive *and determine, from the persistent rumor circulating throughout the Nether World, that his advent is both the Cause and Reason for the phenomenon that all the seasons seem to be changing.*

Three straw hats, six billed caps,
And a solitary city-police hat,
Braided and tasseled, float like bobs
On a lake in the thick Crystal Café air.
They are halos sustained in place by anima,
Surmounting, crownlike, the faces of angels
Congregating at the late breakfast hour,
Instead of flying to harvest, because rain
Has fallen without cessation for two days.

But the delayed rain won't unstunt crops
Or save cattle from being fed on silage.
These angels agree that it's cold
Beyond recorded belief for this season
In their nether world. Usually, the heat
Commits them to an endless futility of flames
That scorch the heartland relentlessly
And drive them to blaspheme the King
Without fear of extenuating culpability.

Suddenly, nervous Beelzebub explodes.
His grotesque shape informs speech
That emerges staccato, like a snake slithering
Out of molted skin, from underneath
The policeman's braided, tasseled hat.
All the bills attend words he slurs;
Their reverence is eternal. Rumor has it,
He postulates, that the seasons are changing
To accommodate the arrival of a President.

8/7/74 — [1] (00654)

Luncheonette †

An attempt at decor: lobster nets

8/7/74 — [2] (02953)

Necromancers △

A thousand enchantments can't recall
The original forest in which we camped.
No philters or tonics taken to relax
Chronic forgetting can release the spell
That befell us by accident long ago.
We were seduced by our own easy spirits,
Going about their courtly arts of loving,
Reveling in gentleness, sculpting fantasies
From delicate dreams seeded by us both.
We were slow to see the forest losing leaves,
*

Becoming wintry in an extended summertime
We ran through, believing we'd outlast
The fancies we knew had deceived others.
We never realized that it was happening
Or saw eyes peering into our sacred clearing,
For privacy the dying density provided.

Where we ran naked and played at being
Woman and man completely in love
And gave birth to a girl named Trilogy,
They stared as though we were of time zones
Unknown to their scientists. Our own naiveté
Changed us into people gone blind and left
In an open field to defend ourselves
Against mindless fear of our uniqueness,
Which threatened the lives inside the eyes
Hiding in copses at Earth's edge.

God had failed to warn us that importance
Might be accorded any human pair
Too essentially concerned about each other
To care about others not caring enough
About themselves. God had forgotten to tell us
That they would gyve our effigies to trees
Burning without flames, make us martyrs
In a universe we'd not been invited to enter,
And that they'd blacken to treelessness the earth
That once forested our fantasies and deeds,
Our singular birth. Then, as if to cleanse
Their sins, they cast our symbolic ashes
Into an invisible lake, that never again
Would any citizen of the state dare emulate
The strange ones who had come to the forest
Long ago to live alone and with their God.

8/7/74 — [3] (00414)

Ends of the Continuum △

The infinitesimal length of a minute,
As registered by rainfall, is infinity
To a skin diver drowning in ten fathoms

Or a farmer waiting for row-crops to mature
Under drought conditions. Time becomes
Acres irrigated by inches deep, feet

Wet to the taproot, bushels and bales
In one tray of a scale being outweighed
By husks, stunted beans, dry wheat

Plunging into poverty's rank and file.
And all the while, nail-biting speculators
Pray their harvests never reach market.

8/8/74 — [1?] (00653)

Tortoise and Hare △

The creaking, two-seat, wood-spoked buggy
From Fortuna, parked on the tarred front lot
Of Gerbes grocery store, is no metaphor,
Nor is it the premeditated distortion of minds
Discontented with conventional travel and time,

Rather a ragged pair of nags, patient
Despite the heat, their tails busy with flies,
Letting drop cakes of manure on the pavement.
They belong to an old couple dressed in convent cloth,
Who've come twelve miles, from need and duty,

Out of the private, tightly knit community
Where their relatives have settled for generations
In precise continuity with their forebears.
Twice weekly, one family is chosen to buy
Foodstuffs for the rest, journey from the quiet

They've provided themselves outside the furious life
That uses heavy-duty shock absorbers,
Relies on power steering and brakes, radial tires,
Automatic transmissions, and air conditioning
To persuade people they're making daily progress

Toward escaping their sweaty bondage to the past.
Meanwhile, these Amish have made the decades
Slaves to their exigencies, teaching trades
*

To cooper, wheelwright, blacksmith, and farmer,
Pursuing the beliefs that not every gewgawed thing

Related to change is really worth pursuing
And that each newly contrived mechanical intrusion
And scientific breakthrough does not simplify life.
Creaking, wood-spoked wheels take to the road
Unnoticed, the buggy a chariot flying to God.

8/8/74 — [3] (00126)

Exeunt Omnes

The guillotine's gleaming steel has finally fallen
Through its constitutional guideposts,
Like a newly christened ship sliding down
Dry bedways. The rusty blade,
Which shuddered briefly, comes to rest again
In its raised position. The tedious inquisition
And its fatigued executioners have gone to sleep
To recover hours lost during the siege.

The severed head of state is returned intact,
In quiet disgrace, to its place of origin.
The golden gate swings on stiff hinges,
Admits the cortège and caissons. No boots
Turned backwards in stirrups lead the procession
Accorded heroes. Ghosts of close friends
Hang awash, circle overhead like souls
Waiting to reunite with an exploded corpse.

The castle, built with people's contributions
To reelect a leader, is his mausoleum.
Some nights, the neighbors claim they hear
Lamentations, see a crazed Hamlet
Pacing the moon's shadows, feel doom
Looming like a colossal Sphinx come to muse
On lands gone to seed and on a man's image
Disassembled to expose his grossest anatomy.

8/9/74 — [1] (00658)

Preparing a Shipment

I flip the lid on my trip to Tipton.
The sealed box, stapled and taped
For added security, contains hours
And pounds lost to a week's labors
Expended upon an invisible boss.

My container has a prepaid waybill,
With unspecified weight and destination,
Addressed to any hometown
That memory inhabits. The impedimenta
Of the unsettled is deceptively scant.

Uprootings and changes are merely hegiras
To the depots of the soul's city of dreams,
And fantasies extended like permutations
Beyond the mathematics of birth.
They require only one label,

With any name and mental state,
At nonrates. Every delivery
Stenciled **DELICATE PRECISION MACHINE**,
ECCENTRIC DESIGN, **COMPLEX CIRCUITRY**
Confirms my being: I'm the contents

Shipped by me, received and signed for,
Every moment, on my sole authority,
And I alone am the insurance placed
On my self. Only my imperishable soul
Knows the scope of its real valuation.

8/9/74 — [2] (00659)

The Open Road $^\Delta$

For Louie Portnoy,
whose spirit runs free
behind his photography

Just before the end
Of day,
I hike a mile out of town
*

Along the railroad track, on graveled ties
Permeated with diesel oil,
Above ground seeded in corn and beans,
Surrounded by a profoundly tantalizing silence.

No tractors disturb the fields;
No coarse freight scrapes steel.
Even the parallel highway is empty,
Temporarily, of people escaping cities.
Overhead, a clean, deep blue is transmuted,
Far in the distance, into fish swimming in a tank
Strewn yellow-orange and blood-rust —
Dusk festooned with seaweed and castles.

I stand at the wide end of tracks that converge
Somewhere in Wyoming, dreaming the miles
In between, down a thousand contemplative yards,
Evoking the spirit's open road,
Over which millions of souls have transmigrated
During the past century and a half.
Oh, to obey the semaphore's green light

And ride out on a breeze, find gold
In a sieve in a cold stream in a steep ravine
Convoluting mountains by the Truckee River,
Settle in Beverly Hills, on sixteen acres,
Make "mov-ies" in boater and blank frames,
And never hike the mile back to town,
Just before the end
Of day.

8/10/74 — [2] (00657)

[The dense penetrations of the
  inbound soul] †

The dense penetrations of the inbound soul
Seeking freedom from the self mystify even
The mystic

8/10/74 — [3] (02952)

New Athens Rain †

Visibility is like thick cigar smoke
Cloaking the air. A rain-soaked blanket
Stains brown, brittle fields, a reward
That comes too late to revive dead vegetables
And grains.

8/13/74 — [1] (04016)

Her First Toy △

Trilogy's third-month birthday

The fleshy-legged baby lies quietly
On her back, following behind eyes
Turning sideways to imitate the arc
A plastic rattle makes above her.
White, yellow, blue magic granules
Flow into its neck, like ideas
Spraying the brain, disappearing.
Her three-month mind is mesmerized
By the hollow sounds, wild flying colors
Leaving one hemisphere to reappear
In another. Does she see her face
In the glass circle at each end,
Recognize memories out of preexistence,
Or is her preciously reflected image
Merely another brilliant bead
Arriving fleetingly, with each turn,
At a new universe within time's toy?

8/13/74 — [2] (00427)

Release in August

For Helen Lukeman;
bless her.

Hers had been a quiet postponement,
Without promise or remorse. Simply,
*

She'd become more acutely aware she was living
Than the rest of us. Yet nowhere
Did her sterile intimacy with private despair
Collide with the open emotions she cherished.
Never did she share with those of us who loved her
The frustration of being alive inside a dying husk.

She stayed up late at first,
All night the last five days
(We'd see her lights speaking to the hours
And seconds, lambent as gossamer, eerie),
To finish wrapping the minutes she'd knitted
And years handstitched into shawls
And crazy quilts, gifts she'd been making
A lifetime, for a Christmas she'd never survive.

Totally alone of her own volition
And without taking any medications
For the pain, she concentrated her remaining energy
On creating vital cards to be spoken
As dialogues between her gone spirit
And the sweet, grieving souls she was leaving behind,
Tiny reminders to touch them, like kisses
Thrown from a train gaining momentum.

Four months later, we came to the cemetery
Again. Standing in silent highlight
Against a snowy, end-of-December prairie,
We each embraced our departed friend,
Gave belated thanks for her gifts and cards,
And laid presents made of memories at her grave.
We knew she'd wait until we left
To get them; that was always her way.

8/14 & 8/30/74 (00601)

[First, the silent stirs under covers:] † Δ

First, the silent stirs under covers:
Toes, fingers give rise to feet
And hands. Eyes open on twin dawns
Seen from within the waking child
*

Who accompanies us on our trip
Far from the source of her birth.

8/15/74 (01301)

Exiles

> *Mardie and Lloyd,*
> *Koz and Melissa,*
> *Bagel and Marilyn*

The beautifully free-spoken campus people
Too swiftly grew into coat and tie.

Those who excavated Egyptian civilizations,
Hammered Etruscan gold into thin genius,
Sold slaves from Thebes, Tyre, and Corinth
To Roman lords, and carried the Parthenon
One stone at a time to its Acropolis top
Now hitchhike great westerly distances
In pursuit of spirits flying down the sky
In wet streams in a thousand Yosemites
Throughout the blind mind's geography.

Those who ran on edge through Roethke's
Dense greenhouses, talked with Faulkner's Ike,
Dead Emily, and brilliantly crazed Benjy,
Painted in the spaces Jackson Pollock
Almost forgot to leave in his hasty distress
To achieve abstraction of a wasting brain
Now sit with Mylar plans of townships
Proliferating, penciling in new streets
For developers eating away at scanty lands.

Those who carried a football five yards
Every lifetime, gazed from a hot classroom
Toward a courtyard where Lilith lay
In wait for their sexual fantasies to chase her
Now take whiskey sours at lunch,
Circumspectly check their soft waists
Each naked morning in the bathroom mirror,
And arrange to meet Miss Wayward Dream
On impromptu business trips to the city limits.

Those who made promises and loud vows
To support sports, endow scholarships,
Defend their alma mater in afteryears
Now give commencement speeches nightly
While intoxicated on pleasant grass,
Grow less wieldy, totter like cows
At reunions, barely stoop to avoid ghosts
Flying low. They blow transparent bubbles
Whose iridescent glow almost recalls

The beautifully free-spoken campus people,
Who grew too swiftly into coat and tie.

8/16/74 — [1?] (00602)

Reunion

Since our last gathering, the forest
Had filled with new trees and shoots,
And a stream had cut through to its core.
So profuse and perfectly graceful
Was its symmetry that no beings
On earth could beg a loving God,
Even one totally dedicated to creation,
For a more enduring serenity.

Yet as we entered and followed thoughts
Down paths to former conclusions
Now grown, like rings of an oak,
Into static patterns we'd assimilated,
The roads, by subtle degrees, began
To diverge, swerve invisibly,
Until our voices couldn't be heard
Anymore above the forest's roar.

Being lost by being caught
In controversies that kept each
In tense communion, we raced frantically
To escape each other's biases.
One by one, we emerged whole,
As personal interpretations of souls
*

Purged of friendship, leaving the forest
Suspended in harmony with itself alone.

8/18/74 (00676)

Rescue

Mine is the spirit's fluid, the will
That drives toward the sun exploding
And climbs inside the soul in flight
From a dying husk. I am freedom
Measured by breath immeasurable.
My blood rushes as spasmodically as day
Confused by one hundred tornadoes
Funneling through a solitary eye.
Night is blighted by fires
Hell-born and -fed. Lucifer stalks
My mind with fine wine-nets,
Anxious to recapture a free agent
Recently set loose, convinced
Of my susceptibility to weakness.
Doubts about escaping the serpent
And his bite frighten me almost to death.
Yet as the moon comes into view,
I see you, wife, shadowed, subdued,
Racing to take me into the rain
To wash sin away so that, together,
We might bathe naked in our marriage forever.

8/19/74 — [1?] (00674)

[La Salle–Peru, New Berlin, Jacksonville.] †

La Salle–Peru, New Berlin, Jacksonville.
Two bridges two rivers wide collide
Inside

8/19/74 — [2?] (03260)

Naked Baby Trilogy ^Δ

The baby speaks to me in pantomime.
She sings lyrics written on her eyelids,
Writes love notes gently with fingertips
Touching my mustache, whispers wisdoms
She's brought with her from a distance
To enlighten a mind gone blind from life.

I breathe in her ear, wait for words
I've never dreamed of to escape like echoes
Endlessly leaving a seashell's source.
My lips kiss her belly with delicacy,
As though its flesh were a fresh gardenia
That might wilt with a slight disturbance.

So murmurous and groping is the religion
Created by the child crying to be fed
From its mother's breast that I weep.
Ecstasies engendered by this tiny priestess
Call me helplessly to her altar to pray.
In pantomime, I speak adorations to her.

8/19/74 — [3?] (00433)

Noche oscura del alma

Loud sounds drown out the noise
That cloys
            perfectly wrought reason
Caught in a limbo the mind churns
In its burning
                in-sin-erator.

Dim light brightens images of you,
Floating so close
            to the surface
Of this unnatural dusk that I
Can see you reaching out to drag me
                                under.

Our haloed bodies, freezing in heat
Generated by their gone spirits
*

Isolated
        outside sound and light,
Beneath a sea of liquid selves,
Are speeding meteors in brief decline,

Flying ghostlike through a space
In   space
Left behind by the fire they created
In our original retreat from life.
You and I are somewhere in be-
Tween, being   drawntoeachother

Beneath wet-frescoed cloisters.
The great dome containing all sky
Opens   wide to admit our souls.
Distances/close. We come home,
Like babies leaving God's eye,
To grow inside our innermost night.

8/19/74 — [4?] (00675)

Preliminaries ^Δ

The baby sleeps in steep, gleaming clouds
Crowded in eastern flower beds. She dreams
Destinies conceived by God, climbs stairs
Made of stars braided in time-webs to hold
Firm for the few loose years bequeathed her
On her Earth-journey. She stirs, turns
Her tiny head, whines quietly. Symbols,
Like sand granules, stream by hemispheres,
Toward interpretations not yet released.
She is our newborn creature, Trilogy,
Whose unformulated brain patiently awaits
Final instructions for her first free fall
From the dark side of the mind's full moon.

8/19/74 — [5?] (00431)

Music, Wine, and Isolation

For Wishbone

Electric organ, electrified guitar,
And electrifying drumsticks strap sounds
To the chair where my shivering brain sits.
The ears cringe in electrocuted ecstasy
As the pulsing voltage from transformed wine
Surges down the spine, through the veins,
In alternating spasms of berserk current.

I can sense my mind going slowly insane
Inside the synthesizer's uncivilized asylum
And feel the entire weight of my lonely existence
Hanging precariously from taut strings vibrating
As if to loosen sanity's weak grip on my life.
I fall free, soar, a prismatical phoenix
Flying through a fiery horizon, into fantasy.

Soon, the music breaks into naked components
Tumbling like dust motes over the mind's Niagara.
Each note tornados across my vision,
Lingers, undresses, and waits for me to enter its eye.
I fornicate with the whores of my solitude,
Who scream for release from tube-tied overtones,
And awaken, next morning, with a child by incest.

8/19/74 — [6?] & 9/5/76 (00672)

Up from the Land of Pharaoh

God,
　　　how the body needs such drastic release

From its rigidity! Yet, Shem and Japheth
Rebel against their brother; I rebel from them,
Fighting to defend Ham against demons
Mounting forces within his unyielding soul.
In disgust, I throw the holy stones to the dust.

Evil is the people come to rape the golden calf,
Parade naked into the Promised Land
To sleep with pagans awakened in Sodom and Hades.
I can't save them from their new-gained freedom.
Lot's wife is salt poured on their open wounds.

God,
        how the body grieves such drastic release!

8/19/74 — [7?] (00673)

Cold Companionable Streams ᐞ

> *Among what rushes will they build,*
> *By what lake's edge or pool*
> *Delight men's eyes when I awake some day*
> *To find they have flown away?*
> — William Butler Yeats, "The Wild Swans at Coole"

The wild, clipped swans at Coole
Remain patient in their stasis
As I race to refill the lake,
Which they float on so gracefully,
With new poetic enthusiasms.

The magical liquid is a discipline
Whose wayward nature resists
Cold control. Even Yeatsian
Versification breaks apart,
Occasionally, while in flight.

Trembling into a new morning,
I follow a cantankerous man
On his way, in absolute silence,
To paths that describe the lake,
Around which he spends his days
Floating boats, watching the birds,

And I wonder why his clothes
Are metaphors, why he mumbles similes,
Throws old poetry, like feed,
Against the breeze, believing
The wild swans will swim to him.
He's been dead for fifty years.

8/20/74 — [1] (00671)

A Decorated Veteran Returned Home ^Δ

All the late passenger and freight trains
Pass on time through my unscheduled mind.
Their destinations bear no relation
To actual places connected by tracked miles,
Rather to my way stations I dream into being
Whenever my ears fill up with sounds
Of steel wheels rattling my window frames.

Time is two legs lost from the waist down;
Minutes are hours expanding into day on day
Alive with mistaken identities and dying lives.
Each is me. Those fleet faces I glimpse,
Flying by in silent, tinted isolation,
Remind me of calendar dates anticipated, arrived,
Then finally misplaced in the eyes' wastebaskets.

Often, I've wondered what it would cost for a train
To stop in Tipton, wait long enough
To let me board, take me to K.C., and connect
With the *Chief* for the City of Angels and beyond.
Only, Vietnam can't be bought and sold
By an imagination amputated just below the soul,
Nor the stumps of dreams be taught to walk again.

8/20/74 — [2] (00669)

Unlaundered Accounts ^Δ

The master of ceremonious defeats
Has left his seat of power to appointees
He himself personally offered
In nomination. Such a gracious
And uncompromising abdication
Merits not only our praise
But our appreciation as well.
The nation that regularly cleans house
Sleeps in bedsheets spread
For kings and queens. The people fear
A sovereign who neglects to tell his mistress
He hasn't bathed in forty days.
*

How will they be able to differentiate
The truth from lies, next time
He seeks to proposition them, when
He won't even wash in Peoria?

8/20/74 — [3] (00670)

Fission

> *There has never been any doubt that man was meant*
> *to die, but that all men might die at the same time is*
> *frightening to the very marrow of flashed bones.*
> — Dr. Haber Mendenhall

> *Prospects of annihilating a tribe always existed, even*
> *with cave dwellers, yet it took a forgetful chemist to*
> *arrest certain elements sufficiently volatile in isola-*
> *tion, then bombard them with neutrons, to teach us*
> *how to explode an entire planet.*
> — H. Compton Steiglitz

Man's chain of being has a weak link,
Located, geophysically, near Los Alamos.
A concatenation of atoms
Explodes fifty thousand Japanese faces
In one preconceived balance of trade.

This generation's McGuffey is a diplomat
Trapped by clichés he spawns in daily speeches
Presaging doom, whose tired exhortations
Are homilies on peace at any cost.
All people exist on a face-to-face basis

With "destructive capability" and "annihilation."
Human achievements have reached a peak of disbelief.
Mortality has never been so grossly exposed
To the elements. All we have left is the hope
That no once-and-future Prince of Sarajevo

Elopes with a President's mistress. Even hope
May be the very enemy flying down the sky
As unborn mushrooms. I turn my eyes upward
And see a very old man hoeing the clouds,
Carefully preparing the air for broadcast seeding.

Images of patriots hearing "fireside chats,"
Cheering the first mail dropped, listening
To Mary's little tinfoil lamb, reading Freud
Surreptitiously beneath an incandescent light
Explode my stammering, answerable mind, and I weep.

8/21/74 (00668)

Plant Manager

The staccato of splotched silverware
Being carried from the dishwasher
And thrown into place doesn't drown
The buzz-saw droning in my head,
Nor does my wife's silence,
Gnawing at my patience like rat teeth,
Mollify the unabating roar
Of the blade that cuts our years to dust.

She chides me, like a phlegmatic child,
For relaxing on my ass, at the table,
Malingering before dessert. Her scorn
Reflects service poorly rendered,
As though I must redeem myself,
Do penance forever
For sins I've committed by my very being.

Taking coffee and cake,
I envision the ladies, in netted curlers,
Sewing isolated parts of garments
They never see completed or wear.
Each is my Liza Doolittle;
I'm their Higgins-magician,
Mystifying lives measured by seams,
Dozens completed, and coupons glued

To afternoons. Amidst the staccato
Of silverware, the hair curlers disappear.
I suspend my fifteen-year headache
By stumbling to the sink with dishes,
*

Then fade into our bedroom, alone,
Where my only dreams are of waking,
Leaving my wife with her magazines
And painted nails, retreating to the factory.

8/26/74 (00667)

[It's not like members of Silk Stocking] †

It's not like members of Silk Stocking

Despite a young man's singular efforts
To stave off the onslaught of nature,
So fecund is [t]he
Whose fecund body continues propagating

8/26? – 9/1?/74 (03321)

Keepers of the Castle △

Each thick stalk of the poke plant
Is an umbilicus connecting leaves to earth to God.
The garden, crowded with wild, thorny bushes,
Sumac, ivy, and climbing euonymus,
Grows profusely in uterine soil.

Termites thrive inside the wooden frame
Of a massive cast-iron cider press.
The corn drill of 1878,
Stationary beside a cistern pump,
Accumulates rust like dust on years.

Spiders, disguised as flowers, rocks, twigs,
Let their gothic nets undulate and hover
From tree to leaf to ground cover like buttresses
Flying through sunlit, cathedraled air,
Or Piranesian ropes dangling in the mind's nowhere.

The grass is a goat's coat of dirty hair
Worn by our mansion and stable in a crazy quilt
Of alleys and rights of way unconceived in abstracts
Dated in *ans*, measured in *arpents*,
And deeded forever to successors of DeLassus.

Rounded eaves, ornamental steeples, turrets,
A widow's walk with wrought-iron scrolls
Gaze on the acreage like executors
Of the original will, wearing judgmental periwigs,
Trying hard not to betray their dotage.

Although the gingerbread sags, chimneys lean,
Paint flakes in blatant places,
Gutters refuse even the slightest rain,
Caulking cracks away from plate glass,
And the attic leaks occasionally,

The demesne and its occupants hold firm
Against onslaughts time devises.
There's so much that needs to be done
By the two of us, who've emigrated from the city
To Canaan to renew our faith in being alive.

9/1/74 — [1?] (00666)

The Ritual of Babbitt Arising

Leviathan breaches as abruptly as disease rising
Inside a sleeping baby. The whale floats in close,
Too close for accident, as if intending to beach itself
On unseen shoals its dreams have allowed to accrete
At the edges of a vast and deeply complex ocean-sea.

The mammal groans; inaudible squeaks touch the air;
Heat lifts from its stretching body like ineffable fog
Shadowing dawn. The colossal creature has been caught
On a hooked yawn baited with invisible plankton
Daylight supplies. He awakens sweaty, ready for Zenith.

9/9/74 — [1] (00664)

Ephemerae

This house is a winter's night iced over in silence.
Everywhere, dream-people on skates finger-paint the sky
In slow-rolling silhouettes. Shadows within my eyes
Glisten like invisible singers I listen to for hours.
I might be Clyde Griffiths escaping Dreiser's mind,
Forsaking the strict, mission-oak confinement of religion
And environment for the essence of ephemerid, moth,
Butterfly, which clothe the wind in perpetual bow ties.
Each poem I fancy as a design too intricate to grasp
Slides into stride inside the climb to which I adjust
As the flight and the pilot become one with thin sky.
The unequivocal mastery of the tiniest space that people
Like myself occupy is their greatest victory over bone
And feeble cortex. It's the space taken up in pursuit
Of the skaters our dreams paint, the quest for sight
Described to Oedipus by frightened ghosts, and open roads
Left chaste and cleanly cropped of all wired skylines
That create a climate for cave drawings at Lascaux
And brain waves that electrify ancient cities of the soul.

9/9/74 — [2] (00665)

Seducing the Muse

My typewriter's taciturnity, this crisp morning,
Reminds me of a thousand lonely late last nights
Confined to the celibacy of my cork-lined library.
It whispers infinity's vocabulary with the inconstancy
Of illogical Satan persuading his compatriots to mutiny.
It reiterates myriad chases and prolonged escapes,
Searches and seizures creativity exacts from her suitors,
Caught up in futile quests for the perfect verse.

Wistfully, I reminisce of my capricious mistress.
Memory sees her undressing my voice in silence
Refined to obsession, senses her slender fingers
Reshaping my face, lips, teasing me to her body.
Abortively, this morning, I attempt to seduce her
And revivify the ecstasy that lingered ephemerally
*

In adolescence, when my poetry, still a virgin,
Dared, for the only reciprocal time, to seize her soul.

9/14/74 — [1] (00663)

Gestalt

Shadows scattered on the lawn from high trees
Are pieces of a jigsaw puzzle without a theme.
I race through their maze, try to find a place
To begin. The image contained remains a secret
To my senses as I fly behind a gas-powered machine
Hewing away at the grass, making the rows even
As if plumbed with chalk line, cutting short
The September fescue. Each pass fails to eradicate
Shadows pasted to our land. Like obnoxious beggars,
These afternoon vagrants, cast on the breeze
That confuses, superimposes, then returns them
To their original positions on the ground, seem forever
To wait for glances and handouts. Their outlines arrange
A strange form of mosaic on the inlay of eyes
That try to distill meaning from shapes and weight.
My mind's fingers manipulate, nudge them,
Lift one, then another, slowly as nuggets
Sifted from a freezing stream, until a black chunk
Is fitted contiguously to a less dense hunk,
Another, another. Formulations in dislocation
Coalesce as shadow seats into swaying shadow.
The image arises alchemically under a bright sun.
At once, I become aware of my wife staring at me
As I contemplate this congregation of trees
And earth. Out of the obscurity, she comes to me.

9/14/74 — [2] (00662)

A Transcendental Fugue $^\Delta$

I

I see two squirrels encircling the oak tree.

II

Each is me
          chasing myself, identical species
Day and night trying to discern a difference
Worthy of leaving behind
                              for others to emulate
When all my dusty parts are scattered.

III

The oak tree is a space-bridge;
                              it is me,
Whose changing length accommodates to forms
Of growth
          dependent on additional hours
Devoured by my unpredictable desire for life.

IV

I am the squirrels creeping on fleet feet
Along taut power lines
          stretched from a generating station
Hidden within my consciousness
                              to the house
Of my pumping heart.

V

                    I am also the tree's
          pith;
My blood is its fluid juice flying upward
Through primary paths that defy gravity,
Emotion flowing
          toward its celestial home.

VI

                                        I
Am tree/squirrel/iris perceiving my
Self
          as all of these beings at once,
                    in God's wide iris
                              perceived.

VII

I see two squirrels encircling the oak tree.

9/15/74   (00603)

Going Stale

The gilt-edged, leather-bound brain
I set to rest, each night, on retiring
Fits into its morocco slipcase
For tight protection. It leans on the shelf
With my old dreams, accumulating dust.

Such extravagances I've indulged in
Not from boredom, rather as a crazy profligate
Breaking pencils in half, biting nails
While waiting for original thoughts
To sail ashore, allow me to stake claim

To lands inhabited by ancient laureates
And barter meticulously inlaid philosophies
For ideas rhymed with verities of the heart.
Such grandiosities I've indulged in,
All these years, without choice,

As if singled out to gather words to be worn
Like an ornament of shore-washed shells
Around the neck of a voice in a chorus
Of one, an orchestration of sea and me,
Whose deep resonances have been doomed

Never to reach the surface as music
Audible to persons walking in the sand
Or working on plans for condominiums.
The brain, hidden away in its stifle,
Takes on a disquieting odor of decay.

The urgency for nonverbal purgation
Doesn't persist. Making joyful noise
No longer engages the smooth soul-flute.
I weep for our first walk in the zoo,
Poems we carelessly threw to the day,

And love notes we wrote on Easter eggs.
These lamentations of my aging heart
Are rhapsodies cast on an avalanche
I'm both in front of and underneath, alive
Inside a pile of dusty rubble, dying.

9/16/74 (00661)

Christ Sees Himself as a Poet

I'm hunted by packs of snarling clichés
Unleashed by policemen wearing suits.
Their tedious, high-pitched, feverish wails
Assail me as I scratch at cell walls
Of this forest that guards my anonymity.

Finally, I'm treed, held at naked bay
Until the critics wound me with epithets,
Concentrate my entire reason for being
Into easy syllogisms and clean hypotheses
To be frozen or fed instantly

To an unhungry public glutted by feasting.
They leave my intestines and severed head
In the forest as carrion for lesser beasts.
My mind is the prize they've finally captured
By constant bombardment of my sensibilities,

And I perish in a very convincing paramnesia,
In which new readers step heavily
Over my fragile verse, trip into sleep,
While the rest revert to Seuss rhymes
Without realizing I'm the one they crucified.

9/18/74 (00660)

The Brief Ecstasy of Icarus's Escape

Green-yellow-blue neon mirages;
Three throttles; hands in midair,
*

Knotting a cockpit macramé, testing gyros;
Eyes scanning pressure gauges; OK —
Radio to tower; taxi over bumpy concrete,
Rolling, revving without lost motion,
Lunging down the runway like a sleek porpoise
Humping through rough seas, breaching,
At an outrageously steep angle of attack, into oblivion.

Inertia defied, gravity totally overcome,
Takeoff is achieved with mathematical certainty.
Mastery of weight over space is cleanly executed
By a smooth grouping of cables and hushed thrust.
In this man-made fantasy, I've become as excited
As an unrealized idea reaching synaptic life,
Ecstatic to be 25,000 feet from everyone
Everywhere in time, as I fly a planet's curve,
Into the sun's eye, at horizon's periphery.

The high of sky is long as the mind is wide,
Quiet as dreams in shallow sleep are deep,
Peaceful as the ego floating in fetal solitude.
My heart, skittish as if it had hummingbird wings,
Hovers, drops through a fathomless air pocket,
Drifts, dips, reduces its airspeed,
Loses lift, recovers. Friction on the leading edges
Dissipates, drips away as if made of melting wax.
Spent, I descend to a sea of bumpy concrete.

9/20 — [1] & 9/23/74 — [1?]   (00609)

Reflections 25,000 Feet Deep

An involuntary marriage of spirit and

          Psyche

Is consummated in flight. The hot bones

          Vibrate

Inside a frighteningly gentle-appearing

          Turbulence

Silenced by the noise of rotary engines

          Pulsating

Between cold galaxies. The hollow eyes

          Come alive,
          *

Redefine images suspended in original

Déjà vu.

The blocked ears hear exploding cells

Of babies

Not yet born splitting their zygotes.

Mitosis

Ordered by God goes on inside the mind,

Dividing

The lives of my life into love living

Forever

In memories of the sweet birth of baby

Trilogy

And the uncertainties of a wife become

Mother.

9/20 — [2] & 9/23/74 — [2?] (01406)

Supplemental Income

The Transtar runs weekends between Farmington
And Fruitland, then north on 66 to Pontiac and back
In less than a single sun and moon —
One way a trailer-load of impatient cattle,
Before highballing empty all the way home.
For five days, the driver teaches daydreaming.

Summer becomes a three-month-wide haul
Over the Rockies. His intermountain express
Presses lightly as rabbit feet over concrete,
Washing highway sides littered with mesquite,
Snow near Lake Tahoe even in June,
Dehydrated grasses across Kansas flatlands.

His ports are a hundred numbing truck stops
Scattered haphazardly as red Monopoly plastic
Over the main-traveled game board he covers
On whining, oversize tandem tires
Eighteen times flying. The geography teacher
Believes in practicing what he preaches in class.

Once behind the wheel, he becomes Master Ahab,
Pacing every lane across the broad sea
Of states pulled by the same tides.
His scintillating eyes are obsessions in quest
Not of a mythic leg or a breaching whale,
Rather the mastery of captaining his own *Pequod*.

9/21/74 (00608)

Phaëthon

The four-horse chariot runs wild
Without a skilled driver to rein it in.
It streaks too close to Earth,
Burns the stratosphere, singes green grasses
Growing thick as populations in places.
Oceans boil, bubble; steam lifts
To ammoniacal fog seen from great distances.

Inhabitants of the kingdom begin retreating
To basements, spelunking in spacious caves,
Converging hastily on subterranean ethics
As vast waves of lava spew
From Vesuvius. Zeus awakens too late.
Thunderbolts and rain he hurls incubate
Amphibians slithering in spastic coagula

From mottled eggs breaking slowly open.
A swollen universe wobbles out of true
As the son of the sun finally comes home,
Prepared to bear all consequences
For his carelessness. He waits quietly,
Anticipating immortal extinction. Instead,
Helios pardons his deeds unequivocally,

Reasoning that divine justice without mercy
Would be tantamount to atheism on Heaven Hill.
Gods who rose from the holiest souls in the cosmos
Have no recourse. Retaliation
And debate are deep-sixed, inoperative.
Soon, only a slight cicatrix on infinity
Will exist in place of the dismantled planet,

Until a new creation divides the firmament
And life starts inching from gills to lungs.

Phaëthon: alias of a former President gently censured from office

9/22/74 (00607)

Aging

The alabaster moon, in whose lithophane gaze
I see suggestions of faces dying and dead,
Arouses passions to breaking, assails me
Like a creature seeking revenge for being neglected.
She invites my mind to undress
In a splotchy forest and lie down
For a turn at lovemaking with her. Ideas of order
And serenity bleed where cold years
Scratch the flesh, and I'm reminded of soft curves
Sculpted to fleeting perfection by my heated tongue,
Sinewy spines and supple, climbing thighs
Attaching like ivy tendrils to my body's length,
My mind being cradled between female legs.
These were familiar enticements my memory
Has obliterated. Gentle reminiscences
With which the moon tantalizes old men
Contented, finally, to consort with themselves
Are spider bites that drive them to lunacy
Or suicidal flights from the graceful bridge
Spanning youth and death. I see faces
Dying and dead in the alabaster moon; one of them
Resembles me. I can feel myself going cold.

9/24/74 (00606)

The Truant

I daydream a thousand truant officers
Hiding behind patrician oak trees
Sprouting out of the nineteenth century,
*

Waiting for me to come skipping home
After playing hooky from my identity.
I try to imagine who reported me missing,

Who might object vehemently to my being
Off by myself, ambuscading the day,
Boarding corvettes brought up in irons
By Edward Teach, or reading poetry
That has nothing to preach about life,

Ghettos, hieratic religious practices,
And death thinly disguised as metaphor.
Faint suggestions of personal guilt
Knit a web that suspends my attention
In gentle confession. Certainly, I wouldn't
Have turned myself in to the mind's authorities,

Suborned my will, or been forced to surrender
Private documents assuring my liberties.
I've always avoided the ease of academies,
Roll-top security, and quarter-size-
Collar-and-tie self-esteem.
There's no vest pocket

In my work shirt for the gold railroad watch
My father bequeathed me for good luck.
Yet, I find my personal freedoms
Threatened by specters concealed in trees
Shading paths my imagination pursues
As it races to elude absolute truths.

Perhaps, inadvertently, I dropped clues
To my hiding place or to the motivation
For my peculiar behavior. Hopefully,
When I awaken, a new daydream will have formed
Through whose Victorian doors I'll escape
To a nameless kingdom where nothing is sacred.

9/25/74 (00605)

The Poet's Confession

Such controlled emotional outflow
Accompanies his mellow moaning
That the gods stop, look down
*

To take note of the tiny being
Brought low to his knees in prayer.

He's unaware of peering eyes
And ears straining to differentiate
Implied meanings in his weeping.
Someone may have deceased, escaped
Incarceration in a decaying soul,

For all they know. He withholds
The reason that has driven him here,
As though he himself might not know
Or because he needs firm assurances
From those to whom he might disclose

His secret that they will keep
This humble beseeching for help
From reaching his loving public.
Effete, a tree without fruit,
A bum stumbling in dizzy retreat

From life's numbing impoverishments,
He submits his verse to search
And seizure by fathers of the temple
Of godliness. His haughty past
Is examined line by line

For promise of rejuvenation.
Words from his lips crack from thirst
As he begs to be taken whole
Through pestilence, famine, and fire
To arrive at the very beginning

Of himself again, when he was afraid
And uncertain of being seen by people
Rushing up to greet him with praises,
Naive and meek, when writing
All night was to experience ecstasy

Incessantly, not Armageddon.
Now, after flabby years,
He's returned. Such controlled
Emotional outflow conjoins his voice
With agony that God draws near.

9/27 & 10/1/74 — [1?] (00614)

First Insights ^Δ

The tiny child raptures me with her smiles.
Such smooth and unassuming contortions
On a face untrained as yet in deviltry
Contain no seeds of pain and disillusionment.

Her wide smiles are signs of contentedness
With a pristine world unspoiled by those
Who'd try quietly to insinuate her modesty
With graceless displays and tasteless games.

She squeezes her moist lips together happily
On recognizing the glints in my eager eyes.
We are friends of the most individual kind,
Who've accepted each other without compromise.

Two moments are we in the sum of a lifetime
Divided once, as we touch cheeks
Like roses gently nudged by a breeze.
We've become not just playmates, neighbors,

But, without *La Gioconda* smiles anymore,
Father and daughter blended in embrace,
Who seem, on this occasion, to perceive a feature
Of the other each has failed to see before.

10/1/74 — [2?]   (00434)

Preparing for Incarnations

My childhood lies in shadowy crosshatchings
Etched by light passing through curtains
Hung from ceiling to floor in foreign corridors.
I am the maze my mind occupies when it dreams
Of dying or retreats from dreams altogether
While straying, like gas trapped in natural caverns,
Between strata, waiting to pass from one life
Into another. Changes are sometimes slow to come.
The body can anticipate the accidents of autumn

Before leaves, hovering vigorously as hummingbirds,
Quit their fluttering. Books, games, and fantasies
*

Fade like exhaust and are lost, in dusk, to an older day.
Rusted cast-iron toys, gewgaws,
And boats that sailed imaginary lakes are antiques
Brought to auction. Only the lakes remain,
Constantly filled with rain draining from gutters
Catching lamentations, splotched with pollen,
From skies that have sheltered my life sixty years.

I am, and my wife is, an element of cycles
Ever operating. We're the vapors ascending,
Spent and empty, the way of Abraham's descendants,
Returning original through the Great Cloaca
By being reborn. The light I see right now,
Funneling through foreign corridors I pace,
Touches my face like snow, reminds me the time
Has again arrived to gather up things.
What I leave behind will have to await my return.

10/3/74   (00604)

Plant Manager

For John Gulla,
my mentor
and godfather to my family

I arise at five each morning
To open the factory by 6:45.
Even sleep conforms to the schedule
Of routine elements comprising a life
My three self-winding stopwatches
Record in dazzling synchronization.

My eating habits during the long day
Are erratic, digestion questionable at best.
The stocky body is a spotted leopard
Trained at stalking lesser prey,
Yet my tired brain, top-heavy,
Can't maintain the strenuous pace

Of making commands seem relevant
Or polite anymore. Now, my patience
Becomes thread that breaks when ladies
Screw their tensions too tight
*

Or lift presser feet too quickly
Before they finish edge-stitching a seam

Along my stomach or between my ears.
By nightfall, when all the machines
Are silenced and the piecework egos
Desert their dirty stations, I remain,
Indistinguishable from any bundle of slacks
Stacked on its spindly wrought-iron truck,

Too blunt to complain. I drag
Through cluttered aisles as if I were a pair
Of pants being sewn from components of a soul
Moving sequentially, on an assembly line,
Toward final inspection, before being shipped
To wife, food, endless 5 a.m.'s.

10/7–8/74 (00613)

Colors †

October's leaves are ingredients
In a feast being laid before me;
Celery, mustard, curry, and turmeric
Are stirred by invisible breezes,
Blended to soaring euphoria the eyes
Imbibe like sweet, indescribable liqueurs
Before I settle into the routine stupor
Of driving ninety miles into the Prairie.

Each tree emits a different odor,
Tastes completely original to the senses,
As though

10/11/74 (01366)

Homecoming

The town's three major flower shops
Have been unceremoniously busy all week,
Creating original bouquets for a queen
*

And her attendant maidens, corsages
For an entourage five hundred people deep.
Homecoming for a Prairie-town university
Coincides with our unplanned arrival home.

We've returned, with reasons unannounced,
To our clapboard roots during this season
When leaves, squirrels, weaving spiders
Incorporate eternity into their schemes;
We've come back to recapture a soaring euphoria
From October's sweet, indescribable liquors
Before hibernal stupors force shut

Doors excited eyes held open to summer guests.
Soon, the parade of crepe-paper floats
Will begin assembling. We'll climb aboard
As it passes us, being passed by shadows
Cast against time, then realize why
We drove such distance just to see others'
Festivities: love is keeping memories alive.

10/12/74 — [1] (00959)

Official Program

The eyes of every local merchant
Peer out in flat, black offset focus
From the official football program,
Hawked for a quarter before the game.
The cover is a queen recently elected
For a plethora of questionable deeds,
Arbitrary qualities, and a languid education.
Between her legs of stapled pages
Ride the bravest knights, known as
All-LeagueAll-ConferenceAll-District
Smallcollegeallamericanathletes.
The rest get mere alphabetical mention
As bodies ready to participate in the melee
Diplomatically scheduled to yield victory
On homecoming weekend. The crowd grows restless.
Well-dressed professors
*

And their doting wives whisper from hills
Invisible to students who worship words
They carefully choose. Two by blue-jeaned
Two, youths touch, kiss unabashedly, talk
Softly about the new night pursuing them
Like a hungry creature.
Long after the group of running humans,
Having fully engaged in the game and reinstated
The queen's name statewide, has exited
Its playing field, they touch yet, leave
En masse, clutching official programs
Like Dead Sea Scrolls about to be thrown
To history, ready for a lengthy death,
Each retiring to a private celebration.

10/12/74 — [2] (00960)

Her Five-Month Birthday △

Like a spaceshot soaring minutes
Into orbit, baby Trilogy has reached
A five-month high, and still
We plot her curve, watch nervously
For slight deviations in her flight pattern.

Savoring has finally moved from tongue
To brain, like arterial blood to veins
To heart, and makes faint impressions.
Once, only mother's milk sufficed,
Then cereal mixed with formula; now,
She has taught herself to hate peas,
Tolerate carrots and beans, and relish
Sweet peaches and pears and apricots
As if each one were her sucking-thumb.

Tiny hands, having mastered grasping
Not wholly by design or only accidentally,
Are just now touching exotic objects.
The stubby fingers are subtle antennae
Beginning to differentiate hot/cold,
Rough/smooth, sharp/soft/hard,
*

Wet and dry, like diapers metamorphosed
Without warning or clean bedsheets
She alters overnight in sweaty sleep.

We've seen the slow head, connected
To a stiff neck, grow alert
To quick movements not merely from reflex
But fear of intruders bearing gifts.
She chooses who will hold her folded
In smooth shoulders, refuses dignitaries.
Only her father, with his special voice,
And the gentle lady who breast-feeds her
Soothe the baby into lasting quietude.

Even as the day recedes, we watch
Her momentum fulfill its expected trajectory.
Hers has been a perfectly executed launch.
This little being is certainly poised
In her graceful ascent into the life-sky.

10/13/74 (00437)

Divorcée

The slurred words she murmurs
Disturb her perfectly curving lips.
Excuses trip from her tongue like sermons
Expurgated from scripture rewritten
By thieves in search of altar gold.

Lies, like toads cloaked in beads
And queenly ermines, assault truth,
Assume disguises whose fraudulence
Excites the king to renewed faith,
While youthful suitors pace unseen

Beneath their obese ruler's balcony.
Rumors of illicit romance illumine
Her deep obscurity, widen her eyes
Into wafers, offered the unredeemed,
To be eaten as earthly sacraments.

Finally, she's banished from the castle,
Balancing life like a juggling mime.
Outside, she awaits her spectators' applause.
Only a lover with kingdoms to offer
Will gain her slightly stained glove.

10/16/74 (00612)

Initial Stages of the Race ^Δ

Without a sign of growing weary,
She passes the halfway barrier
In the steeplechase she entered as a free agent
Six months ago, when the contest was announced.

Calisthenics accomplished on her naked back
Consisted of making her hands move,
Like northern lights, toward her face,
Then away, in order to calculate distances
Once the race got underway. The links
In her sensorimotor chain hadn't been closed

When hands that merely flailed the air
Like mechanical arms in an experimental lab
Began making the same discoveries:
Fingers gently enmeshed in flesh
Formed symmetrical equations between nerves
Designed to coordinate touch with brain.

Finally, all prerace preparation ended
With sets of knee bends by the limber participant.
After many attempts to reach and hold
The tiny, kicking feet and toes,
She succeeded in keeping the position intact
While perception connected the act to memory.

Now, she leads her pack of one
In a steeplechase predetermined by a genius
Who forces choice and rewards determination
With a glorious victory over nonexistence.

10/20/74 (00542)

Manimals and Other Beasts

You and I lie paralyzed on a bed of days
Lighted from somewhere above by an ecclesiastical sky.
We're robed in sin woven around our minds
Like ideas knitted by a guru sitting at his loom,
Preaching free love among beasts and beings.

We lie awake, while lying completely asleep,
In sky-gardens seeded with germinating dreams
Clustered in egg-swarms warmed to ecstasy
And hatched by the eyes conceiving the wide earth
Drawn out across an endless, bending horizon.

Eventually, the snakes of creation emerge, wormlike,
To the brain's fertile surface, beg permission
To search out and bite persons who've strayed by accident
Too far from each other's corporeal touching.
Lunacy scrapes interconnected nerve endings

We once used to communicate our gentle telepathies
To each other. We've become our own vipers' prey,
Obeying fears that drive us deeper apart.
The edge rises up like a spectral beggar
Stretching out its arms to take us down,

As it divides forever our wired, sensual attentions.
The snakes seduce us into making love in quietude,
Then distract us from private animal appetites
By inviting every terrestrial beast to our bedside
To observe firsthand the final, impotent orgasm

Recorded by the last two surviving manimals
In a defunct kingdom of civilized human creatures.
Somewhere beyond our ears, we hear the music
That sleep provides its wakeful ghosts. It cries,
"Kyrie, Kyrie, eleison! Save us from dying alone."

10/24/74 (00611)

Time-and-Motion Analysis

Six and fifty-hundredths
Snatch me from weekend revelry.
*

Motion chases stasis
Jerkily around a circular dial
Of days calibrated in elements,
On a job of life and death.

Hundredths concatenate like seeds
Lifted from a severed pumpkin.
They cling in a mass of memory
Before forgetting they belong to me.
Dissipation is the funnel they use
To escape from hour to hour to day,

Until new data is collated,
Expectations are graded and measured
Against my previous performances,
And age is requested to set
A tighter rate on my operation.
Now, the accuracy of my quota defeats me.

10/28, 11/16?/74, & 1/2/75 — [1?]   (00624)

The Foul Rag-and-Bone Shop

The very awareness of days passing
Dazes the engaged apparatus whose gauges
Register pressure in human calibrations.
Boilers occasionally explode unnoticed
By all but me. I feel steam escaping
My veins, float-valves closing my eyes
When anyone comes near to inspect
Unrepaired damages from past accidents
I've failed to report. One more citation
Could close the doors without further recourse.

The worrisome business of operating full
On a daily basis and the maintenance required
To keep burners cleanly fired
Exact too grave an overhead
Just to produce replacement parts
For a body whose guarantees are obsolete.
Lately, I've requested all major repairs
Be postponed pending word of a merger
*

Or, more probably, a permanent shutdown
Of furnaces that powered a proud soul.

10/30/74 (00610)

Epilogue to the Twenty-third Sermon

*Listening to John Donne's echo
on Allhallows Eve*

At one time, the human stranger seated here
Among his lifelong neighbors was given a name,
A distinguishing feature, birthright, franchise
To quickly locate and draw him out of a crowd,
And his empty sack of being began to expand.

Later, he dreamed of making his name known
Above all equal and greater creatures on the plains
He frenetically roamed, legally staked and claimed,
Deforested, tilled, made verdant with wheat and feed
For beeves and pigs. Yet, he only succeeded

In becoming rich with overinflated conceit.
Failing badly to evaluate his modest accomplishments,
He frantically demanded offspring to keep alive
A dying reputation the oceanic soil would wash away
With his decayed hulk when the last wave broke

Onto his isolated promontory to bury his voice.
No amount of totemic energy or insane urgency
Could promote a male baby to perpetuate his name.
The girl he created in old age, "Sky Smoke,"
Scattered his ashen vapors across a bald horizon.

Now, he sits here, a stranger even to himself,
Unable to recall reasons for all the meaningless rush,
Whose resolute disbelief in his still being alive
Slowly transforms him into a ghostly apparition
Clothed thinly in skin tinted with disappearing ink.

10/31/74 — [1] (00621)

Drizzle △

Beads of rain pressed against my wind-screen
By high velocity are motile sperm climbing
An invisible tube to reach my uterine mind.
Above the roof, where vision goes blind,

In a dark compartment illumined from far below,
They latch hold in thick suspension, explode
Into figmental children without family names,
Who depend solely on me for their nourishment.

Not necessarily against, but without, my consent,
I've fathered another baby from out this drizzle
To grow up in the City of Poetry, where I've dwelled
The last twelve years with my fastidious mistress.

10/31/74 — [2?]   (00622)

Approach-Avoidance Conflict

Mile by mile, my speed climbed higher
Along an undeviating maze of straight road,
As though no destination might be reached
Unless it were the ultimate fatality achieved
In unpremeditated, totally asocial suicide.

Such clinically introspective ruminations
Deprive periods of rest I take from driving
Of any release, quietude, peace of mind
I might find before pressing ahead.
Even the coffee tastes like arsenic dust.

Instead, these breaks create a malaise
Whose trance I can neither deny nor defeat.
In one, I'm a rat vacillating between cheese
And an electrified grid plate, safe only in stasis
Yet conditioned to reach home by nightfall.

10/31/74 — [3?]   (00620)

Suggestions △

Our growing cub is touching earth,
Gumming whatever those robot hands
Can latch onto and draw to her mouth:
Thumb, pages of a convenient magazine,
Sheets, her mother's teats, heated
To expectation — every anything in reach.

As gentle benefactors of a brain arrived
At the end of divine silence, a being
In training, we wonder what gospel
Predicted this creativity, which disciple
Prophesied the coming of such purity,
Why her arrival was so vigilantly awaited.

We can only guess at the life she left
By the way she still smiles in her sleep.

11/4/74 (00728)

Winter Catches the Moon in Its Teeth

Finally, the deep freeze,
Inevitable as death accepted
Unexpectedly by humanity,
Has arrived. Indian summer
Is gone in a perfidious breath,
Smoke-cold, forgotten
As foot-trod leaves
Strewn like ruins over the Palatine.

It's almost time, now,
To make wide postponements.
Adrenaline slows in my veins
Like arctic ice floes.
Something the senses anticipate
Makes me take shelter;
A severed moon bleeds
In dawn's steely jaws.

11/5/74 (00619)

The Dragon

At the very base of the shaft that connects me
By way of the brain, through supple vertebrae,
To the earth lives a nameless dragon who guards
Passages to the Kingdom of Endless Dimensions,
Where my mind reclines in guilty lassitude,
Waiting to be set aflame, devastated.

I remember every breath and forget only
The energy required in climbing so deep
To reach the source of uneasiness, where demons,
In repulsive profusion, strangled the weak spirit
Trying to surface. Even then, the dragon
Refused reunion to elements of my broken soul.

Cradle and grave coalesce. I see babies
Alive in dead fetuses in bellies of queens
Washed ashore on beaches where life assembles
For its prolonged surge toward reincarnation.
Babies from chrysalids explode into a golden rope
Hung from the base of my identity. I climb down

And realize the dragon was me all the while,
In sleepy disguise, trying to outwit wisdom,
Deceiving the deceiver. Soon, I break through
The layered maze of complicated justifications
For his remaining all these years
And discover my fear of solitude made him wait

Until I finally arrived here to protect me
From myself once the long journey was made.
At this depth, the air is dry ice.
The lungs of the animal within the dumb animal
Collapse. Overexposure causes the brain,
Long obsessed by chimeras, to seal its shaft.

11/7/74 (00618)

Visiting Grandparents ^Δ

An old bedspread brought up from the basement
And thrown over the living-room rug
*

Is a playground for flailing legs and unacrobatic torso.
While trying to swim through invisible water,
The self-amused baby moves backward like a crawfish.
Each noise distracts her fleeting concentrations,
And at play, after sleep, before feeding,
She acts out sideshow antics in pantomime
With the ceremonial daring of a trapeze clown.

Her Prairie-raised grandparents remain mesmerized
By sweet reveries of childhood her performance evokes.
Their recent days recede like beads through a funnel,
Spill onto the floor by the eager girl,
Whose eyes convert them back into a gentle dream
Her mind can absorb. It's almost as though she knows
They've also upstaged a similar audience before
With the untranslatable syncopations heritage bestows
On the children of man's oldest traveling show.

11/10/74 (00961)

Miscellaneous Man

He who chooses his destiny is doomed to undergo
Each vicissitude as intimately as a wife who knows
Her baby was immaculately conceived in another's mind,
As a prostitute who realizes she's a Brancusi seal
Anchored beneath a busy museum's spotlights,
And as a lost child who has forgotten his father's surname.

If Everyman be judged by the quality of self-discovery,
His degree of sweet and gentle ego-esteem,
The evocative depths of his free-fleeing fantasies,
And the sheer, naked need to emancipate the spirit
Enslaved in pedantic casuistry, then whore, virgin,
And truant must be roused from his poet-sleep and adored.

11/11/74 — [1?] (00616)

A Christmas Eve Hymn

Where were you when the first Christmas burst through
Its tight-wrapped, cold-blown bloom, into flower?

Who knew the beautiful human who sat so alone
Beside the tree, touching its rose-odor needles,
Supple even after the first hard freeze?

What became of connubial birds, worms, tigers in branches
Above a white paradise, thriving on delicate fruits
The man was instructed to leave and only once tasted?

Why do we celebrate the beasts and beings, this evening,
As static reminders of those who died or are dying now?
They live yet in our existence. We're their memories.

When will another Christmas bring us all back together
For the first time since flowers grew in Gethsemane?

11/11/74 — [2?] (00617)

Pieceworkers

Disheveled spirits pass through the factory door
    Like parts slightly vibrating on a conveyor belt,
And as with numbered pieces, each worker arrives
    Sequentially at her designated machine on the floor

To stitch time, mind, and daydreams into frills

    Svelte, breastless New York ladies will soil
Before donating them to tax-deductible charities
    For consignment and resale to bony, spirited daughters
Of 39th Street–loft sample-hands from the Bronx.

11/14/74 & 1/2/75 — [2?] (00615)

Rites of Baptism ᐃ

From minutiae, two specks grew:
Moon chasing sun, sun moon,
One dependent upon the other,
Both nearly invisible without emanations
From the fiery core of an orbiting Source.

Their union engendered a new hope
Of keeping alive the delicately shaped bloom
*

Of human kindness in mankind's garden.
A godly image ripened to womb fruit,
Exploded, emerged as a third speck,

Resembling flesh of our respective origins.
We've come today to bless the baby, Trilogy.
She's the newest star in a galaxy
Defined by love edging ever outward.
Her birth connects us with Genesis.

11/17/74

The Dream-Tree △

I

Beyond this earth, on the planet of Zilla,
There lived a baby named Silly Nardilla,

Who dreamed of a tree filled with namels
And nakes, nippos, crackoons, and nowls

Instead of the usual Christmas ornaments.
She prayed all year long that her wish

Would be heard in the far-distant garden
Where dream-creatures slept peacefully,

Side by side, serene in the green forest.
Leones and ostricks, *tigres* and tortoyses,

Even her wise, old, slow-moving pachyderm
Friends, Undulant and Silliphant, heard

Pleas she made on her knees each evening
Before being invaded by fleeting elves.

II

Deep in her mind, a meeting was convened.
When all the animals reached agreement

On the terms of their roles on Xmas Eve,
They boarded a dreamboat like Noah's

Ark and floated her storm-torn streams
Of fantasy. Finally, they arrived safe

At the hour when she awakened in surprise
To find those gifts she had desired

All before her on the floor, in the branches,
Like animals of night kissing her eyes

Or future friends come alive to greet her
On her first celebration of eternal love.

Meanwhile, her parents stood silently by
As their baby dreamed her future dreams.

                    Jan   L.D.   Trilogy
                         12/25/74

11/18/74   (01407)

Intimations of Futility

If only I had
A biography of my life
To go by,
I could rely on hindsight for answers,
Refer to causes célèbres,
Read portions
Where I needed to make decisions
At forks in the road.
The sheer idea of perfection,
Heroism, statesmanship,
Scrupled nouveau wealth,
A Picassoed physique
Buckles my stagnant mind.

It's the second-guessing
We lack, vision with a voice,
The crystal discipline
That allows death's finger
To flick its rim without breaking it,
While achieving an outbound ring
Whose sympathies unloose
*

The introspective I,
Set it free
To scribe its autobiography.
With tabula rasa, we arrive;
We leave with the slate erased.
Everything in between is all we are.

11/24/74 (00623)

Zola's Requiem

For dear "Aunt" Gerry Carp;
God bless "Uncle" Zola.

Spider mums have netted in a white-
And-red web the outer shell
Of the vessel that will transport his soul
To the highest reaches of deep.
Within that silvery coffin
Lies the perfectly still synthesis
Of love contained forever by the will
And labor lived by a gentle creature
Who called his fellow beings "Honey."

We've come to witness a burial
Of our grief consecrated in his name.
He kisses each of us, hugs us each
For the last time. As the cables
Lengthen out, I reach to touch him.
My palm pats the disappearing casket
As though christening his new boat
Or shaking hands with memories
Of Zola until today forgotten,

And I'm left with a velvety, wet petal,
Whose delicacy reminds me of his love.

11/25/74 (00626)

[The people convene to discuss the meaning] †

The people convene to discuss the meaning
Of survival. Basic themes are repeated
With tedious frequency: crime, inflation,
Populations unable to feed themselves,
Individual freedom under constant attack
By anonymous industrial-militaristic
Complexes, polluted air, heart attack,
Almost every convenient excuse and
Cause

11/30/74 — [1] (01367)

Flower Shop on the Square

Outside, beneath a slow-blown snow,
Townspeople pass this plate-glass eye
Like abrupt shooting-gallery ducks on hinges.
I take careful aim, speculating intuitively
On what makes them refrain from pausing to gaze
At the tableau — china icons and thriving plants —
And cleanly hit the mark on each moving target.

Hurriedly they stir, this Saturday after Thanksgiving,
Three weeks prior to Christmas Eve,
To purchase love featured on TV screens.
They search for oblations to assuage the ancient guilt,
In full-page catalog displays,
On sensually molded mannequins, atop tables
Laden with chrome- and gold-plated gewgaws.

The occasion dictates conspicuous moral extravagance,
Promotes material worship, spiritual bankruptcy,
By virtue of life's eternal commemoration of the death
Delivered so many ethical centuries ago.
What a pity our unfavorable balance of trade
Remains perpetually unrepaid and can't be satisfied,
With the least ceremony, by merely exchanging nosegays.

11/30/74 — [2] (00625)

Stranded

Like a German occupation, the unexpected snow
Invaded us abruptly out of a predawn hour,
Engaged us on foreign soil, made us take cover
Under its white mantle, indoors, frightened
For our outbound lives. We'd meant to leave
This prairie town early this Lord's morning,

Yet being stranded appeared more defensible
Than driving through imaginary Maginot lines
Already infiltrated by a cold enemy. Escape
Seemed suicidal: against such whiteness,
Everything, even nakedness, silence, night,
Shows its outline, becomes visible to death,

Requires absolute willed stillness to avoid
Being captured by the claustrophobic mind
Or going slowly mad inside its darkened shelter.
All day, through glass, we saw the flakes
As bombs containing insane doubts about the future,
Exploding all our old notions of freedom.

12/1/74 (00628)

Pleasures

Jan, beautiful Jan!

We penetrate invisibility, enter all the days
Escaped from memory, dreaming of when we were virgins
To each other, knowing, now, that nothing pure
Ever dilutes the shadow of its recaptured past
And that love sculpted from clay, once fired,
Never breaks. How beautiful we still are!
Suggestions of growing old fade like myths
Twice told vestal maidens. Our bodies invite us
To the precarious ceremony of tender, naked lust.

Like outlines fleshed in by an unexpected light,
Darkness illumined by our touching eyes caresses us.
We disappear in a torrid, yet fertile, valley,
*

Hot as ice on fire. Scorched by ecstasies,
The eyes are torn clear of their burning orbits,
Blown by soaring blasts lifting erratically
From the soul's exploding sun. We emerge whole,
Having achieved continuity with all creatures,
While reaching beyond pleasure, to selflessness.

12/3/74 (00627)

Sad Song of Ecstasy for Jan

Like invisible beads of moisture
Seeping through wintry impenetrability,
People we've always known,
Who have touched our lives with love,
Keep disappearing. Everywhere,
Uneven extremes in density and pressure
Set up vacuums. Someone is forever
In transit from low zones to lower,
High positions of distinction
To higher private elevations
In the collective public anonymity,
By the endless transmigration of souls
Made ultimately unstable
For having aligned themselves with mankind.

Why are we doomed to drowse
In a perpetual twilight of dying?
Why do the beautiful, smooth physiques
We've been endowed with accrete fat
Overnight, lose their curried scent
As the mind is drawn to senescence
Or early death by accident?
And what of those cowardly few
Who, having seen the specter gnawing
From within, spurn the future
By climbing back on all fours
Through sleep, toward a lambent candle
Eternally burning at the far end?
Do we deceive ourselves? Is life a dream

We teach our kind to believe is real,
Or are the tight throats of remorse
And swollen eyes of grief
On the leaving of a close friend
Meant to alarm us and awaken us
To a precarious corporeality
We possess? Touch my eyes with yours,
Dear, blessed wife, and try
To explain away the radiance we transmit
As mere Mosaical phenomena! Kiss me
With your vital light and be persuaded
That our mirrored images transcend
Precious reflections of Christ. While alive,
Let us be each other's faith.

12/15/74 (00629)

Sowers, Reapers, and Gleaners

With daily confusion, we sow seeds
Of our souls' misdeeds. It's as though
We're desperately seeking refuge
From the godly possibilities
Of living the monk's asceticism,
In perverse, upturned furrows
Of previously undisturbed earth.

The crooked rows we hoe
In a garden not of our choosing
Follow us with the rootlike persistence
Of fugitive, trailing shadows
Assailing an alien sun
The entire length of existence
Recorded by curious man.

Between each hard ridge
Stir stillborn dreams
Ancestors bequeathed us in genes
Never completely formed
In their gentle resurrections
Below warm rains. Colder
Than swollen oceans, their hopes,

Like bodies of forgotten prisoners
Left to rot in cells, decay;
Medieval souls lie coffined
In silence, in anonymity
Visited by worms and moles.
I hear all the ancient generations
Calling without being answered,

Warning me to fear an easy harvest.
I weep for my feeble estate.
Never have I been able to succeed
At eradicating the weeds
That molest, like flies a dog's eye,
My mind's germinal ideas.
The only thing I've ever grown

Is old. Soon, my very being
Will be planted, a death vegetable
Set in black invisibility
And tended by watchful nematodes.
All I ask from my brief season
Is a reasonable hope that God
Will notice me growing toward Him.

12/16/74 (00632)

On Looking into Baby Trilogy's Eyes ^Δ

Into her blue, blue eyes, I stare,
Hypnotized by antic reflections of my hair
And handlebar mustache: a strange face,
Attenuated as El Greco's anonymous saints',
Floats in two azure pools
Like identically slender blossoms of a flower
Never before recorded or echoes
From a solitary shofar forever trapped
Inside a perpetual festival of atonement.

We are pieces of a correspondent seed,
Excommunicants from a collective womb.
Through her, I see myself as a clot
Ontologically racing from age to age,
*

Species to species, in awkward regeneration
Of the ultimate God-conceived creation,
For whom human speech is the blessed key
That opens the mind's silence, conscience
The lock that keeps the instincts caged.

She is my home away from the home
I abandoned on uprooting myself at birth,
Moving quarters to the tenemented universe
People use as their way station
In time. I am her pliant landlord
And tenant, who remains ever steadfast
Day and night at the wrought gates
Of her eyes to guard against satyrs
Disguised as nursery-rhyme blue-boys.

As we share the strange, pained face
She watches me strain to recognize,
I imagine the hour when I'll sit alone
Without her eyes of the bluest blue
In which to gaze to remind myself
That the inhabitant of the flabby face
Bereft of hair and handlebar
Is a scion of Heaven's flowering tree
And that she's the daughter of his ecstasy.

12/18/74   (00963)

As Christmas Approaches

For Mom and Dad

A family scattered like October leaves
Reunites. Adjourned committees of people
Seeded in the same furrow and harvested
Return from afar to complete the table
Spread with the bounty of Christmastide.

For a moment, the forgetful mind recalls
Its adolescence, revives old hopes
Of discovering trade routes to the Moluccas,
Its fright on stepping aboard a caravel
For ports beyond Atlantis, and the consequences

Of conquests hastily made. For a moment
Only, the enlightened eyes illumine
The soundproof booth of rooms
Where the growing spirit moved
Through peaceful sleep and secret glooms

To arrive at the day it would fly away
On liberated, untried wings. The same
Stained carpets and smudged wallpapers,
Window shades, headboards, and desk
Give rise to images of a known paradise.

Despite its unchanging stability, home
Is never quite the way we left it,
Nor is memory, which alters the height of shapes
And the size of basic configurations,
As easily verified when tested by fact.

Yet we've returned, on this Christmastide,
To rejoice in the blessed hour at hand
And participate in a celebration of renascence
For a man, his life's companion, their children,
Congregated under a common roof.

12/23/74 — [1?] (00631)

Just Crawling ᐃ

The baby moves like a gentle ameba.
She crawls, sits, and falls over,
Takes up a new direction,
Achieves distance measured in feet
Across a dirty rug,
Tumbles like a bear cub,

Reaches, strains, totters sideways
In a sky diver's soft, sensual roll,
While alternating between smiles
And surprised, wide-eyed sighs
Of disbelief and relief. Trilogy
Is the sum of her energy.

She becomes what her parents see
As an extension of their mentality.
*

Her being calls all eyes
To crawl with her on bended knees
Up trees whose leaves are snowflakes
Or inchworms spinning gold.

12/23 — [2?] & 12/25/74 (00964)

Flight

As I look outward from the cabin,
    The sleek wing tip I see
Reaches halfway across a universe
    Whose horizon is in diminishment.

Upward, momentarily blinded
    By invisible white sky, emergent,
The eyes leap through blue
    High above receding land.

Gone as melting ice
    Transferred eventually to oceans,
We're unearthed, assuming otherworldliness
    As time aligns itself with dreams

We energize with heartbeats
    Freed from bodily intervention.
Life is a matter of staying awake
    In cryogenic sleep,

Avoiding demons that would lure us away
    From the healthy soul's animation.
Our flight today is being made
    In preparation for incarnations

Assigned to our particular fate.
    We are tiny pieces of humanity
Caught on a sourceless wind,
    Being carried to a new beginning

At the far end of the mind's sky.
    Whatever awaits our arrival
Remains to be conjured by us alone,
    As we descend inexorably to earth.

12/26/74 — [1] (00633)

A Sky Filled with Trees

For Stuart and Jeffrey Fabe

Even if a hundred bodhi charms,
    Drooping like plump Buddhas
From pear trees planted in the sky,
    Fell from the ivory heavens
And landed in my open eyes
    Like orient moon-fruit,

I doubt if I would realize
    They were tokens of fortune
Meant to keep me alive,
    Not as food to be eaten,
Just by being reminders
    That the mind can harvest the sky.

12/26/74 — [2] (00101)

Incarnations

Although only hours have elapsed,
This Christmas is already a thing of the past,
Whose passage through space is a comet
Casting sparks across known galaxies
    Of vision and reminiscence.
We gasp at its fleet and searing flame.
    Such novas only come once
Every seventy generations of man,
    Then lapse into legendary darkness.

All across the vast stage on which
Day and naked night exchange the hours
    In a graceful rape of solitude,
We're resigned to our own blind silence.
    Face to face, we gaze
Into the inscrutable faces that linger
On the flickering images and symbols we worship,
Wondering if, when the next nova returns,
We'll be there to recognize ourselves.

12/26/74 — [3] (00630)

Deep-Sea Charter ^Δ

For Mike Köepf,
the fisher king of Half Moon Bay

I

Exhaust floats off
And is caught in the raw wake
Of twin diesels churning full throttle.
Gulls dive. The swells divide
Across our heaving prow, grow wide,
Wider, then disappear behind us.
Open ocean invites us to drop lines,
Play its expensive games
Of finders-keepers and make-believe.

II

Going at 900 revs,
        We troll for live bait
In slow circles,
        Hoping to hook bonita.
Big fish know the difference!

III

Now, an hour has elapsed,
        And still no signs of activity.
My impatience grows steadily,
        Yet the ocean has no set schedule.
No force can suborn it,
        Nor any amount of persuasive charm
Break down its inviolate soul.
        The ocean, like every element
Except man, is without shame
                or guilt.
        Its will derives from its size
                and depth,
Not from heredity, omens, and death.

IV

After being out two hours,
We finally hook a bonita
*

On a trolling fly. Within minutes,
The large line is weighted
And dropped over the side,
Above an airplane wreck sighted
By triangles made with a Fathometer.

Below us, the monsters strafe,
Fluting through silence
Like dead souls flying in space
On their way home. Anxiously, we wait
For the bait to touch bottom
And the oversize reel to take up slack,
Become completely taut,

Then drive back out
Against smooth, oiled ratchets.
Only, this time, the tautness is grouper,
Caught inside a rocky grot,
Bloated, intractable, taut,
Taut to the edge of pain's threshold,
Then tensionless — our first strike, lost.

V

The fishing boats lumber
Between buoyed channels,
Pass Port Everglades, the Point,
Then diminish into ocean.
As they climb my salt-spewed bedroom window,
I try to remember our expensive venture,

How, yesterday, we plied a stretch of sea
Three hundred feet deep,
Comforted by radio, compass, twin engines,
All the while in sight
Of calcified, condominiumed land
And within reach of the fleet,

All of whose chartered crews
Were engaged in making systematic passes
At the same square acre of ocean reef,
How our money guaranteed us,
If not a mountable trophy, at least
Another cash-carry chance at a "catch."

Yet, this morning, my memory
Can only recall *pescadores*
Mending nets on Alicante beaches,
Their inebriated nights
After meager catches, the dust, flies,
The families surviving by a stingy sea.

12/29–30/74 — [1] on 12/30 (00634)

Song for Trilogy ^Δ

You're a little soul growing older,
Baby Trilogy,
Grabbing sandaled feet and toes,
Plastic beads,
And everything that neatly fits
Between teeth
And upper gums. You're sitting up
Without leaning,
Crawling without resting every
Two feet,
Reaching for walls and tables
To steady
The flabby legs not quite ready
To walk free.
You're a little soul growing older,
Baby Trilogy,
Growing older as your little soul
Is released.

12/30/74 — [2] (00967)

The Door ^Δ

As wide as the eye can slide from side to side,
There is only ocean and, of course, its voice,
Whose gentleness is a loving lady's soft touch.
Above, ubiquitous sea gulls reach down
To extract fast-fluting shadows from a surface
Almost completely undisturbed by light breezes.

Beyond the ears' perimeters are deeper voices:
The throbbing, ceaseless drone of propeller shafts
And airborne blades churn cohesive firmaments,
Exceed the audible limits of unconcerned bathers
Just entering the beach. Everything has its place
Except me; I look for day's opening to penetrate.

12/31/74 — [1] (00635)

[Didn't want to be the one to say the end] †

Didn't want to be the one to say the end
Has come 'round, yet the old year

12/31/74 — [2] (02955)

Do You Believe in Magic?

The earphones fill with liquid music,
Mellifluous, sensuous as promises of love
Whispered through soft whiskey swilled,
Hinting of nights to come, lost in flowers
Petaling your body, lifting to climax;
Electric tremulations, borrowed guitars,
Da Vinci cartoons flying us to heavens
Upon spacy moon-ships; and ocean spray
Identifying us as sea urchins awash
After a tumultuous night of storms
At sea together. Such passional melodies
Break down the most substantial brains,
Explode all decent preconceptions life
Prescribes, through conventional ceremony,
For the diseased spirit trying to survive
Its daily self. Such strident sounds
Make us slaves comfortably caged
Within the peaceful framework we set
Around ourselves to allow that freedom
At any time to the species contained
*

Deep inside the breathing spirit,
Freedom to hold and be freely held
Without bars, chains, nets, soft arms,
Or the gentlest poetical preludes
Draped in invisible veils overhead,
Freedom to receive ethereal music
With our plain ears and transform it
Into a bridge connecting the mind with
The Magician who turns life into love,
Love into profuse emotional explosions
Whose velvet ashes never stop falling,
Life back into magic made by the wind,
To be carried through the human heart
As blood tuned to music set beyond time.

12/31/71 — [3] (00953)

Knothole

The tail end of another year,
Like a wily child peering through
A knothole in a stadium fence,
Focuses all its intensity on us.

It runs behind and in front of us
Simultaneously, straining to see
The future and recall the past,
Grouped like players on opposing teams,

The outcome of whose fierce battle
Will never be decided. Its eye blinks.
Our actions become nonexistent;
Then the sides change

And different-colored shirts
Take the field as the game resumes.
We're the players and spectators, combined
To witness the trophy pass hands

Or remain with the defending club
For yet another season. Soon,
The score is 12:00 a.m.
Morning checks in with the referee.

Last year peers through
Its knothole, unaware
We've already changed uniforms for events
Scheduled in a newer stadium.

12/31/74 — [4] (00636)

New Year's Celebration

I

His blood feels like slow-flowing sap,
December-cold, clotting against the air.

Night is awash with streamers, confetti.
Noisemakers rattle the ears to deafness,

Scatter debris of shattered past memories
Into tiny pieces as if this were the first Eve

His aging body had ever spent in celebration
And all the rest were a telegrapher's code

Tapped out and recorded by a blind man,
Rather than the last punishing blow

Inflicted on his wounded soul. He seeks refuge
In his mind's treelined lovers' park.

II

The romance of their first secret meeting is history.
Its articulation is merely the weak evocation

Of a feeble poet who's forgotten how to rhyme
His identity with the lonely life he leads

By himself with a confined, ectomorphic wife.
No words flow between them at supper.

It's as if the menu they read reveals scripture
Intended not to be preached or discussed

But eaten by starved and emaciated inhabitants
Of the house of bodily solitude. They order

Without hesitating, then lapse into silence,
Waiting, watching, seeing beyond themselves.

III

Strange how, now, he almost seems to distinguish
The orchestra playing, nearly hearing notes

Above the patchwork surface of his blindness.
With their eyes, they ask each other to dance.

Iris and retina refuse to accept the pressure
Set up by the pleasantries of survival

In a reeling eddy of sociability.
They decline the invite by focusing on the chiasma

Connecting immediacy with dim twilight.
Together, they witness the last few strokes

Of the post meridiem fling them over midnight,
Into a wide morning of a wider new year.

IV

The two people who've celebrated the eve
Of changing years prepare to leave

Through the quietude of their inebriated stupor.
The drive home to a furnished apartment by the ocean

Is a short thread quickly unwinding
From an eccentric spool sixty years thick.

The loose ends of the garment they stitched in youth,
And have worn mutually since, unravel,

As a rapid, spastic heart attack,
Like an actively steaming volcano, erupts,

Overflowing the ancient walled city
Of the man located too near the edge.

1/1/75   (00958)

The Orange Bowl

Eighty thousand people
Are seated along the cantilevered shaft
*

Of a reinforced-concrete straight needle,
Whose eye lies on a synthetic floor
Where players thread heroic hopes,
Then sew an athlete's dream
To throw over cold memories.

A populace of faces and heads,
Bobbing as if in a locked boxcar,
Threatens the steel bleachers
With stomping feet that show appreciation
For certain diagrammed performances.
Foundations tremble under the unstable weight,
Yet beams maintain their rigidity.

Breathing in and out invisibly,
The stadium takes on an amebic shape.
The crowd becomes a net of capillaries
Feeding the gigantic lungs,
Oxygenating the brain, supplying life
To the Cyclopean eye glued to the profile
Of a nation indulging its vicariousness.

After the last action,
Dense human molecules,
Like balloons released into turbulent air,
Commence exchanging their temporary sense
Of community for obsessive seclusion.
In retrospect, the organism's former size
Seems more important than the score.

1/2/75 — [3] (00957)

[We discuss possibilities, alternatives,] †

We discuss possibilities, alternatives,
Types of bait, all this before leaving dock,
        jigging the buoys
                with hand-held rod, and drop line

Intracoastal Waterway — engines drone,
                        bells signal contact

1/3/75 (00742)

Returning Home

A persistent angle of attack
Keeps his back pressed against the seat.
Uniformities below flow into clouds,
Disappear — they never were at all.

No runway, chaotic streets, or city,
Despotic people, fleshed-clogged beaches
Exist now that he leaves these shores,
Aiming northward home. Or do they?

Forgetting readily can so easily lapse
Into permanent fantasy, become a delirium
Too fragile for his mind to handle,
A memory without fulcrum to balance ballast

Shifting beneath all the days ahead.
A sigh, a series of little deaths,
Travels the cerebellum's slender wires.
The sentient engine alerts itself to failure

In the main circuit of its overriding brain.
A pervasive fear of being forever adrift,
Lost in boiler rooms where identity
Is manufactured, confounds this creature,

Who, until now, has remained comfortably
Sedentary in his steadily slowing existence.
Frantically he tries to remember each grain
Of sand that peopled the face of the beach

Where he sunbathed, as if to recognize a semblance
Of the essential profile of days
Composing the résumé of scattered activities
Belonging to him. The task subdues him,

And as the soaring vehicle makes its approach,
Descends, lands, he discovers he can't recall
His name or claim baggage he checked through
To a destination not even vaguely familiar.

1/4/75 (00637)

The Closet

For friend Mitt Landrum

Like pieces of luggage he used traveling
In search of something up ahead,
Then laid aside once he'd found himself,
The days of his past are neatly tucked away
In recesses of his brain's black attic.

All that innocence, settling like dust
On untouched surfaces, remains unregained,
Suffocating; angels could swirl through it
Without disturbing its opaque layers.
He gropes slowly among the mind's old clothes —

Pressed together, hung in motley disarray —
Reaching for something palpable to revive
And adorn a body shivering in nakedness.
Ghosts tug violently at his fingers,
Try to draw him headlong into their persuasion,

Make him disappear in Pandora's chaos-box.
He resists their sensuous subornations,
Opts for the garments he's worn for years
Without complaint from those who have known him
As a rather gently obtuse sentimentalist,

Who is changeless as a litany sung at altars
Stained with rusty wine-rings.
Yet, he weeps with the faint realization
That nothing achieved requires, equally,
Nothing to resurrect it from depths of neglectfulness.

1/10/75 (00638)

Not Only a Matter of Love △

I awaken to a house full of baby
Babbling on Sunday morning's first floor.
Her babbledebabble reminds my ears
Of a cantor chanting Kol Nidre
In a round repeating endlessly.

The sounds are the growing baby groping
At daytime play, absorbed as a researcher
In heady pursuit of elusive equations
To properly isolate. Her fascinations are
Transitory fixations in a dream machine

She's perfecting with each encounter
Her eyes, fingers, supple skull formulate
In a Brobdingnagian world of objects.
In her new universe, we are both, at best,
The most and least common denominators.

My water seeks her level; hers
Combines with mine in unpredictable currents
Of crazy vocalizations. We float rapids
On tongues buoyed by prattle, moved merely
By the sheer, shrill thrill of babblement,

And end our trips into unmapped lands
Without translator or guide. Like precise Boswell,
I take notes, keep a diary
During her unpatterned journey toward words,
As though it were only a matter of love.

1/12/75   (01009)

Eternal Triangle ᐃ

Baby's-breath, lilacs, heather, oleanders
Decorate this lost and disappearing day.
Sweet magnolias, honeysuckle, lemon trees
Lift, in sifting whispers, into a wilting eve
Galleried between antebellum porticoes,
Before settling beneath breathing whiskey sours.

Through carnival glass, I see Quentin pass
Down murky fathoms of the Charles River,
Weighted with two six-pound flatirons
Tied to ideas of honor tied to a pride
Derived from self-denial of ripening flesh
Rife and alive. His drowning confounds me.

I hear tiny bubbles balloon to the surface
Like off-key carillon bells transposing,
*

In near-melody, once familiar tunes.
Farther out, their overtones go inaudible.
I touch his lips reaching to kiss his sister
As she races from his bursting veins to escape

Death conceived for her sake. Her soul's
Unblessed integrity withstands the pressure,
While his is swallowed whole by a skimming trout
That swims, inviolable, in a nearby stream,
Then disappears. Somewhere, a feisty little girl
In muddy drawers begs me to take her away.

1/15–16/75 — [1] on 1/16   (00052)

Weeping

Coffee detonates the sleepy mind's atoms.
Dreams fixed on surreal escapes explode,
Scattering infinite bits and pieces of me
In every direction. I awaken to strange weeping,
As if someone I left in a past life cycle
Recognized me now, in one of my modern disguises.

An old notebook filled with holographic poems
Rides everywhere with me, in my attaché case,
Like a homunculus offering the only dossier
Known to have survived my final transformation.
I'm reminded of all those old seasons loaded
With cold futilities, debts, foreclosed notions,

And dusty, regressive sessions in quiet libraries,
Where I read myself to sleep atop verses,
Wrote daytime hours into empty notebooks,
Hid, nights, in linings of leather seats;
I even recall how fantasies entranced the spirit
Breathing slowly in hibernation, beguiled the mind

To dark transportations. Perhaps the weeping
I sense is an overtone of the lone struck chord
Tuned to touch the original alive source
That made my spark of being begin to echo
Its destiny, then cease to ignite the pure burn
Needed for the creative flame to sustain itself.

1/16/75 — [2]   (02150)

[All debates, this morning, turn on an axis] ‡

All debates, this morning, turn on an axis
Driven by twenty elders, whose interests lie
With the city of Tipton. The issue is sticky,
Unacceptable to some. A matter of tax-free
State and federal bonds to build a home
For the aging has filled the sky like ducks
Flying south.

1/17/75 — [1] (01368)

Being Passed

Riding westward by myself, doing seventy-five,
As if to escape day's light lifting higher
Each mile out . . . riding westward,
I was overcome by the shadow of shapes
Pacing ahead, although seemingly attached to me,
Trapped in brief solar eclipse, blackened
By a tractor-trailer's passing roar,
And threatened by nebulous death at full speed,
Come for me, pausing, then riding by.

Up ahead, like fireflies, red-blinking lights
Illumined, in eerie flecks, the corrugated sides
Of wreckage jackknifed, one dead driver,
And shadows tangled like notes jangled off-key.
Riding westward another three hours,
Toward K.C., I glimpsed the shadow of shapes
Retreating behind, although seemingly attached to me,
As if some unseen force were not quite satisfied
Or had been haphazard in choosing its proper victim.

1/17/75 — [2] (02172)

[I am a two-eyed Cyclops] †

I am a two-eyed Cyclops

1/17/75 — [3] (02951)

Blind Milton Anguishes Between Poems ^Δ

An unearthly chill fills the solitude
That follows me. With freezing heat,
It cauterizes thoughts that once flowed
Freely as rain weaving tapestries,
Arrests metaphors that connected me
To my eyes. Each constricted lid
Is a turnstile granting admission
To those who produce the proper token.

Now, my mind goes begging for change,
Any combination to open the safe
Containing precious images
Guarded by anguished generations of men
Trembling under the enormous weight
Of their brilliant disorientations.

Only, my doors stay sealed.
I rot inside, outside the vault,
Knowing not which night
Is the brightest in a starless galaxy,
Which unsunned day is the darkest
In my procession of uneven progressions
Leading from sleep, through seeded fetus,
Then back to sleep. In blindness, I weep.

1/17/75 — [4] (02201)

Son of the *Rachel*'s Captain

Tin-winged windmills are still,
Early this morning, as I leave unseen.
The sun has yet to penetrate this land,
As silent people creep from farm doors
To cars and flow like tributaries to jobs
Within Tipton's miniature Carcassonne.

The road I take to the main highway
Is an open sore: state repair crews
Are forever spraying tar, laying gravel
For a million Sisyphuses to carry away.
I awaken to intermittent shotgun blasts
Scraping rocker panels and underframe,

Keep from meeting a speeding vehicle
Head-on by veering too near a shoulder
That eats my tires in voracious bites,
Then spits me out in an icy cornfield.
In an ocean of cow-filled solitude, I drown,
Waiting for Ahab to take me aboard.

1/18/75 (02212)

On Visiting the University Campus After Having Been Lost at Sea Nearly Seven Years

For Janny Hofmann

The days passed are men's pants manufactured
And sent into the marketplace
To adorn naked bodies before being worn out.

I recall almost nothing at all about time
Precedent, except for the long-legged filly
Whose lithe and elusive being
Drew me across pastures,
Through narrow canyons, and onto grass prairies
Dappled with love-spill.

I barely remember sweet-breathing metaphors
Seeded with absolute precision by trembling poets
Who ionized our dry clouds
With images capable of setting
Rainbows between us as we sat
On soft, wet lawns and kissed their lips.

Forgetting has left me absent-minded and weak,
Envious of all those gay-speaking souls
Seizing their seasons without any restraints.

Forgetting has made me aware of a new obligation
To restitch my mind into finely designed clothing
To adorn its naked and empty intellect.

1/20/75 (02550)

Weeding in January ^Δ

The sky is haywire-alive with fire
At the wrong time. Even spiders
Awaken from dazed slumbers, stumble,
On weak legs, to a sunned spot
Of barn siding or holly leaf
From which to suspend their disbeliefs.

Curious, I stray from a heated house,
Outdoors, with light coat, gloves,
And begin pulling clumped weeds
From a garden whose soggy, unturned soil
Lets them loose easily as worms
Freed from hard earth by the rain.

I am piqued to complete the immediate task
Of eradication before winter
Remembers itself or sees me playing
Behind its back as though no tomorrows
Still stood between April planting
And January's coldest hours at hand.

A chill cast by afternoon shadows
Presses against my sweaty neck,
Stifles all my inclination to continue,
Forces me inside just as the door
Between death's edge and rebirth shuts
And snow clouds begin to form.

1/27/75 (00348)

[Only one among all the comedic salesmen] [†]

Only one among all the comedic salesmen
Gathered to reprise the new fall line

1/31/75 — [1] (06161)

Cynic

Words lie dormant as snakes
Twisted in sleep beneath rocks
Thick with snow. The tongue remains
Locked in a natural landscape of mouth,
Like a chameleon concealed in its changes.

Ideas leading to thoughts expressed
Escape silence, slither on their bellies
Over precipitous cliffs, into quicksand pools,
Emerge from molted skins as vipers
Assuming cabriole shape, and strike.

1/31/75 — [2] (02637)

Precarious Season △

IBM to-sell lists, ref cards,
Freshly prepared, hover like gilt halos
Over the aura of zealous men
Who live by every 5 percent portion
Of every total sale they consummate.

Each man regards his stacks of cards
With reverential awe. He'll memorize ranges,
Model options, and in-stock availabilities
Like telephone numbers of clandestine whores
He'll meet biweekly on trips away from home,

Then set out, traveling the stony roads
Laid one cobble at a time over many seasons.
None knows the distance he'll finally cover
Before learning if his draw against commission
Makes expenses or whether he'll be eating filet

With crabmeat appetizer and sticky apéritif.
All the apostles know a death-moth hovers close,
Hear its wings frantically beating stale air
To stay aloft as they leave with their lines.
The noise becomes a roar they've never known.

1/31/75 — [3] (02211)

Demolition

Such a clatter of utterly understandable
                                    clutter
Shatters sleep
              that the ears explode;
                        headache balls
Fall like rain through lobotomized air.

        Foundations supporting the eyes'
                                    skyscrapers
                                         co
Llapse onto a plain littered with dead butterflies.

        Bulldozers, bellyloaders, snorting tractors
Power away the debris,
                           pour it into trucks
        Waiting to take it to dumps.

                        An immobilized poet
Awakens amidst frenzied termites
        Nibbling at his abandoned landscape.

1/31/75 — [4] (03542)

[Falling out of bed,] ‡

Falling out of bed,
        falling through a hole in what was said
Last night,
        recalls the original fall
                    from grace.

        She regretted how strangely, steeply
                    the hill increased its pitch,
How sad it seemed we'd been falling
        out of love
                    over a distance of yawns.

I reprised our journey through sleep,
    hand in hand in green lands
Blooming blue skies, blue eyes,
    lighting flame-blue horizons
Falling softly forward, through love-vortices,

Toward us, in those new and gentle zoo days.
    Now, the blues begin their secondary
        hue transformations.
Our brush strokes don't quite touch the canvas;
    they fall short,

Painting an invisible family portrait,
        in which we sleep separately,
Two people burrowing upward,
        through a downward drowning

2/1/75 (00784)

Soccer Practice: A Reminiscence [Δ]

The notion of her crawling on all fours
Recalls the stupendous energy expended
During my days in training for sports,
Frustrations of failing to make a score
Right in front of the goal, falling
To frozen ground from a block thrown
On the blind side, grasping bars
Spaced in a cage of bruised bones
To keep from buckling to hardwood floors.

Suddenly, the game is being replayed
Atop an oblong clock face,
With a referee at every boundary line.
A body dashes past, alone
In open field, balancing her blur,
Racing noisily toward uprights.
Accurately, she zeroes in, kicks,
Becomes a victory ball penetrating the net,
Caught up in her father's outstretched arms.

2/9/75 — [1?] (01031)

Silhouettes

Mingled branches cling not to air
But frozen lawn they share with shapes
Of cupola, turret, chimney stack
Smoking billowy, evasive shadows
That shift unreasonably from driveway
To sidewalk. Somewhere down there
I, too, must be, peering up at myself
Through weather-etched glass,
Wondering just how long the strong sun
Will last before I disappear.

2/9/75 — [2?] (03930)

Mutoscope Reel △

Already her nine-month birthday

A penny for my thoughts
Sets the optic machine spinning.
The revolving reel
Reveals a baby crawling naked
In quarter time,
Stopping frequently to suck her thumb.

The little girl
Moves as if each frame flipped
Were a rug slipped
From under her in a shifting room,
Infinitesimally
Caught between interlocking planes.

Hands and kneecaps
Give way to soft feet arching
Tiptoe taut
To see valleys beneath the furniture
She scales
Fist over fist, on wobbly legs.

Such ascents
Leave her peering in every direction.
*

An invisible entity
Distracts her, suggests screaming a litany
Of erratic ecstasy,
Brings her gracelessly to her knees again.

Her mother waits
Somewhere beyond the slowing frames
To remove her to sleep,
Let her escape the circular path
That rims her days.
I watch her laid gently to bed,

As the last slides
Dissipate and the hot light fades.
Vacantly, I fumble
For a penny to buy more time.
When I return,
Someone else is behind the machine.

2/13/75 — [1] (01085)

Queen of the Stardust Ballroom

What strange places our lives are!
We honeycomb such elaborate hives
With our soft bodies, old clothes,
Rocking horses, and unsurfaced hopes.

God bless the relics that tell us
We wore, like bright scarves,
The sweetest debris about our dreams,
And bless the restlessness that sent us

In search of secrets to keep
From ourselves. Who knew emptiness
Would join our broken family
When everyone else took leave?

And who could ever have guessed
That shattered glass glued
To a slow-spinning reflector-ball
Might relight a dead face,

Illumine a light-footed dance
In the late hours, after living
Lost its love-lettered cadence?
Only those new to dying alone,

Old at loving life, can survive
The final fling. For them, the years
Remaining are a wide summer night
Kissed by fireflies, filled with wings.

2/13/75 — [2] (03932)

[What a sad scene:] †

What a sad scene:
TV and a magazine —
Can't see, can't read.
Distractions seduce me
Now that you've left.

2/13/75 — [3] (06162)

Early Morning in the Kitchen

The plates off which we eat
Are crusty and soiled with shards
Of dreams we dine on in sleep.
I awaken before she does,
Each morning, to clean,
Then neatly cupboard, the things
Strewn in our cluttered kitchen.

Machines do our dishes,
Spin mixtures systematically
Into hot or cooled conclusions
Long after we've pressed the button,
Left, and forgotten to check
The subtle transformations
Unintentional alterations
Have made to our identical spices.

Unsighted, by heart,
My nostrils distill the air
For just one deviation,
Praying that someday when I awaken,
They'll have transported me to Polynesia
To taste green leaves
And watch my wife run,
Absolutely naked,
From a savage wearing my mask.

2/26/75 (04070)

Snow

Long after I've finished this lonely trip,
I still see snow seeding oceans,
Growing in fields tilled in a somnolent sky.
White weeds streaking toward freedom
Emit sweet, secret scents of poppy,
Encourage an enfeebled mind to leave toil.

But the joyous clairvoyance that accompanied me,
Once, on explorations to the soul's lighted core
Has diminished. The need to grope blindly
Through low-hung night entirely by myself
Releases off-white, mosquito-like furies
On the air. I cough dust beat from God's rug.

I've become the snow this country withholds
From the sun, an organism of driven flakes
Frozen in shade cast by fast years
Reaching across a face of living crystals
Rubbed smooth by seasons exchanging places.
Soon, even tenacious drifts will evaporate.

3/2/75 (04407)

The Scribe

The quill point, seen head-on
In a widening eastern summit,
*

Is pressed against a book of hours
Whose leaves are numbered to infinity.
Such delicate red strokes,
Blotting slowly over a page
Of daily illuminations,
Leave certain areas raised
Above shaded tents and pennons.

Somewhere below, a naked monk
Leaves sleep, takes up his robe
And sandals, sinks to his knees
In a pool of accumulated fat.
Reassured of gentle redemptions,
He goes outdoors to seize the day
Between thumb and forefinger
And scribe his name, in gold leaf,
Across the side of a fleeting cloud.

3/3/75 — [1] (04015)

Plant Manager

Wherever I go, these needle machines
Sew inseams up and down my eardrums,
Blindstitch each eye from side to side.
Steam hissing from an innocuous teapot
Registers 125
P.s.i. in my pressurized head.

An invisible air compressor inflates veins,
Floods adjacent cells with undrained water.
Afternoon becomes a colossal vacuum unit
Drawing the breathing spirit out of me;
Raw suction extrudes the straining body,
Breaks down molecules, attaches, painfully,

A whirlwind to my belly, makes it a taut fetus
Filled with refractory pockets and linings,
Belt loops, bands, and serged pant legs.
Am I being pilloried by piece-rate dreams
For practicing an occult brand of manufacture,
Or is disaster flattening my sacred precincts

Gratuitously? Soon, the funnel goes smooth,
Disappears into still air, and I am left
Knee-deep in tatters and zigzag scraps
Cut from patterns spread my body's length.
Somehow, each piece must be numbered, bundled,
Then stitched, before parts are forever mixed.

3/3/75 — [2] (00812)

Remodeling

Recently, he had his brain
Equipped with piped-in philosophy,
Added expensive chrome fixtures
To replace all the old porcelain
In his eyes' pull-chain bathroom.

He replastered cracks in his skull
To keep daylight from disturbing thoughts
He'd been seeking, so long, to nurture
Like mushrooms in wet, spongy beds —
His head became a perfect hothouse.

After updating and insulating his attic,
He commissioned air-conditioning units
For his dream-conceiver complex
And heating so the roulette room
Might be used throughout the year.

Then, when all standards were approved
By special inspectors he'd bought,
Coupons were circulated to lady friends,
Entitling them to free admission
To the world's first one-man whorehouse.

3/3/75 — [3] (00813)

Disciples Gather at the Farmers' Lyceum ^Δ

The garrulous disciples decide their fate
Around a breakfast table, formulate theory
*

Conforming to Hadrian and Machiavelli,
Debate the merits of heresy and ethnic bias
In private enterprise, affirm the values
Of farmland, floating municipal bonds,
And using Funks Hybrid or Pioneer seeds.
Elevators, shortages of cornfed beef,
Prices of beans, acres, commodity investments,
And fluctuations become epithets, metaphors,
And every other voluble form of speech.

These ethical men cajole each other
About going to Cocoa Beach for the winter,
Letting the local Ford dealer
Sell them everything except black rebates,
Feeding cows on milo, donating wheat to Russia
As a charitable deduction. They ruminate
On Mayor Daley's reelection, a president
Suckling on Congress's teat, how far
The mercury's dropped, and what they'll do
For entertainment, with fields too wet to plow.

When they finally disperse, a wide silence,
Like water undammed from a man-made pond,
Inundates the space I occupy inside the café.
My mind drowns in such an abrupt deprivation
Of human intercourse. Furtively, I look for
Another source through which to surface,
Since breathing depends on feeding the brain
Constantly oxygenated sound. In silence,
I watch lake tourists observe the rain.

3/4 & 7?/75 (00814)

[And just when we thought we were shot of winter,] †

And just when we thought we were shot of winter,
Here comes the most hellacious blizzard
Out of nowhere, so that all at once, we
Were caught without coats, doing Sunday groceries

3/10/75 — [1] (03258)

Entering Ten Months ^Δ

She's a chipmunk with puffy cheeks,
Three upper teeth,
Seen when she decides to smile,
Two below perpetually,
Like rare museum pearls.

She opens and closes drawers
And doors, challenges mountaintops,
Escapes imaginary enemies
Through passes she locates behind tables
And chairs. Every floor

Is a field for unrehearsed sport,
Where she stays constantly absorbed
In play with various paraphernalia
From the exotically shaped world
Of eggs and Saltine tins.

Often, she'll completely undo
A mound of disheveled clothes
By throwing each piece
Over her shoulder, then find
An identical pile rising

Behind her. We laugh at ourselves
For having created such
Outrageously pleasant companionship,
Then cavort at peekaboo
By hiding our eyes behind nothing

But the lighted corners of her mind.
Every time she sneaks out,
We're where she left us, smiling,
Until sleep assails her
And she feels herself gently

Being drawn away from play.
Softly, she trills a sonata
Familiar to her mother's ears
Before a sweet, brief stillness
Overtakes what God has made.

During these interims, we wait
Outside her door of dreams
*

For each new awakening.
Precious rebirth for us three
Is such a blessed occurrence.

3/10/75 — [2] (01096)

Paleontologist

The great mastodon,
So long buried in sandy tarpits
And neglected by those
Walking along dream-paths
Over its soundproof roof,
Awakens, surfaces erratically as gas
Escaping deep strata,

Assumes a shape decidedly identical
To the human being
As I assemble it. Similarities and
Variations resist
Description, for arrested vestiges
That stay etched
In fossil design on my blunt mind,

Viewing the skeletal metaphor
With skeptical fright.
The surprise of elemental discovery,
Such as touching
An exposed self rising from fogs
And piecing together
Broken bones of dissociated dreams,

Is both quintessence
And unapplauded reward for a life
Of endless expeditions
Into malarial rain forests and bogs.
Many days, I gaze at
Ancient giants I've placed in a museum
Of labeled nightmares,

Wondering if anyone would pay
To see or study
These wrecks exhumed from the depths
*

Depressions penetrate
If I were actually ever to open my doors
To public scrutiny
Before they bury me in my metaphor.

3/16/75   (00815)

Delay

Due to Chicago rain and fog,
An unanticipated delay
Has left us isolated, bereft,
Caught in mid-journey.
Our stride is broken on an ocean
Floated with people crowding
Scheduled currents. Motion
Is a notionless processional
Leading from conclusive plans,
Made many months ago,
To a tentative, endless waiting.

Waistless tandem mannequins
Pass corridor gates like grey-
Hounds chasing motivations,
As heated hours press wrinkles
Into our foreheads and clothing.
And we have no place to go,
No safe refuge to lie down in
Without fear of molestation,
No peace of mind to divide
Among ourselves like a deck
Of well-worn playing cards.

While she reads and I write verse,
Something hovers above us
Like nothing surfaced in dreams;
It hangs aloft on the jet stream,
And we're caught right in between
Earthly disturbances and dragons breathing
Just beyond the ears' door.
*

We reach to open it and listen for
A swarm approaching or a storm
Already broken. Only, the loudspeaker
Mutes the noise with a call to board.

3/17/75 (00816)

New Orleans Sketches

W.F. — an appreciation,
1925–1975

Wherever we walked today,
Through Ponte Vecchio-like streets
Within the Vieux Carré,
We saw Faulkner strolling in the wind,
Heard him whispering to Slim,
The bootlegger. We even listened
To his clackety portable play
Insatiable music as he sketched
Cobblers, psychotics, and jockeys
From his blossoming bohemian mind.

In St. Anthony's Garden, we stopped
To muse on sylphs, naked satyrs,
And nymphs he'd set free as tears
From the sad eyes of a marble faun.

Through the door at 624
Orleans Alley, ground floor,
We watched his restless phoenix
Rise with untrammelled abandon,
On a kite's quick-flicking lift,
Over Jackson Square, over fifty years,
To this wrought-iron afternoon,
From which we've followed it back
To his ashes to wish him luck
On an exciting new writing career.

3/18–19/75 — [1] on 3/19 (00818)

[Business-suited men, in convention gray,] †

Business-suited men, in convention gray,
Drink noon lunch through visions
Of eternal expansion, reminisce about
Days spent at UVA and Ole Miss,
In heady, lascivious reveries
Identical except for the faded faces
And blurred dates

You wonder how one more pigeon will
Light on the statue for the gulping swarm
And what will be left for our daughter
After the Mechanical Goat sucks away
All the debris.

Zip up my butt and
My lips and I'll become
Your duffel bag you can dump
In the most convenient ocean.

3/18?/75   (02152)

Rebirth of the Blues

For Bobbi and Al Karraker;
a souvenir

Not even wealthy bums and the slovenly young
Can afford pads in the Vieux Carré.
Numb poets have retreated to Mason City
And Eugene, with notes on tap-dancing blacks
Shaking money cans and hats. Painters
Have taken to hand-hewn mountain shacks,
With sketches of Rubenesque nudes
Caught in degrees of unimpassioned striptease.
Each has escaped intact, with memories
*

Of drunks splayed in shadows lying zigzag
Up alleyways, clutching opaque bottles
Like babies stroking satin-smooth blankets.
No new musicians tune their instruments
To Bourbon Street blues. Only the barkers
Sing cheerless lyrics for bemused crowds
Dressed in freshly pressed symphony clothes:
"Come *on*! Come *in*! Get it *on*! *Get skin*!"
"Get it *on* . . . by watchin' her *take it off*!"
"Come *on*! Can *you* get it on?"

3/19/75 — [2] (00817)

[The lines waiting to dine at Antoine's,]

The lines waiting to dine at Antoine's,
The Court of Two Sisters, and Brennan's
Are drawn taut as rubber bands stretched to
Their breaking points. Nerves shatter;
Patience snaps. From a thousand beaks,
Silent anthems screech, as people eat
Expensive table scraps wrapped in French
Adjectives. One bus goes, one arrives,
With birth and death at zero-growth
Impasse. Pegged floors strain, warp.
Wrought-iron balconies corrode one rain
At a time, invisibly, for a long time,
Until everyone is asked to please
Excuse the inconveniences of survival.

3/19/75 — [3] (01369)

Sutpen's Grand Design

For those desolates of the Vieux Carré

After the war, nothing of value was left

Except the women to sew burial clothes
For those perished. The rest went naked.

Everywhere, lying in obtrusive silence,
Drunks sputtered like fired ruins
Smoldering where, once, plantations stood.

They begged of no one to be taken back
One Philadelphia brick, square nail,
And filigreed cast-iron portico grille
At a time to their slave-laid foundations.

Even they knew renovation was unfeasible
In a reconstructed land where absinthe bars,
Art shops, and massage parlors,
Like ubiquitous carpetbaggers and scalawags,
Crowded them in against parking lots

And condemned freight entrances to sleep
Among packing crates filled with gewgaws.
Now, the horizon between cement and sky
Is continuously clouded by cigarette smoke
Rising from a hundred abandoned shanties
Beside a river soaking its banks with wine.

3/19 — [4] & 3/21/75 (00819)

Hallucinations at Houlihan's Old Place

Sweet hysterias rush up toward me
Like furies unleashed on a tired giant
Rising out of a mythical sea
To threaten a prosperous city with hurricanes.

I swat awkwardly at their invisible bodies
As though they were gnats gnawing at ears
And sun-seared eyes of a neglected dog
Whose laggard hulk I might have occupied.

Beyond the glass, the flickering lights
Become reflected insects weaving and passing
Above a murky summer surface, become people
Who've accidentally taken me for a Goliath

They must swarm and defeat. I can't even eat
Potatoes and meat steaming in a frying pan,
And I leave by the rear-exit door
Before the waitress notices my vacancy.

Outside, there's no escaping. Contagion
Crisscrosses time like a lost ship
In a shoreless sea. I search for the eye
Of the hurricane to climb into, out of the noise.

3/19 — [5] & 3/22/75 (00820)

Balconies

Beautiful Jan;
her birthday poem,
3/23/75

As we leave the restless city behind,
Even the Cabildo and Presbytère
Are cast in half-light latticework.
All the way out, my eyes persist
In tracing lacy intricacies of balconies
We touched last night, from below,
As though all the earth were newly formed,
In cold Parisian molds, of hot-poured iron.

Now, I see you indefectibly wrought
In a pointillism of tiny fleurs-de-lis.
Your mild beauty becomes beads of rain
Being strung by my delicate memory
Into grilles enclosing a portico
Over which you lean, whispering to me.
I listen to the design of your gentle voice
Dripping from years connected by our love.

3/20/75 (00821)

Jennifer's Poem ^Δ

She dreams such supple children

My poems are the home
I sleep in
When returning from trips
To the waking hours.

Each crowded room
Is a beautifully dressed metaphor
Waiting to be unclothed
One tentative article
At a time,
For the unveiling of her naked soul.

Each night,
I choose a new room
To take a new muse to bed
In a dream turned on a tilt,
In a home built on a hill, in a head
Filled with fertile verse.

Each morning,
I wake with a new child,
Whose head lies beside mine
On the pillow. I kiss her goodbye
As I disappear, once again,
Into the business of living alone.

3/25/75   (00822)

Easter Flood

Entreating us to remember the soul's
Ancient emancipation from the self,
The paschal mystery of resurrection,
The priest kisses his leatherbound missal.

He prepares us to meet Christ again,
Through gifts of the Eucharist feast.
"Our hearts are restless until they rest
In Thee." "Certitude of a joyful eternity

Is guaranteed those who seek His face."
"He was among us in an empty tomb
And is risen." Such transcendencies
Stir the wobbly memory to rectitude

By asking us to question our intentions.
I listen to bits of twisted theology
*

Disappear somewhere between stained glass,
A marble altar, and the congregation.

Everywhere, lips on little faces
Repeat liturgies in oblivious mime,
Adults spew antiphons like food
Too large to chew, and babies cry out

As though, within the crowded church,
A vagrant spirituality were rife.
Isolated voices and shuffling feet
Become cacophonies whose noise is water

Flooding levees, as everyone, except us,
Surges toward the Communion rail
For wafers and the breath of God.
We huddle in an abandoned landscape

Of desolate pews, waiting for a sign
To evacuate to higher ground
Before the creeks run backward
And drown us in the final benediction.

3/30/75 — [1] (00350)

Local Bowling Alley †

Not only Sunday evening but Easter

Sunday evening TV ricochets off
Sunday evening people playing Sunday
Evening pinball machines, as Easter's
Fading frequency fills with static

Bells, flippers, and digital tabulations
Snap with the erratic precision
Of machine guns biting blindly into the night

3/30/75 — [2] (01370)

Easter Unobserved

Through the Crystal Café window,
I see, in deep and wide perspective,
Gas pumps, stop sign, telephone poles,
And dawn dripping like a hooked trout
Hung broadside from a bending rod.

Somewhere above the wet horizon,
The spirit of a fisherman quietly hovers;
Below, every solid object,
Cross street, and piece of farm machinery
Assumes the shape of a crucifix.

Within, the rabble concerns itself
With fertilizer costs per acre
To feed cows, the great rebate,
And how the law protects the farmer,
Without even a mention of Easter Sunday.

Now, the objects beyond the window
Dissolve in morning's bleached shimmer.
I see a thousand withered bodies
Nailed against a dripping earth,
Shivering in naked rigor mortis,

And each distinctive face out there
Belongs to a person seated here,
Cursing inequities, bemoaning the law
That requires each to die alone
And hang together in eternal life.

3/31/75 — [1] (00800)

Paean to Machines

An outsize Corliss steam engine,
Charging light to the eyes,
Rumbles the skull's floor.
Dual turbines, propelled by noise,
Spin the ears' blades.
A Scotch Marine boiler
Powers the throbbing veins
*

With oxygenated, blood-colored bubbles
Floated in liquid suspension.
The entire body shudders wildly,
Like an out-of-true tire
Wobbling down a smooth highway,
As it moves away from birth.

Fuels required to energize
Such a highly integrated vehicle
Are too volatile for human minds
To manage alone. They arrive
As ideas, packed in dry ice,
For the heated brain to break down
And distribute to each substation
Beyond limits of the physical city
Within the imagination.
In its raw, awkward simplicity,
The machine achieves a godly grace
Unknown to the most complex contraptions
Tinkering man has ever conceived.

3/31/75 — [2] (00801)

Finding *The Marble Faun* ᐃ

Delicate words I follow
Trail off like deer tracks
Into a covert woods.
Stealthily, the mind creeps
Through bay leaves and laurel
To see where they sleep.

My eyes gather their prints,
Like fingers picking up crumbs
A child dropped quietly
To remind him of the way out.
At times, I find twigs
Snapped, catch glimpses

Of fleeting objects leaning
Into the wind's scent,
Retreating deeper into thickets
*

Constricting vision and insight.
I follow anxiously
In fresh, uncompassed directions,

With intimations of arriving
At a subtle nestling place
Where warm words rest
Breathlessly in family clusters,
Almost waiting to be touched.
The softest fawn leads me home.

4/1/75 (00802)

Gentle Lamentations ^Δ

Preposterously yellow forsythias
Sear the eyes to ecstasy.
Like slowly inflating balloons,
Trees everywhere fill out
With gauzy hues of buds in bloom,

And I am reminded of my wife
A year ago, nearing
The end of gestation, tumid
And flushed with her lush blossom
Rushing headlong into May's calyx.

Last April, we shared
With spring the secret of beginnings,
As though she were Trotaconventos
And we Calisto and Melibea,
Meeting in a dark, forbidden garden

To choose the name "Trilogy"
For the seed of our sweetest hour.
We didn't see the lady go
Who left us earthly wisdoms
In which to swaddle our baby girl.

Now, the outrageous forsythias
Frustrate us with haughty games
Of renascence. They summon forth
A covenant we made with nature
That can't possibly be kept this season.

4/3/75 (01110)

The Golden Chain ^Δ

Sweet Maya is on her way.
She comes dressed in brocades
And green, lacy crinolines
Everywhere bustling. A dervish
Fancifully freed on the heartland
Entertains us with her quick changes.

Her first birthday imminent,
Her second spring begun,
She has become a piece of the seasons,
Recapitulating,
Connected to us by an umbilicus
Attaching the days to God

And God to every generation
That has perpetuated itself in us
Through love and soft compassion.
The leaves are ancient people
Returned to witness her rebirth
As the golden chain is lengthened.

4/20/75 — [1] (02093)

Epilogue ^Δ

So far from the city yet near
When grandparents get lonesome,
She has merely to dream herself there,
And the clean air will part
Like waters of the great sea
To let her pass unscathed.

She will be their gentle link
To us, we her guarantee
That those who made us breathe
Will carry forth into her future
Through memories of our beautiful past
And meet the husband of her years.

4/20/75 — [2] (02125)

The Patient

I

The sidewalks are occupied by people
On leave from the state hospital
To spend Friday evening
Beyond interstices and sheets
That landscape their business district
Week after tranquil week.

Trees that canopy their pilgrimage
Are clotted with cackling grackles
And chimney sweeps screaming
Like patients in shock therapy.
Leaves and wings and screeching
Become indistinguishable as they pass.

Headlights scratch the shadows
Dusk deposits like skin
Over the bones of another day.
Evening bleeds light on them.
The tourniquets of their weak minds
Have lost their grip.

Night becomes dead weight
Clinging to a body of hours
Each inmate wears
Under a baggy cotton outfit.
One runs, and then
Another follows, while a third

Stumbles awkwardly to the curb,
Splits her wrist on a beer can.
Beneath a mercury-vapor
Street lamp, they gather
To watch her, and wait without words
As she stares frozenly at the wound.

Afraid to move and unable
To beg help, she remains
On the dirty pavement, while cars
Fly past undistractedly
With taillights dripping blood
And their sounds drowning her moans.

The birds continue to pose
As leaves and screeching wings
In the trees she sees as shrouds,
While the people she's known for years
Eye her with fascinated abandon
And a fear of acting in her behalf.

II

Night becomes four walls,
An army cot, and metal end table
Lighted by a forty-watt bulb.
Day intrudes on rays
Slanted from a sun hung
Above carbolized waiting rooms

She uses to socialize with herself.
Last evening recedes
In a labyrinth leading from birth,
Through forgetting, to the new scar
That patterns her stitched wrist
Like a bracelet. She begins to weep,

As if something buried in silence
Were surfacing to touch her tongue,
Make her speak what her mind
Sees through curtains draped
Across a field of blossoming poppies
In a greater field thronged

With Queen Anne's lace.
Her fingers pluck a flower
From the vision, draw it to the wound.
Soon, only smooth skin
Is visible above her blue veins,
And her world is flooded with light.

She rests her delicate head
Beside the generously blessed man

Out of sand, with healed hands,
Near a sea whose tides they control
From the soul of the land they inhabit

With the people she's known for years.
Together, they share a dream
*

Of disappearing through Heaven's iris,
To be seen in God's eyes
And washed in a stream of blood
Flowing into their future lives.

5/9/75 (00803)

[Off in a corner of mid-May,] †

Off in a corner of mid-May,
He sits dismayed

5/17/75 — [1] (06163)

[In an unfamiliar town of familiar
   Gothic houses] ‡

In an unfamiliar town of familiar Gothic houses
(Trees lining streets connecting forgotten antecedents
To residents who recognize themselves on color TV),
We are waifs set free on restless tides
That never touch shore yet never cease
Reaching toward the edgeless extremities of life.
We float, for years, over billowing days
Oceaning over civilizations buried below us
In coffins carved from the soft bones of dreams
Abandoned by people creeping out of the slime.

5/17/75 — [2] (01371)

Silences △

                                        For Jan;
                                        a spring gift

In this May-green park, where silence grows
Profusely as rain-soaked grass,
*

My ears strain to hear the sounds
Of breathing and play dropping from lips
Of disconsolate men on hard benches,
Slipping off the fingers of deaf-mutes
Sculpting air into communicable shapes,
And dancing on stages
Within supple hip-cradles of females
Skipping carefreely across the Square
And riding bicycles without wasted motions
Or vain concupiscence.

And as I listen to all these distant voices,
The tufted grass that completely surrounds
My seated mass of peaceful being
Distracts me with a gentle rustling noise,
As though each blade were a cat's tongue
Licking the smooth back of my mind,
Or sandpaper scratching the inner ears
To a fine dust, instead of bare feet
Slowly closing in on me, from behind.
Inside the void where I've searched for sounds,
My smiling wife stands with our child.
Their silence reminds me how blessed is mine.

5/17/75 — [3] (00804)

Wilderness ‡

My silences are lakes arrived at
Only by portaging. Everything in between
Is pothole and low-water stream
Floated with noise, algae-spun noise
That buoys the vessel containing my gear.

Each time I leave, the maps,
Like children with familiar toys,
Seem more reluctant to give up secrets

5/28/75 (00739)

The Books, the Woods, and Us ^Δ

For Dr. James W. Webb,
Oxford

All the fine old signed limited editions,
With decorated boards and gold-stamped spines,
Contain uncut rectangles of rag-paper pages
And colophons neatly tipped in and inscribed
With the dateless names of forgotten skeletons.

Like bones, they remain buried in graves
Steeped in the stale air of locked library stacks,
Waiting for sunlight to eat their cloth,
Moisture to fox their pages. Soon, the brittle leaves
Will break down to fiber and odorless dust,

Until only hidden memories of the private mind
That created giants from apocryphal idiots
And noble Quixotes out of frightened convicts
Will live untouched within the wide cedar-silence
Of vine-woven wisterias and old magnolias.

Finally, the seething woods will overrun Rowan Oak
In nature's embrace and leave it inviolable
To all but a solitary few, who, like Ike,
Will come unarmed, compassless, unafraid
To be lost inside the dark mind's Bailey's Woods.

Then, the library that coffined the books
And the woods that guarded his spirit will become,
Like Campo Vaccino over the Roman Forum,
Open fields covering man's oldest sanctuary,
Above which peasants will loll with their sheep.

5/30 – 6/1/75   (00071)

The Party Dress ^Δ

For Dr. Frank and Mary Long
and
Margaret – Jan – Trilogy

All week, she labored at a machine,
Stitching memories — of delivery,
*

Returning with her baby to the country,
The first bath,
And feeding from breasts aching for release —
Into a dress her child might wear to her first birthday.

Only, when she'd finished repinning it
And making a few alterations,
It still wouldn't quite fit,
And the delicate blue-felt appliqué she'd styled
With grosgrain dreams and rickrack hopes,
Embroidered on a lacy membrane of spacious days,

Refused to assume her mind's dimensions,
Required more time
For beading each blessed hour by hand
Than she'd allotted before the party began.
So she dressed her child in a hand-me-down frock
Her own mother had sewn from memories

For her to wear so long ago,
That her girl might share the innocence
Of baby flesh pressed against crinolines
And know, for a moment, anyway,
The nearness of three different women
Become one in a garment of sheer creation.

6/2/75 (00806)

Impasse ^Δ

The keys look at me inquisitively,
As if waiting to see
Which typebars will strike my fancy
And which faces in combination
Will memorize their chance meeting
With me on this white plain,
Unknown to antecedent and legacy alike.

I peer into the glass-capped circles,
Hoping to awaken reflections
Sleeping in the ooze
And have them surface inside bubbles
Exploding against the fingertips.
*

Only, each white-ruffled ocean
Keeps its deep secrets from strangers,

And my eyes continue to stray
Among a forest of keys
Growing impenetrable as cedar trees.
I find no signs of creatures
Living or having passed this way,
To lead me to the place
Where white light breaks into flame.

6/8/75 (00787)

The Captain Has a Close Brush

Outraged like angry Ahab,
I fly urgently by my years,
Searching out the personal leviathan
Everywhere lurking in an ocean
Whose tides my breathing controls.

Despite their changeless designations,
The highways I float
Are never the same;
Destinations are always uncertain,
Never predetermined,
Ever evolving as word arrives
That a sighting has just been made
Someplace other than where I am.

On a thousand occasions,
With astrolabe and compass,
I've shot the unpredictable stars
Hung from the brain's retina,
Recalculated the breadth and depth
Of dreams, consulted the orrery
That revolves on the mind's axle,
To tell time in civilizations
Buried under a hundred feet of sea.

Lately, I haven't been able
To stabilize the flabby ballast
*

In the bone-ribbed main holds.
Storms have thrown the whole boat
Unreasonably out of balance,
In places fractured its skeletal frame,
Damaged its sturdy twin masts.

For years, the vessel has traveled
In an inwardly winding spiral
Without its master knowing how or why,
As though it were a long spring
Being tightened to its breaking point.

Now, it reels inside the seaborne eye
Of the heart's violent hurricane.
Through an open hole in the ocean,
Leviathan finally surfaces to meet
Its servant and master face to face.

Harpoons I let fly
Graze the writhing body without penetrating it.
Wearily, I unwind and heave
One last barbed epithet
At the pearl-gray giant breathing death over me
Like an airless cape.

From somewhere deeper than death,
Blood rushes up through its spout,
Tinctures the water with rusty spray.
Wounded, yet alive, it plunges,
Dives back through black gravities,
While I hover above, treading the years
With a belly full of salt water
And eyes blurred by salty tears.

6/11/75 — [1] (00807)

The Gardener

The years till wrinkles in my face,
Burn its topsoil, upturn the furrows
I pace like a mule forever caged
Behind its leather-sweaty traces.

Harvesttime arrives early,
Yet always I've been too late
To create a market for my commodities.

Soon, ripeness will seep into rot;
Then, weed-inundated and abandoned
To sad afterthoughts and imagined ills,
The plot will lie fallow again.

In times before records were kept,
The only crops that grew in my garden
Were impatience, regret, and old age.

Now, even this last planting
Refuses to bear fruit, be harvested,
And I live on, immutable,
Seemingly untouched by new seasons.

6/11/75 — [2] (00809)

Left Behind △

Out here, silence is a balloon hung high,
Hovering above day fading away to night.
As far as the eye can penetrate,
No animate beings, except mourning doves
And meadowlarks, disturb the landscape.

Beyond the tremulous wheat field,
Ruffled to Titian suppleness
By the wind, a tin mill spins.
Stark green trees at fence-line and brake
Scrape the horizon. Goldenrods bend,
Fill the earthy air with spice;
Their yellowness frustrates my nostrils.

My eyes follow rails
Receding into the other world.
For only a moment, my feet repeat
The precarious balance of a trapeze man
As they glide atop a gleaming T,
Then rediscover the gravel bed below.

Old telephone poles,
Whose green- and white-glass insulators
No longer embrace black nerves,
Still reverberate with old dreams
When a train speaks shadows between them.

And as I stand alone, a pickup truck,
Heading home, turns off the highway,
Cuts through fields of two-foot corn,
And disappears in cumulus dust.
I watch its cloud join clouds, dissolve —
Lost, forgotten — as my eyes awaken
And retrace the road to my car.

Although I'm a stranger in this heartland,
The rude familiarity of candy wrappers,
Empty Jack Daniel's pints, Winston foil,
And crushed grapefruit-juice cans
Strewn in the highway's backwash reminds me
That I've returned intact, been debriefed,

And that I'm no longer an alien
Adrift in an ocean of gold daffodils.
Oh, for that brief evening hour!
Ah, that sweet, sleepy silence! It's late.
The mercury-vapor lamps are flickering.

6/11/75 — [3] (00808)

Helen Among the Twelve Disciples ^Δ

For Margaret and Dick Haxel

Chair legs claw the terrazzo floor
With raw and bawdy screeches
As the men in feed hats take their seats,
This autumn-cool June day.
The blond, rouge-cheeked waitress
With blue-shadowed eyelids,
Wearing too-tight jeans
And a gauzy blouse over pert breasts,
Arouses their sleepy minds,
Brings blood rushing into fat, flat veins.

A hundred undramatic voices
Reach, like hands groping in the dark,
To touch her white arms.
She stands naked before them,
In the middle of the cold floor,
Unabashed. They order eggs,
Gravy biscuits, a pot of coffee,
And three fresh plates of gossip,
Then turn momentarily stony
As her bouncing body floats away.

She awakens before five, each dawn,
To be violated by viperine tongues
And eyes used to guiding sows and cows
To troughs. Their bib-overalled protocol
Has failed to reduce her silky silence
To snide rejoinders and caustic asides.
Just now, she returns with their food,
Flies in and out like a bee,
Pollinating their base desires with a smile,
Driving them crazy as bulls in stud.

She breathes urgent fertility over them
Without words, as though she were queen
Of the Nile, newly arrived
In a region of dislocated people
Thirsting from drought. All eyes
Succumb to her beauty with prurient intent.
They would worship her pagan form
Were she not the town's whore, Helen,
Eldest daughter of Reverend Brown,
A harlot among disciples of the Lord.

6/12/75 (00123)

Was

It used to be that a man could meet
With friendly men for breakfast
And record a community's doings
In a testament of easy laughter.

Cabals convened to review
Viable relationships between the law
And those it governed. They legislated
For people who couldn't read

And agreed on sacrificial rites
To be made prior to harvesting.
They translated sacred scriptures
To coincide with fickle weather.

These arbiters of tiny economies,
Whose hard-core philosophy
Blossomed in orchards and fields
As broad as a long season,

Couldn't escape the earthy smell
Of dirt, forget hellfire
Smoldering in Gothic woodcuts,
Or remember to pray to the saints

Or imagine Paradise in a halo
Above the face of a mother
Wearing nothing but pallor
As she suckles the Lamb of God.

Yet in their coarse living,
They wore the tattered robes
Of prophets and kept the secret
Of their common source to each other.

And at night, when they retired to fires
To untwist day's flames,
Grandparents, wife, and child
Reminded each that the ancestral name

Had survived in his immediate family
And that the unique animal, man,
Still ruled the beasts
Of the jungle. Such was the past,

Before all the land was dismantled
And gardens had to be planted
Between spaces in worn sidewalks
Connecting city with countryside.

6/13/75 — [1] (00810)

At Rest △

For W.F., 1897–1962;
his epitaph

Sweet, sleeping William
Lies undistracted
By occasional passersby
Come to lay praises on his grave.
He's completely serene
Beneath the grieving earth,
Below a white-oak sky,
Rooted to the other universe
By endless lines of prose
God wrote to him.
Now, like descending Moses,
He returns with the stones intact.

6/13/75 — [2]   (00070)

Father's Day

A few hours spent in a jewelry box
Filled with time's links and studs

Pass quietly away like a celebration
Of winter slipping into April daytimes.

At easy play, the mind's curious fingers
Sort them into memory's tiny compartments,

Lined in rubbed plush and crushed velvet
To keep from bruising beautiful heirlooms.

They isolate a gold design of tiger's-eye
That watched a boy of nine years

Play gin rummy with a traveling man,
From the Wabash to Grand Central Station.

Another pair, with blue star sapphires,
Applauded three graduation ceremonies,

Shook hands with a proud young man
Standing with diploma, touched his cheek.

A set of diamond-inlayed shirt studs,
Scurrying across the cluttered box,

Adorned the broad form of two generations,
Who shared each other's formal attire.

A jade-mounted tie tack and silver-dollar
Money clip from 1921,

Secreting a million histories beneath its date,
Linger in a limbo of forgotten hopes

That an old man had for his growing son
And the obstinate boy learned to cope with

And enjoy on joining his father's company
As a scion of his lifelong ambitions.

Now, the accessories of yesterday's dreams
Are tucked neatly away in drawers,

And each knows where the gems are stored
When the time comes for them to be worn.

6/15/75 (00811)

The Poet Papers His Walls ^Δ

The fingers are grasshoppers springing
At mindless keys
That wait, like TV addicts,
To have their thinking done for them
By an omniscient brain.

The machine suffers delirium tremens:
Ideas shudder and jam,
While their stuttering mannequin
Dictates his amnesic biography
To anyone willing to listen.

Verse he produces at random,
On invisible pages
Rolled tightly around the mind's platen,
Resembles rejection slips
Received for poems he's never submitted.

6/18/75 (00823)

Flowers for Pharaoh

Black-eyed Susans and blue wildflowers
Line the highway like blurred quotations
From myriad poems I've penned in solitude
And abandoned in dank motel rooms.

Four days out of each week,
I spin in the whirlwind of tractor-trailers,
Seem lost as bewildered Moses
In a cement desert, waiting for words

To take to the people, inscribed in stone
By light emanating from empty air,
Rain-words to nourish God's flowers
And give them names to be recited aloud.

6/24–25/75 — [1] on 6/24 and [4?] on 6/25 (00824)

Clothesline

An old bleached bedsheet,
Connected by two wooden clothespins
To a line sewn through a clean breeze,
Wrapped me up in its flapping shadow.

I was its captive, held suspended
As though the tightly sprung pins
Had caught my mind by its thin edges
And hung its imagination out to dry.

Naked, I laid my thoughts to sleep
On a hazy sky, tucked them in with clouds,
Nuzzled tight-limbed into myself,
And pulled the wind up over my eyes.

While concrete miles stretched taut
As a sheet over duskbound earth,
I loitered peacefully in a dreamless daze,
Wondering what sort of gentle lady

Would soon be gathering in clean laundry.
Then, I recalled seeing my wife
*

Outside, this morning, as I left for the week,
Pinning our wash to an invisible line.

6/24/75 — [2] (00825)

[So short is the time]

So short is the time
    To know both the mind in hiding
And the one you find.
    So many are the blessings,
So few the opportunities
    To repay them in kind,
That when the chance finally arrives,
    We often mistake it
For an intrusion on our privacy.
    Frequently, we assume it to be
A mandate to withdraw from the enemy
    And spend eternity contemplating the life to come.

6/24/75 — [3] & 9/4/77 (06295)

Willy ^Δ

So myriad yet so immutable
Are the mind's stopping-off places
He chooses to occupy nightly,
On gloomy trips away from acquaintances,
He doesn't even know when he's gone.

Loitering in dim-lit crypts
Separating the empty outside air
From an even emptier plenum,
He personifies wandering Moses.
His fleshy pores are eddies of sweat.

By constantly wiping the glass
With his narcissistic tears,
He successfully escapes recognition
By eyes peering through smudges
On the mirror hung from his brain.

When fatigue comes near,
He resists circumventing desperation
Leading through no-man's-land
By declining tiny tablets and capsules —
He's crossed entire Saharas on his knees.

Sleeping beneath sleazy sheets,
Inside his forsaken bag of being,
Without solace of a female body,
Evokes a monastic stoicism
That almost glorifies his loneliness.

Each dawn is his apotheosis.
He blends into clothing, sifts the dark
For an opening, and sets out prophetically,
With swatch cards and sample garments,
To service the bargain basements of his heart.

6/24/75 — [4] (00078)

Rehearsing for a Public Reading ^Δ

I ignite in the flickering flames
Consuming brain-shadows
Cast by a fire-breathing creature
Reciting Milton's verses as his own.

In an empty and airless auditorium,
Backstage, I watch, in amazement,
An unsheathed bank of machines
Shuddering in stuttering repetition,

Watched over by a genius
Synthesizing words and meters
Into fantastical concatenations
Spewed from a rusty computer.

Rigid and afraid to breathe,
I wait until the session is over
And a packet of keypunched cards
Drops, with a thump, to the floor

Before introducing myself to the poet
At the dials, behind the microphone,
*

Then congratulate him on a performance
Unsurpassed by the original master.

A vague facial resemblance
Connects us. We sense that a heritage
Of ancient, dissolute troubadours
Has catapulted us to this podium

To corroborate the nature of fraudulence
By celebrating our plagiaristic craft.
As he explains the controls, I insert
My punched stack of Macbeth, and recite.

6/24/75 — [5] & 9/5/77 (00201)

[Misty is forever in the thought] †

Misty is forever in the thought

6/24/75 — [6] (06299)

Midnight Blue △

Linda and Emily

Twins spin identical silken songs
Ever entwined whenever hymned
For reasons no matter whatever . . . sisters —
Two beautiful blue spiders
Frozen behind their mild music,
High above a thousand midnights,
Their web holding up the earth's air . . .

Sisters transcending hand-me-downs
Wherever, then not explained.
Surrounding with sound while spinning,
They tantalize, like lyred Amphion
Charming Theban stones in place,
Unwary prey, paralyze memory
By singing them forever into their lair.

6/24/75 — [7] (00203)

The Bindle Stiff ^Δ

The long train, running forever
Through crossing gates my eyes operate,
Is a naked, nameless, evasive lady, an eidolon.
Frantically, I grab at the caboose's rail
As though it might free me from the wind,
Let me fly in the spinning wheels' backwash.

Destinationless, released from all environments,
Unbound from time's tight-wound spring,
Dissolving in infinite dislocations,
Exonerated from gravity, Freud, the loins,
I pray for a slow, steep grade,
To make my leap, near the peak of the Great Divide.

6/24/75 — [8] (00204)

[A boy went to bed on the sand;] [†]

A boy went to bed on the sand;
When the sun rose, he was a man

He walks slowly through public places,
Looking for a strange face to befriend.
Every airport, subway station, bus,
Baseball stadium, restaurant, and store
Through which he wanders teems with people

6/25/75 — [1?] (04359)

Memberships ^Δ

Each of them held the required credentials
For admission
Into the private country club
Called Life,
Recently completed on one edge of an island
Bequeathed
By a man too old to be considered a leader
In the community.

Each had the right people owing
Favors.
All needed the facilities to further
Opportunities
Ensuring a steady source of ego, income,
And stability.
Eagerly, they sold their mortgaged souls
For membership,
Despite the prospect of monthly dues
In perpetuity.
Once the list was filled, new applicants
Were taken
By reputation, not on a basis of time
Subscribed.

Lately, there's been talk of starting a club
In the desert,
Where ukases won't be issued on a whim
Or limits
Set to restrict those who are eligible
Unless
A quorum of the democratically elected board
Objects.

6/25 — [2?] & 6?/75 (00205)

Convergences [△]

Somewhere inside afternoon,
A train rumbles over decayed ties.
An engineer poised in his lusty diesel
Nears a crossing, tugs the horn rope,
Passes through, squeezing the throttle,
Shining a rusty stretch of T's
To the lustrous highlight of a pearl.

Paralleling the sway-racing train
Shadow for dusk-crouched shadow,
A trucker high in the flip-over cab
Of his whining Transtar presses hard,
Waves a hand, blasts his air,
And waits for a shared highball reply,
Before each diverges forever,
*

Divided permanently by wheat fields
And hours that push them outward.

I alone have returned unsundered,
Within a persistence of vivid images
Captured like whales by the eyes' harpoons,
To describe to my heart this brief gam
Of men and machines I accidentally spied,
Come home knowing the frozen romance
Of choosing always to be on the move.

Landlocked, I convince myself
Of the absolute mandate for breaking away
From parochial nine-to-five trades.
In desperation, decrying the futility
Of incarnations, I grasp a semi's door
As it clears a weigh station hellbent,
Clasp the shaking handrail of a caboose
Tracking a never-quite-final horizon,
And beg to be taken aboard once more.

6/25/75 — [3?] (00206)

Lepidoptera ^Δ

Each twin is a solitary wing
Floating tenderly out from the body
Of the godly music they sing.

Within the shared, muted transparency
Of their voices, I see Gothic-hued
Stained glass showing through,

Climaxing like a thousand tiny pieces
Taken, in the quiet blink of Creation,
From a perfectly focused rose window

And released on the nubile air
To seek the sun's migrating light.
My eyes' gently woven nets

Sieve the loud and furious night,
Where they've strayed from day,
Catching only their soaring notes

As their colors escape and return
*

To the cathedral on the golden plain.
The mystery of their brief passage

Brings my stunned mind to its knees
And remains unexplained, as I search
The world's coverts, with nets poised,

To recapture what was never trapped.

6/26/75 (00207)

[The bee-ravaged blooms are people] †

The bee-ravaged blooms are people
In a city doomed by Visigoths;
The tree

6/28/75 — [1] (06720)

Still Crawling △

Still she moves overland on driving knees.
Occasionally, two- and three-step advances
End in a painless backward thump
To her diapered rump. Urgency, speed, and trajectory
Erratically set each venturing-away,
Remind us of jagged lightning ripping a path
Through afternoon shadows. Before we realize,
The juggernaut reaches our front staircase,
Prepared to tackle Everest without concern.
Her right leg has learned to lift itself
On command, anchor its tiny, ivylike toes
To anything low, like an open dishwasher door
Or carpeted stairs inadvertently ungated,
And pivot the sinewy body into contortions
Of temporary dominance over her archfoe, gravity.

Now, she climbs. Our hands halo air
Edging the hole through which she passes,
In case she loses balance or balks to question
The philosophic nature of human precariousness
In relation to fear and pain. As she nears
*

The first landing, something triggers a desire
To touch earth again. She turns like a tank
Reversing one track, then backs down
Without wondering how profoundly steep
The mountainside is or who might be waiting
At its base, with open arms, to cheer her victory.
Still, at thirteen months, she moves overland
On driving knees, uninterested in walking,
Since her daddy can't resist picking her up
Whenever she crawls within his eyes' wide reach.

6/28/75 — [2] (00750)

Sales Meeting: The Spring/Summer Line ^Δ

For my friend Ed Baum

At midcity penthouse level
Within a soupy, July-droopy sky
Tinctured with faint iodine hues,
The men gather behind cigar smoke,
In air-conditioned insularity,
Sedentary as dissipated deliberating mandarins.

Recaps, ashtrays, and peanut bowls
Are strewn like refuse over tables
Draped in soiled ruffled-satin tablecloths.
Strips Scotch-taped to swatch cards
Convey, in colorful cuneiform,
A soothsayer's coded potential for fabrications
Each prophet will be expected to take to his people
As proof of the gospel's contemporaneity.

Soon, the vituperative haggling begins
Over models, dimensions, trims:
Widen loops; narrow waistbands;
Shorten open bottoms a few inches;
Modify Trad slack from western pocket
To quarter-top; retain flair leg.

The men digress, recess for catered lunch,
Where they pick up strands
Abandoned last January, weaving hours
*

Into the warp and woof of seasons
Unrolled from partially used fabric bolts.
Old ghosts and ethnic jokes are exhumed,
Promotions and retirements added in for spice,
Personal successes boasted before dessert.

The line explodes in an open-ended mitosis
Only a genius could commit to memory.
No man can know enough
To sell one buyer slack items
Along with their leisure-top coordinates,
Sportscoats, suits, and "quadrobes."

The ramifications of bad-credit extension
Are thoroughly rehearsed. Salesmen's commissions
Suffer from canceled shipments.
Discrepancies between gross and net bookings
Grow in relation to overzealous selling tactics.
Monthly draws can be quickly exhausted
Before a first order is ever OK'd,
By failing to heed "suggested" company policy.

These admonitions are a sea monster's tentacles
Squeezing the men's delusions and pride.
Despite IBM sheets
That chart performance crests and troughs
Logged by each for two previous seasons,
None believes the facts apply to him.

They grow restless, anxious to receive,
Like communion wafers, the sample garments
They'll take in their car trunks
When they leave for open territory
Via back road, interstate, Main Street,
Square, and mall. All have been given
The true Word of the Lord to proselytize
To the nation's storekeepers and populace.

Half a year, a hundred lonely motel rooms,
And fifty thousand land and air miles from now,
These disciples of the sacred robe
Will return to this mountainside, go down on knees,
And pray to the gods of Goshen for chutzpah
And merchandise with which to clothe the Philistines.

6/30 & 7/2/75 (00209)

To Canaan and Back ^Δ

Twice each year,
A missionary caravan sets out from the west,
For the lush environs of Canaan,
To renew its collective faith in bodily raiment.
Revivified, each pilgrim returns alone
To spread the Word to heathens
And tell tales of his own grail quest.

The devotees bring back with them, intact,
On stacked swatch cards
And in tightly packed black sample cases,
Fantastic, mystical fabrics
Woven of golden fleece and princess-hair,
To be converted into bookings
Of goods sold two seasons in advance.

Throughout the lands they canvass,
In every thieves' market, mart, mall,
And outdoor emporium,
Their robed, vaguely Hebraic visages are known.
July and August winds, January snows
Will echo their sandy footfalls and accents
Along their client-oriented diaspora.

And when the final amen
Rises from their agonized proselytizing,
These men of the cloth will prostrate themselves,
Pray for purpose, guidance, and strength.
Their return to Canaan, to consecrate sample garments
And bathe in its sacred pools,
Will mark the start of another mission.

7/3/75 & 12/5/77 (00208)

[We walk, abandoned, down corridors] [†]

We walk, abandoned, down corridors
Of the sea that flows underneath the sun

Treveira   Trevera

Doors open, before our voices,
Onto corridors down which dreams travel
Toward the light blazing beyond the end

Gray light strafes, like gulls,
over a late-afternoon sky

caravansary
vexacious
cicatrix

7/3–11?/75   (06301)

The Track of Time ‡

To lose track	Two opposite reactions to the same arbitrary factor,
To keep track	Both irrelevant to knowing the moment of death,
	Each an agreeable notion at times, at times
	A mere persistent idiosyncrasy, like a mosquito,
	Existing for the sake of disrupting man's serenity.

To lose track	Parentheses enclosing all human activity . . .
To keep track	Everything in between is an immeasurable integer
	On a scale used to register the breadth of dream
	And the pressure of life excited to its boiling point —
	The space within is the mind's unclaimed terrain.

To lose track	Two boundaries like mountains, one snowcapped,
To keep track	The other green above the timberline, washed in sun,
	Through whose corridor runs everyone born to the earth.
	On one side, the high peaks

7/11/75   (03610)

Manager of Outlet Stores $^\Delta$

He attends the chamber-of-commerce meeting
Once each month,
For Monday lunch with merchants and professionals,
And modestly regards himself to be
An integral part of the community's growth.

Although he leaves twice a week
In a station wagon weighted with goods
Being transferred from warehouse
To factory outlets in three states,
He considers Farmington his headquarters.

For all the alluring ladies
Loitering along sleazy hallways
Down which his bachelorhood leads,
The whore he best knows
And misses most passionately when home

Is the road that undresses his thoughts.
She fingers his rough spine with smooth hands,
Draws him into her soothing curves,
Releases his scalding semen
In the car's front seat without his knowing.

The attachments he's made by chance
Extend to waitresses, leggy barmaids
He tips at night's climax with room keys,
Night clerks taking wake-ups
And raspy complaints with bored restraint.

He smiles at their "Yes, sir. . . . No, sir. . . .
Right away, sir,"
Then places his advanced reservation
For guaranteed late arrival, ground floor,
Commercial rate for the following evening.

As itinerant minister of surplus and flaw,
Disciple of not-quite-right merchandise,
He reaches multitudes with his bargains,
Preaches God's love of cheap prices
And the gospel of inconspicuous consumption.

He's a youth with a promising future,
Who, by selling his soul wholesale,
Has gained enviable control over his destiny.
Already, the contracts have been signed
For new stores in Limbo and Purgatory.

7/15/75 (00074)

In Praise of Epiphanies ^Δ

For my mother,
with love,
on her birthday

Reaching zeniths and apogees
Used to be considered a feat
Of mythic impossibility,
Achieved only in the misty reverie
Of gentle historians, dreamers,
And sentimental poets listening
For whispers of immortality.

We never did believe in fantasies,
Fairy tales, allegories,
Parables brought to life,
Leaping high over barriers
Placed between us and time.
Always, they were life-lies
Others invented for survival.

Only, now, you've arrived
Pedestaled on a summit of years
Sixty degrees west of birth.
We see you smiling down on us.
Tirelessly, we climb to touch
Such real beauty and cling
Before you ascend again.

7/16/75 (00210)

Spider and Fly Δ

Monotony spins its weblike mist.
Filamentous silence entraps me
On this long drive home,
As my nervous fingers flit feverishly
Over the radio's push buttons
To squash the persistent buzzing I make
Like a fly striking a bulb aching to explode.
I light on the mind's silky circumference

And suddenly discover myself freely hanging
From the fundus of a glassy, incandescent vacuum,
Dangling nauseously in living asphyxia.
Eight fibrous legs, racing on air
Like myriad blades sliding over ice,
Carry me to the edge of self-awareness,
From where I'll view the inevitable entanglement
And ensuing predation of two alien species.

Now, the strands of highway I follow
Vibrate the entire web hung from my brain.
I lose equilibrium, sense of direction
And sink into its weightless undulations.
Slogging knee-deep in boredom,
I can't stop my soggy, spongy plodding
Toward the center of the lair, where fly
And spider are inextricably snared in their own miasma.

7/22/75 — [1] & 12/6/77 — [1?] (00211)

[For the last three years,] †

For the last three years,
He's ruled, with an iron fist,
The Sanhedrin
That administers regulations
To the ten lost tribes of Abraham

7/22/75 — [2] (06298)

Farmer Hades' Wife △

THE ARGUMENT

> *The daughter of Zeus and Demeter, wife of Hades, queen*
> *of the infernal regions, aggravated by the sun's preemptory*
> *blight on lands she'd hoped to subdue through untimely*
> *drought and assume suzerainty over by such catastrophe,*
> *decides to confront Helios head-on, using symbolic ritual*
> *to reverse the earth's elements, confuse its populace into*
> *complacence, and thereby reinstate herself in a rightful*
> *place of authority in the universal scheme of existence.*

In 95-degree heat,
At the edge of a cornfield
In the middle of seething greenness
Stretching horizonless from eyes
That refuse to admit its very existence,
An ancient lady, Persephone,
Inspects her burning pile of rubbish.
The incongruous vapors
Are an egregious affront to the sun,
Hellbent on creating this drought.

The gray-headed termagant in apron,
Oblivious to the sun's complaints,
Rakes the flames to ashes,
Lets them smolder in her backyard,
Then quenches the spent bed
With cobra venom from a garden hose.

Satisfied, she unleashes her hatred
And, aiming the dripping nozzle upward,
Threatens to extinguish the sky.
Further down the river valley,
Tiny rain clouds converge.

7/22 — [3] & 7/22?/75   (00212)

Jacksonville, Illinois △

I

The walled city on the prairie,
Surrounded on all sides
*

By parapets of tasseled afternoons
And soybean moats,
Is impenetrable to wandering hordes.

It's a shimmering, mystical citadel,
Whose pales are water towers,
Electric poles, and chimney stacks
Disguised as windmills and spires
Rooted in earth, penetrating heaven.

As we approach focal point,
Depth and dimension realign
To accommodate our inventive myopia,
Admit us as distinguished guests,
Come to bathe in its sacred fountains,

Taste of temptations to guess time
From unset clocks,
Touch its enclaves of artisans
Busy stitching gossip into Gobelins
Stretched on frames of their lives,

And take their modest crafts
Into our eyes for safekeeping
Until we arrive home again.
Such pilgrimages to the site
Where our original seeds were dropped

Into seething black furrows
Notched by God's fingers
And covered over by grandparents
Forever changed by His visitation
Remind us of our rural origins.

They take us back to a faith
In nature's distillations
And renascence, away from the rubble
Of collapsing cathedrals and factories,
Rats, graft, and stubbly winos.

II

As distances between cities decrease
And the fresh air we're forced to share
*

With neighbors we've never seen
Diminishes to a thin nimbus above us,
Our leave-takings increase.

Journeying to the prairie-buried city
Provides the only escape from a fate
That's changed us into wreckages of destiny,
Scattered us over a land
We cleared by hand before inhabiting,

And left us for dead. We've survived
Inside the sweet delusion
That freedom is a state of mind
Arrived at through hallucinations
Inspired by doleful Quixotes

Ranging unaided across the plains,
With pride, in search of courage
To liberate the individual soul
From loneliness. Only by going out
Have we found castles in which to lodge,

Yet only by returning home,
Via the dirty posadas
And vibrating factories, can we recall
With excitement the last urgent flight
And contemplate future sojourns.

Just now, the walled city
Shimmers like a string of beads
About the exquisitely shaped neck
Of a lady in need of being saved
From the silence of an empty day.

7/26–27/75 (00213)

[I leave Ladue's lushy green acres] †

I leave Ladue's lushy green acres

7/29/75 — [1] (06296)

Joseph K.

From dawn, through day's inexorable yawning,
Into restless nightmare again,
His existence is a prism filled with stills
Attached to an invisibly spinning axle
Fixed in the aimless void of illusion.

Before, he advanced from court to court
Crowded with bemused, empty faces.
Obliviously, they listened to his piteous appeals
And not-unreasoned pleas of innocence
For ostensible crimes against the psyche.

Yet his conviction was predetermined;
He never even had a beggar's chance
To free himself from the stigma of martyrdom,
With which his habitual and abstemious lifestyle
Had branded his soul in the eyes of his jurors.

Now, constraints levied on his brain
By the unrelenting Draconian executioner
Of his mind's easily swayed Sanhedrin
Have left him raving in a padded cell,
Beseeching commutation of his life sentence.

Occasionally, he steps out of his solitude
For a smoke or scribbles his name, in chalk,
On the granite walls, to reassure himself
He's still there. Even as they lead him
Down the dark hall, to the stale room,

He repeats his profound litany of innocence.
They strap his legs and white wrists
To the chair. The lights dim into quietude.
His vertebrae fuse; nerves snap.
Returning from his amnesic journey

To the edge of the sea, where sleep flows,
He leans in bed, on numb elbows,
Dumbfounded by the degree of his self-deceit,
Troubled only by not knowing
In which room of the dream he's awakened.

7/29/75 — [2] (00117)

[Time passed is the flower picked,] †

Time passed is the flower picked,
A garden tilled and harvested,
Sorrows floating like jetsam
On the pond rippled by a daughter
Growing up, getting engaged, leaving.
Time is our constant companion
And confidante;

7/29–31?/75 — [1] (01372)

[Traffic stalls behind an orange tractor] ‡

Traffic stalls behind an orange tractor
Lugging a double rack of disks
On the highway bisecting his property.
Cars following close behind swerve
To avoid hitting me. I cringe
In anticipation of being hit,
Developing whiplash
Or chronic bad back. I envision
A claims adjuster squaring with me
For a substantial settlement.

7/29–31?/75 — [2] (01373)

The Candidate △

Existence is a persistent slogan
That both follows and precedes
The whistle stops I've scheduled
In every state of the union,
On my whirlwind campaign for election
To the Congress of Merciful Souls.

I've taken my call to participate
In the ways of decent men
From the creeds of Plato and Socrates,
Whose faith in logic and reason
*

Embraced God's mysteries —
I believe; therefore, we are.

The planks supporting the platform
From which I sing my issues
Withstand the tramplings of filibusters
And rhetorical cant employed against me
In debates on individual freedom
And the right to privacy by all.

Despite fierce opposition,
I've expressed the interests of Everyman
Through self-respect, integrity,
Words turned to actions,
By charity given unattached,
And with an abiding love for my parents.

Now, I beseech you
To review my credentials and vote.
Although you don't know me personally,
We'll meet when you cast a ballot
For peaceful change and equality
Of ambition and success surrendered at death.

And if chosen, I'll bear the weight
Of your incomplete dreams and the agonies
Affluence may have caused you.
I'll fulfill my disavowals of gain,
My promises to improve your state
Of holiness. I'll legislate for your survival.

7/31/75 — [1] (00215)

Visiting the Artist ^Δ

Somewhere beyond my range,
Someone pencils the blue sky
With nubile outlines and strokes
Plumbago-shaded in nervous gradations
Of invisibly accumulating rain.

Locked in the car, I watch afternoon
Change from a two-dimensional plane
*

Into a ragged mountain chain
Held in place by rooting sunrays
Snowcapped above its timberline.

Next, I see sheep wading the horizon,
Nudging their plump, fleecy bodies
From side to side, bumping as they follow,
In tight chaos, their unseen leader
Through turbulent thermal currents.

Finally, all vagaries dissolve,
As the vast space before the vehicle's glass
Compacts to the size of black vacuum
Inside an inflated paper bag
Grasped at its neck by a vicious fist.

Sullenly, I wait for two palms
To smack the wrinkled sack of sky,
Explode it in my face. Only, now,
Someone has begun to erase the design,
Replace it with a smooth cerulean hue

Of luminous wash. My squinting eyes
Limit their vision to the white highway,
As I settle, again, into a daze,
Among a pile of crumpled sketches
Strewn about a painter's studio floor.

7/31/75 — [2] (00202)

Distress Message

Lacking wife and child beside me,
I'm an unguided, absent-minded navigator
On a terminal journey to the edge
Of a squared-off earthly existence.

Nowhere can I locate their faces
Among the leaping phosphorescences
And grotesquely enmeshed seaweed
Or resurrect my baby's cries.
I've forgotten how my lady's love
Touched my rough, uxorious ears
Without her speaking one word.

Now, absolute inarticulateness
Dismantles my prevailing sanity,
Throws the boat in a violent yaw,
Spiraling it inward, toward loneliness.

Neither debris nor creatures
Reminiscent of sea gulls
Appear as hopeful visions
Of my returning, soon, to sleep with Jan
And wake with mercurial Trilogy.
I've ranged too far from Argos
To catch the changing tides.

In a Madeira bottle, I seal a tear,
Stopple it and drop it overboard,
Into the larger eye of ocean,
Without watching to see if it floats.

7/31/75 — [3] (00216)

Breaking Stallions ^Δ

I ride bareback
Atop the sweaty genome of chromosomes
Bucking dizzily in a corral
Where generations of my forebears
Have been thrown
And broken their spines in the dust.

Ancient eyes are on my performance,
As I try to break the leaping creature
Trapped in its frenzied fear
Of not being able to unseat me.
We hang as one on the hot air,
Each obsessed with maintaining stability

And prevailing in the face of a history
Racially oppressed for ages.
Damn the whiskered ragmen
Who've tracked me to this time!
Goddamn them for reminding me
Of the proud and threadbare tailors

Who rose from crude peasant stock
That ravaged the Steppes beyond Kiev!
Why, for so long, have I eluded
Their hereditary nets and thrived
In an academic nether world,
Only to be dragged back

And forced into a raw saddle
Atop survival's frothing wild stallion?
I reel in a drunken paraplegia.
My feet rip loose from the stirrups.
Caught in the vortex of old dust
Blocking my nostrils and throat,

The stench of my flowing blood
And the shame locked in my brain
Can't mistake the truth of my defeat
Or negotiate another compromise
With genes that have permanently hurled me
Into a factory of trouser-making machines.

7/31/75 — [4] (00214)

Willy's Evening Entertainment ^Δ

Light beams copulating frantically
On naked, heated air
Unload against faceless blurs
Bound by a tremulous stage.
Each dancing body
Attracts tiny, luminous particles,
Absorbs acid lyrics
Wrapped in sensual melodies
Like flowers lifting liquidly
Above a Christmas cactus.
I fornicate with articulations
The strings, keys, and skins make
With their close, open lips and thighs
And surrender my entire being
To the fellatio of their persuasive overtones.

Somewhere behind the drapes
Separating the syncopated noise
My mind grudgingly differentiates
From live primal vibrations
The group routinely evokes,
A vague premonition of death
Rises to my eyes like smoke.
I sense a hot, wet explosion
Go frozen below my fly.
Soon, the music concludes
And is hastily packed in suitcases;
It leaves. I remain behind,
Stuporous, feeling cheated by the whore
Who brought me to climax,
Then rolled me for my wallet.

7/31/75 — [5] (00217)

Groupies ^Δ

Teenage odalisques collect about the groups,
During break, like slavish metal filings
Drawn to the seductive overtones of sex-notes
Long since diminished. Each daddy's girl
Seizes her first forbidden fruit, squeezes,
Prepares to leave home, take flight,
Abandon her leisure-class attitudes for mindscapes
Not platted for mass public dwelling.
Manifestations of vagrancy and indigence are delicacies
She savors like caviar, pâté de foie gras,
Tequila to be piquantly sipped — unstoppled freedom
Effervescently running from her bottle of life.

Suddenly, the lights rise. Night is packed in cases,
And she's left waiting for a decorated van
To fleet her away. Anxiously, she waits for a ride,
Like the war bride of an ill-fated pilot,
Carrying her nameless baby in stillborn dreams
Of breaking out of the parochial heartland forever.
Even by Cesarean, she's unable to deliver her hopes alive
From the parent-owned environs where she's grown up.
*

Always, younger girls in see-through concupiscence,
Dreaming, in turn, of being liberated from their destinies,
Violate the smoky seraglios of acned musicians
Who, during breaks, lure concubines into their harems.

7/31/75 — [6] & 12/30/77 (00218)

Blown Apart ^Δ

The eyes fasten onto stroboscopic maracas
Chattering, like cicadas, against the close air
Inside my head. Lights divide the darkness
Like Creation happening all over again
For those of us who weren't yet born
At the first performance. Taut, primitive strings
Set the air trembling, tune membranes
To specific overtones in warring vibration
With the guitarist's original picking,
While the room contracts to accommodate our noise
In a claustrophobia inhabited by jungle creatures.

Voices supported by pentameters commingle,
Trip through fields of melodies flowering
Like land mines buried in notes exploding
Over naked tunes floating on oceans
Of mustard-gas smoke. The communal demolishment
Of late hours gives birth to a creation
Never dreamed of or exegetically explained
In classrooms. The music detonates the terrain
Over which I cautiously tiptoe,
Breaking open my brains, igniting flames
That keep the imagination heated for versing.

I peak over the foxhole's edge
To survey the infiltrated stage, then scream
For the enemy to subdue my mind in sweet dissolve,
As the music draws to a crescendo, then fades,
And I'm left, on armistice night, abandoned and cold.
No one runs me through with a bayonet,
Shoots from a distance, or body-bags me by mistake.
Even the saggy, bedraggled barmaid
*

Refuses to bring me a final drink of wine.
And as floodlights illumine the swirling room,
I arise like the first human on earth and surrender.

7/31/75 — [7] & 12/31/77 (00219)

Prelude to Another Day

As piped-in music pauses
Between songs, the hostess
Retires briefly to the kitchen.
The automatic odor machine
Finishes its fifteen-minute cycle.
I alone sit in this emptiness.
The awful silence
Wounds ears used to daytimes.

Before entering the mainstream,
I order breakfast.
Three scrambled eggs and muffins
Remind me of what people
On hospital diets eat
Before and after surgery;
Coffee pits the mesentery.

Only the cryptic blue numerals
Posted on the motel bill
Suggest I actually deposited
An allotment of my life, last night,
In this hallowed repository
For people's transience.
Soon, even that will be lost.

8/1/75 (00956)

Merchant Sailor △

The itinerate Holsum bread man
Wears a pen over his ear,
Cropped mustache under his nose,
White socks, lace-top shoes.

He sits alone, having hot coffee
Between dockings, concentrates
On making an account entry
For his Crystal Café delivery

In a dog-eared leather log
He keeps pressed to his hip
Like an orthodox ship captain's
Talmud of the sea.

Twice, he lifts a salutation
Room's length, reciprocating
Recognitions of his arrival by farmers
Gathered to lament scorched corn,

And townspeople sifting in to discuss
Universal joints, twisted axles,
And snapped drive shafts
From last night's tractor pull.

He greets the teenage waitress
Of local breeding, in tight jeans
Over pear-supple buttocks,
Whose smile is a sun at midnight

Among this lascivious contingent
Of good old boys. He winks
As though they've shared intimacies
Implausible in a community this size,

Then follows her languid path
Back to the fetid kitchen
As if his head were attached by chain
To an anchor capstan and winch

Instead of to a brain set aflame
Almost involuntarily
By visions of her tiny, naked breasts
And belly convulsing in climax.

Something distracts his eye,
Refocuses his mind on the wrist watch
He uses to guide him from port
To port in his Midwest Mediterranean.

He lays exact change on the counter,
Waits while she places each coin
*

In its compartment, copies a receipt
He requests, on which she writes, "Tonight."

Then he leaves with an obtrusive gait
Obvious to everyone but himself.
Outside, he lingers long enough
At the back of his cargo truck

To rearrange the ballast of pastries
And other bakery goods he'll deliver
Along the routed hours of his mind.
Before fastening the safety latch,

Casting off ropes and sailing,
He grabs a loaf of whole-wheat bread,
Squeezes it in slow, profane delight,
Excited about returning at high tide.

8/2/75 — [1] (00220)

[Like a tracked fugitive,] †

Like a tracked fugitive,
I stay just minutes ahead
Of an expanding thunderhead,
Rapidly exhaust all escapes
Other than the straight course

8/2/75 — [2] (01374)

[The highway I travel,]

The highway I travel,
Striated with white dashes
And continuous white bands
Defining both extremities
Of the cement cambium and bark,
Is clotted with nervous termites
Chewing paths through morning's subfloor
And joists supporting afternoon traffic.

Where the creatures incessantly pass,
Tandem discolorations appear
Like indelible tire tracks,
Staining my nearsighted eyes.
It's as if vision were mapped
By black sap flowing down maple trees
Growing in a hundred country towns,
To as many deforested cities and back.

Trees that have lined driveways
To and from my peripatetic mind
Begin to lose leaves, shatter limbs
In storms that age the body overnight.
Now, I use fewer avenues of escape.
My speeds diminish. I get lost,
Forget directions and reasons for needing them.
Soon, even the roots will pull loose from life.

8/5/75 — [1]   (00457)

[A young man without memory of the past] †

A young man without memory of the past
Speaks to his dreams,
As though they might answer his voice
With words made of delicate rose petals
Floating down from an old sky
Through which he used to run with friends.

8/5/75 — [2]   (01375)

Race Day

My nervous mind overwinds
Like an internal-combustion engine
Whose accelerator is jammed wide open.
The machine redlines, peaks;
Brains explode through the fire wall
Separating sight from palpitating heart.

Blood floods the cranial compartment
Like grease and mucoidal oil
Spewing out behind broken valves,
Pistons, pushrods, and scorched crank.
Lobes crack off the overhead cam
Like discs deteriorating along the spine.

The vehicle veers, stutters in space,
Disintegrates into flameless particles,
And is assimilated into oblivion
As vapors expelled by a psyche
Racing time toward a finish line
Stretched between death's checkered flags.

8/12/75 — [1] (00221)

Word-Seeds

For my flower child, Jan

I planted word-seeds,
With delicate articulation,
In furrows of teeth and tongue,
Covered them over with subtle persuasion
To keep them deeply penetrated,
Away from scavenging beaks
And sniffing rodent noses
That might nip meaning in the bud.

Then I waited for their first shoots,
Rooted where the original seeds
Exploded into gentle tendrils,
To pierce my garden's weeded surface,
That her eyes might scan
My perfectly slender verses,
Rising in bouquets of "I love you"s
For her ears to arrange in their clear vases.

8/12/75 — [2] (00107)

The Hours Call Out His Name ^Δ

The oak-cased regulator clock,
Whose face, hands, and pendulum
Bear a striking resemblance to Christ
Crucified, hangs over the bed,
Above his slanted, sleeping head.
It drips drops of raucous tocks
Ticking to sandy Calvarys,
Where, naked in nightmare,
He listens to the minutes and hours arrived
Being announced to consciousness
Like witnesses summoned to an execution
By hanging. He becomes the victim,
Swinging from the long-drop pendulum
In a monotony of tedious arcs
As though dangling by his neck from a rope
Knotted on a hook in the skull's roof.
He gasps. His spine snaps,
And all numb sleep ceases.
Life bleeds furiously
From clogged ears and stuffy nose.
His inflamed eyes open,
Focus on a hulk slumped in the corner.
Reluctantly, they funnel his thoughts,
Like helium, into the shapeless form,
Until it fills with a dizzy semblance
Of the new day's design,
And he climbs down from night's scaffolding
To rewind invisible clockwork.

8/19/75 — [1] & 1/3/76 — [2?] (00223)

Mowing Crews ^Δ

Two mowing crews line the edges
Along the highway I drive home.
Their machines' portentous, faded orange frames,
Cluttered with whisperous sidebar sickles,
Rear-mounted brushhogs,
*

And reiterating scythes, remind me of lobsters
Set free from live boxes to die
In the implacable heat of the heartland sea.

Traffic adapts to their meandering speed,
As wide blades shear the dry grass
Into clumped silage. Road men,
Bare-chested, beaded with sweat and grease,
Wave caution signs periodically,
Alternating from STOP to SLOW and back,
To keep people from assaulting each other
Or crashing into a tractor, from distraction.

Long after I've driven out of their sight,
My mind persists in asking why
These men and machines have been assigned
Such an essentially Sisyphean task
And if, in fact, they might not be
A few of Dante's sentenced offenders in disguise,
Doomed to labor in the Devil's service
By paving our way to his flaming dominion.

8/19/75 — [2] (00224)

Ceaseless Weekend ^Δ

Today, I've embezzled eight hours from work
To range as far from home, before dusk,
As our old car will go. We slip away unnoticed
Except for a fat gas-station attendant,
Who scrutinizes the few trappings of flight and escape
We take along on the journey for assurance's sake.
He leans over the hood — the last man on earth —
And cleans the windshield, with distracted apathy,
Leaving indelible streaks I'll disentangle
From the real horizon for the next two hundred miles.

Meanwhile, my wife and I scan a map,
Whose intersecting lifelines withhold clues
To the future. We choose a route we've never used,
Then set out, with a tank full of fuel,
On the crusade we've planned so long to make
*

To a land beyond the limits of familiarity,
Just inside the outermost extremities of memory.

Now, in a susurrant hovering above the earth,
Sealed in our machine, we enter freewheeling,
Coast through a warp of weekend hours,
And are lost within a gentle cloud without borders.
Weightless, we tumble toward moon's day,
Blind to all roads that might convey us home.

8/29/75 (00226)

[Today, the Bagel bites the dust] †

Today, the Bagel bites the dust

8/30/75 — [1] (06300)

Two Stones Cast in the Rain

For Marilyn and Bob "Big Guy" Neagle

We awaken to the rain's persuasive wash
Cleansing the remaining hours, making room
For the nuptial celebration of two souls
Approaching the sacred pool, from out of oblivion.

Soon, Marilyn and Bob will leap together
And leave behind their individual selves,
Like tiny, finite rings infinitely widening
From the original source of both thrown stones.

An earthly church awaits their arrival
To house, for seconds, their gestures and vows.
We watch the hours rush toward 2:00,
Then witness their spirits forever coalesce.

Now, we hear their whispers across the distance,
Connecting the present with their faces in that rain.
A beautiful shimmering of mind-circles
Imitates, in steady emanations, their wedding embrace.

8/30/75 — [2] (00225)

The Casket Truck

For miles, I hover above the highway,
In the backwash of a vault company's truck,
Staring at two caskets juxtaposed,
One silver, one bronze.
In the morning sun, the ornate skin
That covers these twin containers
Resembles crinkled foil I've often used
To wrap leftover meat and cheese.

Mesmerized by the sight of these sarcophagi
And frightened by their stark, funereal obtrusiveness
On an otherwise quiet and private drive,
My mind squirms, turns apprehensively
To Yeats's apples and Sir Thomas Browne.
I feel myself being buried alive
In a catacombed potter's field
Of gurgling intestines, lined with urns.

For miles, I linger behind the speeding coffins
As if connected by an involuntary curiosity
To confirm their destination is different from mine.
Ahead, my turnoff looms.
Nervously, I watch to see which way
The hearse will go, then exit alone,
Toward the river, heading west,
Into a raw fog stalking me from above.

9/3/75   (00116)

Learning Languages ^Δ

In all tongues, love is itself.
Trilogy's vocabulary has grown
By permutations, degrees of sophistication.
She used to call everybody "mama"
Regardless of genus, species, or gender.
Then, her daddy became "da,"
And she assumed the recognizable identity
Of "bay-bee." The caged creatures
*

That pace beneath her amused eye,
Outside, are "bow-wows."
Thrice daily, after eating and play,
She tugs her ear, slaps her face,
Loses her smile, and can't be held.
We say, "See-pee . . . see-pee,"
And she knows we've spoken the code that, broken,
Transports her to the satiny land of sleep,
Where her blanket stays and Maxine waits
To be wound into the most beautiful sounds
That ever a magical cow did make.

Despite Trilogy's last three months of learning,
Her words are only minute crystals
Atop her tiny mind's iceberg;
Below, we imagine a cavern
Dazzling with myriad glassy refractions,
Flowing slowly toward tropical climes.
We ask, in wild abstraction,
"Do you want to go for a ride?"
And realize, as she sidles toward the door,
How much more than the deliriums
Of sheer joy are locked in her storeroom.
When asked "Do you want juice?"
She goes to the "ice-cream table,"
Violates the debris above the edge
She can't see, being so close,
And gropes for the half-filled glass
She remembers her mother placing somewhere
In the landscape of past hours.

"Do you want to hear the big music?"
Elicits a mixture of trepidation and ecstasy
From the baby, whose head barely reaches
The antique Wurlitzer's keyboard.
She flounders beneath the giant orchestrion,
Desires to be lifted high in my arms,
Guarded against the anticipated din of triangle,
Two drums, flute and violin pipes,
And mandolin piano, which reverberate
At the touch of a button. We dance wildly
As turtledoves flirting in jagged flight.
Beside me, she's mistress of her fears.
*

Peering into the brightly lighted kaleidoscope,
Composed of revolving "wonder light"
And stained-glass panels, she shapes
Her own private designs into seedlings
That, someday, in rapt and passionate density,
Will forest the aura of her creative self.

The bridge consisting of slender vowels
And consonantal syllables braided with sounds
Woven with words and tied, like hemp,
Into concatenated phrases
Spans Trilogy's childhood reservoir.
As we three cross the invisible chasm
And turn back to reflect on the hour,
The shore is clouded in a gentle haze.
Before us, the distance has no terminus.
Signs along the way change from lines
To symbols to ideas spelled out in a dialect
We repeat to each other without tiring,
As though to remind us that growth
Is not confined to stages nor aging
Wholly related to social exposure.
By translating the holy scrolls, together,
We're learning to articulate love
And make it accessible to everyone.

9/4/75 — [1]   (00751)

Toasting an Old Foe

The restaurant's dimly lit anonymity
Impregnates my unsubstantial identity
With a million seething sterile seeds.
I'm born unto myself, this evening,
A stepchild of my lonely discontents,
Conceived out of a dour relationship
Entered into by my wayward soul
And a brooding, nymphomaniacal notion of freedom
That climaxes on journeys away from home.

In cribbed recesses of my dark mind,
Muffled cries, like vagrant winds
Slipping mysteriously under a front door
*

Or whimpers from a baby craving breast milk,
Rise through insulation in my ears,
Beg admission as valid rebuttals
To arguments I've tried mightily to sustain
In order to justify these flights
Despite my feisty body's antagonism.

A protracted moaning reverberates the bones
That barely keep my being intact.
Momentarily, I look up from my plate,
Afraid that someone has recognized me
And is now about to demand my companionship.
But no one is out there before me
Except the specter of a vaguely familiar
Elongated face in the wineglass
I touch to the air in toasting my insularity.

Suddenly, the apparition staring back
Breaks into laughter as if tickled
On its bare feet. With unsteady fingers,
I check my lips to register a reflection
Coincident with my own self-image.
But all my features are alien.
Something's taunting me. A misty nemesis,
A spirit, draws near. To make it disappear,
I fearfully swallow the wine.

9/4/75 — [2] (00227)

Firefighter ^Δ

The pen's pointed end is a nozzle
He directs toward invisible objects
Burning behind his mind's keen eye.
Agents he drains off the brain's reservoir
Are not quite chemical, not liquid
In any absolute sense, but a kind
Of ineffable powder flecked with energies
Flying around under expanded pressure.
Once released, word-clouds
Raining down in seething torrents
Occupy the spaces created by fiery ideas.

After hours of fighting flames
Exploding out of nowhere and tongues
Rekindled by drafts of windy indecision,
He brings the conflagration under control,
Deems it completely benign. Only then
Does he stow his equipment in pockets,
Leather case, and easily accessible boxes
And leave the splintered chars on the page.
He's never arrived early enough
To save more than the basic foundations
Of any originally consecrated edifice.

9/5/75 — [1] (00228)

Time Is the Lady's Name We Gave Our Child △

Time is the lake in which I bathe,
The garden to whose furrowed earth I genuflect
Feeding squirrels, touching lushy petals
Without notions of plucking them from rose,
Cymbidium, and lady's-slipper plants.
She's the street down which I go,
Toward the home I've known so well
Through repeated mowing seasons and snows.
Time's gentle, naked thighs and tiny breasts
Are those of my wife, whom I kiss nightly,
When we synchronize our private lives
With the hall clock's insomnious ticktocking
To guide our breathing through sleep.

And time is the name we gave Trilogy Maya,
Our tiny messiah, to commemorate her birth,
When she descended our minds' canal,
From the lake by the garden down the street,
Toward the gabled home where we labored
In Maying fecundity, awaiting the epiphany
When days prior and unrecorded
Would converge on her and make of our mortality
A love-flame perpetually burning.

9/5/75 — [2] (00756)

En Route

The vibrating tires are mental centrifuges
Spewing out ultrasonic circles
My ears clutch like a child's hands
Cupping exploding soap bubbles
Floating on air. Their elusive music
Seduces me. I enter their sensual whirlpools,

Where motion becomes a series of explosions
I fail to notice: road holes,
Pistons pacing in tunnels, like moles,
Eighteen-wheel buffaloes stampeding,
Shoulders misgauged, carcinogenic exhaust
Brazenly invading an impotent countryside.

Only the radio's cat-o'-nine-tails,
Lashing the mind's bleeding back,
And fog, punctuated by blunt objects
Overtaking me every so often,
Keep sleep from sweeping me away
From my primary business of staying alive.

Yet, traversing this silent land,
I can almost hear its Septembering voices
Calling me to abandon my travels and plans,
Join their transmigration of harvested spirits.
Until today, I never estimated
My destination was so near at hand.

9/16/75 — [1] & 1/17/78 (00229)

In Harvest Time

A love song for Jan

The distance between these honeyed fields
And green ones we've recently seen
Is measured in seeds planted in furrows dug
In earth plowed, sowed, and showered
By clouds crowded with distilled days
Evaporating from our confluent lives.

Their tributaries, refilled as they radiate
From our hearts, meander over a land-dial,
Whose shadowy hands are vines
Attaching flowers and fruits to taproots
That stretch flexibly toward the core,
Where harvests from our marriage are stored.

Annually, from one planting to the next,
Our love-blooms ripen to a delicate affection.

9/16/75 — [2] (00230)

Death Comes to the Salesman

It happened so fast —
The sun slipping past the black gates,
Into this hoary morning —
I felt compelled to frisk the mist
Lifting from roadside hills and valleys
To allay my anxiety that sunlight,
Not the ocherous body of death,
Had thrown its shadows
Over my future with so little notice.

Yet when I sent out my eyes
To scrutinize its vapors, they were gone,
And in their place, everywhere,
Vision was a painfully blinding haze
Clawing across a tender sky.
In defense, I drew the visor down,
Limiting sight to the pavement on fire —
A bubbling river Styx —
Until I was no longer the driver

But a victim drowning
In midstream, in a nether world,
Ferried to the earth's furnace.
By the time I finally arrived for my meeting,
I'd completely forgotten the reason
For leaving home so early
Or even in whose body I'd slept, last evening,
*

Before dying with such abruptness
On this perfectly normal Saturday morning.

9/20/75 — [1] (00081)

Closing In ^Δ

Parents of arrogant, broken-home children
Weep Hail Marys, hallelujahs,
And hosannas on New York streets.
Their cries reach all the way back here,
Where we raise soybeans and corn
To camouflage radiation plants
And silos wombing SAM's instead of grain.

An aroma of disillusioned youths
Caught smoking grass and sniffing coke
And pinned, like clothes, to a police lineup
For pushing coats of many colors
Filters all the way back here,
Where the slow odors of floating waste
From refineries, dynamos, and sewage depots
Penetrate pig trough and salt lick.

Beastly teenage murders and rapes,
Dismissed for false arrest or bargained away,
Are delivered in prime-time slots,
Like candies and chips from vending machines,
To anyone with a short-changed education
Or stricken with TV narcolepsy.
All the way back here,
The pterodactyl flies inland from the sea,

While the heartland grows weary
And suspicious of this autumn upon us,
As if an irreversible oracle
Were commanding us to dig in,
Beware of clouds bearing bouquets of flowers,
Lions crouching to be petted, and P E A C E
Needled on time's penal-colony chest.

9/20/75 — [2] (00231)

[I step out into an awareness of winter] †

I step out into an awareness of winter
Riding invisibly in on summer's backdraft.
At first glance, there are no relics,
Only a landscape filled with images persisting
Long after they've ceased their growing.

On closer examination, the old mimosa,
Whose green fronds are still closed from night,
Is blooming with yellow, mummylike seedpods,
Not delicate, peacock silk-plumes,
And the single black walnut in the backyard

Is loosing its leaves side over side
Like trading cards skillfully flipped by a boy
From my youth, who also bartered for and bought
Sought-after comic books, fought battles
Without motive, ran, through shortcuts, home,

Eluding imaginary truant officers,
To lie beside his father, below the radio
Cathedraled above the bedstead of a hundred Sundays,
Listening to voices weaving mysteries
From the most implausible balls of yarn.

9/21/75 — [1] (00468)

Cellmates △

The books scattered about my study
Glance back like chased felons.
Titles on their faded spines are prisoners
Sentenced by my impoverished mind
To remain isolated and forgotten for life.

Although we're not even allowed
To touch the screen separating us,
I often exercise my visiting rights,
Consider it a privilege to sit alone
For hours with protagonists and old foes.

Just now, the guards leave.
I reach over the inviolable barrier
To feel the breathing pulse
Of a bulky volume of Paradise Lost
And savor its freely sprung meters.

Only, in doing so, it eludes me
And bolts toward the yard wall.
I race after it, fall behind
In a pool of turbulent searchlights,
As it leaps over the top of my mind.

Soon, the guards reoccupy my room.
Shot through with anxieties,
I withdraw, wondering if they've seen
My foolishness and don't actually intend
To taunt me in my open cell.

9/21/75 — [2] (00232)

Retrieving Leaves ^Δ

The three of us step outside,
By the glassed-in back porch, and breathe
Like perplexed strangers recently admitted
Through Ghiberti's golden doors to Heaven.

All around is a sibilant whispering
Of swaying trees stayed to the earth
By chunky roots yet shaking furiously,
As if a thousand housekeepers
Had taken hold by their lower trunks
And begun to broom clean the October sky.

We lie on our backs, watching the bushy tops
Of locusts, oaks, sweet gums, mimosas
Brush aside scudding clouds
On their way toward day's steep precipice.

The leaves Trilogy chases are love beads
Skittering away from a severed necklace.
She screams as they tumble nervously by her,
*

Reaches awkwardly to capture one
Between thumb and forefinger
And finally succeeds. She brings it back,

Stumbling as though inebriated.
We accept her offering to us as an oblation
Made to Demeter and Aeolus, twin minions
Participating in a celebration of seasons

Shaping time around us like facial expressions
Applied with clay by an excited sculptor.
Watching our little sheep run free
Among the leaves, we share the wonderment
And disbelief of having become shepherdess
And shepherd for a flock of one tiny creature.

Suddenly, she sees a squirrel gather something
Beneath the walnut tree, scurry, and leap.
Her eyes follow it through thinning limbs,
To the sun-tinged pinnacle,

Where fall waits to paint her mind.
Briefly, she's lost to our concern, alone
In a zone unknown to all but those
Who've penetrated Ghiberti's doors and returned.
She starts from nuts pelting the lawn,
Then swings into our gazes

And retraces their emanations to our hearts' heart
Partaking of her innocent exuberance. This time,
The leaf she brings us is from the heights
Where color begins. It's still attached.

10/5/75   (00752)

Vicissitudes ^Δ

For so long, the woods around us
Stood monolithic and rough-edged
In every direction, like an unworked slab
Of green travertine. Now orgiastic,
Each tree has been fastidiously chiseled
*

With plum, mustard, and blood-rust,
Deliriously notched out of space
By terra cotta, moth dust,
Crimson and assigned its exclusive shape
In this one-of-a-kind fall mosaic,
Which titillates my retinas to ecstasy —

Cones pulsate, rods twitch. My nerves
Are swollen creeks filled with adrenaline.
Each tree is an individual impulse
Sent over invisibly strung conduits
Running from the woods, through my eyes,
To the mind's color-coded filing system.
The overload explodes my concentration,
And this day's poetry drains away
Like debris on receding floodwaters,

As a spectre of souls flaming in Sheol
Rolls over me. I choke on intimations
Of the woods solidifying again and fading
Into chalky, oxidized shades of gloom,
Standing monolithic and rough-edged
In every direction, like an unworked slab
Of clay waiting to be shaped into skeletons.

10/6/75 — [1] (00233)

Confirmed Bachelor ^Δ

The diurnal hours are naked ladies
Taking provocative positions on the bed
In which I sleep. Posing, they coax me
Out of my comatose state of sterility,
Taunt me with breaching filled with love-spill.
Their feline moaning splinters my memory
As though it were the resonating tremolo
Of a voice shattering fine crystal.
Fastidiously, I sweep up the pieces,
Glue some into scrapbooks,
Store others, banded with elastic, in drawers,
*

And hang the rest in plastic frames
As reminders of time arrived and dead.
Dateless faces, disembodied and faded,
Portraits of sports teams, class pictures,
Diplomas shriveled beyond straightening
Decorate dreaming's morbid corridors.

Constantly, the ladies change stations on the dial,
As if the malaise of impending doom
Were unbearably thorny.
I awaken with a sympathetic stiffness,
Disentangle myself from a net of minutes
And pesty seconds, and peer from the clearing,
Which fears of dying young have worn clean
And in which I've lain for three decades,
Waiting to recognize the lady of my dreams.
Only, no one embraces my solitude
Except a collection of female skeletons
I vaguely identify by the lengths of their hair.
Viciously, they tear my nightclothes, stare,
Then squeeze my bare testicles and penis
Until the shrill pain knocks me back,
Facedown, in a drying pool of ejaculate,
And the clock hands cut me in half, in passing.

10/6/75 — [2] & 1/19/78 (00234)

[Life is an unscheduled direct flight]

Life is an unscheduled direct flight
From parturition to dying.

10/10/75 — [1] (06297)

False Start

The revolving fan blades
Impatiently wait for radio communication
To unleash them from their cabled reins.
*

Suddenly, push-back of the shuddering craft
From its boarding dock is aborted.
Someone has noticed the brakes dragging,
Summoned the maintenance crew,
Ordered engines shut down.

Now, we sit in uneasy silence,
Secretly wishing to forget our peripatetics,
Deplane, and go home.
As a jack maneuvers into place beneath us,
Three mechanics, wearing white gloves,
Swarm the gear, from out of nowhere,
Like lampreys attaching to a shark's belly
To hear its dark heartbeat.

Wrenches, ratchets, screwdrivers,
Like bones of a shattered skeleton,
Lie strewn beside anodized parts.
The left outer tire and drum assembly are removed,
A new one installed
And loaded with fluid; the hub is replaced,
The plane leveled. Frictionless again,
It's wheeled back into starting position.

Although the delay's duration has lasted
Scarcely thirty minutes,
Passengers eye their watches with unveiled disgust,
Accept complimentary drinks contemptuously,
Deride the captain's reassuring apologies,
As the plane overtakes inertia
And lifts into its programmed angle of attack.
Heedless, they unfasten seat belts,

Invade the aisles, and resume disparagements
Aimed at American-made machinery,
Fate, and every conceivable absolute
Capable of stimulating cynicism.
I recline, hypothesizing what might have happened
Had the line mechanic driving the tractor
Not noticed the suspect drum or, seeing it,
Decided not to waste our precious time.

10/10 — [2] & 10?/75 (00235)

The Perfect Crime

Three generations of a close-knit family
Kidnapped a solitary week from their routines,
Blindfolded and transported it to Fort Lauderdale,
And held it captive for the exorbitant ransom
Of an untraceable series of memories to spend forever.

After a week, they exchanged their prisoner
For five seats aboard a slipstream
And return passage to their places of sleep and work.
Even now, they talk about the perfect caper
They got away with, heisting their lives

By taking a vacation together, just for the sake of it.

10/18/75   (00236)

Exploration Party ^Δ

Our baby spies three plastic potato containers
Squatting, in yellow stasis, on the carpeted floor
Of a pantry filled, like the back of a pickup truck,
With miscellaneous cans, bottles, and rifled boxes.
Suddenly, she begins her juggling act
With the excitement of a center-ring circus performer,
Rearranging the slightly spongy spuds
To please her special sense of symmetry
Each time they come thudding to the rug.

Satisfied with the indecipherable order she's made,
She lets the door squeak slowly shut,
Revealing a stand of soda cans patiently waiting
For her inquisitive hands to discover its presence.
Stacked like a castle of building blocks
Her daddy might have fabricated for her diversion,
The snap-top cylinders ask to be rattled, dislodged.
Towers, parapets, the bastion itself, lose dimension
A shape at a time. Ultimately, they lie scattered
Like flotsam rising from a sunken ship.

Again content with her unintentioned destruction,
She turns to a plate of leftover toast,
*

Set too close to the table's edge and neglected.
Her searching fingers, like snakes' tongues
Hunting sounds, touch the crusty shards.
She waits for admonitions from her surveillant companion,
Then, with obvious pride, takes a dainty bite.

Next, she bows before the closed oven door
As if asking, in formulistic refrains,
For the magical combination that releases its drawer.
On contact, it comes open, disclosing a trove
Of stainless-steel pots and pans in varying diameters.
Like a lady playing carillons,
She registers tintinnabulations
That form pleasing hymns to her shimmering tympanums.
Lids strewn everywhere are wind chimes
That sing when her knees accidentally strike them.

Now, she sidles against my legs, grabs hold,
Pets me to see if, in my silence, I'm still alive.
Finding my smile, she sits atop my boots,
Squats under my amused eye like a female Gautama
Accepting ineffable praise from Above.
From this vantage, she peers ahead,
Dead-reckons the future looming in her pupils.

She's lead surveyor in our exploration party of two,
Sent into unknown territories
To chart maps, give names to all phenomena
Found in the new world, barter with natives,
And proclaim her undeviable religious persuasion
Toward individual freedom to speak out
Against whatever she can't satisfactorily explain
Or accept on faith, and her sense of direction is gospel.
Success will reflect on her majesty, the queen mother.

Meanwhile, I travel behind her lead canoe,
Carrying packs, retrieving forgotten socks
And shoes, cleaning camp before moving,
Dousing the fire's embers after she beds
In the profound, cribbed sanctity of satin blanket
And musical cow. And I feel privileged to follow,
With words, her journey across the unspoiled geography
Earthing the million virgin miles of her curiosity.

10/20/75 (00753)

Accident-Prone ^Δ

Today, while digging a sandcastle
In the morning news, my curiosity
Edged too near its sedgy moat.
Bending to touch a Coole-white swan,
It fell in and almost drowned.

Recovery was an all-afternoon matter
Of forgetting about a decomposed body
Sighted at the side of the highway,
Ignoring increasing threats to peace
By Red Chinese insurgency in the universe,
And tuning out repeated pronouncements
About probable sun, rain, and heat.

Full extent of damage from the fall
Has not been determined and confirmed,
Yet from metastasizing scar tissues
Revealed on x-rays my mind screens
With consulting Furies, I should guess

The psyche's life expectancy to be
No more prolonged than necessary
For the ears to go deaf, the eyes
To turn black as potting soil,
The brain to fill its death-sack
With electrolytic acid that once sparked
The pulse of the dreaming heart to ecstasy.

Now, I lie on an operating table,
Waiting for the numbness to take effect
Before they make their diagrammed incision
And deliver my soul from the frontal lobes,
Which have distracted me from completing my castle.

10/23/75 — [1] (00237)

Rearview Mirror

When I stare in the mirror too long,
The jagged edges of my reflected identity
Scratch my eyes, make them bleed;
Their lids yellow like wilting orchids.

The strange face pasted to flat glass
Is a gross facsimile of a classroom doll
Cut from rough, colored stock,
A Halloween mask, a shadow puppet,

A fractured Picasso with both eyes
On one side of the nose and the mustache
Of a Guernica bull rising up
To puncture the skin containing its own image.

Although the portrait has neither signature
Nor date to show its provenance
And destination, I recognize it anyway
By the way it speaks, in pantomime,

The vocabulary of crow's-feet, double chin,
Ingrown stubble. The phonetics of old age,
Projecting my face on a silvery screen
The size of my confined lifetime,

Recite a dialogue between my eyes
And insight the future casts from backlight
Dripping off the dying afternoon,
As the past absorbs me in its lunatic gaze.

10/23/75 — [2], 4/6/76 — [1?], & 1/27/78 (00121)

Witnessing a Birth ^Δ

*For Dr. Frank B. and Mary Long;
our thanks*

Before floating away from home, alone,
Into the empty, unlighted morning,
Like a balloon accidentally released,
I tiptoe up the creaking steps
That connect me with my sleeping wife
And baby girl. And I am vexed
By the absolutely perfect peaceful glow
Their breathing casts over the silence.
It's like a fragile pathway of light
The moon, on a warm Wisconsin night,
Sprays across a shellacked lake.

I fumble toward its sibilant source,
Hover like a gold Byzantine halo
Above my lady's face, which seems
Still enough to have been cameoed from the pillow
Beneath it. Her nose twitches.
Unconsciously, she lifts a peaked finger to itch it,
Before stasis overtakes her again.
The kiss I place indelibly in the space
Between our lips, to keep from disturbing her,
Is a wet, fragrant bouquet I've left
At dreaming's door for her to retrieve on waking.

In the hallway, just outside
Temple walls, I linger, transfixed,
Listening to our baby chanting fantasies,
And I imagine her as an olive-skinned Jewess
Trying to break from Egyptian bondage,
Instead of sleep, through her mournful hymns.
I peer in at the tiny, cribbed body.
My eyes see one, yet focus
Both mother and child simultaneously,
Superimposing the two as persistent images,
Although each lies in separate rooms.

They float in a mutually protective womb
My mind stretches taut about their breathing,
And as I leave them in the cushiony bud
Of this blooming day, I assume, with certainty,
That on my returning, my two muses
Will be delivered for me to nurse with love.

10/28/75   (00754)

The Origin of Species ^Δ

Tin cans and glass litter the lot,
Occupied by pickup trucks,
Whose blunt front ends
Loom like lightning clouds ready to explode.
As I pass toward the café door,
*

They cast jagged shadows at my alien shape.
When I look into the eyes of the storm,
Searing light from the rising sun,
Multiplied by twenty windshield lenses,
Blurs my vision. I'm blind to rifles
Mounted on cab racks, CB's,
Whose antennas protrude conspicuously,
Outrigger side-view mirrors,
And oversize bumpers covered with mud.

Inside, tables and booths are islands
Floating in a terrazzo archipelago.
Each is crowded with Caucasic natives
Speaking slightly different patois
Of a language completely distinct from mine.
I might be Darwin, recording variations
Of related species: some have work boots;
Colored, billed hats, whose identities
Owe allegiance to MFA,
John Deere, the local country club,
Funk's Hybrid and Pioneer Seeds,
Wave like pennons on the grease-soiled air;
Blue jeans and work shirts
Socialize with the lawyers' loafers, brokers' ties,
Plumbers' and gas-company overalls.

Similar in structure, size, and physiognomy,
They all appear to have inherited characteristics
Of identical origin: faces equipped
With movable lips, squinting wolf eyes,
Hands that respond to word-manufacture.
Everyone displays tropistic motions,
Goes from cause to notion, changing bias
According to pleasure and discomfort levels.
Unlike protozoans, they show signs
Of abstract logic, insight. This I realize
By the way they've begun watching me
Taking cryptic notes, here in the corner.
Their silence is a fusillade of hurled spears.
Fleeing, casting off the Beagle's lines,
I barely escape Terra Incognita.

10/29/75 — [1] (00239)

Willy's Elegy ^Δ

I

Solid or intermittent yellow lines
To the left of my life, a bright white one,
In a continuous parallel stripe, to the right,
And in between the two, asphalt or concrete
Takes the weightless glacial flow
Off my forward motion without my noticing.
I adhere rigidly to the allotted lanes
That form corridors in space I penetrate
Every hour of every blessed day,
Year to chain-link year.
I see, through glass before and behind me,
With a kind of spectacular, oracular vision,
Driverless vehicles, like split atoms,
Rushing to or from the scene
Of a recent accident, whose victim I was
Or will be or am, right now,
Without even knowing how it happened
Or who caused such a catastrophe.
I concentrate all my visual energies
On maintaining equilibrium, not swerving
When little death-breaths,
Like mind-parasites eating my brain,
Lure me momentarily into sleep.
My speeds vary imperceptibly,
And I frequent the exact motels and cafés
I've always stayed in overnight
Or stopped at for routine coffee breaks.
Only the fluctuating seasons remind me
That nothing stays constant, remains inviolate.

II

For ages, I've made no changes in my routings,
Taken no major detours,
Followed no wrong road signs.
I don't even feel that I've grown older,
These last thirty years,
For having outlasted fifteen autos
And a couple million miles of driving
*

Throughout four states, border to border.
Yet, lately, much of my original territory
Has been reassigned, my accounts
Gerrymandered among two younger men,
Who've just come with the company,
From a Chapter 11 competitor,
With lists of clients they've previously sold.
Sixty-five is no time to retire.
I can still sell men's clothing
And open new accounts
Without fear of credit cancellation
As well as any man on the road today.
What will I do? Who will I lunch with
If they recall all my samples
And swatch cards, my stacks of order pads?
Where will I go when I haven't a date,
No exact time to be somewhere punctually,
At a specific café or store,
With a familiar face waiting to cordially greet me?
What will be left when strategies evaporate?
To whom would my insurance revert if a wreck
Accidentally occurred? Yet, who would suspect . . . ?

10/29/75 — [2] & 1/29/78 (00240)

Energy Shortage ^Δ

Power lines tie the sky in knots,
Connecting every edge of the horizon
In a net a trillion perverse spiders
Might fabricate in a communion of violence,
To entrap a radar-equipped passenger fly.

Each slender wire is a solitary fiber
Of a great man-made rope bridge
Woven by hand to span the vast valley
In which people live. Nothing animate
Except birds and squirrels traverses its paths.

Every person is a cell in the giant skeleton,
Whose vertebrae are shaped to accommodate
*

Spinal cords slung in graceful curvatures
That transport ichor over its back, to the brain.
The earth's nervous system is fragile as gut

Straining to exceed its breaking point,
Scored with gentle speaking voices
And raw, awful force, taut and flexible
As a skyscraper, containing life-source
Crucial to the organism's continued survival.

Yet, now, the men who invented the threads
And those who spun them skillfully
Have lost touch, leave off their trades
To hunt substitutes to reenergize the conduits
With a newer species: nuclear dinosaurs.

10/29/75 — [3]   (00238)

Letting Go the Moorings

This morning, I set sail from Redriff
In a mind-blinding fog.
Taking leave of one's sweetest refuge
Is not easy to set down
In a dog-eared log stowed in a trunk
Unopened for ten years.
Yet I've stayed here too long
Unstirred, landbound,
An alien to the ocean world,
In whose Medusa-filled lacunae
I used to find my sensual pleasures.
Now, I climb the mizzenmast,
Isolate myself in its tight crow's-nest,
To taste of a rife, saline sky.

A 360-degree horizon locates me
Equidistant, everywhere, from nowhere,
In this vast, uncompassed circle of sea
I've entered at life's midpoint.
Finned monsters, cruising beneath,
Encircle the ship like a halo.
*

Extravagant screeching birds
Trail in my spumy wake,
Thirsting for my amphibious soul,
While the crew I've hired aboard
From ghosts assembled in my memory
Grows restless on spying flying fish,
Sargasso weed, and floating atolls
Without sighting a known landmass.

Now, I've entered a liquidless still,
As if the ship were breached in dry dock.
I descend the rope ladder, to the deck,
Drawing my hallucinating mind behind me
Like a thin, cylindrical intestine
Turning inside out. All my emotions,
So long contained, flutter, scatter
Like doves released from an open green,
And I realize I've finally arrived
At my mortal point of no return.
Stranded in irons, at the mercy of elements,
I wait impatiently for a vagrant breeze
To locate and blow my vessel ahead,
To the outer edges of my second childhood.

10/30/75 & 4/6/76 — [2?] (00241)

[Deer sign, loblolly pine] †

Deer sign, loblolly pine
                    peanut-butter-and-jelly sandwiches

11/12/75 (01120)

The Highchair △

Arms out wide, legs astride like a bird
Flying on a high, violent slipstream as she eats,
A creature Italianate in her gesturing, fanciful,
An aviary of noises coming from her very being.

Everyone pays obeisance to the queen,
Seated firmly with belts in the highchair,
Such a stately throne, cleaned after each session.

Drops dolls and plastic pop-beads as easily
As a scientist trying to discover gravity.

A rattle contraption affixed by a suction cup
To the wide tray, where stray scraps of cracker
Reside and she plays out fantasies and games
Of chance and circumstance with unbreakable toys.

11/18/75? (03608)

Survivor of the Ten Lost Tribes △

His eyes glisten like mica crystals
In sun-scratched sidewalks.
They wince from migrating irritants
Loading up under puffy lids,
As their twin scintillas, like needle tips
Threaded with thin intelligence,
Skip through hunks of fluff
And scattered scraps of afternoon light
That vision tries to stitch
Into the poet's many-colored coat.
Soon, pewter dusk encircles them
Like a nervous dervish genie
Released, in a fog, from day's spout,
Drugging his insight with death wishes.

Now, it wraps around his brows
A mummy's gauze. His forehead aches
As if a bed of blood-crusty pins
Were imperceptibly pricking the skin,
Inexorably penetrating to the core
From which all motivation emanates,
Etching in his mind's cliffs
"A WAK EN" and "SOAR."

Only, night's moonless sheet,
Under whose influence he sleeps,
*

Prevents his escape from the wilderness,
Reinforces the fate that has chosen him
Scapegoat for a tribe of writers
That repays its gifts of alliteration and rhyme
With coffee, whiskey, cigarettes,
And a ubiquitous fear of dying alone and unknown.

12/2/75 — [1] (00509)

The Passing of Orders

A horizon-long train of overloaded cars
Rumbles from ear to ear,
Using the tunnel cut through his skull
To cross the great mountain chain
Separating twilight from night.
His stunned brain reverberates.
Chambered chaos, contained forever
Inside this unmaintained pass,
Where thought, in black abstraction,
Festers irresolute, resonates like devils
Bemoaning their damnable entrapment.

The gravel bed covering pia mater
Is stained gray-brown and spongy.
Ties supporting rusted rails
Buckle under the elephantine weight
Of freight being transported
At such tremendous, screeching speed.
Sight and speech remain paralyzed
In their wide, hollow holes,
Like dead men left in uncovered graves.

Once the ultimate sparking wheels
Have passed and their hissing has ceased,
His mind is again overwhelmed
With the terrible awareness of its own silence.
His dazed and empty gaze
Slips back into the drowsy landscape
Few trains pass through anymore.

12/2/75 — [2] (00508)

Waving Good-Bye

For Joe Frager,
*   whose memory will be our blessing to him*

Until yesterday, I'd completely forgotten
How tenuously tied to the land of the living
My cord is, how deftly thin fingers
Can slip the knot that draws us together,
How quickly and quietly they can sever threads
That anchor our spirits to the air we breathe,
Dropping us into the waiting earth forever.

I recalled this then, descending the stairs
Fastened to grave faces of an abandoned family,
Standing with a man in his changing room
At the base of a lake filling with their tears,
As he strained to break the surface and return
By waving good-bye. Only his reflection
Accompanied my flying spirit home.

I recalled this then, ascending the stairs
Carved in the hearts of his bleeding family,
Standing with a wife, beside a gleaming bier,
Reciting Hebrew for his departed soul,
As she tried to reach into the sinking coffin
By waving good-bye. Their farewells
Linger yet on my spirit's fingertips.

12/4/75   (00507)

The Dancers △

Three nights a week,
Baby Trilogy and I
Set out to explore the house
For treasure buried in the eaves
And symphonies not yet scored.

We exit the real world
Through violin and flute pipes,
Bass and snare drums,
And triangle screwed precisely in tune
To a stuttering Wurlitzer orchestrion

We release from silence with a dime.
As the perforated scroll
Begins its smooth unrolling
Across the vacuumed tracker bar,
My dancing partner curtsies; I bow,

Lift her high into sound
Stretching through stained glass
Like rainbows begot by clouds.
In opalescent swirls, we hover.
Blood rushing from my palpitant heart

Touches us temple to temple.
We're Greek lovers locked in stone,
Freed by a fanatical worship of the dance
We perform, father and child,
Alone in our own private theater.

Both hands cupped
As though playing an ancient recorder,
She passionately sucks her thumb,
Hums something to her own accompaniment
I can't quite recall from memory.

Her voice, hanging above my shoulder
In such gentle suspension,
Is the haiku of a fluttering butterfly;
Her head, against my neck,
Is a ladybug on a fingertip.

Soon, I hear the inaudible yawn
That concludes each flight. It lingers,
As if waiting for the machine's last notes
To recede into collapsing bellows
Before enveloping the poppied air.

Carefully, I ascend the staircase
With my drowsy, dancing lamb
And prepare to tuck her into the dark.
I wind her musical cow,
As she hunts a comfortable location

Beside her wadded blanket, and wait
Until all choruses have faded
And only my baby's breathing remains
*

To orchestrate the steps I take
From her room, onto my silent stage.

12/8/75 (00755)

December's Trees

December's trees, except evergreens,
Resemble the thorny red locust
In their alien nakedness, out there.
They envelop me in a briar patch
Of dreamless air as I drive nowhere,
Very carefully avoiding their barbs.
As long as I've stayed on the highway,
My ivory skin has remained unscathed;
The mind has escaped bloodletting and pain
That comes from accidental deviations
And random fumblings down cul-de-sacs.

Only, now, like a prospector for gold
In a vein scraped clean as dead bones,
I seem victim and tar baby,
Both willed and willing to be lured away
From main-traveled moods and attitudes,
Toward the forest's dark vortex,
By a formless vision of even more security.
In here, there is nothing but decay,
Paths wandering back on themselves,
And a wind gnashing its fanged teeth
Against my numb, bleeding face.

Perhaps I've imagined finding a companion
For my divorced and lonely soul, an expatriate
Who, like myself, may have strayed
From the beaten path long ago,
Without knowing it, and needs leading home.
Only, no one stirs.
Against a crimson sunset, weeping,
My eyes pierced by frozen tears,
Blinded to all escapes from my solitude,
I've become one of December's trees,
A red locust rooted in dreamless air.

12/10/75 — [1] (00505)

Triangles

His paper-thin face
Is a vaguely scalene triangle,
Point down, that aging has yellowed
And grayed in irremediable ways.
It shows eraser marks
Between forehead and chin,
As if different mathematicians
Had been perpetually dissatisfied
With its ever-changing dimensions.

His mind's oblique trigonometry,
Determined by straight lines
Placed between symbols and images,
Defines his earthly shape.
When people attempt to formulate
The design of his ultimate growth,
Sine, cosine, and tangent
Mirror, in angles of incidence,
His obstinate, irregular soul.

12/10/75 — [2] (00504)

The Wizard of Gewgaw

Inside the windowless A-frame,
Near the roof of its inverted base,
Behind sealed doors
Separating brain from breathing apparatus,
He keeps daily vigil
Over his delicate machinery,
Religiously prays to gauges and dials,
Recalibrates his clockwork hourly,
Takes no breaks for eating and sleep.

He rarely even leaves for funerals,
Marriage ceremonies, or christenings.
No one else has ever been trained
To operate the controls in case of emergency;
He's taken no definite precautions
For such exigencies, named no one
*

To execute the terms of his estate:
In the event of an irreparable malfunction,
His unit will revert to the alien earth.

12/10/75 — [3] (00503)

Narcissus Imprisoned

I drive, by the seat of my venal dreams,
The vessel my irredeemable life occupies
As it deviates from the cool spawning pool
In a cave where night's heartbeat
Echoes the cries of stillborn babies.

I fly by vaguely familiar skeletons
Breaking from the unfertilized egg
Whose shell contains my brain's humors,
Gray matter, and DNA.
Bones without muscle or flesh

Rise inside bubbles, through the slime
That keeps my viscid eyes moist,
Creating tides, between the cornea and iris,
On which visions of flying fish falling
From great heights wash ashore, upturned.

No amount of begging forgiveness
Can expunge these dying reminders
From the memory I have of admiring my face
For the last time, as it changed forever
In my sight, before my coffined lids closed.

Often, I return to the cave, alone,
Wander in, and immerse my head
In the spawning pool to listen for cries
From just one child who might, by chance,
Have survived the birth of its assigned identity.

Blind frogs brush my submerged legs;
Bats scratch the air beside my ears,
Yet no voices kiss my lips,
And I'm left for dead, to reflect on myself
In the casket that keeps my black dreams alive.

12/15/75 — [1] (00502)

The Pioneer Spirit

For Mike Köepf,
author of Save the Whale;
writers like him
comprise our most endangered species.

I fly from state through state to state,
In too much haste to be detained
By tiny, virulent microbes and viruses.
My insides and skin are perfectly pristine,
The walls of my heart without lesions.
My body aches to take permanent leave
Of its human limitations and soar free
On mind-wings caught atop thermals
Reaching from infant earth to burial sky.

I pass through fertile river valleys
Frozen over with impermanent glazes,
Move beyond enclaves of hibernating people,
Turn due west in quest of trails
Taken by dreamless half-breed trappers,
Scoundrels flashing decks with extra cards,
And speculators bringing in, by the wagonload,
Cheap Eastern ladies and counterfeit deeds
To recreate Eden in the wilderness.

I trace their wheel ruts and hoofprints,
Etched yet in the face of time's landscape,
Examine the clouds for premonitions of snow,
Then slog through inchoate drifts
Threatening to close all Wyoming passes.
My valves pulsate. I'm the lithe fox
Grayed safely against space, the rabbit
Blended into itself. Nature envelops me
Like one of its own. I thrive on silence.

A hundred sunsets locate me in an ellipse
Of lengthening days, until I finally emerge
On the far side of the Continental Divide,
Arrive at the town named Yerba Buena,
Where the land slopes to watery expanse.
After I've traveled such improbable distances
In unmolested vagrancy, the certainty of stasis
Reverses the blood's flow in my veins,
Staggers the gasping pump with its backwash.

Like Balboa, I recline in the high grass,
Contemplating my deed's enormity. Weakened
By the realization of having reached impasse
And saddened to see the vast mass of America
Poised on a fulcrum of beach below me,
Balanced against an entire ocean,
With nobody to make the seesaw teeter,
I leap. My weight is just enough
To unhinge the land. I'm buried under its tons.

12/15/75 — [2] (00501)

Paean to Wordsworth

As though he'd known it firsthand,
The English poet once wrote
That life was a sleep and a forgetting,
The soul's sweet interlude,
During which it leaves its sylvan home,
Journeys far from celestial retreats,
And comes briefly to rest,
With clipped wings, in the child's mind.

Such flights of gauzy dreaming
Informed his gentle lines,
Composed along the Wye, saved him
In reveries of childhood evoked at will
When standing, in medias res,
On Cheapside street corners
Or in Fleet Street pubs serving rancorous
Political cant, saved him from craziness.

He ever believed that man's mortality
Were a paltry thing when judged
Against the death of his inspiration,
That in cloud, stream, foxglove,
And cottage isolated in green to its steps,
God could be seen,
His constancy praised by human beings
Living forever in natural piety.

Even in old age, despondency,
Whose melancholy of bodily change
*

Attended his descendent creativity,
Couldn't keep him from seeking a faith
That looked through death,
To see the philosophic mind
At peace with its binding earthly destiny.
Nor could Dorothy's passing shake him;

Rather, it brought him to his wobbly knees,
Focusing his grief on the remaining hours
Before rejoining her and on the need
To guard against demons
That attack the wounded, unwary spirit.
A chronic, sleepwalking insomniac,
He never forgot his debt to God,
The father of the manchild he became.

12/16/75 — [1]   (00511)

Turnkey

When slightly jiggled or turned
Behind the escutcheon, between lips,
His tongue becomes a skeleton key
That unlocks every word
Kept in the mind's sprawling mansion.

The process of opening each door
Leads to search and seizure
Of every vagrant dialect
And wayward inflection, and arrest
Of incontestable violators,

Whose pronouncements and moans
No longer satisfy the laws
From which proper sentences are made;
They suffer ultimate incarceration
In cells of forgetting beneath the brain.

Only dramatic adjectives,
Nervous verbs, naked modifiers,
And nouns from the most profound
House of earthly worship are freed.
They scurry through the slender slot,

Whistle off the key's smooth surfaces
As they pass like smoke rings
Blown into airy oblivion.
No one sees them reaching ears
Or hears them arrive as minute truths,

Yet they manage persuasively
To infiltrate their neighbor's house,
Penetrate recesses where sounds
Wait to be called at their master's behest.
Soon, union is accomplished,

And the turnkey, having gained an ally,
Begins anew the tedious process
Of weeding out useless words
And changing the locks to conform
To his tongue's new skeleton key.

12/16/75 — [2] (00510)

The Crows ^Δ

Three crows, like granite gargoyles
Affixed to a cathedral's lip,
Cluster at highway's edge,
Oblivious to my passing, for the rabbit
Their beaks and talons obliterate.
The image of the trinity they project
On a screen that drops from oblivion
Persists as if the repugnant birds
Were mounted tissue slivers
Magnified by an electrified microscope.

Now, they begin tumbling, floating
In the zone behind my windshield
Like crows gone insane
Inside the tube my eyes,
In their urgent desire to control
The adjusting screw, can't contain
At absolute stasis long enough
To bring them back to original focus.

Pain chews through my forehead;
I squint, lose visual acuity.
*

The eyes confuse the center line
They've used as a guide for track,
As a nightmarish locomotive
Rumbles through the ears' tunnel.
Mirrors lining the mind shatter
As though viciously pecked at
By crows escaped from a cage
Hung from the brain's rafters
By a Piranesian chain.

Suddenly, shadows, like flapping wings
Attached to blunt, black bodies,
Penetrate my irises. Scorched flesh,
Singed feathers permeate my senses
As if something in my attic has recently died.
And I hesitate going upstairs,
Into the angular eaves of sleep,
For fear of corpses that might be lying there.

12/22/75 — [1] (00515)

Christmas 1975 Δ

For "Dr. Al" and Bobbi Karraker,
dear friends

The asymmetrical shape of love
Touches our baby's face
Through the smooth wine horizon
My hand holds up to the eye
As I toast her first real Christmas tree.
Behind, before, and in between crystal,
She's reflected, in a parallax, as ornament,
Papier-mâché angel, blinking light.
Her fragile fingers decorate our imaginations
With gentle attempts to fill up spaces
In the future we've left for her designs.

Having watched us weave strands
And hang shiny dangling tinsel
From pine-spiny limbs, she reaches to find
What makes them stay in place
And discovers that the laced popcorn
Is neither hot nor tastelessly metallic,
*

Rather, good to eat. She grabs a handful,
And every suspended image shimmers
Like breezed leaves, releasing prisms
Of fascination and laughter that cast her,
Urnlike, in our perpetual lovers' gaze.

12/22/75 — [2] & 5/2/76 — [1–2?] (00757)

Lines Composed a Few Miles Above Christmas Eve

Surrounded by this early morning silence,
I try to find an opening
To break through, into dialogue with myself.

I stand in white sky
Fallen to earth last night,
Listening for familiar voices requiring reply.

Invisible noises lift sourcelessly.
My ears grasp at birdsongs,
Church bells, the electric wires' hum,

As though each might relinquish answers
Or at least give some reason
For my captivity in this unbarred cage,

To which I seem confined for life.
Only, they don't see me eavesdropping,
And the secret of their frequent releases

Is guarded like freedom of speech
By people who cherish their will as God's.
Standing outside, I'm tongue-tied.

On this luminous gray day,
My profile casts no disclosed shadow
By which my identity might distinguish me

From icy trees, houses, solid objects
Without feeling and unable to breathe.
Yet as my being fades into the landscape,

Something changes. My name becomes the snow,
Through which I trudge in frozen boots,
This Christmas day, on my way home.

My eyes retrace footprints they made
On first taking the path
The child in me used when growing

And going away from its friends.
They lead me back through an opening
In memory, to a vaguely familiar doorstep.

My uneven heartbeat pounds nervously.
I enter its sound, follow it
Into a warmth that thaws my tongue,

Then speak to all the lives inside me
To see if, once again,
We might live in peace with each other.

Their voices, so long stifled,
Embrace mine with cadenced love.
Our touching liberates me from silence,

And I enter myself, as at birth
I did, a naked son
Speaking the untranslatable language of angels.

12/25/75 (00514)

Daddy's Turn ^Δ

I sit here in the kitchen, this snowy morning,
Alone with nineteen months of Trilogy,
Watching her out of my mind's quiet corner.
Such absorption in commonplace objects
Makes me wonder if there might not really be
A philosophy of xylophone and pine cone,
Plastic bathtub, blocks, and telephone,
Whose relevance I never realized before.
She seems at perfect inner peace with her world,
Capable of drawing me into her sea-nymph serenity.

To a wood hull with three drilled holes,
She aligns and inserts corresponding cylinders,
To form a boat she sails around Cape Horn
Without even leaving her port on the floor.
Reward is never far behind accomplishment:
*

She takes up her dirty piece of cake
From the rug, holds it, with both tiny hands,
To her teeth, like a squirrel nervously shaving a nut
On hind legs, and devours the crumbling silence.

She opens a miniature lunchpail without fuss,
As though it were a Chinese puzzle box
Whose maze of interlocking planes she's memorized.
Slowly, in my most straightforward English,
I suggest placing the remains of her cake inside
For safekeeping. To my unpremeditated amazement,
She's able to translate and fulfill my gentle command.
How she's learned to interpret and understand the code
Of tribal communications without reading lips
Or speaking is mankind's conundrum, and now it's mine.

Suddenly, she abandons some toys in a wide yawn;
Others she hands me to set neatly on shelves
Lining the endless walls of her drowsy mind.
Only, while I paint Desitin on her chafed bottom
And drape it in a Pamper, she begins crying, "Mama,"
As if this ritual, or possibly something intuitional,
Has made her aware of an absence. On our way to bed,
We peek at her sick mother, floating near the surface
In a shallow pool of sleep. Our silence awakens her,

And she swims up quietly to greet her tired baby,
With a weak smile and a feeble, peaked hand
Breaking from beneath the sheets that quarantine her.
Trilogy reads from the bedroom's deep gloom
The scripture of illness on her mother's wan cheeks.
Fearing to draw too near, I step backward.
The baby waves good-bye, pats my head,
Beseeching me, in her own intelligible sign language,
To make her "Mama" healthy and well enough
To join us when she returns from her solitary journey.

12/28/75 (00758)

Cause and Effect

Metamorphosis
Is the shortest path toward change
In identity crises,

Change the quickest way
To reestablish life
In stalled flight.

Life is
The least painful means
Of escaping death,

And death the best time
To forget everything except
Metamorphosis.

12/29/75 & 1/3/76 — [1?] (00513)

[This is the poetry margin] †

This is the poetry margin

This and this
And this

this is going to be the new margin from here on   out
I feel that you and I, machine, are going to have the nicest

  When all the grass turns brown and the armies go home,
then will we find our true shadows eating together
from the table of waters, drinking from the lake of
friends, located in the vast, depthless recess of the riverbed.

this   is the barest space
this is single-space

this is double-face, and never did we see the sun set
after all the snow geese flew south. I am certain
that when the seasons come, once again, upon our faces
and shadows burn the skin and flesh to apple-sweet,
we will leave the coverts, run toward each other, naked
as rain, and lie down together beneath a tent of stars

The world explodes like oceans drying in the eyes
that cry for a dying friend, then stop, as the earth
opens like a wound torn before being sewn shut again,
with the integuments replaced.
When integuments come to seed, all the world of art a

Then
    the
        rivers
            go
                dry
                    and
                        the
                            sea
                                runs
                                    back
                                        into
                                            the
                                                land

and we go in pirogue, in search of the lost Cajun whom
we left hunting alligators in the bayou; and all thoughts,
like sand dollars, rush onto the shore to dry and decay.

Write Johnny
      Jenny
      Mamo
      Mrs. H

1975? (04676)

[Once again, dislocations descend] †

Once again, dislocations descend
In endless permutations. I am the ghost

1/5/76 (01122)

Cold Feet

Half-asleep, I elude my waking shadow
Momentarily and leave it loitering
In the warm, fluorescent kitchen,
As I descend the creaking basement stairs.
In near darkness, I release the dogs
From cages. They shake their sedentary selves
Into shapes of shelties, then scurry
Through the cellar door, into the snow.
I follow their hasty prints to the pen
And secure a tenacious gate behind them.

Although my senses retreat indoors
To be heated by coffee and to read Roethke
For breakfast, my eyes arrest and detain
My fleet and unengaged spirit.
They cause me to pause long enough for the snow,
Coating pine needles and tree limbs
Like myelin sheathing on tender nerves,
To infiltrate and freeze my bare feet
Stuffed in low boots. I'm discovered
Trespassing on the stark moon's desolations.

Once again within the actual warmth,
Urged ahead by caffeine, charged
With intermittent neon lightning bolts,
My thoughts coalesce, reach contact position
On their cam-driven timer, explode.
Reality transports me to office and desk
Cluttered with P.-and-L. sheets, projections,
Target dates. Despite my concentration,
My feet stay cold. I squirm,
Change seats, sneeze occasionally.

Yet those intrusive flakes persist
All day. Nothing I wish or invoke
Will eradicate that frozen moment
That bit through my outer layer
And made me bleed silent blasphemies.
I still see my blood burning a path
Through the snow, to the floor of the skull,
Where I descended its basement stairs
*

Half-asleep to release drowsing demons
And fasten the clasp securely behind them.

1/20/76 (00522)

Gone Visiting for the Day

For Jerry Walters,
printmaker

It's been years since I've visited the Bosch house,
And my eyes dance like embers blown alive
By heavy, drunk breath. Hieronymus and I
Touch crystal, guzzle claret by the liter,
Chuckle inside memory's encapsulation.

We are time squeezed into opaque intestines,
Consumed, eviscerated, recycled agelessly.
Like effluvial, transmigrating souls in space,
We're loosed from life, through the earth's bowels,
Severed from consciousness to resume dusty nothingness.

Every generation, we gather to retouch a landscape,
Remove petrified piles of human dung,
Whose weight threatens to crack the gilt frame,
Pull the nail, on which it hangs, from its wall.
We're always painting out multiplying faces

To retain the ever-diminishing sky and grain fields
He originally drew to scale in his thronging tableaux.
Just now, the wine we share turns to vinegar.
My brain is caught in a vortex draining light
From the eyes. I see my own bony skeleton

Being extruded, like heated nylon through an orifice,
Into a filament to sew closed night's seam
Behind my retreating, needle-stiff corpse.
Suddenly, I return to the sanity of daily existence,
Collide with strangers I've known my entire life.

A few tiny paint splotches on my spectacles
Beg speculation, allow for the possibility
That I might be someone other than the shadow
*

My imagination casts on its scrim curtain.
Only, the smears disappear in the tissue I use,

And I'm blinded by the stark faces that take their place.
Vision has never seemed so precise.
Before wiping them, I suspected continuity,
Accepted myself as Hieronymus in a more recent skin.
Now, I realize my aloneness is uniquely mine.

1/22/76 — [1] (00524)

Teleology ^Δ

Mobile trailers and sparsely settled farms
Share the desolate, snow-specked land
With sleeping sows, empty fields, cows,
Hours that pass in single file like a cortège.
Even the bony trees are naked prisoners
Standing in line behind a winter door
Leading to the lethal showers, where ghosts
Disappear, exhausting through gas stacks.

In this baleful daytime Sheol,
My mind would have me invent a quiescent God
Manifesting His will and accept as merciful
These specters of doom that infiltrate my brain
Without so much as questioning its motives.
I refuse to acknowledge a season so drear,
Void of birth, rife with death, brooding,
As an occurrence worthy of His purposive force.

Yet one must never forget
That God's is a positive continuity, infinite,
While mortality is incomplete and ephemeral.
What I've witnessed today, I must confess,
Could be pure subjective speculation,
Mere death wish, mind-mirage,
The soul's attempt to locate a warm corner
In a formless universe by making itself heard.

1/22–23/76 — [2] on 1/22 (00512)

Time Assumes My Wife's Smooth Shape

For fragile Jan,
my love

The fluid shape of time
Is my wife's unobtrusive bosom,
On which I lay my moony head.
Beneath her metrical breast,
I hear the earth's valves working,
Every breathing heart
Keeping beat. My opiate mind
Circulates through her arteries,
To the frayed peripheries of imagination.
It returns by way of decades
Linked by years to the great atrium
Where eunuch death waits
To savor whiffs of wasted air,
As the exchange of old cells
Into new selves occurs.

Along her eternally sweeping curve,
Two infinitesimal specks
Reverberate in sympathetic conjunction,
Undisturbed by accumulating millenniums.
Gazing up, I recognize my wife
In the luminous moon, and myself
Reflected by her nude beauty.
We've been alive forever.

1/24/76 — [1] (00521)

Downtown Reverie $^\Delta$

For Saul, my father, leader of his people;
God bless him.

From where I stand, at street-level vantage,
On Washington Avenue, gazing in a slow sweep,
I see massive plate-glass windows
Framing silver cast-iron radiators.
Rusted fire escapes and flaked water mains,
*

Shadowing ancient terra-cotta blocks,
Are crow's-feet on time's soot-blackened facades.

Like the dust motes and grimy cobwebs
They've maintained despite changing decades,
These empty mausoleums still retain
Painful memories of stitchers, ticket tackers, fellers.
Hester Street runs in every direction
Through my eyes. Somehow, I've just arrived
At Ellis Island, naively anxious to take my place

Beside my father and his gentle, vincible father.
I'm ready to cut gimp from buttonholes,
Push the vertical knife through goods
Sixty plies high, press pant legs
On a manual Prosperity in hundred-degree heat,
Until I realize the past can't translate my gazes. . . .
I've lost all traces of the ragman's accent.

1/24 — [2] & 1/26/76 — [2] (00520)

Hegira: Origins of Schizophrenia

Driving through a country-wide hour
Without eluding the sound of my shadow
Keeping pace with my eyes' microphones,
I finally reach the interchange,
Choose the proper exit on the cloverleaf,
And aim my forward motion westward.
Behind me, a trail of ashen dust
Exhausts as if my mind were steadily urging
A circular saw through raw thoughts.
Behind me, all my juices, like sap,
Flow from the self-inflicted wound
Still exposed a decade after
I caused it, biting myself free
From the academic traps of pedantry and conceit.
Behind me, vision, consisting of the reflected image
Of a mustached stranger I've known forever,
Contracts rectangularly, as though the past were a wave
Inundating the shore my eyes pace.

Now, as I shift gazes to the racing mirror,
The resemblance to my identity passes on the left
And flies into the bright, moribund sun.
Ahead of me, for another hundred miles,
Assiduously as a spotter searching for survivors at sea,
I check every blessed mirage;
I even stare into the blinding dusk,
In the hope that hiding phantasms will surface
And release a clue as to where I'm going
So urgently, what I'm doing,
To whom running, from what escaping,
As I outdistance my disintegrating soul.
Only, there are no traces,
No dust, no juices,
And as I drive in every direction the rest of my life,
Vision continues to diminish before my eyes.
Behind me, home keeps changing addresses.
Finally, memory becomes a hitchhiker.

1/26 — [1] & 5/2/76 — [1–2?] (00519)

Frozen

An unnatural freeze turns everything outdoors
To brittle bones, squeezes out every last degree
Of humidity, rubs static electricity
Down the earth's spine. I touch the air,
And my body goes into shock. It burns
Like a child's tongue stuck to an icy windowpane,
Refusing to tear lose or be prized free.

My ears cease distinguishing heartbeats
From the sun's explosions. My eyeballs crack
Like crazed porcelain fired too soon after glazing.
They fail to differentiate people from trees.
Even my nose becomes a clay trunk
Stuck in cosmic jest to a flat, unfleshed skull,
From which two lips slip into silence's abyss.

In such a devastating desolation, I turn to stone,
Blend into space as if my shadow had found a crack
*

And I'd followed close behind it, into a cavern
Spiny with stalactites. Inside, the mind trips,
Stumbles into its numb imagination.
The bones disintegrate. Splinters infiltrate the blood,
Cut veins. The lungs reswallow their own air,

While the spirit fights to escape catastrophe.
In a final lunge, my being, assailed by frigidity,
Reaches a knob, dreams itself indoors, faints
In a warm, relieved renascence. Agonizingly slow,
Nose, eyes, ears, lips, and tongue creep back
Like blasted survivors of a concentration camp.
I weep for their return, weep for my vast frailty.

1/26/76 — [3] (00518)

Elegy for a Child Prematurely Returned

> *For Gary and Sharon Cleve,*
> *in memory of baby Craig,*
> *and for beautiful Dolores*

The tiniest voice barely lifts its whisper
Over the coffin's velvety edges,
Reaches up to touch my eyes,
Place tears there, make me taste
Our common salt. I gaze at his still face,
Stare at his diminutive feet in white socks,
His body contained by man-made vessel,
And visions of gardens within gardens
Growing behind life scent my nostrils.
Rivers falling gracefully to rivers
Falling from rainbows bathe me in colors
That water Canaan, where he plays by himself,
Patiently waiting to fly home.

Rumors circulate through the funeral parlor
That God, with ineffable passion for beauty,
Requested a fresh flower for His bouquet
And personally picked this bird-of-paradise.
Just now, as I stand by my wife,
*

In the full bloom of our precious union,
An image of life infinite, not dying,
Arouses gentle envy in us, as though
We might wish to join his soul in flight
And arrive earlier than foreordained,
At the outskirts of fathomless afterlife.
His premature departure is his great fortune;
Ours is being present to bid him good-bye.*

*God be with ye.

1/26/76 — [4] (00517)

Nickelodeon

The "Root Beer Rag" scoots through the room,
Attracting ears as it travels, picks up speed,
Then dissolves from view like a screeching locomotive
Reaching crescendo down a steep, bending grade
Before disappearing into a cloud of smoke.
All that's left when the notes stop pounding
Are a quavering overtone, an old roll rewinding,
And eager anticipation of the next train's approach.

1/26/76 — [5] & 8/19/78 (00516)

[Coming from the Gumm Sisters to Judy Garland] †

Coming from the Gumm Sisters to Judy Garland
Was, in retrospect, the greatest transformation
That a small-town girl could have ever made.
A rainbow, a trolley, and the Swanee River
Became   the sweetheart of the '40s screen

1/26/76 — [6] (01119)

Lemuel Gulliver Sets Out

The wasted faces of a hundred unknown souls
Grimace in abstraction like tragedy's mask
Hovering at the brain's point of no return.
They are death-moths soaring about my eyes,
Shipwrecked victims screaming to be saved.
Their identities, never retrieved, weren't atomized
Among the broken flotsam and drifting debris,
Rather, sank as slaves in the cargo hold,
While the captain, his mistress, and closest mates
Were freed briefly, taken aboard ships
Sent to their rescue, only to be washed away
And drowned later in the jaws of voracious waves.
I alone survive to lament the tale.

I floated toward a rotating beacon on the Island
Of Dead Souls, whose reflections beckoned to ghosts
And abandoned waifs. Against a fierce current,
I swam to the lee shore, toward safety,
And fainted on the sand, below mangoes and palms,
Asleep for a millennium, in a land of aborigines,
Until revived by a frightened witch doctor,
Who took me, mistakenly, for a weird white god.
Despite the naked Polynesian maidens
He sent into my tent as propitiatory lambs,
No sacrifice was enough to placate their paganism,
And the island erupted with an ashen volcanic flux
That overran their paths and thatched huts,

Cut ruts in the equinoctial jungle,
Where they danced and played lustful games,
Until nothing was left of the land that adopted me
Except the white god called Lem,
Who comprehended the phenomenal upheaval and fled.
Finally, a ship sighted my bottled map
And arrived. I, who'd succeeded at finding in primitivism
My one hope of living outside
The boastful, grandiose scope of scheming senators,
Odious sycophants, religious zealots, and hawks,
Was brought home to Redriff to write and rot,
A fractured, disoriented soul returned to his origins
To navigate the unmapped reaches of Catalepsy.

1/26/76 — [7] (00523)

[Drunks, one-armed blind men, drug addicts] †

Drunks, one-armed blind men, drug addicts

1/26/76 — [8] (01121)

Running in Packs ᐃ

I race from a frozen outdoors,
Into the spastic blasting of a space heater,
And take a seat out of its immediate beam
As though it were a laser that might divide
My caffeine-deprived mind, this morning.

The radio is a coop of roosting hens;
The Seeburg Discotheque and cigarette machine
Are swayback horses asleep on their feet;
The empty chairs, four to a table,
Are piglets stuck to the teats of stolid sows.

For a moment, I squeeze my eyelids to pain,
Remembering how children hide from the universe
Behind cupped hands placed over their faces;
Only, no transformations transport me;
I fail to dematerialize, reappear in another guise.

Through jalousie windows, I watch splintered dawn
Being steadily carpentered, see the sky
Nailed piece to tongue-and-groove piece
Into a partition separating light from darkness.
Soon, the spacious room will be completed

And ready for occupancy by all waking souls.
The singular bark of a vagrant dog
Scratching at the café door distracts my gaze.
Eight senators, in bib-overall togas,
Feed hats, and boots, jeer lasciviously,

Their bellies rippling like waves made by a stone
Thrown into a stagnant pool by a fool
With nothing better to do with his daytime hours.
*

At first, I fail to grasp the connection
Between cur and waitress, who admits the stray pet

Belongs to her. They discern a deeper meaning,
A taller humor, in her futile antics to shoo it
From the entrance, send it on its way home.
Visions of sodomy polka-dot their prurient grins,
Spot their eyes with obscene images of her body

Mounted by the scraggly animal, her lover.
Their whispering snickers alternate with guffaws.
As she shrinks into the kitchen, I listen to them
Pontificate on the virtues of leading a dog's life,
Rewards for letting a sleeping dog lie,

And the importance of keeping a promiscuous pet
Fenced in one's own backyard.
Leaving, I glance at these arbiters of equality
And see eight canines, paws on the table,
Barking at each other, wagging their tails excitedly.

1/28/76 — [1] (00129)

Herr Diogenes Teufelsdröckh

I record my dropsical waist and chest sizes daily,
With a tape measure calibrated in hours, not inches.
Fluctuations in weight depend on what I ingest
And evacuate, which makes it more complicated
To achieve a consistent fit, even more difficult
To ascertain the degree and cost of tailoring.

By night, I've handled so many indecisions,
Given trivial judgments on fit
And style, made myriad minor alterations,
And done so much refolding of unsold opinions
That I can hardly look at a garment and not regurgitate,
Let alone undress for bed without prayers.

In sleep, I see every plebeian design repeated
As if programmed into the twill of my dreams.
I reel dizzily in a shimmering hypnosis
Of optically enervating patterns and feel trapped
*

Under a cross-stacked mass of fabric bolts
Waiting to be spread, cut, and sewn into costumes

To adorn the taut physique of each new week
That comes to me for a personal fitting.
Ironically, my clients compliment me on neatness.
They say I'm resplendent sartorially, impeccable,
That I take inordinate pride in my wardrobe.
Intending to emulate my natty personality,

Desirous of owning an "original Teufelsdröckh,"
They arrive in droves to patronize my raiment.
With due humility, I wish, just once,
I might tear off my clothing, disclose the bones
On which hang, in the soul's empty closet,
The wrappings of the breathing mummy I've become.

Then they might gaze on me in mortified disgust,
Recoil from the nauseating stench I keep perfumed,
And finally discover the slovenly truth of lies
We buy and sell throughout our lives.
Only, I won't; rather, I'll continue recording sizes
On the mannequin wearing my identity's death vestments.

1/28/76 — [2] (00527)

Willy's Fantasy △

I wonder what it really means,
That through all the strange mattresses
On which I've tossed in sleep this week,
I could feel the barely perceptible
Proverbial pea beneath my belly.
Am I royalty shabbily disguised,
An underachiever without prior reason
For pursuing my rightful patrimony,
Vanderbilt in traveling Willy's shoes?

Or is it that I've actually detected
A foreign mass thriving in silence,
At the onset of metastasis, inside me —
The first whirling pearl of my diadem?

1/29/76 (00526)

Factory

From the varnished-hardwood sewing floor
At the base of the active mind's factory,
Stertorous snorts and continuous short roars
Escape through the brain's fenestration
And ventilator ducts draining in the spine.

Frantic machines, handwheels spinning
Like turbulent whirlpools, stitch ideas
With penetrating deliberation, as presser feet
And feed dogs free their designs of wrinkles.
Tensions tighten and release, as nerves vibrate

Like thread sliding through tiny guides,
To the plunging points of double-needle eyes.
Scintillant heat is generated beneath the surface,
Where thoughts fuse and conclusions are tied
Like loops, safe from unraveling persuasions

That would unknot the entire concatenation
In a single slip of the original inspiration.
When each creation is completed and examined
For sizing, fabrication defects, bias shading,
It's ferried to the warehouse, properly placed

By classification, then held on shelves
Lining the mind's distribution center,
To await dissemination. Ceaselessly,
The machines stitch, three shifts a day,
As if their supply could never exceed demand.

1/30/76 (00525)

Convergences

Up from the country, skirting the city
Via its clogged circumferential highway,
I feel as if a flock of honking geese
Had suddenly plucked me up,
By the seat of my senses, in its collective beak
And carried me off on its flapping draft.
As I head west, caught in the mass exodus,
*

Thoughts metamorphose from fowl to rodent.
In the scope of my rearview mirror,
Visions of riverfront, civil buildings,
Hotels, and corporate rectangles overwhelm me.
I see these colossal structures
Heaving, quaking, igniting from reflected flames
Of a dusky sun. Like frantic water rats
Fleeing a sinking ship, people in hordes
Are racing to avoid them, and I'm trapped
In their rush-hour wake, unable to escape
For the next eighteen miles, treading for my life.

Gradually entering night's impenetrability,
I see, behind me, headlights
Of vehicles exiting the highway like termites
Seeking channels leading to the safety
Of thirst-slaking, earth-dug foundations.
I proceed outbound, wading deeper
By the hour into unfathomed anonymity,
Pinned at my bright beams' focal point,
Guided, not guiding, freewheeling.
In this cavity, I'm a locust groping,
Preparing to molt its crusty husk
Before assuming a more commodious growth.
The wall inside my drowsy mind opens.
I climb a rickety stile, unused for years,
And set foot on the sanctified burial lands,
Where ancestors, standing with candles,
Chant orisons to ward off demons
And release mares and evil-smelling humors.

Suddenly, I realize I've reached my destination
Ahead of schedule, alive, afraid of dying,
Yet beguiled by the vibrant lilies of the valley
Coloring night with their deathly sweet scent.
Delicately, I bend to pluck a bouquet.
Darkness gives way to daylight,
And I find myself approaching a city,
Coursing over its skirting circumferential highway,
Converging on souls making their morning journey
Into dawny flames. Briefly trapped,
I weep with almost fanatical gladness,
As though I'd plunged off the earth's edge
*

And been hoisted back up by reverse gravity.
The sheer appearance of people is God speaking.
I accept my entrapment as a great liberation.

2/9/76 — [1] (00531)

The Poet's Slatternly Verse ^Δ

My words wear the strangest faces tonight.
I barely recognize them for the heavy makeup
They've obviously taken hours in applying
To disguise blemishes, discolorations,
And a birthmark common to each individually.
Something beguiling attracts me. I lean closely
To hear every sibilance and coy syllable spoken.
Their careful articulation teases me,
As though each were undressing to bare flesh
Before my eyes, asking me to take her
At her word alone, without knowing the whole body.
Passionately, they draw me into their persuasion,
Make me kneel beneath their metered lines,
Supple feminine endings, and internal rhymes.

Soon, entangled in their strangling embrace,
I can't step back to gain perspective.
My mind trips on the hypnotic alliterations
And fickle similes that litter the air.
All in a spin, I begin to grasp at metaphors
To keep from falling through false profundities
And empty philosophies. Grown too weak
To resist, I join my own ferocious applause.
Even after leaving the stage, I can hear
The raucous audience clapping encore, encore.
Once more, I return to parade the words
I've always believed expressed beauty best.
For some reason, they've all become whores,
For whom I'm merely an itinerant pimp.

2/9/76 — [2] (00530)

To His Coy Wife △

I measure the cost of our being apart one minute
In eons of squandered and empty eternity.
Our briefness is so coldly calculable,
So extremely impermanent and fleet
When gauged against the inexorable forever,
That the slightest separation is a death-bite.

We can't afford the increased interest
On interest forfeited when we withdraw from each other
Too often in vain argument,
Then reborrow our love at a higher rate.
Such fluctuations only create imbalances,
Debase the pure ingot. I beg you, lady,

Don't remain aloof. Invest your gentleness in me,
And I, in turn, will remunerate you with my soul.
Anything less than our absolute mutual confidence
Will result in a bankruptcy neither of us can survive;
Anything greater will ensure us earthly perfection
And a currency we'll spend together in afterlife.

2/9–10/76 — [3] on 2/9 (00110)

Drummers Carousing in Surinam

Lascivious faces in black makeup,
Seemingly disconnected from their bodies,
Float behind the floodlights,
Jeer, scream at unpredictable intervals,
As the blond girl making the music
Gyrates behind the loud sound of guitar,
Electric piano, Moog, flute, and drums.
Something they desire and can't possess
Writhes up there, behind a shield,
Kicking, miming every possible position
In the Kama Sutra. The faces slobber,
Crave drink to sustain their high.
Reflexively, their hands reach for paper
To pay for their depraved pleasure-quest.
Glasses repeat themselves frequently,
*

As the faces lapse into silence
During break, then slobber again
When their bella donna remounts the stage.
Completely uninhibited in her stance,
She prances loose-hipped, bare-toed,
Open-bloused, her mouth biting her words
With vicious, masochistic concupiscence.
The faces leer at her, bite back
In futile, unrehearsed exuberance,
As each, by degrees, leaves the music room,
Escorting an inebriated image of Cleopatra
Back to his room, in his brain's sedan.
In the first few frames of slumber,
She still gyrates before climaxing sumptuously
In the collective polygamy dreams reinforce.
Soon, not even his laborious snoring
Will awaken Ozymandias from his disorientations.

2/9/76 — [4] (00529)

The Funeral Procession

The highway I drive this morning
Is a seventy-five-mile yawn
Stretched tautly across dawn's gray face.
I peer through her impersonal eyes,
Focus on roadside corpses, and wonder why
Nobody's bothered to remove these wasted souls.
Every radial blink of landscape
Comprises a vast, fog-diaphanous cemetery
Whose cenotaphs are ramshackle silos,
Sagging barns, rotted fence posts,
And parted farm machines furiously rusting.
Faint ululations of hoot owls
And stray dogs' howling infiltrate the ears
I huddle between, trying to differentiate
Life signs from the sounds dying things make
Just prior to leaving their shapes forever.
No distinctions arise between my breathing
Inside this vehicle and the outside air.
Perhaps my shadow is still buried out there,
*

Waiting for the sun to resurrect it from sleep.
Possibly, my drowsiness is to be held accountable
For such tenacious anomie. Whatever the reason,
I sense a million invisible faces
Wearing my chalky features, glaring at me,
Stripping off my flesh in layers, like sod,
With their deep, biting stares. Above me,
Predacious, curve-necked birds hover,
And suddenly I know why crews don't assemble
To cart away the proliferating carrion:
The mind's parasites accomplish the feat daily.
Now, scalding talons stab my brain.
I'm lifted bodily from my seat, bleeding,
Then dropped by the roadside.
Too late, the pain of needling beaks awakens me.
I'm unable to revive, break free,
Keep from being consumed alive.
The gravelly backwash of my own tires
Blasts my mutilated spirit as it passes me by.

2/17/76 — [1]   (00528)

Rain Comes to Nourish a Dry Plain △

Rain finally intercepts my forward motion,
Restrains my nervous speed, detains me
Long enough for a brainstorm to overtake
My dry ideas. Drops splotching the windshield
Partition vision the same way a fly sees,
So that all landscapes are scroll-sawed,
Objects netted like veins in an oak leaf.
Unable to superimpose any two moments,
My eyes continue to twist day's kaleidoscope,

Inside which each water globe is a note
Synesthesia washes with rhyming mind-light.
I hear a universal clepsydra ticking millenniums
In seconds. Suddenly, all shapes coalesce,
Become something greater than mere rain.
Beneath the silence where I've lain dormant,
Water oozes, seeds twitch, stretch;
*

Shoots begin to lift my thoughts toward bloom
On this plain where poems have never grown.

2/17/76 — [2] (00536)

Knight-Errant ^Δ

For Walter Eichenwald,
the last of a wonderfully Victorian breed

I take to the road again, this morning,
Like a soldier of fortune,
Knowing that somewhere an enemy waits
To engage me in a battle to the death.
Painstakingly, I surround my entire mind
In chain mail and a suit of armor
Made from xeroxed stock sheets and bulletins.
Each hammered rivet and mesh link,
Keypunched by skilled artisans,
Helps secure my body's corporate integrity,
Keep it from being violated by conundrums
Connected to the tip of a skeptic's jousting tongue.

Once mounted on a company horse,
I choose one of ten familiar routes
To seek out the opposition. My eyes,
Like rain ricocheting from roof to walk,
Bounce off posh specialty shops,
Factory outlets, newly opened emporiums.
Soon, my bowels run hot,
Pupils dilate, contract with palpitant dizziness.
My brain yawns from lack of fresh cells.
Even tendons and ligaments relax
Before my energy regathers itself
In a monolithic facade and I attack

With assorted promotional closeouts
Guaranteed to open up
The most inaccessible and opinionated
Anti-Semitic, cigar-smoking buyer.
I feint, lunge, recoil, parry,
Then adroitly plunge my sword forward
*

And write an order for immediate delivery.
We shake hands in good faith. Victorious,
I head home to the Kingdom of Gewgaw
With my lord's glorious name maintained
And my honor saved in a time when the chivalry
Of pursuing 3 percent commissions is obsolete.

2/18/76 (00537)

The Flower Store ᐃ

For Margaret, Harry, and Mamo Hofmann
The thick, purple scent of hyacinth clusters
Saturates my nose and eyes simultaneously,
As though they were growing inside my head.
A wine-dark gloxinia, floating on the floor,
Beside myriad mums and potted kalanchoes,
Is a genuflecting nun in velvet robes,
Attracting me to holiness by its silent repose.

In this land where glazed shapes
And plastic plants, unfragranced and spiritless
Amidst the living, also wait
To be given purpose by human hands,
I stand on the edge of inspiration,
Gazing through opaque drowsiness,
Into mirrors multiplying visions of God.

Suddenly, I see myself blossoming
Somewhere between Genesis and eternity.

2/22/76 — [1] (00143)

Great-Grandmother ᐃ

For "Mamo,"
Mrs. Harry Hofmann, Sr.

Not her palsied fingers and hands
But eight decades and a solitary year
Memorized to their craft fashion a nosegay
*

That our child, Trilogy, watches materialize
From paraphernalia scattered within the shadow,
Named Mamo, that covers the table like dust.

The slow metamorphosis of a wedding bouquet
From individually clipped miniature carnations,
Unopened Joanna Hill roses,
And baby's-breath sprigs enraptures her.
The magical appearance of a perfect bunch
From nothingness frustrates her imagination.

Unable to ascertain the nature of creation
Or fathom the tricks of mundane conditioning,
Our baby imitates her great-grandmother.
Silently, she unwinds yards of Floratape,
Scatters velvet leaves from their cellophane,
Drains green-plastic water tubes,

Then bends the slender wires,
Used for supporting scissored stems,
Into shapes resembling nesting snakes.
Through the myopia of triple-thick years,
The white-haired maker of corsages
Peers at her tiny apprentice and concentrates,

As if recognizing, for the first time in ages,
In the silk-fine gold hair
And delicate face of her great-grandchild,
The godly design of her tedious arrangement.
Smiling, she hands our toddler a bloom
With which to begin her own bouquet of years.

2/22/76 — [2]   (00759)

Outbound

I awaken from a daze. Preconsciousness fades
Like a rowboat drifting from the shore in wash
From a force passing across a foggy lake.
From this isolated promontory where I've slept,
Naked and bone-cold, beneath a faceless sky,
I look out over an expanse of water
Not breathing, preternaturally placid,
*

Like the still-warm corpse of a deceased friend.
I peer in three directions. No eagles' shrieks
Or cranes' ululations reach my hearing.
Nothing moves along my eyes' peripheries,
Which, on other mornings, have seen beaver,
Muskrat, possum, skunk, otter.
Below me, a nest of conifer needles
Still neatly retains my sleeping shape,
Yet I don't recognize its resemblance to mine.

Now, a final yawn dilates my pupils.
Insight is briefly multiplied. Like a steel probe,
My mind reaches into the perfect vacuum
Sealed by fog, and I can see the rowboat
Floating into smaller and smaller vortices
Of ever-widening horizons. In desperation,
I leap into the freezing water, begin swimming,
To keep open my only means of escape,
And I'm stranded between sleep's vessel and land,
Shipwrecked in a buoyancy of waking hours.
In this hopeless zone, bereft of dreams,
Floating up to my neck in limbo, I tread blood,
Praying either to be flung ashore at once
Or dragged under by a riptide, without a struggle.

2/24/76 — [1] (00535)

The Half-Life of Dreams

The eraser of waking yawns
Only smears the graceful calligraphy
Dreams place on sleep's indelible slate
With disappearing colored chalks.
All afternoon, it stays smudged,
Trapped, like Buonarroti's stone slaves,
Between day's recent caprices
The brain assimilates and classifies.
Poetry scanned for explication,
Exegetical interpretations of Scripture,
Algebraic equations isolated,
And diagrammed battles of Thucydides
*

Cover it over, smother night's visions
With a reality so naked, so palpable,
It gasps for air. Finally, a janitor,
Completely oblivious to its incarceration,
Makes rounds before evening classes
And wipes the blackboard clean.
Like worn shells forming a sand beach,
The dust of atomized dreams cascades, unseen,
To the base of the skull's walls and accumulates,
Waiting for night's scribes to decipher
And reconstruct it in this vault
Where the Dooms-Day Book
Is also precariously stored.

2/24/76 — [2] (00534)

The Cup of Life

The years consist of translucent humors
That buoy my convoluted intellect
In an imaginary glass I hold up to the light.
Its vitreous walls break down,
Return, through the brittle reverse alchemy
Of a heated imagination, to original sand,

And I stand chalky and thirsting,
Transported to the edge of the same desert
I set out to cross a score of years prior.
Behind me lie vast and undulant sands;
Ahead, as before, the illusional horizon.
Yet instead of just another Negev,
A pike lined with eucalypti and ginkgoes
Is rolled out smooth and virgin-white,
Like a wedding carpet down a church aisle.

Nervously, I wait for a choir of archangels
To start my heart beating, set my feet
In step with the ceaseless processional
Exiting Gethsemane, take me forward
Body and soul, shoulder to shoulder,
And marry me to a gentle and doting universe.

Only, no music fills my ears;
Instead, the water of years nearing and gone
Sloshes against the walls of the glass
I hold to the light. In desperation, I drink,
Empty the vessel. Desert and horizon dissolve,
As the shiny patina at the bottom dries,
Until all that's left
Is the abysmal reflection of my unidentifiable face,
Evaporating a blink at a time in my mind's eye.

Somewhere at an arid crossroads,
Oedipus sits in blindness, clawing at his amnesia
To reach the core of his being
And grasp the essence of isolation. His weeping
Continuously refills the glass from which he sips
To keep from becoming the dust he eats.

3/2/76 (00533)

Lazarus Being Raised from the Living

My unawakened shadow races from its cage
As if it were a dog I freed from the basement
Early this morning or a moribund soul
Evacuating my dead essence, heading home.

A vertical corpse possesses my mind's skeleton,
Carries it forward with amebic tentativeness.
The wobbly knees advance, retreat,
Grope for a portal through which to pass.

Exposure to the air neutralizes the embalming fluid
Sleep uses to drug its victims. The ozone
Disintegrates mummy wrappings I wear at night
To protect my bare flesh from putrescence.

I stand naked. My toes are tiny anchors
Stuck in the mud from last evening's rain.
Something twitches the tines of my being;
My mind vibrates on a sourceless frequency.

My triangular eyes, absorbing the entire sky
In their pyramidal gaze, transport me past dawn,
*

Via cloudy elephant burial ground,
Unsurfaced sun scaling the celestial tell,

To an abruptly erupting yawn, and I awaken,
Shaking as though returned from a sealed grave.
The alarm clock warns of another day
Waiting in nearby Birnam Wood

To invade my fortress. A dog's sharp barking
Announces the ritual of renascence about to begin.
My nostrils catch wafts of brewing coffee,
As I decide which disguises to wear today.

Soon, I'll enter the land where my name
Will be pinned to an image others had of me,
And for a while, I'll traffic among the quick
Without making myself available for comment

On the miraculous nature of my escape from death.
My breathing should testify I'm alive,
My handshake assuage doubts,
Allay skepticism about my suspicious identity,

And the authenticity of my claim on afterlife
Should be unquestioned, as future generations,
Forgetting I died in youth, assimilate me,
A ghost among ghosts recycled.

3/5/76 (00545)

The Wandering Jew ^Δ

The miles I travel are recorded in metered verse.
Standard definitions of time can't register
The stressed and unstressed measures of my flights
And explorations to the source dreams suggest.

My mind soars, spirals, hovers in a vortex
Above me like a butterfly and hummingbird
Simultaneously fluttering in the imagination.
Gently, it looses moon-dust in my brain.

Seconds and minutes and hours are not relevant
To my passages except as they relate to vowels
*

And consonants rearranged repeatedly to absorb
The hard and soft beats my soul sustains

As it tumbles uncomfortably in the hourglass
That shifts with each phase of sun and moon.
Final arrivals and departures are lines finished
And started, and all distance between the two

Is mere persistence. Stanzas are townships
Whose business districts detain me on my way home
From emotions I never knew existed before.
The City of Poetry is ever my destination.

Its location is as near as light-years to my future
And as remote as the past I constantly manufacture.
The miles I travel bring me closer to the time
When I'll finally meet the inspired One,

Who has been loaning me poems a lifetime
Without insisting each is a road on a map,
Leading to Heaven, that I'd be wise to follow.
At this time, I'm convinced my direction is right.

3/8/76 — [1] (00544)

Overtaken by Contagion

A collision with spina-bifida visions
Has reduced my mind to quadriplegia.
A tiny, painful cicatrix,
Affixed like a lamprey to the back of my brain,
Festers, oozes, drains continuously.
Demons and angels debate
Administering drugs to sustain my vegetation
Against silence or abstaining
In the initial stages, before death
Takes hold with its grotesque fixations.
Through filmy eyes, I watch
And wait, without making a vocal response,
For my fate to be decided. Suddenly,
A shape enters my wound, divides,
Assumes the likeness of my smooth wife,
*

Becomes my mischievous baby girl
Begging a moment alone with me.

Together, they sew perfect sutures
Around the swollen opening, soothe me
With reassurances that they've come
To deliver me from the affliction of my isolation
And will stay beside me in sleep.
All evening, I feel their healing hands
Reshaping the structure of my skull,
Kneading my brain with their delicate fingers.
When I awaken at dawn, they've gone,
Yet I'm no longer by myself.
Their curative image persists,
And where there was a visible wound,
Even its scar has now disappeared.
In its place is a glass door
I pass through, into sunshine,
Stride for stride with my healthy shadow,
Heading home after an eon on the road.

3/8/76 — [2] (00543)

An Evening in the Trevi Bar △

In a bar, I partake of black transportations
The darkness exhausts against my imagination
Like cold breath blown on colder glass.
An unrelenting blur disturbs my eyes;
It's filled with naked, nameless ladies and gents
Groping on weak knees for wishing pennies
Cascading from a fascinator above the stage.

The coins glint, hesitate intermittently,
While the revelers read their mottoes and dates,
Before they become mere musical notes
Dissolving beneath fountains of whiskey and wine.
Then each person tosses his own profile
Over his shoulder, into the afterglow,
And gazes as it floats slowly, slowly, to the bottom.

3/8/76 — [3] (09004)

[I've arrived the evening after the first day,] †

I've arrived the evening after the first day
(The traumas of Creation have weakened slightly).
When I

It's early, this morning, and the motel dining room
Is a Pullman smoker filled with coughing
And flabby-bellied beings in transit
From one inflated transaction to the next.
Orders for sausage links and patties,
Scrambled thoughts, sunnyside-up ideas
Fail to materialize from the kitchen

3/9 & [4/3/76]? (01376)

On First Turning Earth △

This morning, his pen stutters in ruts,
Like a single-trace plow glancing off roots
And flinty rocks choking an intractable field.

Neither will earth yield nor blade break
As the mind's tenacious mule continues to pull
The dead weight of unawakened metaphors
Against the grain. It takes all his energy
Just to keep the unwieldy contraption straight.

Later, when he returns to survey his labor
Strewn in irregular furrows across the notepaper,
He realizes it's not quite complete for seeding.
It still needs the imagination's steely disks
To finely grind the dirt for his verse to thrive.

3/10/76 — [1] (00541)

In Quest of Destinations

Without sight behind me, I assume
That the concrete rushing up under my hood
*

Is consumed by my momentum or wound tightly
On a reel whose diameter never fluctuates.

Possibly, my vehicle is absolutely static
On a two-lane conveyor belt
Moving ahead on well-greased spindles,
Returning unseen below me, to its beginning.

Occasionally, strange shapes overtake me
Out of the blind periphery of my left eye,
Rush by as if on a private strip,
Then disappear over the horizon.

I search continuously to catch a glimpse of them
Twisting through tenuous bends;
Only, the passing phantoms leave my vision
Without a forwarding address. I'm left

To guess at the highway's mindless intentions
And let intuition track their invisible passage.
As I'm carried along in my silent capsule,
An unsettling image of painted Plains Indians

Chasing buffalo toward an inevitable cliff
Invades my quietude, and I begin to suspect
That everyone before me may have plunged
To the rocky abyss of the skyline ahead,

Where fate might be waiting for me.
I lean sharply to my right, and the car
Slides from its forward motion, onto the edge,
And dies. With my ear to the raised window,

I listen in fear, straining to hear sounds
Resembling war cries, hoofbeats,
Bird points pelting my trunk lid —
Weird noises that might alert me

To a stampede catching my stalled existence.
I wait, as hours become empty decades,
Before finally venturing back onto the conveyor,
Satisfied that I've just been imagining vagaries.

Yet as I proceed, the concrete changes colors;
Pinks fuse with clotted crimson hues.
I cringe, uncertain of what next to expect —
Dusk, death, or perpetuation of the quest.

3/10/76 — [2] (00540)

Highway 185

I ride atop a snake's gravely back
As it slithers across country, in sunlight,
From Sullivan to Farmington
Without any apparent sense of direction.
Its head and tail are lost in trees.
I never even see
More than a few patterned stretches
At a time. Hills and troughs
Suggest creatures caught, eaten, and bulging
In degrees of acidic dissolution
Along its convulsing intestines.
Its uneven breathing juggles me
From side to side with nauseating frequency
As I try unsuccessfully to outguess
Its meandering mind. Finally, it contracts,
Coiling sensually around itself
As if to strike or avoid capture.
As I navigate its cloverleafing vertebrae
And seek access to the straight interstate,
I can see its prominent V-shaped skull
And culminating rattle simultaneously,
Threatening me for the last time.
Within seconds, I'm safely out of reach
Of its venomous fangs, speeding away
From my fear of being unexpectedly bitten
By the viper that transported my intellect today.

3/12 & 3/26/76 (00539)

The Exile's Return

For Jan and Trilogy;
six days away

It's been nearly a week since my soul
Slipped invisibly down the mountains, alone,
Over steppes, desert, out of the Land of Goshen.
Through Phoenicia and Babylonia, it flew
To its epochal, predestined place of servitude
*

And sweaty isolation, a Bedouin led by intuition
From oceans, into the heart's interior gloom.

What, if not some vast, passionate love,
Uprooted me initially from my palace
To purge the old corruptions and lust from my veins?
What, other than the ineffable hand of YHWH,
Could possibly have coaxed me from my pleasure dome
To sleep naked on tree roots, beneath the moon,
Make me appreciate the treasures of a blessed marriage?

Today, my expatriate spirit, aching for refuge,
Stops to ponder a perpetually burning bush
Growing at the edge of the mind's Mount Sinai
And lingers to pray for peace, guidance, delivery.
Visions of my wife and child rise from its flames,
Soothe my singed eyes with deliquescent ecstasy.
Ahead, Canaan invites my famished soul to feast.

3/13/76 (00538)

Dawg-Dawg $^\Delta$

Just up from her afternoon nap, our baby
Disturbs the fading cascades of dusty air
With her chaos. Stubby legs take her everywhere
Within the limited perimeters of living room,
Where a miniature terrier poodle reposes,
In a pool of Sunday hours, by the vinyl recliner.

Soon, she discovers the tiny dog silently lying
On its back like Gulliver, only slightly reduced
To fit the scale of her gnomelike universe.
Slowly, she closes in on it, touches its nose,
Retreats abruptly when it awakens with a lick
On her finger, quick as a snake's slitted tongue.

She laughs off her nervousness, pats its belly
With a rough, echoing slap. The creature flinches,
Remains still as she grabs its twitching tail
And screeches as though she can't fully grasp
How a shaggy black bag of wagging abstraction
Can come to life out of such implacable sleep.

Continuing tentatively to pet the docile animal,
Her hand accidentally smacks its vulnerable genitals,
Attached to an unsuspecting brain. In pain,
It scurries, leaving her isolated in cross-legged awe,
Without a clue to its urgent retreat. For days,
Asleep and awake, she chases its bedouin shape.

3/14/76 (00760)

[The years watch us changing in our seasons,] ^Δ

The years watch us changing in our seasons,
Through eyes flying in clouds or peering from creatures
Thriving close to mud, dark grass, and bark
Or disguised as fenestration for skyscrapers and farms.
Our eyes don't even capture reflections of their lives;
Neither do they echo the retinas' most recent impressions.
We only think we discern their transformations,
Without realizing that they are forever mindlessly alive,
While we, individually, are mere evanescent visitants.
We misconceive the redbuds and blossoming fruit trees,
Shivering through early purple springtimes, as ecstasy
Decreed by God. We misconstrue limbs inhaling green
As mystical inspiration nature breathes into the heartlands.
We fail to grasp that we alone endow all their changes,
Anthropomorphically,
And that if we were without corpuscles, vesicles, and pia mater,
Lacking rods and cones and tridimensional vision,
Everything would be flat black as lackluster shadows.
We forget that each of us is sole proprietor of the universe.
If only we could decipher God's heavenly Rosetta stone,
We might sculpt eternity into an image resembling man.
Yet the years have taken care to advance us, despite science,
In outrageous bafflement. Neither age nor the shaping
Of our vagrant souls makes us privy to secret coverts
Where the tree of eternal life grows beneath celestial light.
The seasons protect us from even the briefest immortality.
The years watch us changing from bones and protoplasm to dust
And name us according to when we arrive and when we leave.

3/23/76 (00301)

Portrait in Storm Time ^Δ

Each window of my fleeing car
Is a Victorian photographer's billowy backdrop
Surrounding me with improbable clouds.
Inside my insulated studio, I watch
An invisible hand draw the storm down
Around me on a series of spring rollers
Attached, somewhere above my roof, to the universe.
I wonder who would busy himself, this foul day,
Moving such heavy apparatus and for what effect,
Considering no one even requested this stormy sitting.

Phosphorus flashes penetrate the unnatural canvas
Before my glassy irises like fired cartridges
Leaving traces of powder burns on my mind.
Stiff-necked, I peer into the afternoon morass
As though posing to gain a more stable appreciation
Of my relationship to nature. Nothing breaks.
The hidden sun's polished parabolic lens
Can't focus me on its dry plate, for the rain
That smears the inverted image of my fear-filled face.
And I drive on without a record of my passing.

3/29/76 — [1] (00302)

Monday Night

For Dr. Al Karraker,
whose Aleutians I used

Monday night is at the uppermost pole
Of my frozen universe. I've arrived here
To set up base on an unmapped ice floe,
Inhabit an igloo in my heart's empty auricle,
Write in isolation, grow tired in seconds,
And die unnoticed in this cryogenic Sheol.
The shape of my disoriented spirit is lost
Among myriad minuscule Aleutian flakes
Mingling and fusing at Earth's galactic edge.

Monday night is on the outermost slope
Of an endless white tundra I scale unclothed,
*

Searching for a piece of my cracking soul to eat.
A blizzard of noisy photons, reversely magnetized,
Shatters whatever stability was left from Sunday.
I huddle under the ground cover my shadow makes
In perpetual daylight. All my old dreams
Of one day becoming master of my anguish
Dissolve in the air like caustic smelling salts.

Monday night is the innermost port of the week.
Like a fog closing on ships, it encircles me.
Main arteries moored to its insomnious zone,
Bordered by agitated latitudes I occupy, pulsate.
As often as I've been here, the arctic ice
Has never appeared penetrable. Now, a peculiar heat
Seems to be melting everything around me.
I feel myself unfreezing, flowing southerly,
Toward Tuesday's great equator, sleep.

3/29/76 — [2]   (00303)

My Thoughts Are Only Light-Years from God ^Δ

For Sev and Fred Meyer;
the Music Room

I stand under the coffered, vaulted ceiling
Of an ocular dome, listening to my own thoughts
Bounce back seconds later as sibilant whispers
Off the tongues of phantoms I've peopled, for years,
With mellifluous dreams and gentle egoisms.

Their deferential tone doesn't violate the silence
In which I bathe my ears. Their voices
Move like blood, from valve to valve,
Throughout the body of my accumulated consciousness.
Our kindred spirits have survived assaults

From vermicular spores floating in the mind
And leeches draining hemoglobin from my brain.
They tell me we still share a common heritage
And that we agree on the sanctity of inner peace.
Now, in this pantheon, under whose golden roof

We gather to commune with each other alone,
I sing myself through the celestial opening,
Into heavenly purlieus where our birth occurred
And my thoughts first met me dressed in flesh.
The song that echoes in my head is God's selection.

3/29/76 — [3] (00304)

Hirsute ^Δ

This particular morning, the Crystal Café
Contains a quorum of filled seats.
Twenty filibusters are in progress simultaneously.
Only by reaching supraliminal thresholds
Is one vested interest distinguished from another.

With one physically visible exception — facial hair —
All senators and junior representatives
Strike an uncommonly common chord of agreement.
They've convened to monitor social mores
And reconfirm Tipton's supremacy over Goshen.

The young bucks drill wells,
Machine farms, keep feedlots,
Set concrete driveways and sidewalks,
Drywall new housing units, raise hell
With their three-speed, half-ton pickups.

Yet the only way to tell them apart
From those in the final, prolonged stages
Of heartland disease, who caucus together,
Each morning, to vote the day into being,
Is by their deviation from a clean-shaven face.

Reluctantly, the older men accept their appearance
As the price paid for future progress:
Wide sideburns, resembling a mule's blinders,
Protect the ears from direct frontal assaults;
Clipped mustaches support insecure noses;

Scruffy beards, like golf-course rough,
Landscape the perimeters of sparse smooth surfaces,
Over which other eyes roll toward recognition;
Under blue- and green-billed insignia caps,
Hair presses toward a bumper crop.

Despite their feigned public disapprobation,
The heavier senators look to this new generation
With confidence that continuity will be maintained
And that they too will learn to bury indiscretions
In the potter's field of their daily debates.

And as if to cast aside any lingering doubts,
They've fastened onto an image from the Bible, reasoning,
"If Christ could go around half-naked
And wear hair coming out his ass,
Then these young brush apes can't be all that bad!"

3/31/76 — [1] (00306)

Downpour ^Δ

The center of every cloud floating in my eyes
Is dropping out. Tight, striated wisps
Are being extruded down toward the ground
Like miniature funnels. Is the heated air
Kneading them as it rushes upward, or is water
Weighing inward to each fluffy tub's drain?

From every direction across the wide expanse
Below which I pass on my perpetual trek home,
Invisible faces surmounting these whiskered masses
Peer out from an increasingly cluttered sky.
I imagine their vaporous brains analyzing me
Through a chain of magnetized, interrelated ideas,

Calculating what conceivable reason I might have
For being interested in their corporeal existence.
Within seconds, my fear, which they've probably guessed,
Turns to hysterical, paranoid trembling
As I realize their shapes are changing to mushrooms
Growing from bombs broadcast-seeded around me.

Now, I'm certain that something greater than demons
Playing with my insecure sense of place and time,
Something higher then even my imagination can reach,
Is up there, refusing to relinquish its anonymity,
And I wonder if I'm actually under attack
Or if this siege has merely been mounted to alert me

That my mind is in danger of being subverted.
When I look again, my eyes are fluid blue.
There are no traces of an enemy either fantasized
Or otherwise. Only a few dusty splotches remain
On the windshield and hood to corroborate the rain
I never saw or heard falling at all today.

3/31/76 — [2] (00305)

Redbuds ^Δ

My excited eyes take me by the hand,
Lead me through a pure fuchsia net
Of redbuds stretching, yawning into bloom.
We awaken each other with our touching.

As I pass from one room to another
Within this seething, open-air greenhouse,
Apple trees and dogwoods arouse me
To taste their white, lacy fragrance.

I stop long enough to memorize their scent,
Then continue along the labyrinthine path
My eyes cut through winter's blindness.

Everywhere in April's aquamarine sea,
Along whose lee shore I leisurely loaf,
Clipper ships, frigates, whalers, and packets,
Rolling in irons this early springtime,

Begin raising green sails up their masts,
Prepare to lift anchor for summer oceans.
I wave to invisible crews active as bees
Aboard the mind's fleet, secretly contrive

A means of booking passage, securing release
From the landlocked harbor, where my eyes
Have lain in dry dock, keeping me earth-tied.

No escape outlines its design on my irises.
Yet as I retreat from this isolated beach,
My feet go forward toward the new season,
And I realize that freedom is nothing other

Than the eyes' way of leading us to discover
That life connects us, through endless cycles,
To each other and each to original Creation;
Past and present achieve the universal *now*.

The eyes sow my seeds, plant my soul
In the fertile earth, fuse my bones with air.
I become the redbud, growing, everywhere, profuse.

4/2 & 4?/76   (00139)

Gulliver's Departure

It's so quiet here in Redriff
This fine, pink, spring morning
One might think the entire population
Had died of virulent floating spores
Or rats breeding beneath garbage heaps.

Gulliver paces dusty cobbled streets
Toward the wharf, where ship and crew
Wait to transport his flustered imagination
Away from conformities of church and state.
A sullen face belies his inner excitement

On leaving behind wife, childhood,
And Anglican life, for the open sea.
As he passes the cast-iron fence
Outlining a tiny green cemetery
In lacy design, his spaced mind buckles;

Reflections of his mild mother and father,
Held silently in skeletal suspension
In this earth where his birth occurred,
Gurgle to the surface of his brief reverie.
His weeping disturbs the invisible pool,

As he recalls their futile attempts
To guard him against straying from reason,
Deviating from traditional regimen
By administering too-gentle punishments.
Remorsefully, he kisses their sweet memory;

His heart breaks with hermetic affection.
Yet, knowing, even as in youth he'd realized,
*

Salvation lies in setting sail,
He abandons his melancholy, and bolts.
Now, the vessel fills his entire vision

With a palpable reality beyond dreams.
He throws up his duffel,
Climbs the hemp ladder, and boards.
Within hours, he'll be out of land's sight,
Past the lighthouse, over the horizon,

Without any identity or forwarding address,
And all his credentials will be invalid,
And all his academic scholasticism passé,
And all his expectations for the future useless,
And all his dreams irrelevant, his fears numb.

Toward this day he's gravitated and schemed,
Laid aside and sacrificed a lifetime
To let the moorings come untied.
Soon, the sea will set his mind at ease,
As he steers for Lilliput unsuspectingly.

4/3/76 (00112)

On Leaving Home

A love paean for Janny

As I recede further and further from home,
Mile by mile, hour by hour,
Memories of little Chi-Chi and her mother
Multiply proportionately. I become a total slave
To passionate emotion engendered by their absence.
Melancholy takes off her sheer robes,
Exposes her Rubens-smooth concupiscence,
As though the mere suggestion of sexual transgression
Might relieve the tension my silent weeping imposes.

Speeding, with calculated exactitude, into sunset,
The eyes, twice removed from the eyes I use,
Gaze through the elusive lady's nudity
And, recognizing she's not the muse who inspires me,
Refocus my imagination on my wife and child.
Mystically, I sit at the table where they eat supper
*

Quietly, by themselves. I lie beside them,
Behind the TV, and wait nearby
While our baby goes excitedly to her potty,
Taps her bare toes in mock impatience,
And repeats her most recent achievement.
I share in her deep pride as she carefully pours
The slight contents into the large bowl,
Reaches to flush it, then rushes away
To mount the next yawn flying torward sleep.

Just inside dusk, I envision lovely Jan
Pacing rooms that partition her moody vigil.
She seems to be searching for something lost:
An antique ring unloosed from her thin finger,
A letter left unopened from the noon mail,
An unmade phone call suspended beyond hearing,
Compliments on her beauty modestly accepted,
Too hastily jettisoned. She paces
In the twilight embracing my sad face.
We both know the misplaced object is us
And realize the futility of following solitude
From minute to hour as if it could allow us
A keener glimpse into the future communion
Of our postponed lives. Yet, alone,
Only reveries suffice to mitigate the gloom
And perpetuate hope of coming together soon.
Under the roof of the universe, through which we fly,
We rely on each other's love to keep us alive.

4/12/76 — [1] (00761)

Scintillations [Δ]

A flash within the blackest void
Night ever manufactured fractures silence,
As though someone speaking in dreams
Lit a candle on the moon's dark side
With his feeble voice and illumined the universe.
What absolute truth or profound philosophy
Could have been postulated to spark my mind
Alive inside this cave where I've lived
For thirty-five years without ever emerging
For fresh breaths of daytime light?

Maybe I've awakened inside midnight
And, frightened by not recognizing its environs,
Merely flipped on the nearest brain switch.
Possibly, I've been talking in my sleep again,
Relating myths of other lands and animals
I've not seen. Yet, these noises,
Never before penetrating to such depths,
Have caused the knife guarding my head
Against death to raise up the greased slides,
To the guillotine's apex, and catch uncertainly.

Perhaps the scintillating glint that woke me
From drowsiness was the keen-edged blade
Of consciousness, flying swiftly through space
To sever my dark identity from its destiny.

4/12/76 — [2]   (00307)

In a Daze △

The highway he drives from mid-state home
Passes rapidly beneath his vehicle,
Reappears briefly, in numbing retrograde,
Within the rearview mirror's edges,
Into whose glassy depths he habitually gazes.

Partial sky, wavering medians,
The blank, bony backs of road signs,
Cement extruded like a taut chalk line
Marking the exact two-lane track
That parallels its westbound running mate

All surface at a glance and persist
Like pinpricks sticking his limited vision.
In the distance, tractor-trailers shimmer
Like groupers fluting through a murky ocean;
Cars dart and weave like schools of tarpon

Migrating from one fresh vacuum to the next.
Occasionally, he gets to measure his relative speed
Against someone overtaking and capturing
His invisible shadow on their right door.
Only then does he know beyond a shadow of doubt

That his own motion is not a continuous moment
In an endless, isolated time warp,
Rather a flight whose arrival can be charted
By following any car ahead to its destination
Or any one behind as it disappears from sight.

4/13/76 (00309)

Flight from St. Louis to New York: A Microcosm △

At thirty-five, midway through my poet's journey
Away from the tribe, alone, with only the wife
An ancient Midianite peasant presented me with
To comfort my flight, our tiny blond child
Left behind as a reminder of our mild pariahhood,
I've reached the grassy knoll of a vast continent
And stand into the ceaseless, sand-salted zephyr,
Fearful of looking back over memory's lapsed terrain,
Craning to discern what habitable lands comprise the horizon.

I am Vespucci, Balboa. I am eucalyptus trees
Keeping sentinel along the soggy peripheries of mind,
Where ideas have a tendency to give ground, erode,
Slide into an ocean flowing with broken intentions
And unseaworthy dreams, then disappear into Pandemonium.
I am the energy it takes to get my existence in motion.
I am the place at which I've arrived: a wilderness,
A forlorn beach unpeopled yet alive with voices.
A soaring gull sings my ears aloft, flies my eyes

To Christlike heights of Miltonic vision and inspiration.
Paradise is now. The frail existence of my tiny ladies
Becomes immortal within the halo my love radiates
Around their delicate female shapes. Our future is now,
Below us, as we speed o'er Byzantine-spired cities
And ivory minarets anchored to fleet, silvery moons.
Beneath the wind, all the moments we've ever owned
Persuade every daytime we'll ever breathe to return us to earth
And let me resume my journey toward the frontiers of verse.

4/19/76 (00308)

Impressions

I

Puerto Rican housemaids chattering in abrasive tongues
Throughout the hotel's hallways, complaining of their slavish lot,
Caught inescapably in the cornucopia's neck like dry seeds —
They feel themselves being shaken into a hundred tiny pieces.

II

Saks Fifth Avenue is the screeching of hangers on clothing bars
And the persistent monotony of brass gratings clanging open and shut
On crowded elevator cars lined in Circassian walnut from the 1920s.
People are mere incidentals, undistinguishable from the soiled fashions
They hold up to their invisible bodies or try on. Floor ladies
Stare out from corners to see what face the nearest clock displays,
While I shove my eyes deep into the mind's unlined pockets
To keep them from mounting every young girl examining herself
   in a mirror.

III

I stand in the baby department of Bloomingdale's,
My hand trembling from the combined weight of outfits
I've carried around with me the last twenty minutes,
Waiting at a frequently reenameled, archaic cash register
For someone to disburden me of my hastily chosen gewgaws,
Then further extend my indentured days to my signature.

4/20/76 — [1] (01377)

"The Wild Beasts"* ᐃ

Each canvas is truncated by a peering head
Bifurcated by another peering head
Vitiated by myriad peering heads
Trapped accidentally in the spontaneous cubism
Formulated by crowds moving through the museum halls.

Each painting installed for the exhibit
Reflects the natural tension of unrelated shapes
In close juxtaposition, yet it becomes impossible
To differentiate disembodied human faces
From those composed with broken brush strokes in outrageous hues.

Like Manguin, van Gogh, Matisse, I lose sense
Of where the *I* inside me fits in with time outside.
Suddenly, the corridors pulsate with oily odors.
My eyes blur; focus drips off the framed rectangles.
Each subject comes undone from a prison

Sealed long ago by men waving thick, nervous pigments
Over canvas grave sites where, until today,
They've lain unmolested. Apparently, my anxiety
Has liberated the beasts of these sleeping spirits,
Who pursue me, now, as I flee the peering heads,

Toward any void that might give my paranoia refuge.
They chase me all the way to the turnstile
Insatiably clicking off paid admissions,
Then retreat to stalk the dazed multitudes
Come to gape at them — caged felines in a zoo.

*The Fauvist Exhibit, the Museum of Modern Art

4/20 — [2] & 5?/76 (00310)

A Moment of Solitude ^Δ

I wash away all the day's accumulated pollutants,
In a shower that changes from hot to cold
And slowly back at unannounced intervals
As though an oracle from the shady groves at Delphi
Were sanctioning its unnerving transformations.
Now, while my wife recuperates from fatigue
By searching in sleep for sweet, delicate glimpses
Of her child, a thousand miles beyond her reach,
I sit dripping, shivering by the air-conditioner,
Behind undraped plate glass, inside a silent veil,
Imbued with a timorous indolence, unable to move,
And afraid to disturb the precisely screwed balance
That holds my present state of solitude in place.

My ears hear neither the bell captain's whistle,
The horns' stichometry in the streets far below,
Nor screeching taxis. The drums cease reverberating
*

From subways and jet planes touching, each minute,
The taut, concrete-covered tines of this skyscraper,
Which fleshes the spine inside my breathing being.
I'm blind to the late-afternoon pewter horizon
Squeaking on shoddy hinges as night's flap
Follows its hours around. Myriad sounds
Funneling through twenty-four stories of conduit,
Exhaust vents, elevator shafts, wrapped ducts,
And exposed plumbing become the mewings of a fawn.

Musing numbly, I could almost mistake this place,
Where we've come to get away by ourselves for the week,
For a retreat on the shadiest slope in Delphi's grove.
Only, the painful scald-mark on my leg, from the shower,
Has begun to roar. My brain awakens in fear
Of evil omens and oracles foretelling the destinies
Of those who travel from their homes, questing solitude
Or any other unnatural form of disengagement
From the steeplechase of daily pursuits. I rejoice
With the realization that within an hour, we'll leave
To meet friends for drinks, friends for dinner,
And, hopefully, end up being saved by the crowds
That remind us we share the inconveniences of survival.

4/20 — [3] & 5/23/76 (00311)

[It's 5:11, and even yet,] †

It's 5:11, and even yet,
The corporate feet

4/21/76 — [1] (06585)

Wednesday Matinée △

A love song for Jan

We leave the Broadway matinée at 4:30,
Merge at 46th and 7th Avenue
With a colossal ameba of weary people
Extending homeward in every direction.

We're atoms in a scuzzy cyclotron,
Colliding in flight, pressed against walls
Whose sordid surfaces are lighted arcades,
Sanctum sanctorums, and frankfurter stands.

Finally, we escape the Cyclops's gaze,
Slip through shadowy valleys
To an oasis that hotels our souls,
Ascend twenty-four flights, phoenixlike, and undress.

Our tired bodies, lying side by side,
Provide relief from such deathly compressions.
The space our love occupies
Is the private theater we lease from each other

On a moment's notice, without reservations,
Whenever we choose. Right now,
Neither of us recalls the last act
Of the matinée we've just begun to stage.

4/21 — [2] & 6/4/76 — [2]   (00312)

The Masters Call Me to Their Service △

For Janny,
*   who loaned me the ending to this poem*

Having long ago abandoned the strict ivy rigors
Of reading romances, essays requiring underlines, picaresque novels,
Histories needing complete memorization, and sciences
That never quite explained the divine right of kings
Or justified the Protestant gospel of wealth,

I was, today, on contemplating three hundred years
Hanging from walls, pedestaled, curatorially displayed,
Reminded that the time elapsed between Brewster chair
And stained-glass panels from the Coonley Playhouse
Was once mine to shape into the design of a promising future.

I'd forgotten the sources from which my mind soared:
Winslow Homer's *Nor'easter*; Thomas Cole
Seated on an outrageous promontory above Mount Holyoke,
Painting the Oxbow into a palpable pastoral Arcadia;
Comfort Tiffany weaving stranded light into leaded Favrile.

Until today, I'd lost contact with big Max Schmitt,
Rowing one of Eakins's single sculls in a painted Schuylkill
So real I could smell his sweat, touch his muscles bulging,
See ripples as his shell delicately checked into stillness
With each stroke . . . we spoke a moment about the river's surface.

All those Newport and Providence block-front desks
And patrician chest-on-chest secretaries, crested with pedestals
And hand-carved cartouches, convex half-shells,
Resting on claw-and-ball feet, comprised the ornamentations
My eyes almost utilized in furnishing their first atelier.

Like them, I'd also set aside the beautiful Revolutionary silver
Kirstede, then Revere, made with delicate deliberation
By repousséing and heating the walls of my malleable imagination.
I'd climbed down to the shadowy base outside the frame
Of Bierstadt's Andes, Church's grandiose Yosemite landscapes,

And wandered ahead of myself, onto a desert plain,
To a house and wife and baby girl, where, to survive,
The flame had to be snuffed between reality's fingers
And the gliding butterflies of my sensual imagination
Had to be netted, labeled, and preserved under glass.

Until today, the spell that had enthralled me so completely,
Keeping me asleep in a waking state of daily tasks,
Had not been assailed. Something about the media
Bathing my blood in magazine print, TV fluorescences,
Political speeches, and endless inane requests for donations

Never would allow my well-entrenched snoozing soul to fly free
From its nest in the tree of my life, hollowing from inside
Without my awareness, or shake me out prematurely
Before it had tentatively scheduled me for cancellation
Or reverse the painless, dreamless drift toward death.

Only now, having been exposed to these museumed artifacts
And touched by their inspired ghosts, my soul's old self,
So long confined to sorting, tying, and filing away dialectics,
Craves freedom, again, to pioneer the unexplored wilderness
Bordering on territories where artists first disappear

To sharpen chisels and leads, tip their brushes,
Mix pigments from scratch, gesso canvases, select stones,
Before deserting the working world for a more perfect universe.
Fortified by their courageous, omnipresent legacies,
I vanish unseen into the centuries to search for my verse

And for my own voice, with which to annunciate its metered being.
The reward of the dreamer's life is, precisely, his privacy.
Itinerancy is his declaratory signature of resistant independence,
His artistry the religion of an omniscient, living poetry.
I beg to be taken to the workshop of the gods and taught to escape.

4/22–24/76 — [1] on 4/24 (00313)

House of Books, Ltd. †

For Margie Cohn,
such a beautiful lady

Each morning is a short walk from 55th Street
To Madison at 61st, each evening a brief retreat
From the book-lined rooms where she thrives
Among

4/24/76 — [2] (06584)

A Gentle Lament △

We hold hands, as the vortical world below us
Miniaturizes without our sensing we're climbing,
Until, finally, the clouds become sun-doves
And our clasp breaks in straight and level flight.
We draw back into our private inspirations.

My wife sits across the aisle from me, reading
Without assimilating the meanings of static words.
She dreams herself home before our scheduled arrival,
Touching, kissing, grasping our tiny child, Trilogy,
With distant eyes, while I watch her from my side,

Trying to intercept her misty reverie and ride it
To a source behind her mind where verse begins
And memory stimulates images that sinew the bones
Holding our living poetry together. A baby cries
Some rows behind. Our gazes unite. We smile,

Each recognizing the primal tongue of the young,
Which, not long ago, spoke incessantly to us
*

And now merely reinforces a gentle melancholy.
Separated from our firstborn, returning home,
We realize how vulnerable and how precarious

We've made her existence by flying away together.
Only our awareness of her incomplete mastery of time
Keeps us from accusing each other of unusual cruelty,
Assures us that on entering her life again in hours,
She'll forget, in seconds, we ever really left at all.

Yet we reach, again, across the narrow aisle,
As though holding hands might mollify regrets
We still have and relax anxieties common to everyone
Who has deeply loved a close friend far away
And wondered if ever they'd see each other again.

4/24/76 — [3] (00762)

Morning Flight △

Locked inside the turboprop vibrations
Of a Beach King Air, we fly through 13,000 feet
Of choppy clouds, higher, then out of sleep,
Purged, lean, and feathered above day.

I am the machine that transports me soaring;
My organs are sheet metal and cast aluminum;
Its oil and fuel lines wind around under my skin;
My arms are its wings, its radar my brain.

From the four-seat, pressurized cabin,
I peer into the cockpit, through tinted windshields,
As if inside the eye-pierced cranium of a turtledove.
The horizon ahead is a gray Himalayan chain

Crosshatched in multifarious chiaroscuros.
Turbulence nudges the plane's smooth underbelly,
Translates the earth's quick-cooling heat into shudders
That touch my brain through my feet and the seat.

Somehow, the clichéd fantasy of landed man
Unfettered like a bird begins to diminish
Now that I've consented to enter the wind's dominion.
Queasiness tarnishes the dream's poetical luster,

As a breathing overcast intercepts and envelops us
Midway toward the destination. While instincts
Guide our counterparts, only expensive instrumentation,
Without guarantees, carries us along proper airways.

In my blindness, visions of migrating flocks
Stalled in silence on limbs, grounded by fog,
Arise like bats diving at my head, then away,
And I wonder what made us want to take off today

And why I would have entrusted my life
To such a precarious uncertainty as turbulence
And to so gratuitous a notion as winds aloft.
Not even the fleeting glimpse of farmland

Beneath the scud or the downwind runway
Racing the craft's shadow reassures me
Of a safe touchdown. A furrowed frown
Undoes my disguise of quiet equanimity.

I bury my eyes in the pilot's steady hands
And wait for his sole judgment to dismantle us
Or keep us alive. The blades change pitch;
The flaring plane veers, achieves equilibrium.

I sit listening, while gyros fade into silence
As all switches are flipped off one by one,
Before I finally step out into a blinding sun,
Unable to believe that the day's just begun.

4/28/76   (00314)

My Brother's Keeper ^Δ

As I enter April's last day, this morning,
My lips, for some strange, unexplained reason,
Begin to vibrate the halo containing my head.
I can sense the assembly of stray chords
Being coaxed from memory. Plaintive strains
Of Gershwin's lugubrious Concerto in F
Hover, in my vision, against spring's green gestalt
Like a Sutro mist, as if contiguous May
Were a draped caisson being set into place
*

For a funeral procession. I peer slowly
Into a pool of poppy-blown mind-waves
And imagine myself back, through black vacuums
Behind my eyes, beyond the brain's dark side,
To the generation that fed, bathed, and clothed
The beautiful Jewish Brooklyn-tenement musician.

I hope to locate the ghost who's summoned me
With my unwished-for whistling this incongruous day.
Only, as I gaze, neither voice nor figure lifts
From the subliminal stream serpentining the cave
Beneath my skull. No mystical incarnations
Inspire me to an empathy with the great composer.
Why I should have been made a co-conspirator
To another's creativity remains unassailably baffling,
When I actually consider that until today,
No source of coercive, aural force,
Especially not the snorting of sewing machines
And high-friction complaints of cutting blades
Fusing the pieces of my life into a shroud,
Could transpose my diminished soul into a tone poem
Or reshape the outer boundaries of nature's inscape.

Yet as I pass through April's last day,
The recurring melodies, waiting at my tongue's base
To be given new life, whisper thanks in my ears
For having freed them from their eternal sleep.
They accept me as their most recent creator.
I lean out of a sooty tenement window and weep
As if I were Ira at my brother's first recital.

4/30/76 (00315)

Machines in the Garden ᐃ

At adventitious bruised spots along the geography,
Enclaves of behemoth road machines
Wallow in dull silence, stand in rancid rainwater
Up to their mud-choked half-tracks.
Their cold manifolds, cracked and rusting exhaust stacks,
And empty hydraulic lines suggest abandonment
By another age altogether. A metamorphic force
*

Transmutes these construction sores to tarpits
And their backhoes, bulldozers, belly-loaders, and rollers
Into the perfectly preserved three-dimensional skeletons
Of grazing, wading brontosaurs, stegosaurs,
And pithecanthropes. Yet nothing stirs
Except birds and rain in this atavistic burial ground
Stretching from Springfield, through Champaign, to Joliet.
Trepidation guides us hastily toward our destination.
Afraid even to speak to each other or breathe unnecessarily,
For fear of waking the beasts from their dreamless sleep,
We drive by in awe, cautiously keeping our distance,
And pretend their bright-yellow Caterpillar bodies
Are vibrant butterflies lighting in gardens behind the eyes.

5/6/76 (00316)

Visitation ^Δ

> *For Trilogy and Jan,*
> *whose love for each other*
> *is indefectibly wrought*

All alone for the moment, I float on a drone
Of background monotones welling oceanlike
From the television. *Sesame Street* and *Mister Rogers*
Play to a full house at Edwards' pediatric ward,
Where our baby sleeps between chrome interstices,
Atop poppy-white hospital sheets.
Numerical repetitions and phonetic articulations
Implore my attentions. Yet my dazed mind,
Infected by a succubus, rejects their exhortations,
Stays focused on the crib containing our two-year-old,
Who was brought into this limboed isolation
Late last night, out of the grasp
Of 105 degrees, convulsing toward demise.

Momentarily, the serialized bathos of effete soap operas
Intrudes on this quiet room through thin walls.
It calls to me like Sirens trying to lure Odysseus.
Only, her tiny, unblanketed body, loosely gowned,
And its labored, peaked silence, so absurdly juxtaposed
*

To all that commercially contrived tragedy,
Keep me from being distracted. Instead, my eyes,
In random sequence, review visions of her seizure.
I recall her rolling eyeballs and blue skin,
Cold rags applied to forehead and chest
Heaving violently, her frothing, painful regurgitations,
The unannounced lapse into semiconsciousness,
Before she was finally whisked away by Naperville paramedics.

Right now, it's almost impossible to differentiate
Last evening's emergency-room screams,
Still wrapped in memory's soggy ice packs,
From the inane persiflage and hysterical screeching
That swims sinuously as eels into my ears
From kings and queens reigning over game shows
Clotting the screens. I tune out their extraneous sounds
And try unsuccessfully to grasp the implications
Of a polysyllabic patois that incorporates "Tylenol,"
"Phenobarbital," and "encephalogram" without flinching.
Feverishly, I seek a layman's translation to dangers
Intrinsically related to our baby's precipitous condition,
But our consultation with an Indian pediatrician
Both impatient and condescending yields little insight,
Confuses the issues of fever, epilepsy, and seizure
With unnecessarily conjectural medical pedantries.

Febrile brain disorder, hemorrhages, malignant tumors
Constitute the vague lunar landscape
He causes to fly around in our minds like dust
Stirred up by a cyclonic broom. We refuse to accept
This unfamiliar man as possessing absolute answers.
Yet on his insistence, we consent to submit her
To skull and chest x-rays, extensive urinalysis,
Hemoglobin tests, and periodic sedatives.
My wife's cries are the most primal grief known.
Her maternity is as equally primitive as profound.
My silence extends past the inner limits of fear,
To the outskirts of shimmering immortality,
Where no televisions blare
And angels repair to pray for Trilogy's eventual recovery.

Out of nervousness, I eat the cold food
She leaves untouched each meal. Nauseously,
*

Her mother sips warm juices she refuses to drink.
We hang on every suspiration as if it were ours
And stare at her near-naked body, transfixed,
To identify which of her features belong genetically
To which of us. Not since labor and parturition
Have our emotions been so coincident
And our lives tied so tightly to the umbilicus
Connecting the three of us to each other's thoughts.
For the first time since her actual birth,
My wife and I realize that the only sacred thing
We've ever created is our little baby girl, Trilogy.
And even though she's now in critical danger
Of being taken away from us or changed forever,
We accept her sickness as a visitation from God.
This vigil is our most privileged intimacy with Him.

5/7/76 (00763)

The Origin of Species

A Mother's Day gift

Not against the better angels of our judgment
Or just for the sake of bereft couples
Do we accept conception and endure birth
But to slake the thirst in their dry throats
With the mystic's voice prior to our arrival
And release their hearts from hermetic silence,
As ripeness gives rise to first cries
On taking one of us into their lives.
Despite pleas of tedium and inconvenience,
Even the pariah's indifference to the environment
And distrust of society's dictates are mollified
Or changed by the basic needs we require.

Yet to some, we become incubuses and succubi,
Undesired ghosts and poltergeists,
While others grudgingly assimilate us
Into their egocentric galaxies.
A small group actually recognizes
*

A special essence of gentleness and intimacy
They never expected infancy to beget.
Still fewer, like you, Jan, penetrate
The crystalline layers that halo our origins
And approximate the celestial source of life
You yourself have twice touched,
Once as a baby, once by inviting us here.

5/8/76 (00764)

Sartor ^Δ

The sock-fitted feet slip into his shoes.
The hairy legs and thighs slide through underwear,
Into his trousers, up to a widening girth
That fuses with spongy chest and pectorals
Self-consciously hidden from public scrutiny
By his loose-fitting shirt and corduroy coat.

Almost every part of the body belonging to him,
Laundry-marked with his cellular identity,
Is assigned a specific garment to wear,
As if to maintain the consistent integrity
Of a fleshed set of daily repeated tasks
Despite each new disguise his mind might assume.

Whenever he tries to break free of appearances
And run naked, each piece of clothing
Begins to shrink and contain the rebellious spirit,
Constricting its movement to a few useless threats
Against the tribe. Even plea bargaining
And bribery can't ease the predetermined sentence

The organism has borne throughout the course
Of his entire existence. Solitary confinement
Within recognized, accepted patterns of dress
Has left him threadbare, with frayed edges,
Outmoded, and with nowhere to go for help
In distinguishing the clothes from his ragged soul.

5/10/76 (00317)

The Sisters of Fiesole △

A stranger has violated the sacred city's
Outer precincts, scaled the sedgy moat,
Rappelled the uneven, craggy wall
Seven centuries high, wide, and deep,
Molested two sleepy temple sentries
To reach the inner cloister, and entered
The nunnery undetected by the sisters,
Slumbering in the sweet, protective certitude
Of an abstinence their holy order inspires.

Only one lady, lying naked in the straw,
Stirs from dreaming, shivers in fright
From her recognition of the interloper.
She turns toward his stealthy form
And is absorbed in its orgasmic shadow
Before the others have occasion to awaken.
Next morning, she rushes to hide the dry seeds
She spilled beneath the lover she prays
Will escape nightly from her libidinous vows.

5/11/76 — [1] (00318)

Testing Grounds △

The strangest chain reaction of detonating fantasia
Decimates the brain's subdural equator,
And any expectations I may have had for escaping
From this isolate Wake are carried away
On billowy thermals of cephalic fallout.

My remains peel off a layer at a time,
Exposing sprung steel clock cogs and windings,
Where elastic veins and valves once coursed,
And hook assemblies, needle bars, gears,
Brass parts, and cold, hand-honed shafts,

Which, years ago, usurped the flabby bodily functions
Of a too compassionate, much too gentle,
Unpretentious head and heart, now fill the skull.
*

Even my eyes are reversed to focus inward
On an idiot's screaming stream of consciousness

Previewing on the screenlike optic chiasma,
Revealing ejaculating rabbis and shaved nuns
Kneeling in awe to an obsidian Gautama
Wavering dangerously within a cruciform synagogue
Where I once groped for Benjy's lost quarter.

Now, the lazy, sifting snowflake-ashes
Scatter the atoms of my exploded intellect
Across the eight o'clock horizon. As I arise
And try to collect each dismembered piece
Comprising my sanity's core, I choke.

Tiny phosphorescent dots shotgun my irises.
All my surviving machinery locks tight.
On the floor before me, my prostrate shadow
Comes unhinged from death and enters my body
Like two quintessential old friends shaking hands,

And for a moment, my numb body stutters
From the static weight of its secondary mass.
Once again, I'm the tossing albatross that I wear
As a punishing self-reminder of my entrapment
On this island, where every new idea is exploded.

5/11/76 — [2] (00319)

Table Scraps $^\Delta$

Retiring abruptly, just after dusk,
From an unusually early supper,
The satiated sun
Left a half-chewed moon
On a bone-china sky
Without waiting to pay the check.

Since such scraps are desirable
Late at night or the next day,
We wondered why he wouldn't stay,
While his digestion made room
To assimilate the lunar hunk,
Or at least request a doggy bag.

Maybe his haste was occasioned
By recollections of another engagement
He'd made years before.
Just possibly, he was bankrupt,
Perhaps flustered discovering his appetite
Was not quite as large as his eye.

5/11/76 — [3] (00320)

Synesthesia △

The Facts o' Life

Surrounded by sound, my ears respond
By breathing a pure, energized vibration.
The nose and mouth bow to inspiration.

Touched by flooded light, pushed by blood,
The eyes taste their screaming tongues,
Feel the adder's bite below the throat.

Singed by diminished notes, the frontal lobes
Reiterate a primitivistic, viral beat
That ignites St. Vitus's dance in the gut,

While time rumbles my skull like a drum
Struck to numbness by a crazed musician
Reaching an ultimate synthesis of feeling

Somewhere beneath his sensitive skin.
My psyche releases its cargo into the sky.
I fly after it, beyond the speed of light,

Time, and sound, at a velocity unrelated
To every known measurement, chasing words
Capable of recording my flight to the soul

In phrases soft enough to convey loudness,
Gentle enough to disguise their warlike roar,
Sufficiently sensual to dispel savageries.

Finally, the words revert to simple rhythms,
The rhythms to blood, and blood to what remains
When all else turns to poppied sleep: poetry.

5/11/76 — [4] (00322)

Lobotomized $^\Delta$

After an ageless night, buried in sleep
Six feet deep, one tired body wide,
I mole my way upward through the dirt
In the brain, leaving tunnel tracks,
Like varicose veins, on the surface of yawns
That creep cautiously out of my mouth
As if expecting a predatory varmint to pounce.

Only, no creatures inhabit this land,
And my dead, musty breath dissipates
Without incident. I climb onto the plain,
Wobbly, eyes wincing from the luminosity,
And begin foraging after grasses and leaves
To sustain my dematerializing spirit.
Yet wherever I go, nothing green grows

Except the solitary, stagnant water hole
From which I drink with insane desperation.
I recognize the silence that crowds the sky
And every centimeter of space between me
And the sulphurous horizon as the stranger
With whom I've conversed on several occasions
Without our ever once exchanging first names

Or inquiring into each other's birthplace
And considered destination. Again we meet,
Quite accidentally, inside a deepening shadow
Crawling across the plain. It's captured us both,
As though trying to take us to its source
And explain that we are the same person
Simultaneously, awake or asleep, alive, dead,

Tongueless or when the head is articulate.
Only, I know a person can't be in two places at once,
No matter how common their adjacent boundaries.
I scratch at the shadow's black, deckled edges
For a weakness in its seam. No lesions appear
Through which I might escape back to the brain,
And I am forced to listen to an alien voice

Trapped all afternoon in an endless soliloquy
Of absolutely incomprehensible verse.
The excruciating pain from such constant assaults
*

Screws my mind into defensive semiconsciousness,
Sends me retreating volitionlessly into sleep,
While the poetic node of my breathing heart
Continues futilely to energize my severed lobes.

5/12–13/76 — [1] on 5/13 (00321)

[The rain brings worms to the earth's surface] †

The rain brings worms to the earth's surface
And the early morning rabble to the Crystal Café

5/13/76 — [2] (06583)

Niña, *Pinta*, and *Santa María* △

On sighting Trilogy's second birthday

The cargo tightly tied in our minds' hold,
Over which we've kept close watch
During our two-year oceanic exploration
Into the New World, beyond wombed Atlantis,
Has begun to shift slightly. A few sicknesses,
Changing diet, increases in body size,
Multiplying words concatenating into phrases,
Intensified perceptual coordination
Have contributed to the need for uncrating her,
Allowing her free run of the main deck.

Earlier, our real concerns were for squalls,
Unexpected calms, the treacherous Charybdis,
And ever-present, effervescent Zephyrus —
In short, navigating the unmapped course,
Over two fluid years, from our vessel's hold.
Now, my wife and I take turns climbing,
Day and night, the mizzenmast's dizzy heights
To position ourselves in its crow's-nest
In order to spot seaweed, distant land,
A safe lee and harbor in which to drop anchor.

Sometime during every postmeridian,
Toward the red edges of fading afternoon,
We recheck our logs, annotate our charts
Where modified attitudes of deviating latitude
Bisect widening degrees of acceptable behavior.
Then we make projections, reset our heading
In a direction calculated by guesswork to yield
The Spice Islands, where we might rest awhile
Before repairing toward Haiti, San Salvador,
And undiscovered shores to be named for her years.

5/13/76 — [3] (00765)

In Memoriam $^\Delta$

For "Uncle" Bill Lee,
in blessed memory of Bernice,
his loving wife

This fine May morning,
I once again take to the highway
That interconnects the states of my mind,
Defining, like a giant, winding river,
Boundaries containing old griefs,
Pity, petty hatreds, ecstasies.

From every direction, bold shadows
And imagined poetic reflections
Focus their blunt or pointed weight at me.
My jigsaw thoughts are buried
Under a hundred superimposed notions
Of ghostly specters. I am casketed

In a vehicle speeding, beneath my skull,
Toward a cemetery filling fast,
Of late, with the remains of gentle tenants
Who yet animate my living past.
The wide radius encompassing my parents
And their friends narrows inexorably,

Begins to disappear without a trace,
As though God's rippling stones
Were never thrown or, if so,
*

Without force to disturb the earth's surface.
One by one by one,
I've witnessed the vortex coerce them under,

As the cemetery, like an ocean
Undulating in a storm, engorges the land,
Expands beyond its shores. I wonder
How much farther I'll have to travel
Before this highway ends in desert
And I'm left to survive by myself.

5/19/76 — [1]   (00323)

In the Synagogue ^Δ

For "Aunt" Bernice Lee;
God bless her soul at rest.

As a minute piece of a greater congregation,
We've come to pay our last respects
And listen to the Kaddish, articulated
In its ancient, plaintive Hebraic chant
Over the coffin of sweet, sleeping Bernice.

Arriving before the bereaved family,
I let my eyes wander lugubriously
From pew to Danish-walnut pew,
Glance off hammered-brass candelabra
And menorah, come uneasily to rest

On the perpetually unsealed ark
Surrounded by an elongated tapestry,
Whose muted designs also womb its Torahs.
The relevancy of death and worship
Intrudes curiously on my subdued mind.

I try to interpret the relationship of each
To a modernity so exquisitely refined
As to be entirely isolated from both acts.
Only, seemingly irreverent small talk
Distracts me from my restive solemnity.

Yet as the rabbi begins his eulogy,
Refers to the surviving family members
*

By their first names, recites with them, in unison,
The ageless mystical crystallizations
Fused into the Twenty-third Psalm, I weep

With those weeping for their deceased one.
My voice chokes on the realization
That it's not the kind of worship or burial place
That really matters, rather the tenacity
And delicacy of memories after shadows pass.

Now, I see on the crying air her smile,
Hear in the stifled, meditative silence
Her loving asides. I feel her faith
Rippling my marrow, reminding me that life
Is the depth we reach in loving each other.

5/19/76 — [2] (00324)

Ode to a Barbecued Beef Tenderloin

For Charlotte,
     chef de cuisine de *Chez Brodsky*

It was no mean boneless tenderloin
Or mere marinated chunk of meat
We barbecued last evening,
Rather the most proteinaceous,
Blood-lean beef I'd ever seen,
Splayed over seething coals
To complete the resurrection of the lowly dogie
We sacrificed to our appetites.

From sac to calf in grassy pasture,
Endlessly nuzzling clumped patches,
To full-blown cloven-hoofed creature
Padded with flab,
Turgid and stiff-legged,
Afraid of its own frightened shadow,
You, cow, give selflessly from within,
Desiring neither recompense

Nor justification for existence and death.
We sanctify life
*

Without knowing why
Yours was ordained, by faith, to be consumed,
While we were left to question
And postulate such celestial concerns
As inner tenderness, outer char,
Degree of marbling,

Need for sauce and cracked black pepper
To complement the taste
Or mask its resemblance to our own flesh.
Now that we've lined our bellies
With the stuff of your docile body,
Let us stop and give praise
To the brain that placed us on top
In the chain of carnivorous vertebrates.

5/21/76 (00327)

[Routines guilt me to a consecutive] †

Routines guilt me to a consecutive

5/27/76 — [1] (06582)

One Last Time the Muse △

While on my way to the horizon
At highway's end, I was waylaid,
Detained by a strange lady in black,
Whose only coercive weapons were her eyes.

I was taken a hypnotized distance,
On flutterings of dragonfly and hummingbird lashes,
To an earlier time in my life,
Where the high, thin air was hard to breathe

And each peak in the poppied land
Was impossible to reach without grabbing hold
Of metered lines attached to each other
At precarious points and knotted with rhyme.

From there, I was led into a lacy forest
Treed with dark, artificial reveries,
Pans, sylphs, and classical myths
I'd seeded into my arboretum of Keatsian verse.

Only, no neat rows were left intact
To suggest eclectic allusions and references
Memorized and used; rather, silent worms
Lay buried in quatrains beneath my feet.

Alone, I searched for the vaporous lady
Who'd brought me so far out of my way,
Not just to beg of her my expeditious escape
But learn why I'd been diverted without warning

This morning, while on my routine journey
To the horizon at highway's end,
Where free-associational poetry, personal as sperm,
Once flowed from domes where I'd go daily to browse.

Behind me, beneath a tree, completely undressed
Except for a locket I'd once given away
Depending between her slack breasts,
She waited quietly for me to recognize her,

Then cried as if the mere recognition
Might signal the redemption of something final.
I could see, even in the density,
How solitude and neglect had whitened her skin,

Emaciated her bosom,
Shadowed her hips and sinewy legs
With sinister indications of living death.
Weeping, short of breath, retching,

She began to gasp. Her feeble lips
Whispered that I should sit beside her
And unfasten the gold chain around her neck,
Which she'd protected all the years of our estrangement.

As I reached to touch her, she disappeared,
Leaving just the locket, hot in my hands,
Open, exposing identical faces
Of the youthful poet and the man grown old,

Whom she'd known both as paramour
And infidel. Each portrait bore my name;
*

Every feature was the same
As that which I now wore out of boredom

And defeat. Only, then, I was beautiful
To my mistress of dreams, the lady
Who guided my pen. Long ago,
We drove together to highway's end.

Now, I realized why she'd detained me:
She was dying and wanted me to write
One final romantic ode or elegy for her,
In hopes of guiding me back to my soul.

5/27 — [2] & 6?/76 (00325)

Escapees

I

Wafting mist and drooling fog
Spirit past my drowsy eyes
Like convicts in black and white
Escaping dawn's sawed-through bars.
Briefly liberated from the dark,
These anonymous elements threaten me
As I enter the area of morning
Where they've been reported still loose.
The ambiguous air in which they hide
Provides easy trespass,
Allows them passage to each border,
Where active searches progress
Without resulting in their capture.
I try to avoid chance convergence
By igniting the high beams,
But stark reflections blind me
Instead of illuminating the direction
I might take to circumvent danger.
My vehicle slogs to a stall.
I get out, crawl on all fours,
Feeling with canelike fingertips —
A fiddler crab fidgeting sidewise
Across a debris-strewn psyche.

II

In this white nightmare,
I'm held hostage by netherish creatures
Who've stipulated neither ransom
For my life nor alternatives
To nullify reprisals against them
By future authorities of the state.
Isolation frightens me.
Imagining others lost and groping
Causes me dubiety about the outcome.
That innocent people like me
Should be subjected to harassment,
Gratuitously, is preposterous,
Not explained away
By accusing paranoia or "human frailty"
Of making us captive of our fate.
Clearly, conditions beyond my control
Have brought me to my knees.
For the next two hours, I consume coffee
In a café materializing out of the fog
And wait for a redneck sun
To manacle the escapees, place them
In solitary confinement, and allow me
Freedom to resume my journey.

5/29/76 (00326)

Between Connections

The foggy countryside is dotted with waifs
Occasionally penetrating its glued layers
To make connections, locate junctions,
Navigate cloverleafs,
And reach destinations
Somewhere beyond the pervasive gray
That permeates day's escape routes.

These metaphors, racing through hollows,
Past hedgerows, out of sight,
Might be rabbits, vehicles conveying people,
*

Or vessels fleeting through my eyes,
Containing placid, passive meanings
Imagination assigns to uprootedness
And evokes in defining dead time.

Regardless, as I wait by the roadside,
My mind refuses to differentiate
Among various kinds of transience,
Between symbols stopping briefly,
Like trains, at stations along the brain,
To take on and discharge passengers.
Every fragment of the incomplete vision

Has potential to become the one link
That could connect all images
With what I think about my own location.
But none relinquishes its secret,
As I stand in plain sight of everyone,
In the middle of an inconvenienced identity,
Trying to thumb a ride home.

6/4–5/76 — [1] on 6/4 (00118)

The Inconveniences of Immortality ^Δ

With fierce indignation, I reach deep
Into my skull and rip the sticky webs
From their epoxied struts. My fingers
Get cut on the slender, scythelike
Witches' hair that has infested my brain
For centuries. Although, in the past,
I've complained about the inconveniences
Of immortality, with its ceaseless accumulation
Of Greek myths, Byzantine complexities,
Babylonian and Egyptian sensuality,
My argument with the gods and pleas
To be freed from my body in the Gethsemane
Of each diseased and dying civilization
Have proved useless and gone unheeded.

What pains me most is the legacy
Of unnamed offspring I've fostered,
*

The accumulated moss of dates and data
I've perpetuated by staying around so long,
Consorting with history's nubile whores.
My unchanging, beautifully muscled physique
Aches from the wearisome, mindless repetition
Sex demands of its naked slaves.

Now, the vicious webs I spread apart
To slip through entangle me like tentacles
Of a cephalopod and sting my eyes.
Such lacerations require immediate nursing
To keep suicide from nullifying the punishment
To which I'm doomed. Every time
I've tried to break loose from the cranium,
Arachne has awakened from her sleep,
Seen me leaving, and climbed quietly down
From her lair to bite me into sweet submission.
She anesthetizes my mind, paralyzes
My spine for decades. I lie prostrate
Beneath her lethal, weightless persuasions
To remain. The drugged promise she makes
For tomorrows scattered with opium-kisses
And golden apples laced with hallucinations
Of perfectly peace-loving lotus eaters
And docile Jesus devotees convinces me
That another few millenniums won't matter,
Considering eternity's vast, galactic sweep.

Yet I don't see her uxorial shadow
Descending inexorably this time. My blood throbs
As though every cell knows the hour's arrived
For my soul to finally depart its chrysalis.
As I pass from sanctum to dusty sanctum,
Then through the eyes, into stark daylight,
My clothes fall away from bones decaying
Without pain, and memories gently dissipate,
Like ashes, into the air. My weight becomes nothing
In relation to the ageless concentration of being
Amassed since the earth's first Sabbath.

The relief of nonexistence is an ecstasy
Tithonus never guessed at, unknown
To Prometheus. In this recent dimension,
I realize that even the spirit's renaissance
*

Is possible. The prospect of dying
Excites me to desire mortal life once again.
The elements that comprised my pseudohubris
Purge in the sun's undulant halo,
Regroup within its streaming, earth-aimed rays,
And guide themselves toward a manger
In a land not yet populated by drowsing man.

6/7/76 — [1] (00328)

Breaking Through

> *What time's my heart? I care.*
> *I cherish what I have*
> *Had of the temporal:*
> *I am no longer young*
> *But the winds and waters are;*
> *What falls away will fall;*
> *All things bring me to love.*
> — Theodore Roethke, "Words for the Wind"

A Loire-like shimmer
Rims this entire Mississippi River valley.
Never have such vibrant greens,
Through which my magic carpet soars,
Screamed at me. My eyes listen attentively
For a sign from the incipient sweet corn
Breaking furrowed hymens.
My ears see the fibrous stalks
Winding their slender cords on sky-pegs
Fastened to an invisible lyre. Vibrations
Set my body in sympathy with all things
Procreated, germinated, and about to breathe,
And I'm reminded that just being alive
For another season is the most natural surprise
My winter-weary mind could possibly receive
On drawing back its old ground cover
And admiring the earth from which it came.

6/7/76 — [2] (00144)

Suffragettes $^\Delta$

For Trilogy,
my little girl growing

Each of these women serving drinks,
In tight skirts and breezy breasts,
Or drinking those which others buy,
And being bought nightly by different guys
Is someone's little daughter still,
Back in Jacksonville and Duluth.

By now, they've even forgotten the truths
They either rebelled against or used
In pseudo-good faith — amoral indeed —
To advance them beyond their parents' gate,
Into Prince Real's Skylark,
Mr. Right's '57 Chevy,

And eventually a hundred other backseats
That the slightly less polite procession
Of uncouth suitors questing underwear
Instead of handkerchiefs and scented gloves
Neglected to flush after each use.
Now, they walk from payment to payoff.

How they ever finally decide
On a particular station and arrive safely
Where fate waits to take their bags
And escort them to the next accommodation,
Without at least some familial tie
To ease their uprootedness, is unexplained.

Somewhere back in Jacksonville
And Duluth, locked behind the mutual solitude
Of evening newspapers and dry vermouth
Sipped in perpetual resignation,
Graying couples rummage vacated rooms
For the blessed little girls they still protect.

6/7/76 — [3] (00766)

Kubla's Xanadu ^Δ

For Porpoise

The electric wires connecting their instruments
To the air run conspicuously along my spine.
The insulation falls away, exposing notes
Racing frantically as scared cats through my brain,
Trying to find escape from the vortical connection
Firing my five senses to a spontaneous flashing point.

I am the music they release easily as sperm
Touched into life by breathing. The raving orgasm
Climbs down the web strung across my cranium,
Eight-legged, and bites the arachnoid integument
Protecting my sanity. Something comes loose
Beneath the base, where all formulations coalesce.

Shadows lapse into alligators blowing saxophones,
Scorpions strumming their lyrelike tails,
Elephants playing traps with their tails and trunks,
And fireflies driving incessantly from the ceiling,
Like shooting stars, toward shiny patinas everywhere.
A single synthesizer, tripping in awkward ecstasy,

Carries what's left of me on its powerful back,
Up Giotto's campanile, one narrow, precarious step
At a time, to the upper deck of Western civilization,
To catch fleeting glimpses of every blessed soul
That ever soared, heretical, toward day's lusty lips.
I lean too far over into vertigo's embrace,

And time falls off my face, into the deep abyss
From which no one returns who reaches in to retrieve it
Out of the great Keeper's fisted grip. I enter the air
Free-falling yet not free of my living corpse,
Chasing my shadow past bass and treble clefs, notes
Dripping like dirges from censers swinging, pendular,

Against humanity's deaf ears, and as I pass,
I hear every composition ever written calling me
To participate in its creation by capturing its energy
In the bag below which I hang, loosely parachuted
On sheets of sheer sound sewn together by nerves.
I'm buoyed by the buried geniuses of immolated days,

Come back to soften the shafts of the mind blown apart
By the same demons that infected them. They care!
*

I have shattered. The parts scatter over a landscape
My feet have never before explored. Alien tribes
Assemble to witness this strange creature I've become,
Gathering up the components of something called psyche.

As a vague moon scythes through descending darkness,
Casting half-light in pockets where the music has nested me,
I search, like a miner in a sluice, sieving elusive nuggets
From nothingness, for elements that, combined, might
     constitute
My integrity. I come up with a handful of shadows
And disfigured shapes that refuse to mirror my memories.

Groping feverishly, I beg assistance. No odd wizards
Offer to help me return through the tornado's rifled eye,
To a Kansas plain. Lost, bereft, unmapped, I weep,
Realizing that the spider's marks still exist on my wrist
And that I'm doomed to remain suspended in the silky net,
The victim of Arachne's toxic music, slave to her ways,

As I dangle over the edge, looking up and below, simultaneously,
At a sky no living man has ever imagined, naked with ladies
Bathing in celestial streams, clotted with starving Ethiopians.
I have a choice that must make me come to my senses:
I can leap, jump into the bottomless ages, or climb
Toward the tornado raging above my head and swim within.

Either way, the choice is an axiomatic cul-de-sac.
Sweet Jesus, bring me back! Unshackle me from the air!
Ask the music to energize me one final time,
Reverse me through space, to the place where I thrived
At night's inception! I'll ask no questions, I promise,
Dear God, as to how You performed Your necromancy,

If You'll just get my head into alignment with the life
I left so completely by accident. Do You care?
Can You share my enigmatic fear? I've never been here,
And without marked exits, only the notes can save me.
Now, the sounds wind down; the shadows give way to light.
Syncopation catches up with my slowing heart's metronome.

Nights in white satin parade before my mind's tired eyes;
They dance naked inside the synthesizer that takes me
Into its baffles. My mind is being remixed a thousand ways,
Into shapes imploding in all directions as they slowly return
To the design of my original being. I can sing the words
That confirm me, once again, as a whole soul ready for sleep.

Softly, the notes whisper me into myself. The spider dies
Biting itself, while I emerge purged and unconcerned
About my future. Silence conveys me, whole, toward you, time,
Whom I'd lost. Your quiet beating leads me to myself,
And I realize time is now. I am *now* and *evermore*,
Eternal as any moment I recognize as infinite, and evanescent

As the fading overtones that took me astray. Night ends
In day's beginning. Keyboards no longer own me,
Nor do strings strangle me in their intricate digital scoring.
I'm free to return to the inconvenient routines of survival,
Very careful of every step I take, not anxious to trap myself
In the synthesizer's vibrations or die in its atavistic climax.

6/7/76 — [4] (00330)

Country Cemetery

Just off Highway 50,
Two miles east of Tipton,
Down a gravelly road dividing cows
From wheat, corn from more corn,
The Midwest lies at rest.

Tin windmills,
Long ago emptied of song,
Keep watch for resurrections.
Field wrens and meadowlarks
Gently flagellate the still air;

Their elegiac wings
Are voices whispering musical eulogies
Over green, seething fields.
A cast-iron pump,
Stranded like a nameless statue

In the middle of this vast countryside,
Waits patiently for a shape
To remember it to its task.
I grasp its pitted handle
To see how much it's forgotten.

The water its spout finally speaks
Is an oracle deeply drawn
*

From souls sleeping beneath my feet.
As their words splash my flesh,
I realize they're alive today

Yet choose to withhold judgment
On those still too busy dying.
They thrive on silence, in wet soil,
Where their seeds, though planted
In a hundred different seasons,

Keep growing older each year
Without really growing at all.
My eyes gather in their names and dates
As part of the sweetest harvest
Ever taken from this land.

And as I stand out here, alone,
Their blood circulating through my veins,
My heart renews acquaintanceships
Made, in an ancient time,
With tillers of the tribe of Abraham.

6/8/76 (00140)

The Isle of Lesbos ^Δ

Like finding a dock in the ports of Genoa
And Marseilles, it's impossible
To locate a place to park on this lot.
Beer cans, tabs, glass bottles
Label all the pavement not taken up
By early-morning regulars
With a glinty skull and bones.

I abandon my vessel at the far edge
Of a universe bordered by timothy
And an eroded row of corn
That never accepted its seeds,
Then trip through the debris
Left last night by recent graduates
Of the single high school in town.

Inside, the air is rife with sounds
Scented with hog-trough badinage,
*

Raillery derived from fantasies
Spawned by staying too long
Behind a snorting tractor's wheel,
And cant indigenous to Tipton politics,
In which the victor is nonexistent,

While those he represents go unscathed
By the public indignation they create.
Just now, debates progress
On the life expectancy of private enterprise
In light of higher taxes,
The probability of drought repeating
Last year's debacle, livestock inoculations,

And the enigmatic circumstances intruding
On the unusual case of Red Brewster's
Recent suicide. Speculation runs high
In favor of his wife's estrangement
And abrupt separation of all ties
To take up residence in Vegas,
With a flashy man of vague credentials.

Some conjecture payments come due
On the machinery to make a thousand acres
Produce couldn't be met or postponed
Beyond certain dates. Others scoff
At the basically weak son-of-a-bitch
They always imagined he was underneath
The layers of his outrageous pride.

Brewster's eulogy concludes with silence,
As if every head were bowed prayerfully
Instead of raised in restless attentiveness
To survey two lake tourists
Who've strayed into the café for breakfast.
All eyes line up identically,
Like slot-machine reels on bell-fruits,

As one, then another, recognizes the lady
Wearing leggy shorts, dyed-blond hair
To be the wife of their fated friend,
Red Brewster. Although they strain
To identify her companion, it's obvious
By the unconcerned way both hold hands
That strange demons they've never considered

Somehow invaded a neighbor's house.
Rarely have any of them ever discussed
The stuff of such medieval plagues
Or the possibility of disgusting succubi
Disrupting the peaceful relationship
Of man and wife in their lushy Arcadia.
Eventually, the uneasy hush

Slides back into characteristic persiflage,
Except that all laughter has ceased.
By tentative degrees, the men leave.
As though forced to pay homage,
Each must pass the two ladies at the table,
Who continue their intimacies unabashed.
Each looks back once in disbelief.

6/9/76 — [1] (00128)

Hazards and Satisfactions ^Δ

For Don Finkel,
    whose admiring pupil I'll always remain

It seems I'm always in flight,
Straying from seclusion,
Ranging deep into desolated regions
Where metaphors lie on the ground
Like locust husks hastily abandoned.

Today, I trip gracelessly,
Trying to find my way home
Through the brittle debris
Of naked, sleeping configurations,
And stop briefly to pick one up.

Resting it gently in my eyes' palm,
I inspect the unmolested emptiness
It protects against elements
Threatening to assimilate it into forgetting.
Immediately, I begin filling the vessel

With cells from my own lonely blood
And breath unused as yet
By the brain's extra set of lungs.
*

It beats slowly at first, uncertainly,
Then achieves my nodal sympathy.

The heat it generates burns me,
And I throw my hands high,
Forcing it, like an unnetted butterfly,
To assume the air independently.
All afternoon, I track its path

Back across my mind as it soars
Over a corpse-filled land
Of unfamiliar metaphors, beyond the kingdom
From which I originally began,
To the house poetry built barehanded for me.

6/9/76 — [2] (00331)

Her First Playmate ^Δ

For Jack and Ann Clay,
such gentle people

One slumberous May evening,
When the grass was still exceedingly green,
Faintly scented with sun-seeds
And the beginnings of moon-peppers,

And the twilight was an exposed aviary
Containing the sweetest glissandi of robins,
Peacocks, and fertile mind-birds
Escaped from Hesperian apple trees,

Trilogy and I, hand in tiny hand,
Descended into the dream-tinged landscape
Of our spacious backyard
To follow a "wild" rabbit we'd spied

Eyeing us unself-consciously
From the nearby confines of its docility.
Almost asking to be captured,
It scurried three times around a pine,

As if trying to let our shadows,
Chasing immediately behind,
And the baby's projected shrieks
Override its instincts for survival

From predators and overtake
Its natural tendency to remain free.
Every time she'd reach out
To touch its fluffy white scut,

The creature would capriciously tease her
With an unexpected leap to one side,
Then be away to a new location,
Leaving her dumbfounded and stupefied.

Finally, the "bunky" disappeared
Beneath a caliginous honeysuckle.
She bent down on stubby knees
To see into the mysterious dissolve,

Determine where it was hiding
And why its substance had changed shapes
With the shrub's too-sweet perfume.
Only, nothing moved except bees

Occasionally buzzing by to pollinate
The white blooms surrounding her.
After that, she seemed to lose interest
In the night. Her spirits tired

Of the entire outside environment,
And we retreated silently,
Through a yawny, lunar half-light,
Into presleep routines and bed.

Now, every evening after supper,
When we traipse across the lawn,
Trilogy evokes her old playmate,
And that rabbit is never far away.

6/12/76 — [1–2?]   (00768)

Supersonic Jet ^Δ

Passing two

Her breaking the barrier between sounds
And conscious formulation
*

Was that of a jet racing ahead
Of its own invisible reverberations.

When I attempted to locate our baby
By my memory of old speech patterns,
Only their insubstantial echoes
Clung, like contrails, to my imagination.

Her actual groundspeed
Had eluded my constant perceptions
And my ability to cope with growth
As a series of destinations.

She hadn't shown me her flight plan.
When she said, "No hands, Dad,"
As I wrapped myself around her,
And cried, "Baby do it,"

While I tried to lighten her burden
Of learning certain concepts
For the first time, I felt trapped,
As if in wing-tip vortices

She was emitting as she passed me by.
Now, I look below, into the sky,
Through whose magnificent sphere
She flies at preassigned altitudes,

And realize that glimpses may be all
We're entitled to grasp with creatures
So shimmering, glimpses seized
When she lands near us to refuel.

6/12/76 — [1–2?]   (00767)

Father's Day 1976 ^Δ

For my dear father, Saul

I fumble for visions to enunciate,
Symbols to elucidate,
Fresh metaphors to reshape
*

A hundred times more beautifully
Than originally they existed
In their flat, factual states.

Yet actual images of suitcases,
Perforated wing-tip shoes,
A black attaché,
Cashmere overcoats, and dress hats
Press turgidly to the surface
Of my murky brain today.

Real images of overnight trains
Racing by vacant stations,
Through landscapes vaguely familiar,
As if attached to the isinglass strip
Of a continuously spinning
Praxinoscope . . .

Images of smoke-belching trains
Tracking dusk and dawn,
By inches, across the window
Of a private drawing-room compartment
Keep assailing my memory;
They beg me to climb aboard.

Images of upper and lower berths,
Drop-lid washbasins,
Brass clothing and towel racks,
Tiny fans with rubber blades
Protruding like ears,
And tables appearing mysteriously

From hidden wall slots
Become the intricate pieces
Of a Chinese puzzle
My eyes slide back and forth,
Trying to penetrate secrets
Locked inside the mind's depot.

Even images of passenger trains
Backing in after waiting
Interminably in colossal yards
For GG-1s or switchers
To stitch them into a gate
Pervade this Saturday morning,

Twenty-five years down the line,
With something memory defines
As afterglow and rarely recaptures
When all its locomotives
Have been dismantled and scrapped
And all its travelers retired.

Still, images of you, Dad,
A fastidious student of trends,
Abstract artist of concrete profits,
Spending endless hours, en route,
Behind work papers
To spare me your insecurities,

Flood my astonished eyes.
I weep silently on realizing
That the simulacra of my youth
Are fastened entirely to you, Dad.
Visions, symbols, and metaphors
Pale before this simple truth.

And as I lean over the railing
Of a swaying observation car
To taste the old roadbed again,
I see you waving just up ahead.
Without hesitating, I pull
The emergency brake and leap off.

6/19/76 (00332)

Joseph K. Awakens ^Δ

The sluggish eyes' time locks
Reluctantly arrive, again,
At their preset opening hour.
Silent dials spin, while tumblers
Drop, weightless as racing pistons,
To the base of the brain's vault.

The lids draw back on invisible hinges,
Exposing the irises to visions
*

Of office clerks, secretaries, and inspectors,
In dress shirts and worsted suits,
Preparing to audit the inventory
On residual ghosts from my night depository.

Only, on closer examination,
The shelves are empty. Toward the back,
Where the protective wall is retina,
A minuscule fissure suggests entry
By devious means or leaking of humors
That keep images from drying out and dying.

Consternation pollutes the pristine crew
Come to check my new day's ledgers.
The huge imbalance can't be justified
As mere deficit from mistaken calculations.
They regroup and hastily conclude
That a major embezzlement has occurred.

I arise and stand naked among them,
Trying to fathom their unreasonable concern.
It's been years since I've placed savings
In sleep's bank or received interest
At a rate of return worth investing dreams
In high-risk, low-yield bonds of faith.

Why they've come, this morning, early,
Without warrants for search and seizure
Or even for my arrest
Is beyond comprehension. Yet I shiver
Under their accusative scrutiny
As if I were guilty of a spurious felony

And plead *nolo contendere* unsuccessfully.
Who these people are, why sent
And by whom, escape my finest logic,
Transform what was a routine awakening
Into a gloomy litany of court proceedings
Against me. I'm the key witness

For my own self-defended trial,
Testifying as to my innocence, rebuking allegations
That somehow I've been swindling my life
Of its precious possessions, robbing it
*

Of essential opportunities for dividends
By denying fears and frustration a foothold.

Honorable members of the jury, judge,
I refuse to accept your votes of guilt
As absolute, impartial, or divinely final.
You bastards! Get your sweaty hands
Off my neck! Let me loose, you idiots!
Hey, you're sick! Where are you taking me?

Son-of-a-bitch! That noose!
Hey, I'm as innocent as any of you guys!
Jesus! I told you I refuse to allow you
To involve me in such carping foolishness!
My neck's overheating my head to bubbling!
Ah, death! At last, I'm free to dream!

6/23/76   (00333)

Résumé of a Scrapegoat

Every highway I drive,
With station wagon straining to contain goods
Brought up out of steerage,
Is Hester Street,

And I'm the displaced waif
A hundred ancient diasporas left behind
To hawk rags and stitched shit
Made in sweltering lofts and dank basements.

I'm the entremanure of flawed raiment,
Remainders dead as flounder
Stacked flat on shelves
Or hanging in static masses from racks

The lowest class capitalist,
Searching low and lower for newer Laputas
In whose depraved precincts
I might display my thieves' market.

I'm the wide-smiling, gold-filled mouth,
The glistening, beady eye,
*

The hooknosed, seven-foot shadow
That demonizes Teutonic children's dreams,

The eternal, stereotypical victim
Hanging by my three pawned balls
Outside the emporium with shattered plate glass,
Cluttered with xenophobic bigotries.

I'm the scrapegoat for last season's guilt,
Soiled hopes, dreams with tiny holes,
Spirits returned for overlooked defects,
Mismatched leisure lifestyles,

The robber baron impeding competition
By fixing prices on perfects
I label "Irregular" and flawed garments
I advertise as "Grade A" merchandise.

History's kiss has touched my lips
With the viper's flicking tongue,
Singled me out from the crowd
To toil in dirty gutters and alleys

With cunning and guile, quietly,
By the sweat of my Semitic brow,
While crawling naked on my scaly belly
To avoid being swastikaed by sign crews

Gluing posters, on every available board,
With news of another outlet-store
Or wholesale-chain opening
In a strip mall or shopping center. Amen.

Shit! I'd give my eyetooth
Just to be the solid-gold watch
Tucked neatly in Pierpont Morgan's
Well-stretched Protestant vest pocket,

Instead of a thimble-fingered tailor
Drawing chalk lines and pinning seams
Across the whim of every fat ass
Able to afford his own graded patterns.

Yet history's also nourished me
With fruits from the tree of life eternal.
I've peddled myself from one generation
To the next, a perpetual hand-me-down,

Promoting my own brand of survival
At cut-rate prices, offering my soul,
On a moment's notice, to anyone
Who'd wear robes like those I sewed for Moses.

6/25/76 — [1]   (00089)

Friday Night Exodus △

By sheer instinct, I leave the downtown,
Fearing for my existence
All the way out, following blindly
The steely, serpentining machines
Holding a death grip on each other
At least twenty-five miles tight.
Their direction and destination squeeze me
Between my squinty eyes
To see what weaknesses might exist.
Meanwhile, the sun's scroll saw
Cuts intricate designs on retinal linings
That form portieres ornamenting doorways
Of the mind. Each mile traveled
Becomes a new room I superficially inspect,
Then forget, in my frenzied search
To find similar highway signs
And familiar streets leading me home.

Only, the traffic going toward Memphis
Scrambles my sense of direction.
My brain is heavy with dangling leeches
From having waded in late afternoon's bog.
Escape is a mere antiphon
My lips mumble without knowing why.
Freedom has apparently been captured
Without even putting up a defense.
A safe return to illusion
Is an absurdity as perfectly complete
In its convolution as a Möbius strip.
Reaching for straws to stay afloat,
I tread in the downtown overflow,
Just as the exit that owns me
*

Rises in the distance, then fades behind
As I continue on, in a numb seizure,
Toward the flood's cresting edge, and drown.

6/25 — [2] & 6–7?/76 (00334)

Returning to the Roots ^Δ

For Margaret and Harry Hofmann,
who gave me their love, the prairie,
and their daughter Jan

In this sacred land my mind cultivates
Behind the eyes' double-trace plow,
Granite boulders, haphazardly asleep
In the green countryside we leave,
Dissolve, like powder, into prairie cows
Merely by our taking to the highway
That ends eventually at poetry's door.

Trees metamorphose into cornstalks
Neatly rowed; soybeans and wheat,
Growing rife in black, alluvial soil,
Replace the copious roadside flowers
And weeds that touched us with color;
Crowded houses become isolated farms
Connected by barbed-wire telephone lines.

Only the sky recites the same vapors
From its beautifully illuminated Book of Hours,
While even the sun sacrifices some
Of its intensity, genuflecting westerly
Within the apse afternoon shapes like a robe
Over the body of quiet reveries
We send out ahead to guide us home.

Perhaps it's the changes occurring
Perceptibly,
Mile by mile, that, on our arriving
At our destination, finally awaken us
To the fact that the objects themselves
Are essentially static
And that we've been deceived

By our active imaginations
Into believing that every alteration
To the landscape happens continuously,
By natural design. Perhaps,
On the other hand, it's this stasis
That makes us aware of the need
To create a changing environment

For our shifting lives to accommodate
The meters motion generates
Whenever we go in search of roots
And find ourselves momentarily displaced
By mirages lifting off city concrete
And abstract seas washing prairie shores
In this sacred land, where metaphors thrive.

6/27/76 (00335)

Odysseus: Severe Thunderstorm Watch Extended Indefinitely △

The broken sky is awash
With myriad sulfide marbles
Whorled, swirling vortically.
I see children, above me,
Concentrating on moving their pieces
Strategically. The prairie whispers
With distant suggestions of thunder,
As soybeans and wheat stalks
Flick like snake tongues
In the superheated breeze
That forages ahead of the storm.
Yellow and blue cornflowers,
Maroon clover blooms
Buffer me from the seething crops,
Keep us from discussing precautions
Against flash flooding.
When I look up,
All the glass balls,
Exotically designed from inside,
*

Have fused into a moving mass
Of translucent plastic. I see
An eye, then Cyclops,
Hovering monolithically as a cliff,
Colossal, vagrant, bellicose,
Looking down at me, with rage,
Out of his leaking orbit,
And I pray that the stones and debris
He's wrenched from the sky's boneyard
Won't devastate my tiny ship,
Wallowing in Midwestern seas.
I cringe from images of bleeding
To death by lapidation.
Puny anathemas I hurl
Fail to obfuscate his vision.
Out here, hiding
Is merely a wide absurdity.
Escape escapes me. The storm
Becalms my vessel at roadside,
Where I try to ride it out,
Waiting to discover what reparations
The monster will demand for my annoying him.
After an hour, I resume
My journey home. Ahead,
Just past a curve,
An overturned tractor-trailer
Burns out of control,
Its cab completely smashed
As though hit by an invisible boulder
Rolled purposely into the road.

6/28/76 — [1] (00336)

Una noche oscura del alma*

Otra vez, yo empiezo . . .
Wait! Wait one blessed moment!
There's just no way
My brain can be Lope de Vega's,
Rubén Darío's, *y* García Lorca's
A la vez.

Idiomatic cadences break down.
My racing mind trips
Over accented diphthongs,
Gets lost in caesuras,
Run-on lines, elided rhymes,
And feminine endings bending sensually

To receive exclamation points from behind,
While trying to squeeze meaning
From phonetic, poetic rinds
Floating facedown in *sangría*
That fills my vascular imagination.
Every endeavour *yo trato de crear*

Termina en conquistas dolorosas
En que la víctima es siempre el poeta mismo.
Self-discovery fails to coalesce
Either before or after reaching climax.
The seeds of creativity wither
Like overripe olives in dry heat.

¡Jesucristo! ¡Ave María!
Why did I perjure myself
Before *los jueces de la Ciudad*
De Poesía Mística? *¡Ay, Dios mío!*
¿Dónde está mi mente,
Y por qué existe mi alma?

Yo pensaba que Tú, Dios mío,
Habías decidido protegerme
Contra los deseos del Diablo.
Pues entonces, ya yo no sé
Lo que significan the flames of Beelzebub,
Nagging like hot gnats at my brain.

What in hell didn't I do
To deserve such a disgraceful fate
As to remain *anónimo* even to myself?
Why can't I prize free
The leeches attached to my lungs
And breathe *el aire puro de los ángeles*?

¡Calderón, San Juan, Santa Teresa,
Escúchenme! ¡Recúerdenme! ¡Contéstenme
Cuando yo les llamo!
*

¡Necesito su ayuda, seguramente!
Speak! Tell me you recognize me!
Speak, beggars! I need you

To confirm my precarious authenticity
As a poet of the soul, *el sensible*
Crying tears for us all,
Carrying forth your traditional orthodoxies
Through our years of rampant anomie.
Tell me I'm worthy of your beads.

¡Silencio! ¡Su silencio me mata!
I feel my being spinning, levitating,
Soaring toward a hovering halo.
Ahora, yo entro y veo cuerpos,
Huesos y cajas llenas de polvo.
With preposterous familiarity, they beg me

To lie down beside them forever,
Under the vault where they've rested
Unmolested for three hundred years.
La resistencia se vuelve imposible.
La sangre corre por los pies,
Por los ojos. La cabeza se rompe.

Los pedazos caen por todas partes,
And no matter what I do
To regain integrity, my blown composure
Restrains me from collecting my wits,
Literally. Disintegration is concluded.
The fate for ambitiousness is banishment to Hades.

As I wait to make the endless journey,
The sky surrounding me fractures.
Through a fissure, some unseen force
Extrudes my mind. I feel a strange rescue
Being formulated, occurring exclusive of me.
I am helpless to deduce a meaning

From what is happening to me gratuitously.
Todo lo que yo sé es sencillamente
Que, evidentemente, las fuerzas del destino
Me han juzgado inocente or harmless.
Cualquiera que sea la razón, aunque no obvia,
It must be that I pose no threat

To their already-made sacred reputations.
So I return from the depths, unpurged,
Dry, tired, discouraged, beyond words,
From making further incursions to the core,
Where new languages are constantly forming
To revitalize hopes of keeping poetry alive.

[See Appendix 1 for poem's translated version]

6/28/76 — [2] (00337)

Catching Fireflies ᐃ

A murky dusk announces us to each other
And to the night bending slowly over
Into shadows under which we snuggle,
Waiting for the first emergence of lightning bugs.

As the grass grows imperceptibly moist,
We stand at impasse, exhorting our daughter
To be patient. We hand her a glass jar,
Its lid hastily ventilated by a nail,

And ask her to imagine it filled with moons.
Soon, as if humming an inaudible villanelle,
The first firefly becomes a welding tip,
Lifts invisibly from the lawn, straight up,

Hovers, dissolves in the trees, leaving its dot
As an indelible spot on our memories. Suddenly,
Shooting stars shower our backyard.
Our child runs wild, trying to capture one,

Pull it down from her head-high sky,
Keep it within the grasp her eyes circumscribe.
Missing the elusive insects, she chases to the edge
Of her expectations, then hands the task to her mother.

Within minutes, the vessel is a blinking neon
Projecting, in a logo she alone can decipher,
Delights from previous worlds she's known.
Such brilliantly dazing phosphorescences

Presage sleep for our mesmerized child.
They've touched her brain with persisting moon-dust,
Painted her dreams with dizzying possibilities
For discovering scintillating visions of paradise.

As night resumes its own conversation
Between fleeting flashes and sweeping beacons,
We open the door to the dream's next morning,
Where white rhinos and unicorns already cavort.

6/28/76 — [3] (00769)

Seeking Asylum $^\Delta$

Converging at the edges of metaphor,
Setting webs behind them to snare the curious
Daring to venture too close to explore their recent remains,
The excommunicated poets depart their minds
For saner times, richer environs, climes
More conducive to their peculiar predispositions,
Beyond traditional poetry, where they've lived
With their flaccid mistresses for the last fifty years.

Precariously, one at a time, they cross a hemp bridge
Connecting two sides of an endlessly deep gorge,
On whose invisible floor ossify the bones of giants
That once roamed the land without foe. They climb,
By means of picks, specially fastened shoes, and a rope
Connecting each to the other, a raw-edged mountainside
To horizon's equator, before descending into the land
Where Amazons run and bathe naked under the sun.

Once arrived, and growing accustomed to the thin air
In which their psyches must survive, the displaced poets
Begin to touch, taste of the paradisiacal fruits everywhere profuse.
Nothing profane infiltrates their one-to-one discoveries
Of nature, as it did back in their Academy days.
Pomegranates and figs, female voluptuousness, blond hair
Are sensual and immediately accessible and palpable.
Women bare themselves continually for no other motive than lust.

What kind of strange place would permit them
Firsthand tactile exposure they can't even describe?
*

Here, for some reason, they feel perfectly free to poeticize
Without being abstruse, recondite, or using ancient allusions
To Homer and obtuse Schopenhauer. What seems to be *is*,
Without the slightest equivocation; what might be
Has no chance of becoming mere symbol, simile, or allegory
Unless it can offer credentials of the strictest breeding.

Suddenly, from nowhere, an unannounced blast
Rocks the planet to which the world's foremost poets
Have immigrated. Plaster pulls away; lava boils;
All the temples and grots collapse like a dream
Reaching sleep's waking surface. The men cringe with chagrin,
As if their defection had finally been noticed,
As though a magnetic force were wrenching them back
To plead guilty to charges of disloyalty and heresy.

Fearing for their existence, they pack up their books
And manuscripts, bid farewell to their dappled ladies,
Head toward the fabled mountain, and cross over
The rope bridge, one poet at a time. By cover of night,
Exhausted, they sneak into the City of Poetry, where stands
The Academy, inviolate and unquestioned, ready to accept them
Despite their daring trespasses. Yet to set an example,
Token punishment and minimal bail will have to be set.

First, a trumped-up crime must be carefully determined,
Since, in their native land, nothing is as it seems to be.
Next, plea bargaining and out-of-court settlement
Will have to be publicized in the media. Possibly,
Even a change of venue will occur before they are finally freed
On their own recognizance, having promised, in writing,
That everything they create will meet the state's standards
For fashionable, footnoted poetry readable only by those

Sufficiently trained in the arts of obfuscation
And pedantical cant. Reluctantly, they acquiesce,
On threats of extinction and subsequent systematic anonymity.
They begin again, the very next morning, translating pornography
Into Sanskrit, French graffiti into Egyptian hieroglyphics.
They convert the Dead Sea Scrolls into dirty vulgate
To amuse the newly elected senators of the dominion
And interpret the Torah as a work of pre-Mosaical origination.

Finally, the years advance them quietly toward senescence.
Their youthful revolt slips memory and eludes its shadows
*

And is completely rewritten to suggest that they are survivors
Of early expeditions in the name of the state, that they failed
To stake new claims for their established modes of poetry.
In their dotage, they've become laureates and venerable practitioners
Where their craft is still emulated and pursued by certain few.

No one recalls their attempt to escape the planet,
Their fabulous exploits in the land of touch and taste,
Their ladies who knew orgasm as a matter of course,
Without being forced by pill or mind-speak or rote memory.
In solitude, one by one, each member of the expedition dies,
Taking with him secrets of the metaphor in which people
Could remain themselves while being transformed, simultaneously,
Into flying fish, carpenters, or sons of a God not yet dreamed.

6/28/76 — [4] (00338)

Slipping Slowly Out of the Cradle
   Endlessly Rocking

What, this early, could possibly cause
One escaped verse from all Walt Whitman
To disturb my drowsy journey to the city?
What, if not a curse of some kind,
Lingering like a fading highway sign
Along the road up out of sleep,
Could persist in its off-key glissandi?
"Out of the cradle endlessly rocking"
Calls me to an antiquated cabin
My mind has constructed over the years,
Cutting, scraping, planing, and notching logs,
Placing them in crisscross fashion
To form an image that might house my curiosity.

My eyes attach themselves, like leeches,
To the pendular indentations etched on air
By the cradle's pair of end posts.
My ears bend into its inoffensive screeching
Of unoiled hinges and swivels, whose complaints
Are minute detritus caught in a wind's wash.
*

I listen intently for any clue
To who might be summoning me, just now,
From the grave's shadow, looming there,
Century-deep, waiting for my mind to arrive.
Ultimately, I'm reminded of the lullaby
Every mother has sung to every child
To coax sleep, sieve demons

That cling to tired, helpless, pristine minds,
And the prayer taught son and daughter
To assuage the excitable angels of Thanatos.
My tongue recites words it's heard:
"When the bough breaks, / the cradle will fall, /
And down will come baby, / cradle and all";
"If I should die before I wake, /
I pray the Lord my soul to take."
These lines begin to repeat themselves
Like driving wheels of a steam locomotive
Overcoming inertia. They revolve,
Until their increasing speed churns the verses
To scintillant glints of light and sparks

Ricocheting off my darkling thoughts.
I envision the endlessly rocking cradle
Situated beside a freshly dug grave.
As it swings, I recognize my own face
Changing, moment to moment, with each completion
Of its full arc, as if recorded indelibly
On a rotating Mutoscope reel.
My features, a hundred million times evolving,
Focus my entire existence on this instant.
Suddenly, I see the child inside me
Motioning he's ready to fly home,
Hoping to make room for the next soul
Waiting impatiently to be born again.

The weeping I originally mistook as tires
Whining on concrete floods my head
With ice-white light. The voice of my genes
Begs me surrender my manhood,
Return to my ancestors. I sing my bones a lullaby.

7/1/76 — [1] (00339)

Knights Convene at the Castle $^\Delta$

Once again, the men return to the roundtable
To rehearse complaints about late deliveries,
Credit cancellations, miscalculated styles and ranges
Over- and underproduced against last fall's bookings.

All are knight-errants, trained, in territories
Various as their chivalric mentalities, to compete
For increasing leisurewear sales and reorders.
They've come to preview the new season's offerings,

Make suggestions according to the gospel
Of St. Ego, assimilate the hype being generated
From the throne, and transfer it into excitement
That will help defeat foes who, like themselves,

Are agents of laissez-faire free enterprise.
As proponents of integrity in men's clothing,
They do battle for the honor of Queen Rag,
A marchioness among scrubby wenches.

On disbanding this three-day meeting,
Each avenger will go on the road, well fortified
In chain-mail paraphernalia. Suitcases
And saddlebags bulging with samples and coded recaps

Afford them the weapons sufficient to defend
The fickle lady they zealously worship,
Who is forever threatened by competitive forces
That shrink from view whenever they make the scene

Yet thrive behind sumptuous luncheons,
Free baseball tickets, fifty-cent cigars,
And off-price promotional goods
Enticing enough to undercut superior fabrications

These Knights of the Tailor's Bench offer
Their "fair-weather" trade. When they're successful,
The rewards are window displays, floor space
In major countrywide resource-staging areas,

Where serfs and vassals alike congregate
To purchase their emblems of national security,
And an impeccable, unassailable reputation
For good values, well-made, of domestic origination.

Now, they listen attentively to their king
As he describes an ambitious new enemy,
Who has been ravaging prostitutes and baronesses,
Lieges and plowmen, indiscriminately.

Something about its ruthlessness confounds plans
To counterattack and defend against expectations
For the new season. None of the men
Can forecast the lasting effects of inflation.

Even the king can do nothing except admonish them
And demand that each of his soldiers of fortune
Be alert to prevailing soft-market conditions
Shifting fortuitously on the winds of fashion.

Finally, they disperse to search out alternatives
And fly in the face of discouraging odds.
Dragons are scratching at the queen's door.
The knights' task is to keep her chastity intact.

7/1/76 — [2] (00340)

Dissecting Fogs △

Leaving town, early this morning,
I drive through two fogs.
One hovers in the vacuum
Between a too-humid earth-blanket
And cooler stratosphere;
The other is sleep-induced,
Produced by the slow-spinning dynamo,
Forty feet cerebral,
That powers the awesome needs
Of the wakeful City of Being,
Where my feelings and physiology
Share an apartment with Psyche.
As I go forward, the fog lifts,
Locating me in a strange terrain
Swarming with migrating vehicles
Following lanes, termitelike,
To and from the earth, to the sky,
Past the horizon, beneath the surface,
Then back in every direction.

Soon, the shimmering cars are links
The sun delicately solders into a chain
Girding the planet in noisy gewgawgery.
My eyes strain to see who wears
Such colossal jewelry. A vision
Of this magnitude staggers my lobes.
I shake, imagining the creature
Great enough of height and mass,
Reposing in comatose and numb idiocy,
Sufficiently broad to take the weight
We collectively subject it to daily.
At once, I realize the creature is *us*,
The chain is man-made, the fog is
Administered humanely from time to time
To declaw reality's paws,
And that my yawns are safeguards
Against dying in a polluted nimbus
Of peaceful, breathing amnesias
While being deceived that I'm alive.

7/2/76 — [1] (00341)

Race Day ^Δ

The sedentary men loll on the sedgy edges
Of their fluid stream of collective consciousness,
Watching handmade racing boats
They launched some minutes upriver
Come down toward the finish line,
Gliding by them, on their own momentum,
Toward a plausible consensus by referees
Trained in decision-making and political favors.

Each heat is filled with skeptical questions,
Suggestions and complaints floated by contestants
Intent on winning and gaining a leading position
With their varying regional spectator trade.
As the vessels press to complete the course,
All eyes rest on watches and stock sheets
To register changes. Only one,
This runoff, will know the success of acceptance,

While all other entrants will collapse exhaustedly,
Slump deep into their shells briefly,
Until they recover from their exercise in futility.
Later, having gathered up all racing gear
And showered, they'll convene in relaxed amity
At the bar of the hotel where, for three days,
They've been staying on a company retainer
And discuss the results of the new season's line.

7/2/76 — [2] (02213)

Appendix 1 — Poem Translation

("*Una noche oscura del alma*," from pages 665 through 668,
with Spanish passages translated by Dr. José Schraibman)

A Dark Night of the Soul

Once again, I begin . . .
Wait! Wait one blessed moment!
There's just no way
My brain can be Lope de Vega's,
Rubén Darío's, and García Lorca's
All at once.

Idiomatic cadences break down.
My racing mind trips
Over accented diphthongs,
Gets lost in caesuras,
Run-on lines, elided rhymes,
And feminine endings bending sensually

To receive exclamation points from behind,
While trying to squeeze meaning
From phonetic, poetic rinds
Floating facedown in sangria
That fills my vascular imagination.
Every endeavour I try to make

Ends in sad conquests
In which the victim is always the poet himself.
Self-discovery fails to coalesce
Either before or after reaching climax.
The seeds of creativity wither
Like overripe olives in dry heat.

Jesus Christ! Hail Mary!
Why did I perjure myself
Before the judges of the City
Of Mystical Poetry? Oh, my God!
Where is my mind,
And why does my soul exist?

I thought that You, my God,
Had decided to protect me
Against the Devil's desires.
But then, now I don't know
What the flames of Beelzebub mean,
Nagging like hot gnats at my brain.

What in hell didn't I do
To deserve such a disgraceful fate
As to remain anonymous even to myself?
Why can't I prize free
The leeches attached to my lungs
And breathe the pure air of the angels?

Calderon, St. John, St. Teresa,
Listen to me! Remember me! Answer me
When I call you!
I need your help, surely.
Speak! Tell me you recognize me!
Speak, beggars! I need you

To confirm my precarious authenticity
As a poet of the soul, a sensitive one
Crying tears for us all,
Carrying forth your traditional orthodoxies
Through our years of rampant anomie.
Tell me I'm worthy of your beads.

Silence! Your silence is killing me!
I feel my being spinning, levitating,
Soaring toward a hovering halo.
Now, I enter and see bodies,
Bones and boxes full of dust.
With preposterous familiarity, they beg me

To lie down beside them forever,
Under the vault where they've rested
Unmolested for three hundred years.
Resistance becomes impossible.
Blood runs from my feet,
From my eyes. My head breaks.

The pieces fall everywhere,
And no matter what I do
To regain integrity, my blown composure
*

Restrains me from collecting my wits,
Literally. Disintegration is concluded.
The fate for ambitiousness is banishment to Hades.

As I wait to make the endless journey,
The sky surrounding me fractures.
Through a fissure, some unseen force
Extrudes my mind. I feel a strange rescue
Being formulated, occurring exclusive of me.
I am helpless to deduce a meaning

From what is happening to me gratuitously.
All that I know is simply
That, evidently, the forces of destiny
Have judged me innocent.
Whatever the reason, although not obvious,
It must be that I pose no threat

To their already-made sacred reputations.
So, I return from the depths, unpurged,
Dry, tired, discouraged, beyond words,
From making further incursions to the core,
Where new languages are constantly forming
To revitalize hopes of keeping poetry alive.

APPENDIX 2 — ACKNOWLEDGMENTS EXTENSION

Louis Daniel Brodsky compiled numerous books from 1967 to 1976. With the exception of two early texts (*The Foul Rag-and-Bone Shop* and *Points in Time*), a book about Florida and the Midwest (*Point of Americas II*), and his volumes of poems about his daughter's birth and early childhood (*Trilogy: A Birth Cycle*, *Monday's Child*, and *La Preciosa*), these manuscripts were chronologically arranged collections comprising nearly all of the poems written by Brodsky over periods spanning many months.

While Brodsky's first poetry manuscripts remained unpublished for decades, Farmington Press printed his volumes from the mid 1970s, offering them as signed, limited editions that featured cover art by Brodsky's wife, Jan. In the 1990s, Brodsky returned to all of these early books of poetry, both published and unpublished, to revise them for their release by Time Being Books.

The poems in volume two of the *Complete Poems* series that were comprised in these early Brodsky works are listed below, in the corrected order presented in the Time Being Books editions.

The following poems appear in the expanded version of *The Foul Rag-and-Bone Shop*, an aesthetically arranged volume that intersperses these pieces among seventeen of Brodsky's earlier poems (in volume one of this series), which he compiled into final manuscript form in 1969 and had published by Time Being Books in 1995:

> This Pendent World
> Indian Summer
> Morning's Companion
> Song
> Cycles
> Phantasms of Sleep
> The Nuptial Bower
> The Turning In
> Introit
> FDR Drive and 78th Street
> The Devil's Circus: Chicago, '68
> Visitation   *(00347)*˚

The following sixty-eight poems constitute the volume *Points in Time*, a collection, divided into geographical chapters, that Brodsky conceived as a book in 1971 but left unfinished until 1995, when Time Being Books released the first edition (with a second edition produced in 1996):

> The Fate of a Poet No Longer in Vogue
> The Golden Age
> In the Dying Hospital
> Pacemaker
> In the Dying Hospital II
> [Silence swings its pendulum]
> [The pewter heirloom hangs off to the right]
> [I cannot write. The mind gives in. . . .]
> Poet in Residence
> [I am all loving.]
> [He stands in his driveway, coffee in hand,]
> The Old Beauchamp Place
> 1513–1906

Song for Jan
[I taste this day!]
The Everlasting Nay
[A sick, thick aroma of quick-frying hotdogs]
The Funny House
[A naked Pharaoh kneels down to kiss the ground]
{As sure as I'm standing here now,]
[Through the glass I muse:]
[Already, since last night,]
The Point
The Fishing Dock
Invocation
Marianne   *(01058)*
Marianne   *(00011)*
The Onset
Pathétique
Vindication
The Sisters of Fiesole   *(01103)*
Marriage of the Shadows
Schoolteacher
Norrie
The Indisposed
A Valentine for Sir Kells
Retired   *(01098, with the title "Litany")*
[How I loved her!]
[Naked as an unnested sparrow,]
The Beautiful Flowers
Widow
The Garden
On Leaving a Flat River Motel
The High Side of Night
This Familiar House
The Landlocked
The Lynching
[A shabby darkness scars the ruffled shadows]
For Eldridge
Jan's Song   *(00105)*
Covenant
Buffy
Mistress Jan
Jack's Bight, Coconut Grove
Four Fragments for Jan / Prayer   *(0111 & 04671, comprised within one
    poem, titled "Five Fragments for Jan")*
For Jan
Jan
[Splinters, disintegration . . .]
Nocturne   *(01099)*
Unwed Seraph
The Progress of Dreams
After the Untimely Death by Conflagration That Occurred at 2:31 on
    Christmas Morning at the Home of J. Martin Brodsky, Involving
    the Father, a Widower, and His Two Daughters
Honeymoon   *(01112, with the title "Carnival's Midway")*
Night
Relics of a Crucifixion
The Baptism
The Tree of Temperance
A Divinity from Within   *(00692)*

These fifty-one poems form the whole of *Taking the Back Road Home*,
a chronological text, created in 1972, that remained unpublished until Time
Being Books' 1997 first-edition printing (with a second edition in 2000):

First Anniversary
A Divinity from Within   *(00351)*

Morning Climax
Premonition
Sunday Morning Has the Smell of Love
The Prisoners
Elegy
The *Wish Book*
Consortium
The Young People
The Lecture
The Actors
Dale's Poem
The Expectants
October
Autumnal
The Visit
Elegy for Mrs. Lycidas
To Love First Discovered in a Cold Country Cabin
A Belated Anniversary Gift
On Approaching Allhallows Eve
The Rise of Silas LeBaron, 1865–1929
Sleeping Man
Late-October Sunday Service
Taking the Back Road Home
Dr. Terraqueous
Ultimate October
Velocipede
A Valedictory Against Insensitivity
House Fly
The Slacks Factory of Farmington, Mo.
The Rough Beast
"Enlistment Notice" et al.
Three for Sister Dale
Bonfire
Above Love in Sausalito
Pescadero Beach
Endless December
The Other Woman
An Attack of the Heart
Deaf-Mutes
The Kiss of Oblivion
Each in Its Ordered Place
Death by Water
Sea Dogs in the New World
Reflections upon Waiting for a Patient to Return from Surgery, 1/11/72
Side Effects of Technology
Tomorrow's Leaders
King of Kings
Self-Recognition
As We Are

The following poems make up the body of *Trip to Tipton and Other Compulsions*, which was organized in 1973, when Brodsky gathered the sixty-eight chronological pieces, and published by Time Being Books in 1997:

Flight from New York to Lisbon
The Spanish Steps, 1725–1972
A Sunday Morning in Florence
Dopo il diluvio: Firenze
Marriage in the Basilica di San Marco Evangelista
End of April: Venice
J and the Beanstalk
Flight   *(03907)*
Looking Through Mutoscopes
Stillborn
Impasse

Peace Talks
Out with the New Line
Ernie Resides with the Angel of Grace
Jacksonville Reveries
Overview of the World Through a Dusty Window of the Tipton Drive-In
The Porch
Stopover   *(03917)*
Yearly Run
Overnight en Route
By Way of Explanation
Morning After the Grand Opening, Crystal Café, 6:30
The Poet
The Outlet Store
Intimations
The Olympics
Prayer   *(00014)*
Eating Place
4:10 Freight to K.C.
Taking Stock
The Returning
Epitaph
Rosehill Cemetery from the Air
Thirty Miles Southeast of Duluth
Thirty Miles Southeast of Duluth II
Sold Out
Jan's Song   *(03935)*
Lament
Passing
Hecht's Café
Calling Card
Sunday . . . Monday
Reverie
Crystal Café Clock
Confessions of a Traveling Salesman
Stopover   *(03943)*
The Last Breakfast
[This wayward conveyance guides me]
Interior Monologues
Truckers
The Auction: Setup
The Auction: Leaving the Village of St. Francois
The Auction: First Day
The Auction: Second Day
The Auction: Last Day
Rainy Drive
The Uncelebrated Ceremony of Pants-Factory Fatso
At Thirty-One
Intimations of Breughel
The First Snow
Sunday Dressed in Deathly Bunting
Thanksgiving Misgivings
Thanksgiving Day Parade
Checked Before Boarding
Privacy on a Crowded Beach
An Occasion for Flowers
Home for the Holidays
Heading Home

These fifty-three poems are comprised in *"The Talking Machine" and Other Poems*, a chronological manuscript compiled by Brodsky in 1974 and published by Time Being Books in 1997:

January 2, 1973
Buonarroti
The Coy Mistresses: A Persuasion to Love

Eulogy for Baker
[My wife rides beside me this morning.]
Butterfield Inn
Planting
Monday in Babylon
The Children of Messiah
Closing the Old Café, Opening the Butterfield Inn
Fugue
The Permanent Journey
Burlington House Viewed from a Tall Hotel
The Vapors
Jean
Up from Egypt
Sunday in the Flower Shop
The Fishing Club
Sunday from Hauser Hill
Radio Station Watergate
Breakfast Reflections
Genealogies
Private Judgments Made Public at the Butterfield Inn
Ahab's Obsession
Prague War Trials
A Stitch in Time
Smoke-Filled Rooms
Three-Day Sales Meeting
The Salesmen
The Impressionists
The Sales Meeting: Last Day
Three Anniversaries
The Turtle
Escape Artist
Evanescence
Trilogy *(03835)*
The Talking Machine
Friday Night Farmington
Just Jan and Me
Among the Chosen
Clockwork
A Time of Butterflies
Mardie and Lloyd
In the Ocean-Sea
Variations in Gray
His Vindication Speech
In Quest of Leviathan
[Always leaving by back doors]
Soap Opera
Reflections upon a Dubious Public Servant
We Are the Parents Our Children Become
Emergency
Dim-Lit Dinner

The following poems form the book *Tiffany Shade*, a fifty-one-piece chronologically sequenced manuscript assembled by Brodsky in 1974 and published by Time Being Books in 1997:

Flight from St. Louis to L.A.
The Friends
Evel Knievel
Growing Older
Soaring Home
Fisher of Men
Alphabets
The Catcher
[Hot-damn for handlebar mustaches]
[Can it be that man is still at work]
Cows

Sleeping Through
Visiting
Nocturne   *(04053)*
Reflections upon Finally Dreaming a Child into Being
Dedication to the Arts
Thanksgiving Day 1973
Traveling to the Capital City
Omens: On Dreaming a Child into Being
At the Midnight Hour
Looking Backward
Paolo and Francesca
La vida es sueño
Continuities
Litterbug
Staying Somewhere near New Athens
Dale
Drinking from the Edge of the World
Excommunicants on Christmas Morn
Bill
The Third Coming
Animus
Repossessed by the Devil
The Old Trouser Factory
Four-Way Stop
After Reading with Buck
Redemption
Skaters
Fueling and Loading
Dreaming the Artist into Being
Tiffany Shade
Skyscrapers
Carousel
The Ages of Man
Heiress and Novelist
The Magician's Demise
Eggshell and Tempera
Motel Stopover
KKK
Waybill
Thirty Years Has Janny

The following "baby poems" form the thematically structured, eighteen-piece collection *Trilogy: A Birth Cycle*, Brodsky's first published book, which was released as a signed, limited edition of three hundred copies in 1974, by Farmington Press, and as a second edition in 1998, by Time Being Books:

And Our Child Asks, "Where Did I Come From?"
Adoration
Crocheting Solomon's Seal
A Strange Kind of Birth
Cruise Ships
Vacation's End
Putting in the Garden
Crew Practice: A Reminiscence
Last Days Before the First Baby
Just Before Birth
Inducement
The Gathering of Pearls
Father's Den
Jan's Song   *(00451)*
Vestiges
First Feedings
Trilogy   *(00454)*
Going to the Land of Canaan

These forty-four poems appear in *Cold Companionable Streams* (a chronologically ordered manuscript that was compiled by Brodsky in 1975 and published by Time Being Books in 1999) and in the expanded version of *Preparing for Incarnations* (a chronological eighty-poem volume released by Farmington Press in 1976, as a signed, limited edition of five hundred copies, and by Time Being Books in 1999, as a second edition):

The Fourth Anniversary
The Tree of Everlasting Life   *(with the title "The Tree of Life" in CCS)*
The Everlasting No
Round Table Café
Plant Manager   *(00641)*
Theft
Islets in the Whirlpool
A Twilight Wedding
Passing of Orders
Stars for Juliet
Flat River
Rainmaker
The Navigator
Leaving Sleep
Buffalo
Grandfather
Haystacks
Gulliver's Discovery in the Land of Farmers
Lucifer's Crew
Ends of the Continuum
Tortoise and Hare   *(00126)*
Exeunt Omnes   *(with the title "Exeunt All" in CCS)*
Preparing a Shipment
The Open Road
Release in August
Exiles
Reunion
Rescue
Noche oscura del alma
Music, Wine, and Isolation
Up from the Land of Pharaoh
Cold Companionable Streams
A Decorated Veteran Returned Home
Unlaundered Accounts
Fission
Plant Manager   *(00667)*
Keeper of the Castle   *(with the title "Keeper of Yards" in CCS)*
The Ritual of Babbitt Arising
Ephemerae
Seducing the Muse
Gestalt
A Transcendental Fugue
Going Stale
Christ Sees Himself as a Poet

These "baby poems," divided into five parts and an epilogue, constitute the volume *Monday's Child*, Brodsky's second published book, which was printed by Farmington Press in 1975, as a signed, limited edition of three hundred copies, and issued as a second edition in 1998, by Time Being Books:

Paean to Jan and Trilogy
Their Song
Ex Utero
The Kingdom of Innocence

Waiting for the Final Release
Beginning to See
Necromancers
Her First Toy
Naked Baby Trilogy
Preliminaries
First Insights
Her Five-Month Birthday
Initial Stages of the Race
Suggestions
Visiting Grandparents
Rites of Baptism
On Looking into Baby Trilogy's Eyes
Just Crawling
Song for Trilogy
Not Only a Matter of Love
Soccer Practice: A Reminiscence
Mutoscope Reel
Entering Ten Months
Gentle Lamentations
The Golden Chain
Epilogue

The following poems appear in the original *Preparing for Incarna-
tions* (a chronological thirty-eight poem manuscript structured by Brodsky
in 1975 and published by Time Being Books in 1999) and in the expanded
version of that text, also titled *Preparing for Incarnations* (Brodsky's fifth
published book, which combines the whole of *Cold Companionable
Streams* and the original version of *Preparing for Incarnations*, exclud-
ing only two poems — "New Year's Celebration" and "The Orange Bowl"):

The Brief Ecstasy of Icarus's Escape   *(with the title "The Ecstasy of
    Icarus Ascending" in the original version)*
Supplemental Income
Phaëthon
Aging
The Truant
The Poet's Confession
Preparing for Incarnations
Plant Manager   *(00613)*
Divorcée
Manimals and Other Beasts
Time-and-Motion Analysis
The Foul Rag-and-Bone Shop
Epilogue to the Twenty-third Sermon   *(with the title "Epilogue to a
    Twenty-third Sermon" in the original version)*
Drizzle
Approach-Avoidance Conflict
Winter Catches the Moon in Its Teeth
The Dragon
Miscellaneous Man
A Christmas Eve Hymn
Pieceworkers
Intimations of Futility
Zola's Requiem
Florist Shop on the Square   *(with the title "Florist Shop on the Square:
    Looking Out" in the original version)*
Stranded
Pleasures
Sad Song of Ecstasy for Jan
Sowers, Reapers, and Gleaners
As Christmas Approaches
Flight   *(00633)*
A Sky Filled with Trees

Incarnations
Deep-Sea Charter
The Door
Knothole
New Year's Celebration
The Orange Bowl
Returning Home
The Closet

These forty-three chronological poems form *The Kingdom of Gew-gaw*, Brodsky's third published volume, which had its first-edition printing in 1976, with a signed, limited run of four hundred copies (produced by Farmington Press), and its second-edition release in 2000 (printed by Time Being Books):

Eternal Triangle
Weeping
Being Passed
Blind Milton Anguishes Between Poems
Son of the *Rachel*'s Captain
On Visiting the University Campus After Having Been Lost at Sea
   Nearly Seven Years
Weeding in January
Cynic
Demolition
Silhouettes
Queen of the Stardust Ballroom
Early Morning in the Kitchen
Snow
The Scribe
Plant Manager   *(00812)*
Remodeling
Disciples Gather at the Farmers' Lyceum
Paleontologist
Delay
New Orleans Sketches
Rebirth of the Blues
Sutpen's Grand Design
Hallucinations at Houlihan's Old Place
Balconies
Jennifer's Poem
Easter Flood
Easter Unobserved
Paean to Machines
Finding *The Marble Faun*
The Patient
Silences
The Books, the Woods, and Us
The Party Dress
The Captain Has a Close Brush
The Gardener
Left Behind
Helen Among the Twelve Disciples
Was
At Rest
Father's Day
The Poet Papers His Walls
Flowers for Pharaoh
Clothesline

The forty-one poems listed here constitute Brodsky's fourth published book, *Point of Americas II*, a thematically arranged volume with first and last sections focused on Florida and a middle section detailing

America's heartland, which was first printed in 1976, by Farmington Press, as a signed, limited run of four hundred copies, and released as a second edition in 1998, by Time Being Books:

Turnout
Arriving at Point of Americas II
Being Beach and Ocean
The Act of Writing
Still Life: Caladium
Point of Americas II: The Rocks
Walking the Beach
Port Everglades Nocturne
Waiting for the Sun
Wading into Sleep
Serene Flight
Mass: Easter Sunday
Sitting in Bib Overalls, Work Shirt, Boots, on the Monument to Liberty
   in the Center of the Square, Jacksonville, Illinois
A Sunny Pre-Easter Saturday in Town
Genesis of the Poet
Instructor and Pupil
Plant Manager   *(00717)*
Exponential Theories
Of Nomenclatures
The Poet Is Asked to Give a Reading
Van Buren Stop-Off: Commensalism
Pine Trees
The Blind Man, the Square, and Sunday Morning
An Early Muse Awakens
Coming Apart
God's Apostles
The Sisters of Fiesole   *(00726)*
Priestly Notions Suggested by a Recent Sales Meeting
Panning for Gold
Rent-Controlled   *(00342, with the title "Senescence")*
Song of Flight
Ancestry
Seascape
Changes in the Will
Spectator
Two Doctoral Candidates in English Meet on a Fort Lauderdale Beach
   over Spring Break
Doleful Day for a Sailboat Race
From Out of Nowhere
Leda Among Pelicans
My Flying Machine
The Voyage of A. Gordon Pym

The following twenty poems appear, along with thirteen later poems, in *La Preciosa*, Brodsky's sixth published volume, which was first released in 1977, by Farmington Press, as a signed, limited run of five hundred copies, and then printed as a second edition in 2001, by Time Being Books:

Still Crawling
Learning Languages
Time Is the Lady's Name We Gave Our Child
Retrieving Leaves
Exploration Party
Witnessing a Birth
The Dancers
Christmas 1975
Daddy's Turn

Great-Grandmother
Dawg-Dawg
On Leaving Home
A Gentle Lament
Visitation   *(00763)*
The Origin of Species   *(00764)*
Niña, Pinta, and *Santa María*
Suffragettes
Supersonic
Her First Playmate
Catching Fireflies

These forty-seven chronological poems constitute the book *Stranded in the Land of Transients*, Brodsky's seventh published volume, printed by Farmington Press in 1978, as a signed, limited run of five hundred copies, and by Time Being Books in 2000, as a second edition:

Willy
Rehearsing for a Public Reading
Midnight Blue
The Bindle Stiff
Memberships
Convergences   *(00206)*
Lepidoptera
Sales Meeting: The Spring/Summer Line
To Canaan and Back
Manager of Outlet Stores
In Praise of Epiphanies
Spider and Fly
Farmer Hades' Wife
Jacksonville, Illinois
Joseph K.
The Candidate
Visiting the Artist
Distress Message
Breaking Stallions
Willy's Evening Entertainment
Groupies
Blown Apart
Merchant Sailor
Race Day   *(00221)*
Word-Seeds
The Hours Call Out His Name
Mowing Crews
Ceaseless Weekend
Two Stones Cast in the Rain
The Casket Truck
Toasting an Old Foe
Firefighter
En Route
In Harvest Time
Death Comes to the Salesman
Closing In
Cellmates
Vicissitudes
Confirmed Bachelor
False Start
The Perfect Crime
Accident-Prone
Rearview Mirror
The Origin of Species   *(00239)*
Willy's Elegy
Energy Shortage
Letting Go the Moorings

The forty-six poems below form the chronological whole of *The Uncelebrated Cermony of Pants-Factory Fatso*, Brodsky's eighth published work, which Farmington Press produced in 1978, as a signed, limited edition of five hundred copies, and Time Being Books issued in 2001, as a second edition:

Survivor of the Ten Lost Tribes
The Passing of Orders
Waving Good-Bye
December's Trees
Triangles
The Wizard of Gewgaw
Narcissus Imprisoned
The Pioneer Spirit
Paean to Wordsworth
Turnkey
The Crows
Line Composed a Few Miles Above Christmas Eve
Cause and Effect
Cold Feet
Gone Visiting for the Day
Teleology
Time Assumes My Wife's Smooth Shape
Downtown Reverie
Hegira: Origins of Schizophrenia
Frozen
Elegy for a Child Prematurely Returned
Nickelodeon
Lemuel Gulliver Sets Out
Running in Packs
Herr Diogenes Teufelsdröckh
Willy's Fantasy
Factory
Convergences   *(00531)*
The Poet's Slatternly Verse
To His Coy Wife
Drummers Carousing in Surinam
The Funeral Procession
Rain Comes to Nourish a Dry Plain
Knight-Errant
The Flower Store
Outbound
The Half-Life of Dreams
The Cup of Life
Lazarus Being Raised from the Living
The Wandering Jew
Overtaken by Contagion
An Evening in the Trevi Bar
On First Turning Earth
In Quest of Destinations
Highway 185
The Exile's Return

The following twenty-seven poems, all of which appeared in earlier Brodsky books, as noted below, and in various journals, magazines, and anthologies, form *Birds in Passage*, Brodsky's ninth published volume (arranged by the dates the pieces appeared in the outside publications), which was printed by Farmington Press in 1980, as a signed, limited run of five hundred copies, and by Time Being Books in 2001, as a second edition:

Endless December   *(Taking the Back Road Home)*
Eating Place   *(Trip to Tipton and Other Compulsions)*
The Poet   *(Trip to Tipton and Other Compulsions)*

Dopo il dilùvio: Firenze   *(Trip to Tipton and Other Compulsions)*
Thanksgiving Misgivings   *(Trip to Tipton and Other Compulsions)*
Reverie   *(Trip to Tipton and Other Compulsions)*
Late-October Sunday Service   *(Taking the Back Road Home)*
Rent-Controlled   *(Point of Americas II)*
From Out of Nowhere   *(Point of Americas II)*
Jan's Song   *(00105, Points in Time)*
Schoolteacher   *(Points in Time)*
The Expectants   *(Taking the Back Road Home)*
Lament   *(Trip to Tipton and Other Compulsions)*
Visitation   *(00763, The Foul Rag-and-Bone Shop)*
A Sky Filled with Trees   *(Preparing for Incarnations [original & exp.])*
My Flying Machine   *(Point of Americas II)*
The Casket Truck   *(Stranded in the Land of Transients)*
Word-Seeds   *(Stranded in the Land of Transients)*
Buffalo   *(Cold Companionable Streams & Preparing for Incarnations [exp.])*
Weeding in January   *(The Kingdom of Gewgaw)*
Triangles   *(The Uncelebrated Ceremony of Pants-Factory Fatso)*
The Flower Store   *(The Uncelebrated Ceremony of Pants-Factory Fatso)*
Rearview Mirror   *(Stranded in the Land of Transients)*
Death Comes to the Salesman   *(Stranded in the Land of Transients)*
Easter Flood   *(The Kingdom of Gewgaw)*
Running in Packs   *(The Uncelebrated Ceremony of Pants-Factory Fatso)*
Ancestry   *(Point of Americas II)*

These forty-seven chronologically ordered poems constitute the book *Résumé of a Scrapegoat*, Brodsky's tenth published volume, issued by Farmington Press in 1980, as a signed, limited run of five hundred copies, and printed by Time Being Books in 2001, as a second edition:

[The years watch us changing in our seasons,]   *(00301, with the title "Omniscience")*
Portrait in Storm Time
Monday Night
My Thoughts Are Only Light-Years from God   *(00304, with the title "Under the Canopy of Heaven")*
Hirsute
Downpour
Redbuds
Gulliver's Departure
Scintillations
In a Daze
Flight from St. Louis to New York: A Microcosm   *(00308, with the title "Intimations of Dante")*
"The Wild Beasts"
A Moment of Solitude
Wednesday Matinée
The Masters Call Me to Their Service
Morning Flight
My Brother's Keeper
Machines in the Garden
Sartor   *(00317, with the title "Charitable Donation")*
The Sisters of Fiesole   *(00318)*
Testing Grounds
Table Scraps
Synesthesia   *(00322, with the title "Correspondences")*
Lobotomized
In Memoriam   *(00323, with the title "Road to Nowhere")*
In the Synagogue
Ode to a Barbecued Beef Tenderloin
One Last Time the Muse
Escapees
Between Connections
The Inconveniences of Immortality
Breaking Through

Kubla's Xanadu
Country Cemetery
The Isle of Lesbos
Hazards and Satisfactions
Father's Day 1976
Joseph K. Awakens
Résumé of a Scrapegoat
Friday Night Exodus
Returning to the Roots
Odysseus: Severe Thunderstorm Watch Extended Indefinitely
Una noche oscura del alma
Seeking Asylum
Slipping Slowly Out of the Cradle Endlessly Rocking
Knights Convene at the Castle
Dissecting Fogs

Because two or more poems bear this title within volume two, the Time Being Books database tracking number is listed, to indicate the appropriate text.

INDEX OF TITLES

BIOGRAPHICAL NOTE

Louis Daniel Brodsky was born in St. Louis, Missouri, in 1941, where he attended St. Louis Country Day School. After earning a B.A., magna cum laude, at Yale University in 1963, he received an M.A. in English from Washington University in 1967 and an M.A. in Creative Writing from San Francisco State University the following year.

From 1968 to 1987, while continuing to write poetry, he assisted in managing a 350-person men's clothing factory in Farmington, Missouri, and started one of the Midwest's first factory-outlet apparel chains. From 1980 to 1991, he taught English and creative writing at Mineral Area Junior College, in nearby Flat River. Since 1987, he has lived in St. Louis and devoted himself to composing poems. He has a daughter and a son.

Brodsky is the author of forty-two volumes of poetry (five of which have been published in French by Éditions Gallimard) and twenty volumes of prose, including nine books of scholarship on William Faulkner and four books of short fictions. His poems and essays have appeared in *Harper's*, *The Faulkner Review*, *Southern Review*, *Texas Quarterly*, *National Forum*, *American Scholar*, *Studies in Bibliography*, *Kansas Quarterly*, Ball State University's *Forum*, *Cimarron Review*, and *Literary Review*, as well as in *Ariel*, *Acumen*, *Orbis*, *New Welsh Review*, *Dalhousie Review*, and other journals. His work has also been printed in five editions of the *Anthology of Magazine Verse and Yearbook of American Poetry*.

Other poetry and short fictions available from *TIME BEING BOOKS*

EDWARD BOCCIA
No Matter How Good the Light Is: Poems by a Painter

LOUIS DANIEL BRODSKY
You Can't Go Back, Exactly
The Thorough Earth
Four and Twenty Blackbirds Soaring
Mississippi Vistas: Volume One of *A Mississippi Trilogy*
Falling from Heaven: Holocaust Poems of a Jew and a Gentile *(Brodsky and Heyen)*
Forever, for Now: Poems for a Later Love
Mistress Mississippi: Volume Three of *A Mississippi Trilogy*
A Gleam in the Eye: Poems for a First Baby
Gestapo Crows: Holocaust Poems
The Capital Café: Poems of Redneck, U.S.A.
Disappearing in Mississippi Latitudes: Volume Two of *A Mississippi Trilogy*
Paper-Whites for Lady Jane: Poems of a Midlife Love Affair
The Complete Poems of Louis Daniel Brodsky: Volume One, 1963–1967
Three Early Books of Poems by Louis Daniel Brodsky, 1967–1969: *The Easy Philosopher, "A Hard Coming of It" and Other Poems*, and *The Foul Rag-and-Bone Shop*
The Eleventh Lost Tribe: Poems of the Holocaust
Toward the Torah, Soaring: Poems of the Renascence of Faith
Yellow Bricks *(short fictions)*
Catchin' the Drift o' the Draft *(short fictions)*
This Here's a Merica *(short fictions)*
Voice Within the Void: Poems of *Homo supinus*
Leaky Tubs *(short fictions)*
Shadow War: A Poetic Chronicle of September 11 and Beyond, Volume One

HARRY JAMES CARGAS *(editor)*
Telling the Tale: A Tribute to Elie Wiesel on the Occasion of His 65th Birthday
— Essays, Reflections, and Poems

JUDITH CHALMER
Out of History's Junk Jar: Poems of a Mixed Inheritance

GERALD EARLY
How the War in the Streets Is Won: Poems on the Quest of Love and Faith

800-331-6605
http://www.timebeing.com

GARY FINCKE
Blood Ties: Working-Class Poems

ALBERT GOLDBARTH
A Lineage of Ragpickers, Songpluckers, Elegiasts & Jewelers: Selected Poems
  of Jewish Family Life, 1973–1995

ROBERT HAMBLIN
From the Ground Up: Poems of One Southerner's Passage to Adulthood

WILLIAM HEYEN
Erika: Poems of the Holocaust
Falling from Heaven: Holocaust Poems of a Jew and a Gentile *(Brodsky and Heyen)*
Pterodactyl Rose: Poems of Ecology
Ribbons: The Gulf War — A Poem
The Host: Selected Poems, 1965–1990

TED HIRSCHFIELD
German Requiem: Poems of the War and the Atonement of a Third Reich Child

VIRGINIA V. JAMES HLAVSA
Waking October Leaves: Reanimations by a Small-Town Girl

RODGER KAMENETZ
The Missing Jew: New and Selected Poems
Stuck: Poems Midlife

NORBERT KRAPF
Somewhere in Southern Indiana: Poems of Midwestern Origins
Blue-Eyed Grass: Poems of Germany

ADRIAN C. LOUIS
Blood Thirsty Savages

LEO LUKE MARCELLO
Nothing Grows in One Place Forever: Poems of a Sicilian American

GARDNER McFALL
The Pilot's Daughter

800-331-6605
http://www.timebeing.com

JOSEPH MEREDITH
Hunter's Moon: Poems from Boyhood to Manhood

BEN MILDER
The Good Book Says . . . : Light Verse to Illuminate the Old Testament
The Good Book Also Says . . . : Numerous Humorous Poems Inspired by
   the New Testament

CHARLES MUÑOZ
Fragments of a Myth: Modern Poems on Ancient Themes

JOSEPH STANTON
Imaginary Museum: Poems on Art